editors

P.S.N. Russell-Gebbett

N.G. Round

A.H. Terry

Belfast

Spanish and Portuguese

Papers

The Queen's University of Belfast

ISBN 0 85389 165 6

Contents

page

Contents                                                    page

Contents                                                    page

Contents                                                                  page

Contents                                                                  page

Contents                                                                  page

# Contents

Preface

It was originally intended that this volume of studies should mark the 50th anniversary of the establishment of the Chair of Spanish in the Queen's University of Belfast. A combination of a certain tardiness in meeting deadlines on the part of some contributors, and dilatoriness on the part of the general editor, have conspired to frustrate this intention. The general editor finds, however, some consolation in the fact that a fifty-third (or -fourth) anniversary is, when all is said and done, more significant by some three (or four) years than a fiftieth.

The twenty-one papers contained in this volume are the work of university teachers past or present who at one time in their lives have worked in Queen's Department of Spanish. Some of them have been in the Department as students, some as lecturers, some as lectors; some enter more than one of these categories. Six of the contributors are on the Department's staff at this time. All owe a debt directly or indirectly to the Department's first begetter, the late Ignasi González Llubera, appointed in 1920 and Musgrave Professor of Spanish from 1926 until his retirement in 1960.

It is I think proper to make clear, in view of my remarks in my first paragraph, that the majority of the studies printed here were received in the academic year 1977/78 (although a good number were received in the session following), and that a maximum length of 6500 words per contribution was set. This latter stipulation was not in the event rigidly adhered to, for the reason that too strict an application of the condition would have meant still further delay.

Especial thanks are due to the Spanish Dirección de Relaciones Culturales and to the Queen's University of Belfast for financial assistance; without them this volume could not have been published. Nor could it have been produced without the ready, cheerful and skilled assistance of Mrs. Jill Gray, the Department's secretary, who alone has retyped every manuscript in a form suitable for reproduction.

Paul Russell-Gebbett
Department of Spanish
Queen's University, Belfast

# Juan Larrea : una interpretación americana del exilio del '39

José Luis Abellán

Juan Larrea es un poeta que, tras su exilio en 1939, había quedado prácticamente desconocido para las jóvenes generaciones de españoles, a pesar de su importancia en los años anteriores a la guerra. Recientemente ha empezado de nuevo a ser publicado y valorado en España, gracias a la edición de su Versión Celeste,[1] en la que, tras la italiana de Bodini,[2] Gerardo Diego y Luis Felipe Vivanco ponen al alcance del lector español su obra poética completa. No nos proponemos aquí hablar de ésta, que ya ha recibido adecuada atención por parte de algunos críticos,[3] sino hacer ver que su poesía y su prosa no son separables, a menos de quedarnos en un entendimiento superficial de ambas. El Surrealismo, de que como poeta Larrea hace gala, no es sino expresión de un pensamiento y pretendida vía de acceso a una tercera dimensión que no se deja aprehender por los canales ordinarios. Sus mismos libros sobre el Surrealismo así vienen a atestiguarlo;[4] en uno de ellos escribe: "lo que el Surrealismo nos revela, como fruto del tiempo, es que en su sentir existe un género de realidad humana, más allá de nuestra conciencia tradicional, que entre la coyuntura de las dos guerras pugna por introducirse en nuestro ámbito, hacerse presente".[5] En el mismo libro señala más adelante como el Surrealismo es un vehículo expresivo para "el establecimiento de un estado de conciencia superior, propio de un concepto de vida nueva donde sueño y realidad mariden sus condiciones". Sólo entendiéndolo así es posible que "no se lo interprete como un fenómeno arbitrario, sin ton ni son en el proceso cultural de Occidente, cosa implausible puesto que prolonga el impulso del Romanticismo, lo lógico es presumir que en aquel intensísimo momento europeo, tras la guerra del catorce que abrió el ciclo de la gran catástrofe, el Surrealismo empezó a dar, a su manera destructora y pesimista, testimonio sintomático de lo que se gestaba en el subsuelo cultural en virtud de los acontecimientos ocurridos y de los ya a punto de ocurrir".[6] Estos evidentemente, eran la guerra civil española y la segunda mundial, que han tenido importancia excepcional en la génesis del pensamiento de Larrea.

Esta vinculación del poeta - y del poeta surrealista - con el pensador, nos pone ya en la dirección adecuada para un primer acercamiento a lo que podemos llamar su filosofía. Es evidente que ésta ha de tener un carácter poético y simbólico que acerca su concepción del mundo al ámbito de las viejas filosofías cabalísticas y gnósticas. Un catador tan fino de las esencias del pensamiento como José Gaos, así llega a declararlo cuando, hablando del primer libro de Larrea - Rendición del Espíritu (1943) - dice que viene "a representar la reaparición, en pleno centro de la ciudad intelectual, de la filosofía cabalística y gnóstica, con paso resuelto, llamando con estruendo la atención sobre sí, declarando juzgarse plenamente fundada, con expresa voluntad de invasión, conquista y hegemonía. Larrea no califica, sin embargo, su filosofía cabalística y gnóstica de tal, sino, passim, de 'poética', y está muy bien: enuncia significativamente la naturaleza y el origen que la distinguen como nueva respecto a las filosofías cabalísticas y gnósticas del pasado".[7]

Naturalmente, una filosofía de este tipo ha de tener como órgano fundamental la Imaginación, capaz de calibrar cualitativamente los datos de la experiencia, para ejercer sobre ellos una lectura de significación ultraempírica. Este método, aplicado al pasado histórico,

viene a constituir el origen de una filosofía de la historia, que es
el nervio del pensamiento de Larrea.  La intuición que sirve de base
a este planteamiento está ya en Rendición del Espíritu, libro escrito
bajo el impacto de la guerra civil española y el subsecuente exilio
mexicano.  En aquellas páginas escribía Larrea:  "De la materialidad
de las realidades de orden heterogéneo que el pasado propone a la
consideración humana, de su disposición lógica, se desprende un sentido
organizado al modo como se desprende de la articulación de fonemas,
insignificantes por sí, en un lenguage".[8]  La lejana intuición de
1943 no ha hecho sino confirmarse en los escritos posteriores de Larrea,
especialmente en La Espada de la Paloma (1956), en Razón de Ser, o
en algún escrito ya de por sí de título tan significativo como
Teleología de la cultura (1965).  En su último libro - César Vallejo
y el surrealismo - este punto de vista aparece ya totalmente depurado;
en él sostiene que la historia del hombre ha venido cumpliendo fines
universales ignorados por los individuos y pueblos particulares, al
perseguir sus fines inmediatos.  Sin embargo, ocultos bajo esos fines
particulares, la imaginación poética puede encontrar el subterráneo
sentido teleológico a que todos ellos están ordenados.  "Los fenómenos
- dice - en que vivimos intricados son técnicamente susceptibles de
encerrar un sentido distinto al que les atribuye la perspectiva de
nuestra conciencia a ras de tierra, antropocentrada en un islote perdido en el inmenso océano de sombras".[9]  Así aparece un fin universal
diferente a los fines individuales de los hombres y las multitudes
concretas que los viven de acuerdo con las pautas e intereses del
momento, sin percatarse de su sentido teleológico trascendental.
     Sobre la base de estos planteamientos iniciales se va a levantar
un grandioso edificio de filosofía de la historia, que culminará más
tarde en una filosofía social y una metafísica, que toma la forma de
una inédita Ontología de la Cultura.  Ahora bien, esa filosofía de la
historia - la parte quizá más original de su construcción - no puede
erigirse sino sobre la base de buscar una serie de 'elementos significantes' que den sentido al pasado.  Así surge toda una interpretación
de España y de América y de sus relaciones, que tiene como nudo axial
la guerra civil del '36 y la correspondiente diáspora.  En este sentido,
hay que encuadrar la obra de Larrea como una ilustración - si bien
eminente y extraordinaria - de la meditación que sobre el problema
español y el hecho americano obsesionará a los intelectuales del
exilio de 1939.  En esa literatura, creemos que de ahora en adelante
la voz de Larrea no debe faltar, por mucho que se discrepe de sus
opiniones, pues constituye uno de sus portavoces más representativos.
     Es necesario, pues, pasar sin más a la exposición de esa filosofía
de la historia española, que empieza retomando elementos antiguos, si
bien para darles una nueva interpretación.  En el primer capítulo de
su Rendición del Espíritu, Larrea inicia su meditación recogiendo la
versión tradicional del escudo español, ornado por las famosas columnas
de Hércules y su lema "Non plus ultra", convertido, tras el descubrimiento de América, en "Plus ultra", con cuya leyenda no sólo se quiere
significar la existencia de un 'más allá' físico, sino de un 'más
allá' espiritual, testimonio primitivo de la eterna creencia española
en un mundo tridimensional.  En este sentido, se interpreta el 'plus
ultra' no sólo como una negación del límite físico del mundo entonces
conocido, sino también como una negación de la fuerza herculea que
allí implantó las columnas.  Hay un 'más allá' de la fuerza, que es
el mundo del espíritu, al cual España siempre ha sido afecta.
     En apoyo de esta visión se ofrece enseguida una consideración ya
inicialmente teleológica de tres ciudades religiosas por antonomasia.
En el despliegue del cristianismo esas ciudades - Jerusalén, Roma,

Compostela - aparecen como escalas de un itinerario con dirección hacia Occidente. La ciudad de Jerusalén, situada en Asia, aparece especialmente vinculada a la figura del Padre, mientras Roma, en Europa, lo está a la del Hijo y Compostela al Espíritu. No puede pasarse por alto el hecho de que esta última ciudad se sitúe en el Finisterre, paralelo geográfico dentro de la Península de las columnas de Hércules, haciendo como éstas alusión al continente entonces por descubrir. La aparición de la estrella que da nombre a la ciudad - Campus stellae -, así como de las peregrinaciones que hacia ella se dirigían, es evidencia palpable del hondo contenido teleológico de aquellas creencias, sobre cuya verdad o falsedad, por lo demás, Larrea no se pronuncia, ni parece que venga al caso.[10] Si Jerusalén está en Asia y Roma en Europa, Compostela tiene una clara vinculación con América, cuya existencia presentían los peregrinos al hacer el camino de Santiago. Con toda lógica, pues, escribe Larrea: "En cuanto se descubrió América cesaron, práctica y naturalmente, las peregrinaciones".[11]

En realidad, toda la historia de la Península ibérica tiene un carácter religioso, y está hondamente vinculada a lo americano. Larrea constata como la Virgen se le apareció a Santiago, a orillas del Ebro, el 12 de octubre del año 40 d.C., y como 1452 años después (cifra significativa que resulta de multiplicar los 33 años en que murió Cristo por el 44 d.C. en que muere Santiago en Jerusalén) los españoles descubren América en el mismo día y mes. El patrón de España - Santiago - y la patrona - Virgen del Pilar - aparecen, pues, vinculados al descubrimiento de América, y las ciudades respectivas Compostela - Zaragoza quedan así mismo unidas, si bien en un sentido inverso, pues Zaragoza es la Cesar Augusta pagana, representación del predominio de la fuerza sobre el espíritu, y ello es bien visible en la palabra 'Ebro', inversión de 'Orbe'. Y es que en España lucharán durante siglos los dos elementos - el europeo-africano con su acento en la fuerza física y el americano de sentido espiritual -, con triunfo aparente del primero sobre el segundo en la guerra apocalíptica de 1936-39, donde se va a decidir el destino de España y del mundo. Esto queda muy claro en el análisis que hace de dicho suceso histórico, y al que nosotros nos referiremos también un poco más adelante.

Los elementos premonitorios que aparecen ya en el mundo antiguo y que abocan al destino americano de España, cobran sentido patente con el descubrimiento de América en 1492, al comienzo de la Edad Moderna, año en que coinciden - y no arbitrariamente - la expulsión de los moros y judíos de la Península. Es la fecha en que la leyenda del "Non plus ultra" queda desmentida por la hazaña española y en que el fin de las peregrinaciones a Compostela, hace que la figura de Santiago cobre su plena significación espiritual. No es irrelevante que la Virgen y Santiago se vuelvan a aparecer en el Cuzco en 1531, cuatro siglos justos antes del comienzo de la República que originará la guerra civil.

La dirección de la cultura occidental revelada por el sentido del Camino de Santiago, coincidente en esto con el itinerario de las tres ciudades antes aludidas, da su plena significación al Finisterre, que se encarna en el Nuevo Mundo con todo el repertorio de reflejos y reverberaciones que involucra y en el que nos detendremos más adelante. Pero la fecha definitiva en que tal significación adquiere plena resonancia es la de 1936; cuyo comienzo se pretendió que coincidiese por los militares insurgentes con la fiesta de Santiago, que se celebra el 25 de julio, pero por razones imprevistas tuvo que adelantarse una semana, al 18 del mismo mes.

Entramos con las anteriores consideraciones en uno de los temas básicos de esta original filosofía de la historia, que es el de la

significación 'espiritual' de la Segunda República española y de su
fin en una cruenta guerra civil de tres años. La conexión de la primera con el continente americano se le hace a Larrea ineludible por
lo que sin duda constituye una curiosa coincidencia. He aquí como lo
presenta su propio autor: "Las Repúblicas que forman el Nuevo Mundo
decidieron el año 1930 designar con el nombre de Día de las Américas
una fecha conmemorativa. Por acuerdo general se designó el 14 de abril.
Pues bien, el 14 de abril de 1931, en el primer Día de las Américas,
se derrumba en España la monarquía y se proclama la República. Es
decir, rimando poéticamente con aquella otra fuerte coincidencia que
hizo que América se descubriera el Día de España, revalidándola por
alusión, la República, el nuevo régimen político, hace su aparición
el primer Día de las Américas. ¿Qué régimen? El mismo por el que se
gobiernan sin excepción todos los países americanos. De manera que
en puridad poética puede decirse que en aquel esplendoroso día del
año de 1931, en que la instauración de la República desató los entusias-
mos populares en forma jamás hasta entonces en España conocida, el
más allá inminente que hacía batir palmas y brotar vítores, el que
excitaba los corazones populares en una pleamar intuitiva... era el
más allá del Nuevo Mundo que encarna América".[12]
El comienzo de la Segunda República en España representa el
comienzo de una nueva era, en que el triunfo del Amor y del Espíritu
será posible. Y esta idea consta de forma textual en el libro de
Larrea cuando escribe: "Al entrar en España la República el 14 de
abril, entra el Nuevo Mundo, el espíritu colectivo de caridad encarnado
en el pueblo, dispuesto a manifestarse una vez cumplida su misión de
víctima".[13] Pues, efectivamente, el pueblo español iba a ser la víctima inmolada en la inminente guerra civil de 1936, que representa para
Larrea un acontecimiento universal, donde van a luchar los dos principios
fundamentales del mundo contemporáneo: individualismo y colectivismo,
con sus respectivos sistemas representativos: capitalismo, del primero;
y socialismo, del segundo. "Los sucesos ocurridos en España - dice
Larrea - pueden, por su magnitud, corresponder a ese antagonismo
decisivo. Tanto más cuanto que el Viejo Mundo en su integridad se ha
visto obligado a violar mortalmente todos sus principios morales, para
tronchar el ímpetu ascensional hacia su más allá del pueblo de España
y cuanto que la sublimación por la adversidad a que éste ha sido some-
tido, ha liberado su espíritu de verdad y de justicia, redimiéndole
de las tareas hereditarias que arrastraba consigo".[14]
En el párrafo transcrito se alude claramente al Pacto de No-
Intervención con que las democracias europeas violaron sus principios
democráticos en el caso español, pero no les acusa por ello, sino que
se interpreta como un atenimiento inevitable a la lógica de la historia.
En ese sentido hay que explicar la actitud de la Iglesia Católica.
"Su papel estaba determinado por el automatismo del tiempo - escribe -.
Porque si Jesús fué víctima de la Sinagoga que se atenía a la letra
de las Escrituras y que representaba a Moisés, Santiago - pueblo -
español -, siguiendo el paralelismo, debía ser víctima de la Iglesia
Romana. Quienes han soportado la atroz guerra - atroz por lo
inmensamente injusta - que ha quebrantado la voluntad pacífica hiero-
solimitana, del pueblo español y devastado su solar nativo, lo mismo
si son castellanos que andaluces, pero sobre todo si son vascos, pocas
cosas encontrarán más evidentes que esta identidad de la causa española
con la víctima.[15] El pueblo español ha sido condenado a muerte por la
Iglesia de Roma que de este modo viene a negar, como Pedro, y a
negar mortalmente, el espíritu de aquél a quien debe la vida. El
episcopado español con anuencia del Vaticano y asistido por la compli-
cidad manifiesta de la Iglesia Universal, ha desenvainado la espada,

como Pedro, mas no para defender a la víctima sino para sacrificarla. Ha santificado la _fuerza_, el matonismo romano, ha bendecido las armas asestadas contra la voluntad pacífica del pueblo español. Al obrar de esa suerte no defendía los intereses de Dios sino sus propios intereses temporales, al servicio - ella la 'enriquecida con la sangre de los mártires de Jesús' - de aquellos que por hallarse identificados con la estructura terrenal del sistema feneciente, no pueden penetrar, según la parábola del camello y de la aguja, en el reino de los cielos".[16]

Y es que en la guerra de España se hallan frente a frente el principio de la _fuerza bruta_ representado por _Roma_, y el principio del Espíritu representado por el _Amor_, cuya palabra no en balde es lectura inversa y literal de la primera. No es, pues, ninguna casualidad que la insurrección preparada por Franco cuente desde el primer momento con el apoyo de Italia, por ver en aquél la defensa de sus intereses político-religiosos, que arrastrará tras su decisión la voluntad bélica y de poder encarnado en Germania. No es tampoco casual el carácter musulmán que adquiere el llamado 'movimiento nacional' desde los primeros momentos: La insurrección se preparará en África con ayuda de los moros; Franco desembarca en Tetuán vestido de moro, y llevará hasta muy entrado su mandato (1956) una característica escolta africana (la "guardia mora").

La tragedia del pueblo español es, pues, la de una voluntad pacífica de _amor_ frente al hecho despiadado de la _fuerza_, que encarnan las oligarquías seculares (clero, ejército y nobleza). En este enfrentamiento, el 'pueblo' es encarnación de Cristo, que es inmolada una vez más. Por eso escribe Larrea: "A la profecía de Pedro ha sucedido la profecía de Juan, al Cristo como individuo el Cristo como colectividad o Verbo... De esta suerte el pueblo español ha encarnado el Cristo colectivo, que bajo un ideal de paz, en una _visión de paz_, ha dado su vida de _ciudad_, en defensa del Bien y de la Justicia humanas".[17] La guerra española es representación - ahora colectiva, y no individual - de la tragedia del Gólgota; de aquí ese carácter universal que se atribuye al conflicto, en el cual una vez más se juega el destino del mundo. En este contexto se interpreta la afluencia "de todos los puntos del planeta" de voluntarios internacionales - las famosas "Brigadas" -, que para Larrea vienen a representar a los nuevos "peregrinos" de Compostela, ansiosos de "dar testimonio con su sangre del carácter universal del fenómeno que tenía lugar en España".[18] Ese fenómeno es al que se refiere el título del libro que venimos siguiendo: la _rendición del Espíritu_ donde la palabra se toma en doble sentido: por un lado, rendición o muerte del espíritu del pueblo español, que es lo que representa su derrota en la 'guerra civil'; por otro, rendición en el sentido de revelación del sentido de esa muerte, que no es otra cosa que un entregar (o _rendir_) el espíritu español a un más allá trascendente.

Por eso para Larrea en la Península ibérica "se realizó la función suprema y trascendente de la rendición del espíritu",[19] con su dualidad inevitable: la derrota y destrucción de Europa en la Segunda Guerra Mundial, por un lado; y por otro, el acceso inevitable a un Nuevo Mundo. "En España prologalmente se condenaron las naciones", dice Larrea; esa condena era al parecer inevitable para que se produjera la rendición o entrega del espíritu español al continente americano. Se cumple así una fatalidad histórica del destino español, que estaba prefigurado en la República, de la que Larrea dice: "Es la suya realidad de Nuevo Mundo y fué, por tanto, la proyección verdadera de América, en prefigura _política_ en España, lo que ha sufrido la victimación redentora".[20] Pero en realidad, ese no era sino un antecedente inmediato, de lo que no es sino una fatalidad secular. No es sino una coincidencia significativa que Colón, el descubridor de América, lleve el nombre de Cristóbal, el santo cristiano que transporta en sus hombros a Jesús niño y al mundo a través de las aguas, ni que el apellido Colombo signifique en latín 'paloma'. "Este es el nombre de Cristóbal Colombo - dice Larrea -, <u>portador del espíritu de Cristo</u>, precisamente a través de ese mar, de Europa a América, de España a su <u>plus ultra</u>. Para mayor coincidencia uno mismo es el día en que se celebra la fiesta católica de San Cristóbal y de Santiago Apóstol, el 25 de julio".[21]

España está vinculada a América de modo consustancial, pues, y esa vinculación se ha plasmado de modo evidentísimo tras la derrota de 1939, en que el Nuevo Continente acoge a los exiliados españoles. Por eso escribe Larrea con la convicción que le da su propia experiencia de exiliado: "Algunos españoles acogidos a tierra americana saben que existe ya la posibilidad de dar pasos en el mundo situado <u>más allá de la fuerza</u>".[22] ¿Cuáles son los valores que ha de encarnar este Nuevo Mundo espiritual que adquiere su inevitable primera residencia en América? Larrea va explicitando uno por uno todos ellos en el capítulo de su libro que titula "De urbe et orbe". He aquí su escueta enumeración: libertad, paz, anti-imperialismo, verbo o anti-babelismo, universalidad, dinamismo, progreso, espiritualidad, materialidad, unidad, ética, verdad, amor, justicia, derecho, humanismo. Todos ellos valores que ya estaban en los ideales encarnados en la Segunda República, y en los que no nos vamos a detener aquí, puesto que aparecerán dando sentido a la Cultura Universal, propugnada por Larrea y en la que nos detendremos en la segunda parte de este escrito.

En lo expuesto hasta ahora no encontramos sino una versión más o menos original de la historia española en su relación con América, e incluso yo cargaría el acento sobre el "menos", dado que este tipo de literatura habría que encuadrarlo dentro de una temática muy característica de los exiliados españoles del '39, según he hecho observar en otro escrito.[23] Sin embargo, toda esta interpretación adquiere singular originalidad cuando Larrea acude al significado cabalístico de los números, aspecto de su pensamiento al que al principio hemos hecho alusión, pero sobre el que apenas hemos insistido después. Según dicho sentido cabalístico, España y América, pero muy especialmente las relaciones de aquélla con ésta, quedarían comprendidas bajo la mística del número 4, como veremos a continuación.

Por lo que se refiere a España, señala Larrea como la forma geográfica de la Península coincide a <u>grosso modo</u> con la de un cuadrilátero, lo que a su vez parece tener relación con la 'ciudad cuadrada' del Apocalipsis. Ahora bien, una parte del cristianismo español - precisamente aquella que nada tiene que ver con Roma - tiene un carácter juaniano, que adquiere sentido apocalíptico con la 'guerra civil' española. Así resulta que el <u>cuarto</u> Evangelio de San Juan, expresión suprema de la profecía cristiana, tiene especial relación con la Península, como resulta bien expresivo de ello el águila que adorna el escudo español en los momentos decisivos de su historia: bien sea la bicéfala del Imperio carolino o la apocalíptica de la Falange. En este orden de cosas tampoco carecen de sentido las <u>cuatro</u> formas verbales que adquiere en nuestro idioma el patrón de España: Santiago, Diego, Jaime, Jacobo. Y en lo que se refiere a América, no deja tampoco de ser sintomático que aparezca como <u>cuarto</u> continente, y que su forma apaisada aparezca como un águila de grandes alas, <u>cuarto</u> animal del Apocalipsis.

El aspecto más llamativo de esta mística del número cuatro es, sin embargo, el que aparece en las relaciones entre España y América. Así resulta: 1) que entre el año del descubrimiento - 1492 - y la fecha del apocalipsis español - 1936 -, median 444 años; 2) que Santiago murió en Jerusalén el año 44 d.C. y que Compostela, el lugar

donde según tradición está enterrado, se halla a 44° de longitud de
Jerusalén; 3) que la multiplicación de ambas cifras (44 x 44) nos
da la fecha exacta del drama español (1936), la cual se halla a su vez
a 444 años de 1492, según dijimos; 4) que la multiplicación entre la
edad a que murió Cristo (33 años) y la fecha de la muerte de Santiago
(44), nos da el año 1452, que es la distancia exacta que media entre
la aparición de la Virgen a Santiago, el año 40 d.C., y 1492, fecha
del descubrimiento; 5) que la distancia entre Finisterre y Nueva
España es de 90° de longitud, es decir, la cuarta parte de la circun-
ferencia; 6) que el año 1531 en que se aparece la Virgen de Guadalupe
es el resultado casi exacto de sumar la fecha del descubrimiento
(1492) más la de la aparición de la Virgen del Pilar a Santiago (40
d.C.).

Todas estas conjugaciones del número cuatro con distintas fechas
o acontecimientos americanos se refieren a Hispanoamérica, pero no
faltan tampoco las referencias a los Estados Unidos con características
similares. Así ocurre: 1) que 1607, fecha de la fundación de
Jamestown, la primera ciudad dedicada a Santiago en el Nuevo Mundo,
es el producto de multiplicar los días del año (365'25) por una fracción
del año de la muerte de Santiago (4'4); 2) que el año de la Independencia de los Estados Unidos, 1776, es la suma de cuatro períodos
de 444 años (significativa distancia entre 1492 y 1936); 3) que 1539
en que Vázquez de Coronado sale de Compostela (pequeña ciudad del
Pacífico) para descubrir California, se produce exactamente 400 años
antes de la fecha clave de la más dramática diáspora española en 1939,
en que los exiliados realizan el "segundo descubrimiento de América".

Naturalmente, todas estas fechas son curiosas coincidencias que
nadie había notado antes. No las toma Larrea por pruebas demostrativas,
pero sí por uno de esos "elementos significantes" decisivos en que basa
su filosofía de la historia. En una nota a pie de página así viene a
aclararlo cuando escribe: "Es muy de tener presente que este juego
de números no se ajusta a un orden puramente matemático, sino más
bien a un esquema poético, en el que se integra la síntesis entre
algunas razones matemáticas y otras de carácter significativo, verbal.
La insistencia de la cifra 4 que presta fisonomía al conjunto responde
más bien a un lenguaje significante".[24]

A través de este lenguaje descubrimos precisamente la importancia
de América en el itinerario hacia una Cultura Universal, hasta el punto
de que viene a identificarse aquel continente con la realización de ésta.
Es algo que viene dado por la forzosidad de los acontecimientos, todos los
cuales tienden - el análisis que hemos visto - a convertir América
en un crisol de razas y de culturas que la constituyen en placenta inevitable
de la nueva cultura. En realidad, hay una identidad entre Nuevo Mundo y
Nueva Cultura, puesto que el descubrimiento de América rompe la imagen
geográfica de la Tierra como mundo plano de carácter bidimensional para dar
entrada al mundo esférico de tres dimensiones, en el cual América representa
la Tercera Persona, aquella que encarna la figura del Espíritu.

Esta concepción americana de Larrea enlaza con una vieja tradición,
que tiene su antecedente remoto en Cristóbal Colón, según la cual
América aparece como receptáculo natural de utopías. Desde la lejana
de Tomás Moro, que sitúa allí su isla ideal, pasando por Vasco de
Quiroga, los franciscanos de Nueva España y los jesuitas del Paraguay,
hasta las modernas utopías de revolución social, el Continente americano no ha dejado nunca de servir de inspiración a tales anhelos
utópicos, que han hecho de América la tierra del Paraíso. Allí lo
situó Colón y allí siguen buscándolo los nuevos utopistas, que han
hecho de aquel continente lugar de referencia inevitable. No es, pues,
ninguna casualidad que fuese Juan Larrea quien primero descubriese

un texto inédito y olvidado de León Pinelo, titulado El Paraíso en el Nuevo Mundo, donde con pelos y señales de toda índole se ubica el Paraíso Terrenal.[25]  Pero los "redescubridores" de ese Nuevo Mundo han de ser españoles, porque el destino histórico ha ligado a nuestra Península con aquel continente.  Españoles fueron quienes lo descubrieron y colonizaron a principios del siglo XVI, y españoles han sido quienes llevaron el Espíritu, muerto en Europa, a las únicas tierras donde podría cobrar su verdadera dimensión universal.  Al fin y al cabo, la Virgen de Guadalupe, Patrona de América, no es sino una Virgen española trasplantada a la Nueva España, que era México, en cuyo país hacía la función de Nueva Virgen para el Nuevo Mundo.  Así lo supieron también ver los dos grandes poetas de América - Ruben Darío, en lengua española, y Walt Whitman, en lengua inglesa -, a quienes Larrea invoca en apoyo de sus ideas.  Sobre el primero dice: "Las conclusiones a que por sus caminos llegó Ruben Darío coinciden, según se ve, de modo exacto y circunstanciado con las que por los suyos peculiares propone este libro.  Ya no es Roma, sino su antítesis natural, el Nuevo Mundo - Amor - el sitio a donde van a parar todos los caminos.  La realidad es redonda".[26]  En lo que se refiere a Walt Whitman sus expresiones son también definitivas; he aquí algunas de ellas: "Ha sugerido algún crítico que la enigmática personificación de Santa Spirita debía corresponder en el espíritu de Walt Whitman al espíritu de América.  Al confrontar ese poema, como acaba de hacerse aquí, con la Canción de lo Universal la equivalencia resulta concluyente: Santa Spirita y América, ambas caracterizadas con el número cuatro, se convalidan.  Ambas se encuentran más allá del principio del mal, superándolo; de Satán, una, de Babel - puerta de Dios -, indicando su naturaleza de ciudad, la otra.  Más aun, la extraña forma femenina que caracteriza a la primera advocación parece corresponder de plano a la condición de Madre que para Walt Whitman es peculiar de América" ... "Madre Suprema para Walt Whitman resulta ser la prehispánica 'Madre de las gentes' del Tepeyac, la 'Madre de los vivientes' del Génesis, Eva, Ave, Columbia.  Un poco más allá aparece cómo ese cuadrado deífico que concluye en Santa Spirita coincide maravillosamente con la forma cuadrilátera de España, semilla y representación de esa Columbia amada.  Complace comprobar aquí cómo los 160 años que median entre 1776 de Norteamérica y los 1936 de España corresponden a cuatro períodos de cuarenta años.  Así como que entre el 1531 de la 'aparición' de la Virgen de Guadalupe hasta el 1931 de la República española, su representación simbólica con carácter de ciudad, median cuatrocientos años.  Ha de tenerse en cuenta que en el poema que Walt Whitman dedicó a España, América se designa con el nombre de Columbia, detalle confirmatorio si los hay. Este es el objeto de su sujeto, la razón de su modo poético de conocer.  Es decir, la personalidad de Walt Whitman después de identificarse con el sujeto en el plano cósmico, se vuelve hacia su objeto que resulta ser América, la ciudad cuadrada que del cielo baja, la Jerusalén celestial que en otro tiempo y circunstancia se definió oníricamente por medio de la imagen de la Virgen de Guadalupe. Tócale a ella gestar la 'simiente perfección'.  En este advenimiento del espíritu universal, definiéndolo, la cuarta dimensión despliega su esplendor supremo".[27]

En realidad, todo lo expuesto hasta ahora no es más que un punto de partida para la elaboración de una filosofía social y de una metafísica de la cultura muy originales que Juan Larrea expondrá en los libros posteriores a Rendición del espíritu, cuyo desarrollo y análisis nos es imposible sin salirnos de los límites concedidos a este escrito.

# NOTAS

1.  Juan Larrea, Versión Celeste (Barcelona, Barral Editores, 1970).

2.  Vittorio Bodini, Versione Celeste (Torino, Einaudi, 1969).

3.  Vittorio Bodini, I poeti surrealisti spagnoli. Saggio intro-
duttivo e antologia (Torino, Einaudi, 1963). Es importante también
como introducción a su poesía el estudio de Luis Felipe Vivanco,
'Juan Larrea y su Versión Celeste', publicado como estudio preliminar
a la edición española antes citada.

4.  Entre ellos parece inevitable citar: El surrealismo entre Viejo
y Nuevo Mundo (México 1944); César Vallejo o Hispanoamérica en la cruz
de su Razón (Córdoba 1958); Del surrealismo a Machupicchu (México 1967);
César Vallejo y el surrealismo (Madrid 1976).

5.  César Vallejo y el surrealismo, op. cit., 194.

6.  Ibid., 230.

7.  José Gaos, 'Juan Larrea: Rendición del Espíritu', en Pensamiento
de lengua española (México, Ed. Stylo, 1945), 348.

8.  Juan Larrea, Rendición del Espíritu, 2 vols. (México 1943), II,
117.

9.  César Vallejo y el surrealismo, 222.

10.  Solamente en cierto momento de su discurso hace una digresión
sobre este punto, y en la cual entre otras cosas dice: "Habrá
extrañado a más de un lector que en los anteriores capítulos se hayan
tomado las leyendas paganas o cristianas al pie de la letra, sin
crítica ni reserva de ninguna especie, como si realmente respondieran
a una verdadera existencia histórica. Si bien se mira no han sido,
sin embargo, tomadas así. Ni se admite ni se deja de admitir, por
ejemplo, que la Virgen se apareciera a Santiago en Zaragoza, donde
este personaje jamás probablemente puso los pies. Ni se da por cierto
que en Compostela estuviese el auténtico sepulcro de Santiago. Ni la
realidad de Hércules. Ni siquiera se somete a crítica el evangelio
de San Juan. Todo ello, desde cierto punto de vista, carece de interés
fuera del desorden secundario. Lo que se admite como un hecho
incontrovertible es que numerosas generaciones humanas han creído
firmemente en su veracidad, fenómeno que les confiere una realidad
subjetiva semejante cuando menos, a la de los más significativos sueños
individuales sin los que no fuera posible sorprender en funciones al
mecanismo psíquico. Porque si determinadas imaginerías llegaron a
polarizar, desarrollándolas, las creencias y actos consecuentes de esas
generaciones, es, sin duda, porque correspondían a las necesidades del
psiquismo colectivo, porque lo definían y revelaban... Lo que sí se
ha intentado es descifrar el sentido de que se hallan impregnados tales
hechos y mostrar cómo analizados minuciosamente, se engranan de un
modo perfecto con la realidad objetiva, evidenciando que, contra lo
que comúnmente se cree en el mundo de la dualidad, no son lo subjetivo
y lo objetivo colectivo dos compartimentos estancos ajenos, cuando
no excluyentes, sino dos planos en verdad recíprocos, complementarios
en un ámbito significante" (Rendición del Espíritu, I, 102-104).

11. <u>Rendición del Espíritu</u>, I, 29.

12. Ibid., 44.

13. Ibid., 49.

14. Ibid., 43.

15. La alusión a Guernica es clara cuando se refiere a los vascos. Una ampliación de este punto de vista puede verse en su famosa interpretación del cuadro de Picasso: <u>The Vision of the "Guernica"</u> (Nueva York 1947).

16. <u>Rendición del Espíritu</u>, I, 142.

17. Ibid., 130.

18. Ibid., 144.

19. Ibid., 205.

20. Ibid., II, 243.

21. Ibid., I, 221.

22. Ibid., 118.

23. José Luis Abellán, 'Filosofía y Pensamiento: Su función en el exilio de 1939', en <u>El Exilio español de 1939</u>, III, 151-208.

24. <u>Rendición del Espíritu</u>, II, 87.

25. Sobre ello habla Larrea en su artículo: 'El Paraíso en el Nuevo Mundo de León Pinelo', <u>España Peregrina</u>, 8-9 (Oct. 1940). Que Larrea engarza su intento conscientemente dentro de la tradición utópica señalada parece claro, cuando en uno de sus libros escribe: "En virtud de los lineamientos trazados más arriba, se establece dentro de su orden la legitimidad trascendental de este conjunto de fenómenos que se enriquece con otros varios como son: las instituciones paradisíacas y apocalípticas de Cristobal Colón y seguidores; los mitos neomúndicos, sobre los que abre sus alas el de la Cruz del Sur; la figura apocalíptica y patronal de la Virgen de Guadalupe; <u>El Paraíso en el Nuevo Mundo</u> de Antonio de León Pinelo, biblia del disparate racionalizado; la personificación de la humanidad paradisíaca en Santa Rosa de Lima..." (<u>César Vallejo y el surrealismo</u>, 225).

26. <u>Rendición del Espíritu</u>, II, 267.

27. Ibid., 296 y 298-299.

Jorge Amado : populism and prejudice

D.R. Brookshaw (University of Bristol)

In a literary activity spread over some forty years and involving more than twenty works, many of which have been widely translated, Jorge Amado has become Brazil's most well-known novelist internationally, and one of the most popular among the Brazilian reading public at large. His undeniable appeal can be attributed to his lyrically sensual evocations of Bahian life, liberally peppered with the African mythology which makes that city so exotic culturally. For Gregory Rabasa, "Jorge Amado é, provàvelmente, o romancista contemporâneo que melhor descreveu a religião dos negros em uma série de romances. Para fazê-lo, mostra quanto ela é importante como parte da vida cotidiana".[1] Likewise Maria Luisa Nunes considers that "the novels of Jorge Amado are among the most important vehicles for preserving African Culture in Brazil".[2]

Most critics, in assessing Amado's work, have laid emphasis on the different phases in the evolution of his novels, the first phase being clearly one of social and political commitment, the second, dating from Amado's return from exile in Eastern Europe, being one in which the politically revolutionary message is dropped in favour of a cultural or spiritual one. For the Italian critic Giorgio Marotti, Amado's priorities have changed over the years, from a socially revolutionary stance to one which evokes the values of 'Brasilidade negra', a type of Brazilian Negritude rooted in the culture of the black proletariat of Bahia.[3] The severest indictment of Jorge Amado has been expressed by the literary historian Alfredo Bosi, for whom Amado is, and always has been, a populist at heart, more interested in exploiting the picturesque aspects of Bahian life, and more prone to the portrayal of social stereotypes, than concerned with illustrating the real causes and effects of social tension. Over the years the populist behind the revolutionary mask has gradually emerged: "O populismo literário deu uma mistura de equívocos, e o maior deles será por certo o de passar por arte revolucionária. No caso de Jorge Amado, porém, bastou a passagem do tempo para desfazer o engano".[4]

The purpose of the present work will be to highlight inconsistencies and contradictions in Amado which stem from his position as a writer whose most constant themes are based on a reaction against the restrictions and repressions of bourgeois culture, while exalting in a romantic fashion the psyche of the Afro-Brazilian masses as a liberating alternative. However, this nativism, or populism as Bosi puts it, inevitably depends on the maintenance of social and racial stereotypes deeply entrenched in the mentality of the class which is paradoxically being criticised. Amado's novels may therefore be important vehicles for the preservation of African Culture in Brazil, but they also preserve and reinforce white myths regarding the Afro-Brazilian as an individual. Nowhere is this more apparent than in the three novels to be considered, Jubiabá (1935), Gabriela, cravo e canela (1958) and Tenda dos Milagres (1969), all of which exalt in different ways and for different purposes the popular psyche, but which also demonstrate the ambiguities and prejudice in Amado's treatment of blacks and mulattoes.

The novel Jubiabá, reminiscent of the picaresque in its development, illustrates through the experience from childhood to adulthood of its black hero the awakening of a racial consciousness which is at first misinterpreted and misused, but which is eventually placed at the disposal of responsible social action. At the end of the novel Balduíno's racial consciousness fuses with the social awareness which he has obtained. His hatred of whites stems from the tales of slavery and

oppression told him by the elderly witchdoctor Jubiabá during his childhood in the slums of Bahia: "O sentido de raça e de raça oprimida, ele
o adquirira à custa das histórias do morro e o conservava latente".[5]
Balduíno's growing awareness of the wider economic causes of oppression
is accumulated as a result of his travels in the hinterland of Bahia,
for as in the picaresque novel, the moral of the tale is inextricable
from the movement of the hero. Balduíno's travels from Bahia to the
tobacco plantations of Cachoeira bring him into contact with a new type
of slavery: the exploitation of a rural proletariat by factory owners
who represent the interests of foreign capital. His return to Bahia
brings with it a deeper understanding not only of exploitation, but of
the meaning of freedom. At the end of the novel, Balduíno realizes
that freedom does not lie in leading the life of a bohemian as he had
previously been taught to believe, but in participating in the labour
movement. Thus his growing awareness of class as opposed to race causes
him to channel his aggression not against all whites, but against
capitalist oppression. His strength and vitality are therefore placed
at the service of all poor regardless of race. Consequently his attitude at the end of the novel is politically and socially militant but
racially conciliatory: "... ele fez a greve e aprendeu a amar a todos
os mulatos, todos os negros, todos os brancos, que na terra, no bojo
dos navios sobre o mar, são escravos que estão rebentando as cadeias".[6]
        The tone of social and political commitment is moreover reinforced
and enriched by the role of Afro-Brazilian ritual. Balduíno's new sense
of purpose brings with it a new and more vital interpretation of this
ritual. At the beginning the sound of drums emanating from the shanties
resembled a plea, devoid of any hope or dynamism: "Eram sons de batuque
que desciam de todos os morros, sons que do outro lado do mar haviam sido
sons guerreiros, batuques que ressoavam para anunciar combates e caçadas.
Hoje eram sons de súplica, vozes escravas pedindo socorro, legiões de
negros de mãos estendidas para os céus".[7] At the end of the novel the
beat of the drums has assumed its original dignity and militancy and
seems to accompany and reflect the spirit of the labour movement:
"Hoje esses sons de batuque soam aos ouvidos do negro Antônio Balduíno
como sons guerreiros, como sons de libertação".[8]
        The intercourse between black culture and revolutionary sentiment
makes the novel a prose equivalent of the poetry of Nicolás Guillén in
Cuba and Solano Trindade in Brazil. However, the figure of its hero
corresponds exactly to the stereotyped Negro of primitivist fashion,
and it is in this respect that Amado's prejudice manifests itself.
Balduíno is a creature of pure instinct. His vitality, his spontaneity,
and his libido immunise him against material desires. Thus Balduíno
"era puro como um animal e tinha por única lei os instintos".[9] Elsewhere Amado points out that "dinheiro era coisa que não fazia falta ao
negro Antônio Balduíno".[10] Indeed, his insatiable instinct is not
directed towards money but towards sexual experience which, it is pointed
out, he cannot go long without. Balduíno's powerful sexuality, however,
requires him to seek partners who are as lusty and knowledgeable in the
matter as himself. Amado stresses that "as donzelas não interessam ao
negro".[10]
        The myth of the Negro as being sexually more alive, more demanding,
and more depraved than the White forms, for Calvin C. Hernton in his
lucid study entitled Sex and Racism, the basis of a deep and apparently
irredeemable complex in the mind of the white man. Indeed, Amado's
treatment of Balduíno's sexuality coincides very closely with Hernton's
conclusions regarding the white man's fascination with the idea that
the black man may be more virile than himself. For Hernton the myth of
the black man's sexual power developed as the logical counterpart of

the myth of the lusty black woman. If the black slave woman was so
ready to receive her white master in her bed, then it was a logical sup-
position that the male was equally depraved. This led the white man to
see the black not only as a potential avenger of his abused womenfolk,
but that this vengeance might be carried out on white women, to the
satisfaction of the latter.

Hernton's final considerations on the subject are particularly
significant with respect to Amado's treatment of the relationship between
Balduíno and the white girl Lindinalva. Hernton concludes: "The racist
fears that the relationship between Negro men and women are healthier
and freer than those between himself and white women. He also fears
that black men can be better with white women than he is. He therefore
transforms the white women into a 'lily lady', no longer a woman, but
an idol, and he fills her with his paranoid fears of Negro men".[12]
This is precisely what Amado does with Lindinalva. As a young girl she
is filled with revulsion after Balduíno, who is in her father's employment, is unjustly accused of taking surreptitious glances at her legs,
an accusation which causes his dismissal. On her second meeting with
him some years later, her fear and disgust of him are reawakened.
Finally, when Lindinalva is forced into prostitution, her growing
obsession as she moves down the hierarchy of her occupation towards the
dockside brothels and her death, is that Balduíno may find and hire her.
Her fear is translated into nightmares: "... De repente acabou tudo e
ficou sòmente o negro António Balduíno dando grandes gargalhadas de
gozo, com uma nota de cinco mil réis e uns níqueis na mão. Acordou
suada, bebeu água. Noite horrível da sua vida".[13] If, as Hernton
suggests, Amado fills his white heroine with his own fears of the Negro,
he fills Balduíno's mind with a fantasy designed to satisfy his own
sense of superiority, for Balduíno's attitude to Lindinalva is one of
worship. Lindinalva is to Balduíno a symbol of purity, whom he can only
possess in fantasy but not in real life. She is Hernton's 'lily lady',
before whom Balduíno is not only sexless but a slave. Thus Balduíno the
monster of Lindinalva's dreams is cancelled out by Balduíno the black
man who accepts his own inferiority before the white woman. As
Lindinalva lies on her deathbed, his slave instincts take over. The
Beast succumbs to Beauty: "António Balduíno se joga nos pés da cama
como um negro escravo".[14] It could be argued finally that Balduíno's
sense of social responsibility at the end of the novel is as much the
result of his devotion to Lindinalva, whose illegitimate child he is to
bring up, as it is of his own experiences of oppression. Thus the
eternal slave and the social militant coexist in the one character. As
for Balduíno the carefree oversexed Negro, he is the stereotyped product
of a white author's own sexual fears and fantasies.

The other stereotype which Amado includes in Jubiabá is that of the
sensual mulatto woman. Rosenda Rosedá is a worthy descendent of Aluísio
Azevedo's Rita Bahiana, with the same magnetic attraction for white men
as the heroine of O Cortiço. She is also the literary version of the
'mulata vaidosa' of samba compositions during the inter-war years, who
is intent on straightening her hair and lightening her dark skin with
powder. Unlike Balduíno the anti-materialistic black, Rosenda is
socially ambitious. Her sexuality is therefore an implement in her
attempts to better her position, hence her desertion of Balduíno for the
affections of a Portuguese chauffeur, which is reminiscent of Rita's
foresaking of Firmo in favour of a Portuguese immigrant in O Cortiço.
Like Azevedo, Amado lays great stress on her physical attractions, and
in this respect she is another typical product of the white male's
fantasy. On the other hand, her materialism and individualistic ambition
clash with the author's ideology. She is in fact an aspirant to the
petite bourgeoisie, and therefore a counter-symbol to Balduíno.

Very different from Rosenda is Amado's more recent 'mulata' creation Gabriela, heroine of the novel Gabriela, cravo e canela. Gabriela
is the female equivalent of Balduíno, a woman with all the natural
seductiveness of the traditional 'mulata', but without the selfishness
of Rosenda. It is through her that Amado conveys his idealistic vision
of the popular psyche. It is Gabriela whom Marotti sees as being
representative of Amado's growing commitment to the values of 'brasilidade negra': "Com Gabriela efectua-se a passagem definitiva e irrevo-
gável de Jorge Amado para a brasilidade negra".[15] In his interpretation
Marotti applies Senghor's ethic of Negritude to the character of
Gabriela, drawing attention to her ignorance of the notion of sin in
sexual love, her minimal sense of past and future and her response to
her present experiences, her vitality and avoidance of intellectually
complex structures. With regard to this view of the novel, it is not
the existence of an evolution towards 'brasilidade negra' that one
might dispute, but the price to be paid for such a consciousness in
terms of social concern. If Gabriela integrates the notion of free
love, she also represents by her behaviour the advantages of sticking
to one's position in life. The idea that freedom lies in poverty,
already visible in Jubiabá, is an unfortunate but inevitable corrolary
to Amado's main critique, which is directed against the social and
cultural mores of the ruling class.

Just as Balduíno was the happy-go-lucky black of quayside Bahia,
Gabriela is the carefree 'retirante' who arrives in the town of Ilhéus
and becomes the cook and mistress of the Arab Nacib. Gabriela, significantly, has no birth certificate and no surname. She therefore
possesses none of the impositions of established society. Her freedom
from limitation is also manifested in her ability to have sex with
different men upon whom she neither imposes nor desires to be imposed.
Gabriela, it could be said, represents a whole tradition of casual
sexual relationships which has its origins in slavery and the instability
of family life within the Brazilian proletariat. Amado transforms this
tradition into an ideal, a new more humane morality, which is pitted
against the instinctual restrictions caused by bourgeois morality and
the concept of the sanctity of marriage.

Nacib, by insisting on marrying Gabriela to ensure her fidelity,
provokes its opposite. The solution to the problem, it must be admitted,
goes against the practices of patriarchal society which, at the time
described, demanded the death of an unfaithful wife. Amado, however,
causes Nacib to annul the marriage and receive Gabriela back once more
as cook and mistress, therefore as a wife, but without the limiting
influence of formal and legal responsibility on either part. Thus the
humanisation of marital partnership is achieved, but Gabriela, the
proletariat heroine, sticks to her station.

Beyond symbolising free love, Gabriela represents the popular psyche
generally. Her vitality and unselfconscious sensuality are fundamentally
innocent. Amado, on more than one occasion, alludes to Gabriela's spirit
as being that of a child, and of the people. She is referred to as
"talvez uma criança, ou o povo".[16] Apart from this she incorporates,
in the words of one character, "essa força que faz as revoluções, que
promove as descobertas".[17] The point is that the revolution which
Amado has in mind is no longer social but cultural and spiritual.
Gabriela's 'força' and her 'alegria' spring from a tradition of social
adversity. Without the maintenance of such adversity, such a quality
would presumably cease to exist because there would no longer be the
social conditions to nurture it. Amado, in his insatiable romanticism,
has become too attracted by the popular psyche to consider the circumstances which might abolish it.

The still more recent novel Tenda dos Milagres contains elements
already visible in Jubiabá and Gabriela, cravo e canela, and further
develops Amado's philosophy of culture based on his interpretation of
the popular psyche. Like Balduíno, the hero Pedro Archanjo indulges in
Carnaval and Candomblé. Unlike Balduíno, he is a self-educated mulatto
who devotes his life to the main issues of the century. As a bedel in
the Faculty of Medicine, he defends the Afro-Brazilian and his culture
against the racist theories of the academics in the early 1900's.
Later, as an employee of the electricity company, he participates in the
strikes of the 1920's. Finally, he battles for the acceptance of mixed
marriages in the higher strata of Bahian society.

Archanjo is Amado's most complete and explicit representative of
'brasilidade negra', or as we might now call it, 'mesticismo', given
that this term is more universally applicable to Latin American nativism.
As with Negritude, the fundamental quality of 'mesticismo' is that it
offers an alternative to the rigid structures of European logic. For
Marotti, the figure of Archanjo enshrines "uma forma de pensamento
alógico".[18] 'Mesticismo' presupposes that European intellect and Afro-
Brazilian primitivism can coexist in the one personality to form the
true Brazilian, symbolised by the mulatto. As the hero himself explains:
"Pedro Archanjo Ojuobá, o leitor de livros e o bom de prosa, o que
conversa e discute com o professor Fraga Neto e o que beija a mão de
Pulquéria, o iyalorixá, dois seres diferentes, quem sabe o branco e o
negro? Não se engane, professor, um só. Mistura dos dois, um mulato
só".[19]

The concept of 'mesticismo' as being the ability to think with the
intellectual implements of a European while at the same time remaining
faithful to non-European beliefs which are unacceptable to intellect,
brings to mind Leopoldo Zea's conclusions regarding Latin American
'mesticismo', which he compares in its aspirations to Negritude: "No
se trata de negar el ser negro, o el ser indio o latinoamericano para
poder ser europeo u occidental; sino de ser también europeo u occidental
sin dejar por ello de ser negro, indio o latinoamericano".[20] Both Zea
and Amado therefore envisage a Latin American identity in terms of a
marriage between apparently incompatible cultures.

Archanjo, however, does not believe in Afro-Brazilian religion for
its own sake because he is not a religious person. In this respect his
'mesticismo' is a pose because it is the result of a conscious effort.
He defends Afro-Brazilian ritual on principle, for if he openly confessed
his atheism he would be giving up his cultural heritage and thus abdica-
ting from his ethnic dignity, or in his own words, selling his soul for
the sake of social position: "Se eu proclamasse minha verdade aos
quatro ventos e dissesse: tudo isso não passa de um brinquedo, eu
me colocaria ao lado da polícia e subiria na vida, como se diz".[21]
Archanjo's position is similar to that of Gabriela, except that his
choice is the result of intellectual understanding while hers is essentially instinctual. Nevertheless, both choose not to deny their
personality, and by so doing abandon social respectability.

There is a contrast in the novel between the mulatto social riser
Tadeu, who acquires professional standing in white society and jettisons
his cultural heritage out of necessity, and Archanjo, who refuses to do
so and therefore dies in abject poverty. Archanjo, for his part, does
not look upwards socially but forward to the time when race mixture is
complete, and Afro-Brazilian Culture forms the basis not merely of the
popular but the national psyche: "Nesse dia tudo já terá se misturado
por completo e o que hoje é mistério e luta de gente pobre, roda de
negros e mestiços, música proibida, dança ilegal, candomblé, samba,
capoeira, tudo isso será festa do povo brasileiro, música, baile, nossa

cor, nosso riso ... um dia os orixás dançarão nos palcos dos teatros.
Eu não quero subir, ando para a frente, camarado".[22] If one is to
understand Archanjo, and therefore Amado, correctly, there is an identification between national racial unity and national culture. The
darkening of the white ruling classes will automatically erode the
influence of an imposed culture, a culture which, because of its basis
in European aesthetics, has been a denial of the cultural dignity of
Afro-Brazil. The implicit message of Amado's later novels is that im-
ported cultural values cannot crush the resilience of 'mestiço' Brazil,
whether that resilience is symbolised by Gabriela or by Archanjo. The
purpose and result of race mixture must therefore be to darken the
whites culturally and spiritually.

The evolution of Amado's preoccupations from the social and economic to the purely cultural can be measured by a different yardstick,
and that concerns his portrayal of the 'gringo' or foreigner. In his
earlier novels the 'gringo' is invariably an agent of social and
economic exploitation. The tobacco plantations and cigar factory in
Jubiabá are owned by Germans. The director of the tram company is
American. In his later novels, Amado evolves towards a criticism of the
'gringo' in terms of his culture, his lack of spirituality, his materialism and practicality. Hence the brash figure of Levinson in Tenda dos
Milagres, the American academic who is responsible for the ultimate fame
of Pedro Archanjo. Equally, the figure of the Anglo-Saxon woman, sexually
liberated, but essentially masculine in her attitude towards sex, is
representative of the loss of spirituality which affluence, competitiveness
and bourgeois as opposed to patriarchal relationships have brought. Thus
the wife of the English director of the railway company in Gabriela,
cravo e canela has the sexual freedom of Gabriela, but none of her
innocence or feminity, for her sexuality is the product of her self-
conscious and therefore intellectual comprehension of it. Amado's distaste
for the liberated 'gringa' is a measure of his fundamentally patriarchal
attitude. His ultimate commitment to the notion of a type of spiritual
sensuality as being a quality peculiar to the Afro-Brazilian masses, has
brought out in him the populist that he always was.

It is, however, in his continual recourse to racial stereotypes
that Amado betrays a prejudice which the more attractive side of his
nativism might cause readers to overlook. With regard to the Negro himself, the Beauty and Beast aspect of the relationship between Lindinalva
and Balduíno has already been mentioned. In Gabriela, cravo e canela,
it is the black gunman Fagundes who continues the stereotype. His deeds
are ugly but his spirit is innocent, and his instinct is to obey and
protect the 'retirante' Gabriela: "Punha em Gabriela uns olhos pesados
e humildes, obedecia-lhe pressurosamente quando ela lhe pedia que fosse
encher uma lata com agua".[23] In Tenda dos Milagres, the monster figure
is the police agent Zé Alma Grande, whose massive strength is manipulated
by the psychological deftness of Archanjo and turned against his colleagues.
The scene described is worthy of a sequence from a King Kong film, as
Zé Alma Grande turns on his superior and kills him: "Suspendeu-o no ar,
girou com ele como se fosse um brinquedo de menino. Depois com toda a
força o atirou no chão de cabeça para baixo".[24] Nor, finally, does Amado
forget the figure of the Negro homosexual in Gabriela, cravo e canela:
"... um negro medonho, servente na pensão de Caetano, cujo vulto era visto
à noite na praia, em busca viciosa...".[25] The Negro, with all his
excesses, is never portrayed by Amado as a strictly normal person. If he
were, then presumably he would cease to be a Negro.

Similar conclusions can be drawn from his portrayal of the 'mulata'.
She is not allowed to exist either as a wife or a mother, for she is a
symbol of sexual licence. She is respected neither as a woman nor as an

individual. Her function is to attract men, to be exploited by them, and to exploit in turn by obtaining her own ends through sex. Individual ambition arising from talents outside this realm is consistently destroyed or denigrated in the interests of the stereotype. Thus Rosenda Rosedá never achieves her ambition of becoming a ballet dancer because she falls victim to her inherent sensuality. Fittingly she becomes a prostitute in the end. Ana Mercedes, her more educated counterpart in Tenda dos Milagres, is a journalist and small-time poetess, who takes charge of Levinson's entertainment during his visit to Bahia. Yet even in her case, it is the physical and moral stereotype of the 'mulata' which prevails, albeit put in the words of her fiancé, the cuckolded and understandably embittered poet Fausto Pena: "Ah! como descrever esta mulata de Deus, de ouro puro da cabeça aos pés, carne perfumada de alecrim, riso de cristal, construção de dengue e de requebro, e sua infinita capacidade de mentir!".[26] As if this were not enough, Amado causes Pena to continue: "... toda aquela paisagem doirada, cobre e oiro e o perfume de alecrim, mestra da fornicação...".[27] Indeed, it becomes apparent during the course of the story that it is the talent for fornicating and not writing poetry which enables her to publish her verse. The 'mulata' is therefore always the same, the incarnation of the white man's sexual fantasy. When placed within the proletariat, like Gabriela, she is viewed sympathetically and romantically. In the case of Ana Mercedes, her extra-sexual talents are ridiculed. Gabriela's innocence and freshness become Ana Mercedes's lack of integrity and opportunism, as they had been with Rosenda.

It is however significant that the 'mulata' achieves greater respectability the further away she is from her African ancestry, a factor which once again illustrates Amado's prejudice, as the critic Teófilo de Queiroz Júnior has pointed out.[28] Rosa, a medical student who appears fleetingly in Tenda dos Milagres, preserves the bodily attraction of her black grandmother, but the facial features of her European grandfather and father: "Tão igual e tão diferente, quantos sangues se misturaram para fezê-la assim perfeita? Os longos cabelos sedosos, a pele fina, os olhos azuis e o denso mistério do corpo esguio e abundante".[29] These qualities coupled with the fact that she is the product of a legal marriage and from a well-to-do family earn her the title of 'morena' as opposed to 'mulata'. Finally, the even whiter Edelweiss Vieira, secretary of the 'Centro de Estudos Folclóricos', and therefore an intellectual, loses her black sexual attraction (at least this is not mentioned), but assumes the moral qualities of whites: "Mulata branca de rosto redondo e manso falar, sorriso modesto, simpatia de pessoa".[30] In the case of the 'mulata', one could conclude from these examples that there is a strict correlation between colour and sexual or moral qualities: that is, the darker the woman is the more immoral her behaviour, the lighter she is the greater the respectability attributed to her. Such is not the case with the mulatto, who does not carry this racial stigma. Tadeu, a dark 'mestiço' is Amado's monument to Brazil's racial democracy, a clear example of how money can whiten, as Archanjo himself explains: "Doutor Tadeu Canhoto, genro do coronel, herdeiro de terras e de gado, bolsa na França, viagem na Europa, não há branco nem negro, no Corredor da Vitória o dinheiro embranquece, aqui miséria negra".[31]

In assessing these three novels which are so representative of the evolution of Amado's ideal, one has to distinguish the positive aspects of that ideal from the negative myths of which the author is so patently a victim. One has to bear in mind that the incorporation of African Culture into the wider culture of Brazil does not necessarily imply the acceptance of the Afro-Brazilian as a social equal. It is in this respect that Bosi's analysis of Amado as a literary populist is justified.

If one defines the populist as being the creator of myths out of
proletarian culture while equally the preserver of myths which are
traditionally the very tools of social control, then Amado falls, no
doubt unconsciously, into this category.  Thus Balduíno, symbol of
black vitality and popular vigour, is nevertheless governed by his
author's acceptance of the traditional symbolism enshrined in blackness
and whiteness, and is therefore controlled and tamed by the purity of
the blond Lindinalva.  Gabriela and Pedro Archanjo, in their different
ways, both bring about the erosion of prejudice and the modification of
rigid patriarchal values.  They therefore contribute to the evolution
of a more liberal society, while having to choose themselves to remain
in their own social positions.  Within this society in evolution, the
myth of 'mulata' sexuality is maintained.  Her only other function
apart from providing sexual delight is an implicit one, and that is to
act as a passive intermediary between a disappearing Negro and a modified White, a stage on the way to an ideal Brazilian phenotype who will
be more European than African in features and colour.  This is most
clearly portrayed in Tenda dos Milagres, a novel which is so openly
derogatory towards the figure of the 'mulata' Ana Mercedes, while res-
pectful to those who have advanced further along the road to whiteness.
Thus the myth of Afro-Brazilian potential is cultural, but the implications of this are countered and controlled by the author's adherence
to the accepted pattern of Brazilian racial relations in which the myth
of whitening plays such a part.[32]  Rosa, the medical student, adopts
the surname Oxalá when she learns of her ancestry through Archanjo, and
this little detail seems to illustrate Amado's ultimate attraction to
Afro-Brazilian Culture for its purely visual and exotic effect.  As for
Rosa, perhaps she symbolises Amado's national ideal: a 'morena' with a
re-assumed African name, a tribute to a race which is disappearing for
the maintenance of Brazil's racial democracy.


                            N O T E S


1.    O Negro na Ficção Brasileira (Rio, Tempo Brasileiro, 1965), 321.

2.    'Jorge Amado and the Preservation of African Culture',
Luso-Brazilian Review, vol.X, no.1, June 1973, 86 - 101.

3.    Giorgio Marotti, Perfil Sociológico da Literatura Brasileira
(Porto, Paisagem, 1975).

4.    História Concisa da Literatura Brasileira (S.Paulo, Cultrix,
1970 ), 457.

5.    Jubiabá (Lisbon, Livros do Brasil, n.d.), 58.

6.    Ibid., 328.

7.    Ibid., 127.

8.    Ibid., 293.

9.    Ibid., 18.

10. Ibid., 202.

11. Ibid., 93.

12. Calvin C. Hernton, Sex and Racism (St. Albans, Paladin Books, 1973), 106.

13. Jubiabá, 272.

14. Ibid., 279.

15. Marotti, op. cit., 147.

16. Gabriela, cravo e canela, 5th ed. (Lisbon, Europa-América, 1966), 323

17. Ibid., 415.

18. Marotti, op. cit., 124.

19. Tenda dos Milagres, 2nd ed. (Lisbon, Europa-América, 1970), 296.

20. Leopoldo Zea, Dependencia y liberación en la cultura latinoamericana (Mexico, Cuadernos de Joaquín Mortiz, 1974), 75.

21. Tenda dos Milagres, 299.

22. Ibid., 298 - 299.

23. Gabriela, cravo e canela, 120.

24. Tenda dos Milagres, 310.

25. Gabriela, cravo e canela, 111.

26. Tenda dos Milagres, 56.

27. Ibid., 57.

28. Teófilo de Queiroz Júnior, Preconceito de Cor e a Mulata na Literatura Brasileira (S.Paulo, Ática, 1975).

29. Tenda dos Milagres, 340. Also quoted by Queiroz Júnior, op. cit., 110.

30. Tenda dos Milagres, 345.

31. Ibid., 324.

32. This would seem to be confirmed by Amado's statement to an American journalist on the occasion of the publication of Tenda dos Milagres in the United States (cf. Queiroz Júnior, 111, footnote).

# Reality, ideality and a critical approach

Ciaran Cosgrove (Trinity College, Dublin)

Let us begin by a conclusion: art must send back to us ideal images in which we recognize ourselves, but distorted, caricatured – how we should wish ourselves and life to be, if only ... . We must proclaim, against all odds, the survival of the aesthetic presence we see negated everywhere around us. We must live for the 'other' reality which is the true reality, and not the nightmare reality we are asked to live as the only reality. Herbert Marcuse talks of the 'Great Refusal' – the self's determination to decline the offer of the 'is' (reality), and reach out for the perhaps unattainable, but tantalising vision of the 'ought' (ideality).[1] The germ of ideality is inherent in the image art throws back at us; not an innocuous germ, but one that drives men, like lemmings, over the top of the precipice. "Plonger au fond du gouffre / pour trouver du nouveau" – Baudelaire yielded to the temptation, as did Hart Crane who found his tragic destiny in the Gulf of Mexico, all because the Muse had failed to continue throwing the lifeline that connected banal life to the image of life imagined. Herbert Marcuse's recent answer to the criticism that the writings of the Frankfurt School to which he belonged were turgid and unreadable is exemplary: "Ordinary language expresses so much the controls and the manipulation of the individual by the power structure, that, already in the language you use, you have to indicate the rupture with conformity; hence the attempt to convey this rupture in the syntax, in the grammar, in the vocabulary".[2] Language must be given shock treatment if it is to become the vehicle for a new formulation. Why is it that 90% of what we read is permeated by literary cliché, tautology, etc.? We seek painstakingly in a poem for the golden image that crowns what might otherwise have been _just_ a 'good' poem; that rare moment when we feel that the boundaries of expression have been pushed back, and the banal world has been, if only for a moment, abolished. The Argentinian writer Ernesto Sábato has said: "la obra de arte es un intento acaso descabellado, de dar la infinita realidad entre los límites de un cuadro o de un libro. Una elección. Pero esa elección resulta así infinitamente difícil, y en general, catastrófica".[3]

There are three noteworthy elements in Sábato's remark: 1) the ideality of the work of art; 2) the ludicrous pretensions of the artist; 3) the artist's limited reward for considerable effort expended. The artist's inflated task is to encompass the world in a single embrace. The work of art must 'speak' the world, give the world its name, present a microcosmic vision of the totality of the world's functions. It fails if it is not multi-faceted, complete and whole in its minuscule form. The size of a postage stamp, it must yet be the Book of Books, the symphony of symphonies, the form of all forms. The fact that the 'reality' art is dealing with is 'infinite', produces a sense of acute disorder in the artist. If art has to do with setting limits to experience, disciplining the Dionysiac urges with the Apollonian rod, how is the artist meant to articulate that which by definition is without limits? The modern literature of Argentina seems obsessed with this question. Three of its most important writers, Jorge Luis Borges, Julio Cortázar and Ernesto Sábato, appear obsessed with this primordial artistic dilemma. Their work is full of vertiginous attempts (failures?) at disciplining the monster – mirrors, labyrinths, tunnels fold back on the author, bringing him back circularly to his sterile beginnings. Like Kafka's K or Sartre's characters in Huis Clos, there is no way out.

Infinity constitutes the author's being. How can the author stand
apart from the flux and give us an artistic rendering of it? The
Cartesian dualism is a trick perpetrated by a gnostic demon. The author
is nothing but an atom spinning in an infinite universe. Borges' Book
of Books in the 'Library of Babel' may exist, but one sure thing is that
we shall never find it. George Berkeley maintained that "the existence
of an idea consists in being perceived".[4] The radical subjectivism of
philosophical idealists such as Berkeley is at once the artist's victory and his defeat. The paradox resides in the fact that everything
is possible and yet nothing is possible. Ernesto Sábato's comment is,
in a real sense, the negation of a negation. 'Infinite reality' is
what is at stake. The artist is necessarily limited in his choice of
what he may attempt to achieve. Yet, if he is successful, then he has
transcended the limitations and somehow, impossibly, pinned down the
Infinite.

Artistic creation, Sábato suggests, is a matter of choice, a
matter of knowing where to call a halt. It is a "hare-brained" (descabellado) venture; nevertheless, it is somehow compulsive. It seems
to be born out of a restless discontent at how things are, and strives
for a postulation of how things might be. And yet, the 'time' of art
is that of the present. Borges, a supreme writer of fictions, who has
almost become a fictional writer, disclaims idealistically the validity
of temporal succession. Past and future are figments of the imagination.
The time of the present is all; the past is a present memory; the
future is a present expectation. Borges, like his city of Buenos Aires,
is an eidolon, a European dream, centrifugal, off-centre, an eternal
will-o'-the-wisp. His celebration of the present, the 'time' of his
fictions, is real, however. Not for him the 'postponing' character of
Christianity. The beauties and terrors of life are lived completely
for what they are, and are not defined by an eschatology. They are not
experienced as incomplete reminders of what is to come later on in
fuller form. Nature lies there before him complete and beautiful, and
not pointing to anything other than its own completeness and beauty.
"And gather me into the artifice of eternity", Yeats says. That ephemeral moment in time art seeks to make eternal. Hence man's preposterous
attempt to become a god.

The artist is the author of his own catastrophe, Sábato implies.
Driven on by his neurosis, he fashions for himself castles of the mind,
hoping to convert them into hard, permanent artefacts – and, almost
inevitably, he is doomed to failure. But his project is not in vain.
As progenitor, the author gives birth to something called the work,
before he dies. A stillbirth, because the work, like Berkeley's world,
does not exist without the perceiving eye. The work will come to life,
however, once a reader is born. The reader 're-writes the work' as
Roland Barthes tells us. The dynamism of the text is assured. Multiplicity of signification is the keynote. Everything shifts from the
signified to the signifier. The authors, the writer and the reader
(re-writer) generate their own infinities of meaning, which parallel the
infinite flux of the universe. Authorial limitation is negated and art
becomes justified. Catastrophe superseded. Negation of a negation.
It is an all-or-nothing situation, as Patrick Kavanagh realized: "But
he dreamt of / The Absolute envased bouquet / All or nothing. And it
was nothing".[5] Hence the tightrope the artist has to walk. He is always
balanced at the edge of the precipice, but must be careful not to fall
over.

The importance of the reader must not be underestimated. Julio
Cortázar, in Rayuela, gives the initiative to the reader, so that the
reader may choose his own way to read, to re-construct the text.

Cortázar readily concedes that he is only part of an on-going fictive process. That process required the other person, not for its completion, but for its continuation. Antonio Machado, in similar vein, refers to "la heterogeneidad del ser".[6] W.B. Yeats, in the poem "Ego dominus tuus", couches philosophical discourse in terms of dialogue between 'Hic' and 'Ille', the self and the 'other', the self and the anti-self. In his Autobiographies, Yeats says, "If we cannot imagine ourselves as different from what we are and assume that second self, we cannot impose a discipline upon ourselves, though we may accept one from others. Active virtue as distinguished from the passive acceptance of a current code is therefore theatrical, consciously dramatic, the wearing of a mask". Art is artifice, construction of a hard anti-self, the building of a dike to stem the tide of chaos.

In Ernesto Sábato's novel Sobre héroes y tumbas, Fernando Vidal's obsession with the 'infernal' forces of the dark, his lonely odyssey through the sewers (labyrinths) of Buenos Aires, demonstrate, in allegorical fashion, the despair of uprootedness and artistic alienation. Vidal feels "grandioso e insignificante"; he is the hybrid artist who embodies failure and success. Vidal/Sábato desires the ultimate 'issue', emergence from the tunnel into the light. Like every artist, he wants to become god-like or stone-like, i.e. achieve ultimate Being, the cessation of the struggle. Deep down, however, he thrives on the struggle. Like Schiller who opts for the 'sentimental' in preference to the 'naive', though he knows the latter to be superior, Sábato does not allow his hero the consummation of character fulfilment. Fernando Vidal is a 'being who lacks', but who is, nevertheless, free. Schiller says: "the goal to which man in civilisation strives is infinitely preferable to that which he attains in nature. For the one obtains its value by the absolute achievement of a finite, the other by approximation to an infinite greatness".[7] The "approximation", the odyssey to Ithaca, is more important than Ithaca itself. "Ithaca gave you a wonderful journey", as Constantin Cavafy put it. Not so wonderful in the case of some of our modern angst-ridden fictional heroes, but necessary, all the same. At this point in the twentieth century, easy solutions are difficult to come by.

Complexity and ambiguity in art constitute a sine qua non in a world which is only capable of trivialising man's aesthetic urges. Art must consciously carve out its own niche and cultivate its essential 'otherness'. It must generate multiple levels of signification, foreclosing none. If this leads to an unstable relativism (the text can mean what you want it to mean), then so be it. In any case, relativism might be a misnomer. The single all-important negating quality of the text would still be there. It must be said that dogmatism, in art, has no place. Barthes says: "a text is not a line of words releasing a single 'theological' meaning (the 'message' of the Author-God) but a multi-dimensional space in which a variety of writings, none of them original, blend and clash".[8] Pierre Menard can re-write Don Quijote word for word, because Menard is Cervantes, just as we, when we involve ourselves with a play by Shakespeare, become Shakespeare for one perilous, vertiginous moment.

Amid this shifting current of artistic production, what is the role of the reader/critic? Is he someone, apart from the process, who comes to the art object once it is completed? Does he complete the process or continue it? These are the problematical issues we must confront, if not resolve. The structuralists attempt to make explicit the implicit structures of the text. Pierre Macherey, who criticises the structuralists, but is close in spirit to them, maintains that the critic speaks the silences of the text, that the critic can scientifically

know what the author cannot know; a contentious issue to which I shall
return.[9]  T.E. Hulme, in his theory of the 'intensive manifold', denies
the intellect's ability to specify the significations of a text:  "The
characteristic of the intellect is that it can only represent complexi-
ties of the mechanical kind.  It can only make diagrams, and diagrams
are essentially things whose parts are separate from one another".[10]
Hulme suggests that the intellect unfolds something that is 'unfoldable',
flattens it out and observes what it sees.  Only intuition, he maintains,
can seize an 'intensive manifold', not the intellect.  Octavio Paz says
something similar when he writes, "El poema es inexplicable, no inin-
teligible".  We might note also what D.H. Lawrence has to say on the
subject:  "Criticism can never be a science; it is, in the first place,
much too personal and, in the second, it is concerned with values that
science ignores.  The touchstone is emotion, not reason".[11]  There is
the third and largest body of criticism which constructs scaffolds of
interpretation which are designed to accompany the work like instructions to a do-it-yourself kit.  This criticism is ultimately reflective.
It paraphrases and cribs, and is usually 'normative', i.e. if the work
does not meet the pre-ordained norms required of it, it is rejected.
The open-ended quality of the text is thereby denied.

If the third type of criticism is finally to be considered inadequate, and if the second throws grave doubts on the possibility of ever
explicating a text, what of the first type, the possibility of literary
criticism as a science?  Pierre Macherey says that "tout discours ...
suppose l'absence provisoire de ce dont il est discours" (p.74).  The
work of art is necessarily elliptical, compressed, the guardian of
unspoken meanings.  Between the lines of a work of art, we must re-
write the text or else we shall passively receive the text as a one-
dimensional tract and not the multi-dimensional force-field that it is.
When Macherey says:  "Une théorie de la production littéraire doit nous
enseigner ce que 'connaît' le livre et comment il le 'connaît'" (p.11),
we seem to perceive a truth and a falsehood.  The text does not reveal
itself; it remains an 'intensive manifold', to use Hulme's terminology.
The truth resides in the fact that we must 'read between the lines' of
the text if we are to gain anything at all, and thereby 'add to it'.
The falsehood rests in an unspoken assumption that the text can be
deciphered like a conundrum.  Notwithstanding a tendency in Macherey
towards sophistic argument, his observations on what criticism should
be are often acute.  His excellent essay on Borges[12] is alive with
freshness of insight, and gives concrete evidence of Macherey's ability
to apply his 'theory'.  His theory could be summarised in his belief
that criticism must:  "déceler en l'oeuvre l'inscription d'une altérité,
par l'intermédiaire de laquelle elle est en rapport avec ce qui n'est
pas elle et se joue sur les marges" (p.98).  But, what perhaps is most
important is that we should be able to recognize the "altérité" (otherness) as the inherent property of all art, eternally elusive.  Accepting
that the work of art is not and cannot be autotelic, it does not follow
that the subliminal areas of artistic process can be elucidated.  It
could, arguably, be more sensible to leave well alone, to read literature
with the spine, and not with the skull, as a character in one of Vladimir
Nabokov's novels exhorts.[13]  If we share this exhortation, we are back
once again in the field of 'intuitive' approaches to literature, as
sponsored by Hulme, Lawrence and Bergson.  The flux of experience, says
Bergson, cannot be seized by the intellect.  All we can do, and it is
enough perhaps, is to plunge 'in medias res', and experience, in
unmediated fashion, what is there.  The question is effectively begged,
however, as to whether the intellectual and the affective faculties ever
overlap in this kind of experience, or whether indeed the distinction

between the two is more than a methodological convenience. It must be said, in any case, that there are areas of agreement between a Macherey-inspired and a Bergsonian critical approach that would preclude rigid separation of the two. Each in its own way seeks to <u>know</u> the text.

Antonio Machado professed himself a Bergsonian. Time and experiential flux are the stuff of his poetry. But, like Borges, Machado believes in time present, time as it is lived, as the only 'time'. The future does not exist. In his poem "Cantares" we read: "Caminante no hay camino, / se hace camino al andar... / golpe a golpe, verso a verso". Life is a series of juxtaposed presents. When Machado evokes his childhood, he does so in terms of present memory. His experience, like Marcel's memory of 'lost time' in Proust's work, is a here and now experience. In his poem "Retrato", Machado tells us: "Mi infancia son recuerdos de un patio de Sevilla / y un huerto claro donde madura el limonero". The verbs in the present tense do not let us forget that the experience is not a childhood one, but an adult one. The lines achieve their poignancy by virtue of the fact that the remembered moments are irremediably gone and only live on in the imagination. The one illusion that art feeds on is that it can staunch the flow of history, bring the past hurtling to the present. And yet, paradoxically, art is embedded in history, articulating man's needs and desires as he fashions his life in time. Man is involved in a game of self-deception, but persist in that game he will: "y todo el esfuerzo del hombre es dar finalidad humana a la historia", Unamuno comments.[14] "History is a nightmare from which I am trying to awake", says Stephen Daedalus in <u>Ulysses</u>.

The artist is forever attempting to escape reality in order to embrace ideality. He refuses the constrictions of time and place, and allows his imagination to soar. As Sábato puts it, he is: "alguien que ha nacido con la maldición de no resignarse a esta realidad que le ha tocado vivir".[15] In Alejo Carpentier's novel <u>Los pasos perdidos</u>, the musician protagonist attempts to deny the 'civilised' world by escaping to the primitive, untrammelled life of the 'selva'. He hopes to find his true being there, but his hopes end in failure. His need for paper and ink obliges him to return to the decadent, civilised world. His belief that he could ever deny that world completely is seen to be an artist's dream. Significantly, one of the members of the expedition the musician joins clutches a copy of Homer's <u>Odyssey</u>. But the promised land, in twentieth century literature, proves an elusive entity. When the musician attempts a second time to go back to the 'selva', he is unable to find his way.

If what Jung says is true, namely that "there are present in every individual ... the great primordial images ... the inherited possibilities of human imagination as it was from time immemorial",[16] one might extrapolate and say that art, for example, may contain only a very few basic themes which recur time and time again. One of these could be said to be the 'odyssey' theme, that of a journey from a state of unfulfilled being to one of plenitude of being. The 'is - ought' dialectic could be encompassed within such a theme. The notion, if it is correct, that art glimpses a synthesis, an end-point to which all human endeavour tends, is yet another variation on the theme. Art, as illusion, ideality or 'otherness', in contradistinction to reality, is perhaps the most important idea in the philosophy of art, and yet an investigation into the significance of this fact is rarely undertaken. "One thought fills immensity", William Blake tells us, yet how often is artistic criticism satisfied with tautological 'explanations' of what the work says, rather than an enquiry into that "one thought" and how it is conceived in the particular work? Above all, the reader's importance must be stressed. The reader extends, enhances the given work, converts it into a pulsating force, makes it yield its inexhaustible significances – significances which the author had perhaps never intended, <u>but which are there</u>. Whether those significances / 'silences' should be methodically articulated, as Macherey would have us do, or whether it may be sufficient to intuit them, may not be so important. 'Reading between the lines' can be cultivated in different ways. What is important is that it be done.

I should like now to investigate some of the 'silences', the possible significations of two of the most popular novels written in Spanish in the last thirty years or so, one of them Spanish, the other Mexican. Both novels have run into numerous editions, and perhaps one of the reasons they have been so popular is to be found in the blurred possibilities of meaning they engender.

We have the distinct feeling, on reading Carmen Laforet's novel <u>Nada</u>,[17] that the true meanings are contained in the interstices of the text, that Laforet has unwittingly given us a richer novel than might at first seem apparent. In fact, the novel is so interesting precisely because of what it does not, indeed could not, have said. In approaching this novel, we should no longer ask the question, inspired by normative standards, as to how good a novel this is, how well form is married to content etc. Instead, we should seek the values of the text as they reveal themselves to us, in spite of the author. We have attempted to establish that the author is but one element, albeit an important one, in the whole writing process. The epigraph to the novel, from a poem by Juan Ramón Jiménez, is such a telling one that it is worth quoting in full: "A veces un gusto amargo, / Un olor malo, una rara / Luz, un tono desacorde, / Un contacto que desgana, / como realidades fijas, / Nuestros sentidos alcanzan / Y nos parecen que son / La verdad no sospechada". The most remarkable feature about these few lines of verse is the quality of the negative designation: the images "gusto amargo", "olor malo", "rara luz", etc. are negative, de-centred, evocative of a reality they would rather not name. The opening lines lead us to expect some climactic clarification, some positive truth; but even the truth is a negative – it is "la verdad no sospechada", not the truth we would be entitled to expect. <u>Nada</u> does indeed provide us with "la verdad no sospechada".

On the face of it, the novel is about an eighteen-year old student, Andrea, who comes to study in Barcelona, stays with relatives there, suffers from the somewhat claustrophobic atmosphere of that household, and finally leaves Barcelona for a possibly happier life in Madrid. As in Cela's <u>La familia de Pascual Duarte</u>, repressed features of Spanish life are everywhere present. Andrea, like Pascual, 'cannot breathe'; but the significances of the novel lie elsewhere.

Although the world of the novel is filtered through Andrea's consciousness, Andrea's own perceptions are unsure, ambiguous, hermetic. It is finally left to the reader to interpret as he sees fit. In the course of the novel, we are presented with a series of emotionally charged situations which confront Andrea. No interpretation of these situations is offered. They are recorded simply, without fuss. It is as if they had been interpolated in the stream of the narrative without the author knowing quite what to do with them. For example, in the opening pages of the second part of the novel, Andrea finds herself at night in a Barcelona street, after having felt "compelled" to "flee" a soirée in the house of her close friend, Ena: "Casi había huido impelida por una inquietud tan fuerte y tan inconcreta como todas las que me atormentaban en aquella edad" (p.114). Nothing is elaborated. We are as confused as Andrea as to the nature of her anxiety. And yet the

clues are there. Andrea had been strangely moved by the singing of
Ena's mother. She had felt, whilst listening to her, that that moment
of plenitude "was not going to end". The compressed intensity of the
moment had to find release; Andrea was obliged to flee. Here we have,
it seems, an instance of pure, unmediated aesthetic experience. For
one precious moment, Andrea finds herself beyond time, locked in time-
lessness. She has glimpsed that terminal point, the 'point sublime' as
André Breton called it, where all contraries are fused, and is unable
to cope with the experience. She seeks some means of calming "aquella
casi angustiosa sed de belleza" the voice of Ena's mother has awakened
in her. She becomes conscious that she is the only living being in the
universe: "había una soledad impresionante, como si todos los habitantes de la ciudad hubiesen muerto". We can almost hear Andrea's heart-
beat reverberating in the quiet city streets. She has an uncanny meeting
with a beggar: "Vi lucir en sus ojos una buena chispa de ironía" - why
irony? Almost beyond herself, she flails about for some way to calm
her excitation. She feels herself being carried along by some force
outside her: "Pensé que obraba como una necia aquella noche actuando
sin voluntad, como una hoja de papel en el viento". The one thing
capable of stilling her excited spirit is the austere, formal presence
of the Cathedral which stands silhouetted against the night sky. The
stone of the Cathedral is almost alive; it is "piedra fervorosa". She
lets its magic work on her for several minutes, and her passion is
stilled. Thus concludes an episode as ambiguous and exciting as the
'clochers de Martinville' episode in Proust's A la recherche du temps
perdu, or in Moby Dick, as Ahab's monologue in the chapter 'Sunset'.
Like Marcel, like Ahab, Andrea cannot fully understand what is happening
to her. She is the victim of her sensibility. She is driven by powers
she cannot fathom. Unlike Marcel and Ahab, she swims against the current
of her sensibility; she does not want to know herself. Hence her
continued suppression of her selfhood. She sees her ideal self reflected
in Ena and does not wish to acknowledge her own subjectivity. Andrea
is much given to self-denigration: "Cómo podría entender yo nunca la
marcha de las cosas?" she asks at one point. Andrea is not a creature
who understands her fundamental drives, nor does the author seem to come
to an understanding of Andrea. Episodes, such as the 'Cathedral'
passage, are delineated and then abandoned, to work their effect. Andrea,
like Ahab, is a being possessed, an unfathomable wonder.
    Andrea emanates mystery; her 'otherness' is what captivates Ena
from the first. Ena has a capacity for knowing Andrea's world. She,
in truth, knows Andrea better than Andrea knows herself. And yet she
cannot know Andrea's experience. In a long conversation in the middle
of the novel, Ena tells Andrea why she, Ena, has been so attracted by
Andrea. The knowledge that begs to be gleaned from this conversation
relates once again to the aesthetic core of Andrea's being. The sensuous
'otherness' of Andrea's personality, her artistic persona, are recognized
by Ena, but in the recognition lies the bitter lesson Ena must learn.
She can never experience life in the sensuously immediate way of Andrea.
Likewise, Andrea, to whom rational enquiry does not come easily, can
never intellectually come to terms with her experience. To return to
the world of literary criticism, Macherey's assertion that the critic
must specify what the artist is not able to know has some bearing on
the Andrea-Ena relationship in this novel. Andrea is the artist, the
solitary outsider; Ena, the objective eye, the critic: "Tenías los
ojos brillantes y andabas torpe, abstraída, sin fijarte en nada" (p.163),
Ena tells Andrea. Ena recalls the moment in the storm when Andrea was
not even aware that she was being soaked: "Parpadeaste un momento,
como extrañada, ...". Andrea's otherworldly character has a fatal

attraction for Ena: "Me gusta la gente con ese átomo de locura que hace que la existencia no sea monótona, aunque sean personas desgraciadas y estén siempre en las nubes, como tú" (p.165). Ena can see the non-conformity of Andrea's uncle, Román, reflected in Andrea. Even though Andrea, on a conscious level, rejects utterly the insinuation that she is like Román, her every action belies her assertion. She is the anti-thesis of the smug, self-satisfied, 'normal' majority Ena loathes. But she does not know herself or her possibilities. Ena says to her: "Me gustan las gentes que ven la vida con ojos distintos que los demás, que consideran las cosas de otro modo que la mayoría" (p.164). Andrea is different, but, tantalisingly, from the reader's point of view, does not know that she is different. At a later moment in the novel, when she attends Pons' party, she describes herself as being like "el héroe de una tragedia griega" (p.224) in her conflict with the "fuerzas cósmicas". Like Odysseus, who cannot become his true self until he reaches Ithaca, Andrea does not experience existential fullness; she is forever experiencing life vicariously, living for an ideal image that is to be found elsewhere. At no time does she desire to be herself. However, for Ena, Andrea manifests her completeness _in her very being_. Ena wishes to uncover ("descubrir") Andrea's universe as she would a work of art.

In her excursions to the seaside with Ena and Ena's boyfriend, Jaime, Andrea lives entirely for them. She does not experience her selfhood. Like a maidservant solicitous for the well-being of her mistress and master, she is happy when they are happy, and sad when they are sad. She has internalized the stereo-typed Hollywood image of two people in love: "La vi apoyada contra él cerrando un momento sus doradas pestañas. ¡Cómo te quiero!". Her alienation is expressed in the fact that she believes the love experience to be beyond her reach. Love is for other people. She can only experience it vicariously, like the cinema-goer who projects him or herself into the role of the character on the screen: "yo gozaba una dicha concedida a pocos seres humanos: la de sentirse arrastrada en ese halo casi palpable que irradia una pareja de enamorados jóvenes y que hace que el mundo vibre más, huela y resuene con más palpitaciones y sea más infinito y más profundo" (p.139). Andrea experiences herself in the passive mode. She suffers what Octavio Paz has called 'el ninguneo', non-being, perpetual displacement of self. She reflects, towards the end of the novel: "Parecía que me hubiera muerto siglos atrás y que todo mi cuerpo deshecho en polvo minúsculo estuviera dispersado por mares y montañas amplísimas...". Can we easily reconcile our former vision of Andrea as the model of sensibility with this image of the fawning, self-deprecating Andrea? In the concluding pages of the second part of the novel, which deals with Pons' party, we see the two Andreas side by side. Andrea can only exist for herself if others give her meaning. She willingly reifies herself, desiring to be "la Cenicienta del cuento, princesa por unas horas", an object for Pons. Before she leaves for Pons' house, she thinks: "Tal vez el sentido de la vida para una mujer consiste únicamente en ser descubierta así, mirada de manera que ella misma se sienta irradiante de luz" (p.215). At the party, she feels alone and isolated; the mirror throws her back a distorted vision of herself. Her true being is elsewhere: "La verdad es que no conocía a nadie y estaba descentrada" (p.220). The past participle "descentrada" is highly significant. Ena's father is also described as "descentrado" by his wife who later refers to herself as "desequilibrada". In fact, most of the characters in this novel are, somehow, 'de-centred'. In other words, their 'centre' or being is located elsewhere. They are never themselves. This is especially true in the case of Andrea, who appears to be gifted with the most tender

sensibility, yet seems incapable of taking the most elementary steps
towards understanding herself. In fact, it seems reasonable to assume
that if the characters in this novel are not what they seem to be, the
textual interplay itself may point to central significances other than
the immediately obvious ones. What we must do is to displace the
critical terrain, ferret out the silences and make them speak. What
John Berger has said of the photograph may just as well be said of art
in general: "whilst recording what has been seen, [it] always and by
its nature refers to what is not seen".[18] Andrea is never what we
think she is. At one moment she is the naive 'Cenicienta'; a moment
later, she is the acute social observer and satirist of the bourgeoisie -
cf. her description of the "señora gorda ... con la cara congestionada
de risa en el momento de llevarse a la boca un pastelillo", or, again,
"Me hablaba sonriendo, como si la sonrisa se le hubiera parado - ya
para siempre - en los labios", an evocation Federico Fellini would
surely admire. At another time, she is the lonely outsider with the
refined sensibility. Roland Barthes proclaims the death of the author.
Once the novel is written, the author sheds it like a chrysalis; it
belongs to us, the readers. Every work of art traces a journey, an
odyssey. Every work of art envisages an Ithaca, the perfected work
without the defects. But every work of art secretly shuns perfection.
Perfection implies ossification, no more goals to be won. This Andrea
realises as she flees the sound of the music in chapter ten. Absorp-
tion in that music would mean death. Odysseus knew this when he plugged
the ears of his men with wax, so that they would not hear the Sirens.
        The world of Comala, in Juan Rulfo's novel Pedro Páramo,[19] is,
like Andrea's world, the obverse of a paradise, a paradise gone wrong.
It promises so much, but yields so little. As the priest Rentería tells
his confessor: "Allá en Comala he intentado sembrar uvas. No se dan.
Sólo crecen ... naranjos agrios y arrayanes agrios" (p.76). On the
road to Comala, Juan Preciado, Pedro Páramo's son, feels that "todo
parecía estar como en espera de algo". Like the suffering souls in
hell, the characters in this novel await a happier destiny which never
comes to them. Hell is not viewed eschatologically. Hell is Comala,
an agonizing present. Like Nada, Pedro Páramo never turns out to be
what it seems. The first obvious feature of the novel is the absence
of chapters. The novel is composed of sections strung together. We
soon learn that the apparent first person narrative which initiates
the novel is an authorial trick. It is only much later in the novel
that we realise that, instead of a definitive objective voice, we
experience the reality of the novel through the prism of multiple
subjectivities. Time sequences need to be unravelled as the dead mingle
with the living. Depiction of character and event is deliberately
clouded. The incestuous overtones in the novel, the absence of privacy,
the irreconcilability of conflicting passions make for an atmosphere
of repression and claustrophobia. Characters are obliged to confront
the fact of their non-existence. Their purpose in life is to prepare
for death, and death is no release, but an uninviting continuation of
what came before. Like Andrea in Nada, the characters of Pedro Páramo
lack a clearly identifiable selfhood. But, as in Nada, there is one
female character who negates the void and salvages something from the
chaos of life. In Pedro Páramo, Susana San Juan is devoured by the
impossibility of a love relationship. Florencio is dead and beyond
her reach, but like King Lear who sees life in Cordelia when she too
is dead, Susana fondly persists in making Florencio her reason for
existence. Knowing that he is no longer with her, she dreams that he
is. Pedro Páramo knows that Susana is the only person he will never
conquer. All of Comala, its lands and its people, have fallen under

his sway, but Susana San Juan eludes him: "¿Pero cuál era el mundo de Susana San Juan? Esa fue una de las cosas que Pedro Páramo nunca llegó a saber" (p.99). Pedro Páramo's moment of epiphany, like Gabriel Conroy's in Joyce's story 'The dead', consists in his realization that Susana, like Gretta in Joyce's story, is irremediably an 'other' person, an island universe, forever unreachable. Susana's passion and Pedro Páramo's passion are unrequited. Susana's recourse is to madness and Pedro Páramo's to a willed psychic and physical immobility. He spends his final years, sitting in a chair, gazing at the road along which Susana's remains have been carried. Ralph Waldo Emerson describes the state of man as being like "the fate of the poor shepherd, who, blinded and lost in the snowstorm, perishes in a drift within a few feet of his cottage door".[20] Pedro Páramo, likewise, almost gains everything, yet loses all.

Susana, alone among the inhabitants of Comala, is capable of envisaging another life of sensual fulfilment. She also knows how to accept pain and how to control it: "Yo tengo guardado mi dolor en un lugar seguro", she says when she is near to death. She seems to surpass the limits of human endurance time and time again; her torment is unending and, worse, inexplicable. And this is what confounds Pedro Páramo. Susana's 'case' does not fit easily into his logical world. The exploitative relation he has with others and with the world is unambiguous, sure and yields results. But with Susana he gets nowhere.

Susana's experience, like Andrea's, is hermetic. Rulfo, in passages which describe Susana's passion, does not interpret. He stands apart and allows the passion to speak for itself. There is a section in the novel which relates how Susana yields her body to the sea (p.99). There is a sense of hedonistic abandon about the experience, as if that moment were to be lived in all its pleasurable intensity, lest a similar moment may never come again. A few pages later we are given Susana's reaction when she is told of Florencio's death. She inveighs against religion because religion only looks after the soul and does not have to do with the body. Her affirmation of the supremacy of the body, seen in the wider context of the novel, is crucial. The novel deals with the failure of life, the failure of the body to rescue from life a vestige of fulfilment. Rentería's role as functionary of religion necessarily excludes itself, since the premises on which such a role may be founded are disproved in terms of the novel. There is no afterlife for the inhabitants of Comala. Susana's protest is therefore life-affirming and resolutely this-worldly. She has no truck with Rentería's sermonizing about souls; souls in Rulfo's world have a thoroughly paltry existence. Only the memory of Florencio's body, the memory of the passion of lovemaking, will stand out against the dark, dying world of Comala. In the most remarkable descriptive moments in the novel, Rulfo gives us a picture of a crazed woman whose passions rage like a furnace when she discovers that her husband is dead. Florencio and Susana are the living antithesis of the sterile couple Donis and Dorotea. Dorotea will never have a child because she has never known passion. Susana is passion personified. It is little wonder that Pedro Páramo stands at her deathbed, astonished at this emotional epilepsy and absolutely removed from it. Susana's illness is caused, he thinks, by her dreams, "esos sueños sin sosiego, esos interminables y agotadores sueños" (p.105). Like the "murmurings" which kill Juan Preciado, it is the "restless dreams" which consume Susana. Towards the end of the novel, in one of her final conversations with her servant Justina, Susana asks her if she believes in hell. Justina replies affirmatively, adding that she also believes in heaven. Susana replies tersely: "Yo sólo creo en el infierno". Heaven is a postponed paradise; it is a hypothetical future, just as Dolores Preciado's dream vision of Comala is a hypothetical past. Susana lives in and for the present. By doing so, she will not escape the hell of Comala's dead, but at least she can in all authenticity say, as she dies: "Hemos pasado un rato muy feliz, Florencio". No-one else in Comala can truthfully say as much. The effect of Susana's death on Pedro Páramo is catastrophic. Never able to assess his relationship with her, he retreats into silence and inaction. She is still, though dead, the embodiment of an ideal that he cannot understand, but only invoke. Ultimately, the only sure thing he knows of her is the magical resonance of her name.

So, from a reading of Pedro Páramo as a novel about hell, we have progressed to a different reading which focuses centrally on Susana San Juan. One reading sees death in the novel as a continuation of life, thereby robbing life and death of meaning. Another reading sees the novel as centring on Susana's revolt - an affirmation of life. The novel negates its own intent, and becomes something else. Jean Franco's assessment of the novel - "The dark forces of passion, greed, envy, resentment are what rule lives, whereas the forces of light exist only in illusion"[21] - is clearly inadequate. The novel's power and hope lie concealed, 'off-centre', awaiting the reader's re-activating intelligence. Both Nada and Pedro Páramo, notwithstanding the negative implications of their respective titles, have something positive to say about the search for the hidden self. It is at least conceivable that, as Macherey says, the text does not know what it knows, and that we, as readers, must seek out its real, not its apparent, meanings.

If, as Ernesto Sábato asserts, the 'elección' in every work of art usually proves 'catastrófica', the catastrophe may only be the author's catastrophe. The reader may illuminate what the author considered dull. The author takes the risks and the reader reaps the gain. When Barthes proclaims the author's death, he proclaims the life of the text. Blake's 'One thought' or Borges' 'Book of Books' may be figments of the mind, Ithacas of the imagination, but they galvanize that process of art we make it our business to explore. They are its cause.

# N O T E S

1. See Herbert Marcuse, One dimensional Man (Boston, Beacon Press, 1964).

2. See interview with Bryan Magee, published in The Listener (9 Feb. 1978).

·3. Ernesto Sábato, Sobre héroes y tumbas (Cuba, Casa de las Américas, 1962), 195.

4. George Berkeley, The Principles of Human Knowledge (Collins, Fontana, 1962), 66.

5. Patrick Kavanagh, 'The great hunger', in Complete Poems (London, Brian & O'Keefe, 1972).

6. See 'De un cancionero apócrifo', in Poesías completas, 11th ed. (Austral 1966).

7. Friedrich von Schiller, <u>On Naive and Sentimental Poetry</u> (N.Y., Frederick Ungar Publishing Co., 1966), 113.

8. Roland Barthes, 'The death of the author', in <u>Image - Music - Text</u> (Collins, Fontana, 1977), 46.

9. All Macherey citations in this article are from: Pierre Macherey, <u>Pour une théorie de la production littéraire</u> (Paris, Librairie François Maspero, 1966).

10. Quoted by Donald Davie in <u>Articulate Energy</u> (London, Routledge & Kegan Paul, 1955), 7.

11. D.H. Lawrence, <u>Selected Essays</u> (Penguin 1974).

12. Contained in Macherey, op. cit.

13. John Shade in Vladimir Nabokov, <u>Pale Fire</u> (Penguin 1973).

14. Miguel de Unamuno, <u>La agonía del cristianismo</u> (Madrid 1938), 34

15. Ernesto Sábato, <u>Abaddón el exterminador</u> (Buenos Aires, Ed. Sudamericana, 1975), 526 - 527.

16. Carl Gustav Jung, <u>Two Essays on Analytical Psychology</u> (Princeton U.P. [Bollingen Series, 20, vol.7] 1970), 65.

17. Carmen Laforet, <u>Nada</u>, 16th ed. (Barcelona, Destino, 1965).

18. John Berger, 'Understanding a photograph', in <u>Selected essays and articles</u> (Penguin 1972).

19. Juan Rulfo, <u>Pedro Páramo</u>, 12th ed. (Mexico, Fondo de Cultura Económica, 1973).

20. Ralph Waldo Emerson, 'The poet', in <u>Essays First & Second Series</u> (London, Everyman, 1927).

21. Jean Franco, <u>Spanish American Literature since Independence</u> (London, Benn, 1973), 252.

Political comment in the work of the seventeenth-century court poet
Gabriel Bocángel

Trevor J. Dadson (The Queen's University of Belfast)


     Gabriel Bocángel y Unzueta was born in Madrid in 1603 into a
family that already had close links with the court.  In May of that
year his father, Nicolás Bocángel, was sworn into the post of doctor
to the Empress María.  Soon afterwards he became doctor to the Infanta
Margarita and in 1620 was promoted to the post of médico de cámara to
Philip III, a post he kept a year later under the new king, Philip IV.
Angelo Antonio Bocángel, Gabriel's eldest brother, became an aposentador
de su magestad, and Gabriel himself, after completing a degree in
civil and canon law at the University of Alcalá, followed his father
and brother into the Habsburg bureaucracy and served the royal family
in one capacity or another for almost thirty years until his death in
1658.  His first court post was that of bibliotecario to the Cardinal-
Infante don Fernando, youngest brother to Philip IV.  By the late
1630s he was a well-established member of the audit office of the
King's Exchequer and after 1641 the recognised chronicler of court
pageantry and ceremonial.
     We may be too easily misled into thinking that, because he was a
petty bureaucrat and court official, Bocángel was isolated from the
outside world.  Certainly we do not immediately think of him as a
political commentator or perceptive observer of contemporary history.
Yet throughout his works are scattered many references to political and
military events of the time.  The earliest date from about 1625 and the
last from around 1652; in other words, we have Bocángel's opinions on
the major portion of Philip IV's reign.  As librarian to the Cardinal-
Infante and a member of the King's tax offices, Bocángel was ideally
placed for watching at close hand the workings of the state.  Of
considerable interest in themselves, Bocángel's views add a little-
explored side to his work and character.
     That Spain in the first half of the seventeenth century was a
declining power, economically and politically, is a view that we accept
today with few reservations.[1]  Not one, but a combination of events,
seems to have brought about the rapid changes that came over the country.
Demographic decline, famine, plague, the depletion of national and re-
gional wealth, industrial weakness, financial and technical inactivity,
a lessening in trade with the New World, all combined to reduce the most
powerful nation of sixteenth-century Europe to a state of economic and
political bankruptcy.  And yet the reign of Philip IV had begun boldly
enough.  Olivares, attempting to resurrect the ideals of the previous
century after more than a decade of pacifism, set about channelling
the growing optimism of a new generation into a sense of crusade and
self-belief.  Amidst their adversities they took pride in being Spanish,
seeing themselves as the last bastion of Catholicism against the hordes
of heresy.  They looked back with nostalgia to the days of Charles V
and Don John of Austria, and felt a deep satisfaction in past glories.
Olivares fomented all these longings, but based as they were on delu-
sions, sooner or later the bubble was bound to burst.  By the middle of
the century the ideal of Christian unity had been lost and most men
wanted peace under almost any conditions.
     As I hope to show in this paper, Bocángel's understanding and
interpretation of the political situation of his day followed quite
closely the scheme I have just outlined: an initial rejoicing in the
new monarchy and new administration and the long-awaited victories they

will surely bring gives way, almost imperceptibly, to a desire for
peace and unity and an end to unnecessary warfare. Furthermore, underlying all his views we find a solid patriotism that was more in tune
with the feelings of the common people than was the biting sarcasm of
other political commentators and poets of the time.[2]

Philip IV, like his great-grandfather Charles V before him, succeeded to the throne at the age of sixteen. Undoubtedly the Spaniards
saw a happy coincidence in this fact and looked forward to the reign
of their new king as being one of unparalleled splendour and success.
Of Philip as an individual Bocángel has little to say. He equates him
with the idea of the Spanish Monarchy, itself the sole defence of the
Catholic faith, and Philip becomes part of the imperial ideal, having
little or no personal existence outside this embodiment. However, in
the Templo christiano of 1645 Bocángel draws a sympathetic picture of
the King grievously affected by the death of his Queen, Isabel of Bourbon, yet still able to show a stoical face to the adversities that
continually assail him:

> Tu que hasta el dia que espiró ISABELA,
> (Si dia pudo ser noche tan triste)
> Has sido Grande; y viendo ya que buela
> A quenta del dolor Maximo fuiste ...   (BOC, II, 79)[3]

Most of Bocángel's early court life was spent in the service of
the King's two brothers, the Cardinal-Infante Fernando and the Infante
Carlos, and understandably he has more to say about them than he had
for Philip. Bocángel evidently felt a deep affection for his young
master the Cardinal-Infante. Born in 1609 and created Cardinal-
Archbishop of Toledo in 1619 -"with singular inappropriateness"- ,[4]
Fernando was an extremely popular young man and had a lively, animated
personality. In 1634 he was sent as Governor to Flanders, and his tact
and charm went a long way towards pacifying the Flemish. He died in
Brussels in 1641, worn out by constant campaiging, and with him died
the last of Spanish hopes.

Bocángel wrote El Fernando in 1637 as a panegyric on the Prince's
life and deeds, concentrating in particular on his campaigns in Flanders. His description of Fernando in this and two earlier poems demonstrates the almost universal belief that he was the only man capable
of restoring Spain's shattered fortunes. Fernando is seen as bearing
the weight of the Empire on his shoulders:

> Sobre la espalda de vn Christiano Atla[n]te
> Huelga Ferna[n]do el ombro, huelga Iberia
> El cuydado, en el suyo vigilante ...   (BOC, I, 10-11)

> El mismo Impireo sustentan
> Tus ombros firmes de bronze.          (BOC, I, 97)

In similar words a contemporary writer also spoke of the Prince's
responsibilities to the Church:

> Y con sus ombros sustenta
> Atlante la Iglesia Santa ...[5]

Indeed, the two principal objectives of most Spaniards of the time were
the defence of the faith and the safeguarding of peace. The House of
Austria was looked upon as the main guarantor of these:

Si el español de 1635 es férvido austracista, no es por pura
pasión dinástica, sino porque cree ... que la Casa de Austria
es la más firme columna de la Religión católica.[6]

but, as Bocángel indicates, greatest hope was placed on Fernando in
particular:

> siendo braço robusto de la Religion, y de la tranquilidad de
> España ... (BOC, I, 246)

Bocángel calls him "ardiente credito de España" and lays stress on his
qualities as a warrior:

> Alta lisonja es esta de aquel Marte
> Sagrado, que con purpuras, y plumas
> Por los riesgos de Europa se reparte
> Pasmo a Prouincias, y terror a espumas ...[7] (BOC, I, 247)

The culminating passage in the poem is the description of the
battle of Nördlingen, which famous victory raised hopes in Spain that
her misfortunes in the Thirty Years War were about to be reversed.  The
heretics are driven back:

> De aquella infiel ceruiz que herida crece
> Mas sus venenos, y su cuello extinguen
> Azeros de Austria en campos de Norlinguen.  (BOC, I, 254)

and Fernando is everywhere, encouraging his troops, rushing to the
weakest point, reorganising the dispositions.  After initial doubt the
day goes to the Spaniards, and in this moment of glory Bocángel allows
his patriotism full scope:

> Como excede entre roxos arreboles
> El Sol, que los educa de la tierra,
> Los Olimpos de azero, o españoles
> Hazen, y los demás sufren la guerra ...  (BOC, I, 255)

A fierce pride in his country and its long-awaited successes is the
predominant note of El Fernando.  Bocángel refers to "Con sangre del
contrario nuestra parte" and "Nuestra victoria".[8]  That the battle
took place many hundreds of miles distant, for a cause not wholly to
Spain's immediate advantage, was of little consequence.  Nördlingen
showed a sceptical world that Spanish troops and leadership were still
a force to be reckoned with.  This was a moment for Spanish pride to
assert itself, and Bocángel fully joined in, and felt part of, this
general acclaim.

Although he evidently saw himself as Fernando's panegyrist,[9]
Bocángel surprisingly wrote (as far as we know) no poem on the Prince's
death, yet he did do so for his much more insignificant brother, Carlos.
The Infante Carlos died at the age of twenty-five on July 30 1632.
He was on his way back to Madrid from the Cortes at Barcelona when he
apparently caught a fever; he recovered slightly, but was unable to
resist the oppressive heat of that Madrid summer.  Bocángel simply states
(in the Retrato panegirico del Serenissimo Señor Carlos de Austria ...
[1633])[10] that he died from a santo parasismo, thus adroitly side-
stepping a potential minefield, for the true circumstances behind
Carlos's death are still as much a mystery now as they were then.

Carlos is important in Bocángel's poem only inasmuch as he is a symbol of the monarchy. González Dávila tells us that he was named after his great-grandfather Charles V,[11] and Bocángel refers to this in stanza III:

> Carlos, a quien por vnico destino,
> Toda la vida le ha heredado el nombre ...

Nevertheless, the dominant figure in the poem is Spain, a country, according to Bocángel, accustomed to leaving her mark on the world:

> Que España desde Orie[n]te hasta el Ocaso
> No sabe andar, sino rompiendo el paso. (RP XXXIX)

She is attended by her provinces and the whole is read out with undeniable pride and satisfaction like a glorious roll-call: "Castilla, la hermosissima donzella, Y la Anciana", "La matrona Andaluz", "Galicia ... ruda Patria de la verdad", "Sicilia fertil, Napoles hermosa, Fuerte Milan", and finally "America ... Firme en lealtad, y varia en Emisferio". There is a grandiose feeling about it and Bocángel obviously revelled in being able to glorify the Spanish Empire:

> En Reynos y en Provincias numerosa,
> Cetros añade al Español Imperio ... (RP XLII)

Yet there is one notable exception in his list - Catalonia - which is a powerful comment on the state of relations with that troublesome province. From 1626 onwards, after the failure of the Catalan Cortes of that year, Castile became increasingly annoyed with the Catalans, who had never been popular in Madrid. When Bocángel wrote the Retrato panegírico, the King's last visit to Catalonia was still fresh in everyone's memory. Olivares had had to bundle Philip unceremoniously back to Madrid from Barcelona, where the Cortes were in almost open rebellion. When Bocángel does mention Catalonia, he includes her with Hungary, examples both of unhappy states:

> Que del menor suspiro, el mas liviano,
> Cataluña y Vngria oyeron ecos,
> Ambos, siendo sus mares lastimados,
> Muchos entonces, solo de llorados. (RP LXXIX)

Similarly, there is a political flavour in his description of Vizcaya and Aragón. Vizcaya appears wearing the harness of Mars, no doubt an allusion to the uprising there in 1632 over the introduction of a new salt tax. Aragón is described as having gone over to the goddess of war:

> Y và Aragon, que se le dà a Belona,
> Armandole otros Reynos de denuedo,
> Que qual lirios, le texen la Corona ... (RP XLI)

"Other kingdoms give her courage, and like lilies weave themselves into her crown": a scarcely-veiled reference to France, since the lily was the symbol of that crown. Memories of the Aragonese riots in the 1590s continually haunted the ministers in Madrid, and it needed more than a little persuasion to make them believe that France would not one day attack Spain through Aragón.

In his observation that Spain is surrounded by warring states only
in arms against her because of her reputation and power, Bocángel shows
an acute awareness of the international situation:

> A Germania no ves gemir bermexa,
> Teñida a embidias de Olandès pirata?
> Mira la Galia y el Piamonte, osados,
> Solo porq[ue] soy mas, contra mi armados.  (RP LXXXI)

and he undoubtedly puts his finger on Spain's major problem when he
frankly states that she is overstretched:

> Mas no es esto lo mas de tus querellas;
> Lo que te tiene al llanto vinculada,
> Es que te faltan fuerças, que sin ellas
> Oy tu defensa yaze desarmada ...[12]  (RP XCVI)

Another recognised cause of weakness was the size of the Empire; Bocángel was not alone in believing that conservation of the monarchy was
more important that territorial expansion.  As Spain reviews her kings,
she realises that her greatness lies:

> No yà en Imperio, que al nacer acava,
> Sino en Reino felix, q[ue] siempre empieça ...  (RP CXVIII)

And yet, although most Spaniards saw the accession of Philip IV
as the breaking of a new dawn, a far more important and influential
figure was waiting in the wings.  The conde de Olivares made his entrance
onto the political stage at the precise moment when a fervent nationalism
and pride were manifesting themselves in Spain.[13]  Because of his
position of power, Olivares had control of practically everything that
happened in the country.  Little escaped his influence, and for this
reason alone Bocángel's attitude to the favourite is not without
interest.

Leaving to one side for a moment what he wrote about Olivares,
it seems that he avoided contact as much as possible with the Count-
Duke.  He never dedicated any work to him, although many of his contemporaries did, including his close friend Salcedo Coronel.  However, he
did dedicate the Retrato panegírico to the Duke of Medina de las Torres,
Olivares's son-in-law, and he was a member of Francisco de Mendoza's
Academia de Madrid, which came under Olivares's patronage since Mendoza
was secretary to the Count of Monterrey, the favourite's brother-in-
law.  On the other hand, as Olivares packed the King's service with
his family and his men, it was practically impossible for a poet to
survive at court without at some stage dedicating a work to one of them.

Furthermore, we have Bocángel's relations with the Admiral of
Castile.  During the 1630s the Admiral and the Duke of the Infantado
emerged at the head of the favourite's enemies.  The raising of the
siege of Fuenterrabía by the Admiral in September 1638 further caused
the relations between the two parties to deteriorate.[14]  The Admiral
gained little recognition for this feat of arms, most of the lavish
praise going to Olivares.  Soon after the event Bocángel wrote a poem
celebrating the marriage of his cousin, doña Gerónima de Maldonado,
to Juan de Cetina; the latter was "secretario del Excelentissimo
señor Almirante de Castilla, General de los exercitos de su Magestad
en España, &c. Gran Defensor de su Religion, y de su Monarchia".  After
thus boldly stating his allegiance on the title-page of El retrato,
Bocángel begins the poem with a lengthy panegyric on the Admiral:

EN Tanto, Gran ENRIQVEZ, que à tu frente
(Dos vezes impedida
De oliuas, y laureles vencedores)[15]
El ocio se consiente
Por dar à nueuo afan, segunda vida,
Enjuga de Belona, los sudores
Al dulce ventilar del aura pura ...[16]

which is followed by a direct reference to the recent victory over the
French at Fuenterrabía:

Agora solo atiendas
A designar à España nueuas glorias
En sangre noble del Francès teñido,
Amor te ruega, que las armas pendas,
Pues los sossiegos te daràn vitorias ...   (Poesías inéditas,
                                             337-338)

The Admiral had many supporters who rushed to his defence:

No careció de partidarios. Las numerosas relaciones que
circularon describiendo la campaña militar le atribuyen a
él exclusivamente el honor de la victoria; las nuevas de que
el crédito debido al Almirante iba a ser concedido a Olivares
despertaron un disgusto general.[17]

in which case the panegyric opening to El retrato may have been Bocángel's contribution.

Nonetheless, only a year earlier it would appear that he was on
comparatively friendly terms with the favourite. In the Lauro cívico
he praises Olivares for organising such a swift campaign against the
Portuguese rioters, refers to him by name in a play on words, and recalls his relationship to the Duke of Medina-Sidonia who was sent to
quell the troubles:

Y tu, Conde sublime, que te añades
Acreedor y origen deste acierto,
Pues con dictamen belico y experto,
Las violencias à OLIVAS persuades,
Y al General Campeon de Andaluzia
Con tu eleccion laureles ocasionas,
Con que en otro Guzman, Guzma[n] blasonas.[18]

The poem ends with a further oblique reference to the favourite:

Oy con glorioso assegurado efecto
El Andaluz Caton verà su espada,
Verà su fiel Oliua respetada ...[19]   (Poesías inéditas, 336)

To support the Admiral, who had been at loggerheads with Olivares
since the 1620s, was tantamount to placing oneself in the opposition
camp, yet Bocángel's defiant eulogy of him in El retrato seems genuine
enough. On the other hand, there is no doubt that in the Lauro cívico
Bocángel straightforwardly praised the favourite for his zeal and
efforts. The Infante Carlos certainly intrigued with the Admiral (one
of the reasons why Olivares had the Admiral banished from the Court),
and Bocángel was close to both Carlos and Fernando. Alda Tesán has
suggested that Bocángel avoided Olivares because of the latter's

treatment of the two princes.[20] This may well be true, although Marañón makes a good case for saying that Olivares and the princes got on well together.[21] Certainly, after Philip's illness in 1627, Fernando and Olivares came to an amicable relationship and as Bocángel did not join the Cardinal-Infante's household until 1629, he would not have been a party to the earlier disputes. If there were any under-lying antagonism between Olivares and Bocángel, it must have derived from some personal cause rather than from any political motive. The one factor that does suggest itself is that on Fernando's going to Flanders his library was handed over to the Count-Duke; the consequent loss of his treasured librarianship certainly upset Bocángel and may have turned him against Olivares.[22]

Nevertheless, whatever his personal feelings for Olivares, Bocángel was at one with the favourite in his patriotism and concern for the unity of the Peninsula. On more than one occasion he even echoed Oli-vares's grandiose plans for the Union of Arms, and like Olivares (and most Castilians) he was unable to grasp the root cause of the troubles in Catalonia and Portugal. These rebellions engaged Bocángel's atten-tion for many years, for as early as 1633, in the Retrato panegírico, he had mentioned the rebellious nature of certain provinces in the line:

> De vna Provincia y otra rebelada ... (RP LXIX)

where he undoubtedly meant the refusal by Aragón and Catalonia to grant the King the subsidies he requested. Within a short time, however, the situation had worsened and refusal given way to open revolt.

In 1637 riots broke out in Evora and other towns in the Algarve. The principal cause of the troubles was, ostensibly, the imposition of an unpopular Castilian tax the previous year,[23] but there were other issues at stake. The Portuguese nobility felt neglected and deprived of honours as they saw the best posts in the government go to Casti-lians. Fears of total integration with Spain, as advocated by Olivares, also added to the mounting bitterness felt by the Portuguese towards the Spaniards. The riots were fomented and enthusiastically supported by the lower clergy, but hopes of a general uprising were dashed as the aristocracy, headed by the Duke of Braganza, and the middle classes, held aloof. As a result, the riots soon petered out, but, nonetheless, they were an ominous sign of what was to come.

In his mainly factual account of the proceedings in the Lauro cívico Bocángel hammers the Portuguese for their "sediciones plebeyas", and, in a manner not calculated to endear him to that people, calls them "vil plebeyo, infestador de Luso". As with most of his contemporaries, he saw the uprising in religious terms: the Portuguese were "infiel", as though their blow for freedom were striking at the very foundations of Catholic unity. But although he failed to comprehend the justice of the rebels' cause, or even the real cause itself - which was of a poli-tical and constitutional nature - , he did grasp the true significance of the uprising as far as its probable results were concerned: behind it lay an attack on the concept of the patria. The Duke of Medina-Sidonia, sent to put down the troubles, is specifically praised for having preserved the patria and is offered a lauro cívico, for in such a way did antiquity reward "los inmortales Conseruadores de su Patria".[24]

Spain cannot afford internal conflicts with all her international problems, so Bocángel applauds the subjection of the rebels and the harsh punishment meted out to them. In a cynical and cold-blooded passage he describes the fate of the rebel leaders:

> Seis que lo fueron, ya no son cabeças,
> En cañamos infames sufocados;

<pre>
                    Los complices, en aspero exercicio
                    A carceles de Abeto destinados,
                    Lauarán menos culpa en muchos mares,
                    Reduciendo el estrago a beneficio ...25  (Poesías inéditas,
                                                                    336)
</pre>

National unity must not be surrendered, and in words vaguely reminiscent
of Olivares's plans he says:

<pre>
                    Y de vassallos, y de aciertos lleno,
                    El Sol de España reinará sereno.  (Poesías inéditas, 336)
</pre>

In 1641 full-scale rebellion broke out in Portugal, this time supported by the nobles, and the Duke of Braganza was persuaded to become
King John IV.26  To add to her ills Spain now had war on two fronts,
for Catalonia had risen the previous year.  Bocángel returned to these
internal conflicts in 1644, and the depth of his concern can be gauged
from the fact that he included comments on the political crisis in the
middle of a wedding poem, the Triunfo de Amor y Marte.27
The customary figure of La Fama de España28 arrives on the stage
to bemoan the civil wars that rend her land:

<pre>
                    La Fama soy de España, vengo (dixo)
                    mar de rebelde sangre, si antes tierra,
                    adonde emprende el subdito y el hijo
                    contra el padre y señor, ingrata guerra ...  (Poesías inéditas,
                                                                        350)
</pre>

Bocángel accuses Catalonia and Portugal of waging an unnecessary war
-"inventaron morir sin enemigo"- against their rightful "padre y señor",
Philip IV.  While these rebellions continue, Spain's "prescrita Religion"
suffers, and tolerance, although a praiseworthy virtue, may on this
occasion be equated with a lack of resolve: "lidia con ellos, pero mas
consigo FILIPO, siendo equivoca su lança".  An interesting aspect of
the poem is the number of medical metaphors used, a reminder perhaps
of Bocángel's family background.  He refers to the cauterising effect of
"el fuego militar" and then states that the two provinces should be
seen as patients in need of swift medical treatment, preferably by
bleeding:

<pre>
                    No sufren medicina sino armada,
                    por esso el Real Leon su amor empuña,
                    y en campaña de azeros espigada
                    salud sangrienta otorga a Cataluña ...  (Poesías inéditas, 351)
</pre>

In another work of that same year (the Dedication to Fray Antonio de
Castro's El sermón ... a las honras de los soldados, que murieron en la
batalla de Lérida) he repeats the view that the war, from Castile's
point of view, is just29 and is concerned with giving medicine to a
sick patient:

<pre>
                    Guerra (dixe) piadosa de justa:  porque la de Cataluña y
                    Portugal, de nuestra parte, es vna salud armada, que forçosa
                    administra la fuerça, pues la mejor medicina se introduce
                    mejor a vezes violenta ...  (Poesías inéditas, 356)
</pre>

Once again Bocángel establishes the link between religious and national
unity, a favourite theme of seventeenth-century political writers:

Viua los años que merece, en quietas felicidades, para defensa
de la Religio[n] Catolica, y de sus Reinos. (Poesías inéditas, 357)

In the Dedication he suggests that the troubles are due to foolishness
and lack of understanding on the part of the rebels: "bie[n] que es
trabajo superior a las armas, hazer primero al enemigo sabio, que
rendido", and in a later poem, addressed to the King's natural son,
don Juan José de Austria, he cynically dismisses the ideals of the
Catalans:

> Jimio en carcel procurada
> el catalan; los hechiços
> de lo libre imaginado
> en la verdad de cautiuo ...[30]

In other passages Bocángel reveals the same arrogant paternalism
exerted by Castile over the rest of the Empire. The Templo christiano
introduces the figure of Spain who appears wearing a cloak in which
are woven the various "miembros Godos de su corona". They do not arrive
on their own "si no bordadas en el ma[n]to de España, por ser todos
vno".[31] This vainly attempted integration may be seen as one of the
main causes of Spain's peninsular troubles, but in this aspect Bocángel
acted like most of his fellow Castilians, who saw the unity of the
Peninsula as the fundamental goal:

> Las piedras de mayor, fuerte grandeza,
> Los Principes Catolicos explican,
> Las de breue inferior naturaleza,
> A la vnion de la plebe fiel se aplican ... (BOC, II, 87)

As a true and faithful patriot he is wounded by the ingratitude of the
rebels: "La fortaleza estrena por simbolo nueuo el sufrimie[n]to de la
ingratitud rebelde",[32] and the word ingratitud is an illuminating
choice in itself, showing as it does how far the average Castilian was
from coming to terms with the real nature of the rebellions.

Whatever our own feelings for the justice of the rebels' cause, we
have to recognise that Bocángel was right to deplore their secessionist
demands. The dangers of a fragmented country were apparent to everyone; France was only waiting to take advantage of the situation to
instal herself in the Peninsula. In his contribution to the Corona
sepulcral, published by Alonso de Alarcón in 1652, Bocángel attacked the
Catalans for wishing to exchange Spanish overlordship for French Impe-
rialism:

> Que desleal licencia (ò Plebe impia!)
> Te incita à codiciar tan nuevo daño?
> Pues al Frances no debes solo vn dia,
> Que es prospero de engaños vn engaño;
> Es promesa, es lisonja ò es misterio,
> Ceñirte al yugo de vn Imperio? (BOC, II, 461)

The poem deals with the siege of Barcelona and Bocángel vividly describes
the living death of those shut up in the city. Barcelona is finally
saved by don Juan José de Austria who, "austriaco braço milagrosso",
expels the treacherous French. Bocángel is fulsome in his praise for
this new saviour:

> que nunca el mas luengo engaño
> cabal coronò su siglo ...[33]

There is only a minor reference to Portugal in the <u>Corona mural</u>, suggesting that Bocángel had recognised that, by now, Portuguese independence
was a forgone conclusion.
    In general, Bocángel was less interested in wider international
matters.[34] He was incensed by the duplicity of the French in waging
war against Spain and at the same time sending the Princess of Carignano to be maintained at Philip's expense:

> Sabelo con mas avergonzada, y excedida experiencia Francia;
> pues à los tiempos mismos que presume oponerse con màs ciega
> furia à la Española reportada valentia, nos embia y encomienda
> su sangre, que se alimenta y conserva à expensas de este grande
> y esplayado patrimonio, à piedades de esta generosa inexhausta
> Monarquìa.  (BOC, II, 33)

but in a period dominated by anti-French sentiments, he never once
mentioned the hated Richelieu.  Nonetheless, although exposing French
hypocrisy in the case of the Princess of Carignano, he was quick to
recognise the worth of another French princess, Isabel of Bourbon.
While Philip IV was with his troops in Aragón during the Catalan campaign, Isabel effectively took over the reins of government:

> Pero ISABEL, con genio preferido,
> Sustituyò el ausente amado amante
> Haziendole en la Corte su gouierno,
> No tan solo prudente, sino eterno.  (BOC, II, 101)

and she played a major part in organising supplies and men for her
husband:

> ISABEL, Sabia y Discreta,
> Mientras lidia en la Campaña
> FILIPO, con fuerça y maña
> Trata la Rueca y Tesoro,
> Hilando en estambres de oro,
> Quantas Vidas pierde España.[35]  (BOC, II, 77)

    After the death of Isabel in 1644 and that of the heir to the
throne, Baltasar Carlos, in 1646, the most pressing question concerned
the succession.  Bocángel captured the mood of the nation when he hoped
that the new Queen, Philip's niece, Mariana of Austria, would prove
healthy and fertile.  The desire for a prince is the tenuous theme
running throughout the court masque <u>El nuevo Olimpo</u> which he wrote in
1648 to celebrate the fourteenth birthday of the still distant Queen.
His principal attempt to give the work some measure of unity consisted
in his efforts to symbolise the hopes and needs of the Spanish people
themselves.  Previously he had talked of "nuestra impaciente esperança",
which would be fulfilled "en fecunda vnion de su amantissimò Real con-
sorte".[36]  In <u>El nuevo Olimpo</u> Spain's anxiety is clearly expressed:

> O mil vezes feliz, y mil dichosa
> España, en cuyos terminos se espera
> esta nueua Deidad de nieue, y rosa,
> que tiene en nuestras almas ya su esfera!
> O Monarca feliz, cuya gloriosa
> sucessíon no veràn siglos postrera,
> ...
> Salue, España feliz, Fenix serena,
> que renaciendo en dichas oy tus daños ...  (BOC, II, 161-162)

It was central to Habsburg hopes and policy that Mariana produce a
strong healthy boy, for we may be sure that it had not escaped the
Spaniards that the rest of Europe was already dividing the Empire and
simply waiting for the line to die out. In those circumstances the
birth of a princess in 1651 was hardly what Spain wanted or indeed
needed. Yet, if we are to believe Bocángel, the birth of Margarita
María of Austria was the cause of nationwide rejoicing, for it did
at least show that the Queen was fertile:

> Sintiola en estremo nuestro gran Monarcha contemplando aquel
> deseado fruto costoso primero que nacido... Esta variedad de
> sucesos hizo no solo en el pueblo pero en las Aulas Reales
> perderse de vista la certeza unos con esperanza colerica se
> persuadieron a todo el dictamen del desseo y despues se
> holgaron con tasa otros de mas cuerdo discurso agradeçiendo
> al çielo <u>la averiguada fecundidad de su Reyna</u>.[37]

Whereas the Infante Carlos had been named after Charles V and the
Cardinal-Infante after Ferdinand the Catholic, this princess was given
names which symbolised the changed fortunes that had come over Spain
in those fifty years:

> se le impuso el nombre de Margarita y el de Maria en memoria
> de su perfecta madre y de su sancta Abuela nombres que
> significan la union y la paz que son los suspirados votos
> desta gran Monarquia.[38]

Significantly, the meaning drawn from these names is almost certainly
Bocángel's own interpretation, for other narrative accounts of the
baptism suggest "Vnion, y Conformidad" and "Estrella, y Señora de la
Mar".[39] Thus we have in these words -"union y paz"- a good indication
of Bocángel's hopes for the world in which he lived. Unity and peace:
how different from the aggressive aims that had signalled the beginning
of Philip IV's reign; now his characteristic wish is for a united
"reino feliz".

He viewed the ideals and aspirations of the Portuguese and Catalans with, if anything, dispassioned cynicism, yet for the times in
which he lived he was not a cruel man, even though we may find it hard
to accept his gloating over the fate of the rebels. In his general
approach he is a moderate. Fear, through the show of force, and love
will, he thinks, educate the rebels to be faithful subjects, and he
proclaims the values of peaceful persuasion and understanding:

> Porque delito que enfermô de ciego,
> Se cura con dexarle iluminado. (<u>Poesías inéditas</u>, 336)

He placed his faith in a monarchy ruled by love and concern for its
šubject peoples and calls our attention on a number of occasions to
Philip IV's unwillingness to take harsh measures against his rebellious
subjects:

> Como que solo el pelear es Arte,
> Donde mas con amor vencer estima ... (BOC, II, 85)

Conciliation, not confrontation, is what he advocates in his oft-
repeated motif of the <u>consejo</u> being stronger than the <u>espada</u>, and his
feelings on the political world are perhaps best summed up in the line:
"triunfando en pazes, hijas de victorias".[40]

Equally as strong as his desire for peace was his intense patriotism. It is rare to find a Spanish poet of the seventeenth century who
professed such love for his country as Bocángel did. Quevedo felt a
deep sense of pride in the glory of Spain and the Empire, but frustration at her lack of success often embittered his views. Nowhere in
Bocángel is there the political sarcasm that characterised the author
of "No he de callar, por más que con el dedo". Bocángel's imperial and
political stance is much closer to the writers of the preceding age:

> Frente al pesimismo escéptico y al amargo desengaño que
> caracteriza a los grandes poetas del barroco, Herrera nos
> ofrece la insólita faceta de un sentido imperial y afirma-
> tivo de la patria ...[40]

He took pride in reciting the number and extent of Spain's provinces
and kingdoms; amidst all her troubles she is still "Religiosa y valien-
te en toda parte"; and in words that recall Camões's Lusíadas Bocángel's
love for his country rings out:

> Salue, ó tu gran Cabeça de la Europa,
> respeto de los Dioses, noble España ...[42]    (BOC, II, 164)

However, he does not let his patriotism blind him to Spain's
obvious deficiencies. He knows that she is weak and is being attacked
only because there are many countries that want to see the power of the
Habsburgs destroyed once and for all. The arguments used by the French
to justify their declaration of war in 1635 did not delude him; he
appreciated the real reason behind the attack:

> Iuzgo que España está doliente, y lidia,
> no solo ya con Marte, con su embidia.  (BOC, II, 163)

Con su embidia: in one political pamphlet or writer after another this
phrase is present.[43] Spain was suffering from the legacy of Charles V:
there were too many who had a score to settle with her.
Bocángel clearly saw in the Cardinal-Infante the type of leader
his country most needed, and it is to his credit that he continually
praised the only dynamic member of the royal family. Of course he
flattered the King and Court. The majority of his observations on the
Infante Carlos are more politic and tactful than a realistic appraisal
of this princely nonentity, and in the case of Philip IV he is no
worse than many of his contemporaries when, for example, he likened
that diffident monarch to Jupiter and Mars. And after all, he had
little choice in the matter; his career depended on showering the
King with exaggerated epithets and lavish praise.
But whatever his slight failings as a purely objective commentator,
we can see quite clearly that for one who held only minor court posts,
Bocángel displayed a rare perception at times. He loved his country but
it is not uncritical love; he saw Spain's weaknesses and was disillusioned by the waste of human and material resources that went into
waging unnecessary wars. He knew in his heart of hearts that her present
kings were not to be compared with the "Enriques grandes y Sanchos
inmortales" of an earlier age; nor were there many glorious deeds and
heroes to sing about, in comparison with the exploits of a Charles V
or a reconquista king. Yet he still believed in Spain, which, in an
age of pronounced scepticism, disillusion and despair, says much for
his patriotism and sense of the past. All through his life Bocángel
had shown a strong disinclination to follow the latest poetic trend

simply because it was in fashion. Now that it was fashionable and, given the disastrous political and military circumstances, relatively easy to decry patriotism, Bocángel constantly strove to uphold the values of the past, to retain a belief in the institution of the Monarchy and the person of the King, and to treat the, undeniably grim, political situation in as positive a way as possible. He offered no easy, immediate solutions such as were continually being urged upon the government by the arbitristas.[44] His verse simply mirrored the hopes and preoccupations of a minor government official in the tax offices, yet it may not be going too far to suggest that through his verse we hear the voice of the ordinary, perplexed Castilian of the first half of the seventeenth century, who was trying to come to terms with the drastic alteration and reduction in the world rôle of his country; an alteration and reduction he was beginning to feel but whose extent he could as yet scarcely perceive.

# N O T E S

1.  J.H. Elliott makes a good case for seeing the decline of Spain in terms of the decline of Castile, as most of the other regions were wholly or partly unaffected by Spain's financial and military losses. See 'The decline of Spain', Past and Present, XX (1961), 57.

2.  It is worth recalling that during the years 1617-1625 there was a considerable movement for reform of Spain's social, moral and educational values, often led by literary figures. The style of language adopted by these erstwhile reformers was "now profoundly didactic, now aggressively satirical, now bitterly polemical" (R.L. Kennedy, 'The Madrid of 1617-25. Certain aspects of social, moral, and educational reform', in Estudios hispánicos. Homenaje a Archer M. Huntington (Wellesley, Mass. 1952), 276). In this context we could perhaps put Bocángel's two major works on court life, El Cortesano español and the Consexos christianos, though they are by no means as satirical and polemical as the works mentioned by Professor Kennedy. For details of Bocángel's approach to the social world of the court, see T.J. Dadson, 'An Autograph Copy of Gabriel Bocángel's "El Cortesano español"', BHS, LIII (1976), 310-314. The views expressed by Bocángel on the political situation fall outside the scope of Professor Kennedy's article both in time and substance, but we would do well to bear in mind her analysis of the zeal with which poets took up the cry for reform and the effect that contemporary social and moral values had on their works. A similar interplay occurs in Bocángel's poetry.

3.  Abbreviated references in this style are to the Obras de don Gabriel Bocángel y Unzueta, 2 volumes (Madrid 1946), edited by Rafael Benítez Claros.

4.  J.H. Elliott, Imperial Spain 1469-1716 (London 1970), 323.

5.  Romances varios de diversos autores (Zaragoza 1643), 372.

6.  J.M. Jover, 1635: Historia de una polémica y semblanza de una generación (Madrid 1949), 184.

7. Cf. the description of Fernando in the Romances varios poem already mentioned: "Assombro de luteranos, / terror de las Suecas armas, / castigo de los Hereges, / miedo y espanto de Olanda." (365)

8. The italics are mine.

9. Cf. the following passage: "Admita pues V. Alteza, estas execcutadas premissas de futuros, y mas heroycos partos, pues oy se conciben en sus inuictas hazañas, para lograrse el dia que haziendo inmortal clarin de su ya merecida fama, escuche el Orbe mis heroycos numeros, en merito de su inmortal assunto." (BOC, I, 245).

10. All references to this poem will be abbreviated to RP and the stanza number.

11. See González Dávila, Historia de la vida y hechos de Felipe III, MS 1257, Biblioteca Nacional, Madrid (BNM), fol. 192$^r$.

12. When Bocángel revised the poem some three or four years later, that is after Nördlingen, he changed desarmada to minorada, so that the last line then read: "Oy tu defensa yaze minorada", which is a fair reflection on the upsurge of Spanish hopes after that victory.

13. Cf. J.H. Elliott: "Philip IV himself, with more intelligence but no more strength of character than his father, hardly represented a very inspiring herald for a new dawn, but in the conde de Olivares he had chosen a favourite of a very different calibre from the favourites of Philip III ... In his intense nationalism, in his desire for a thorough reformation, and in his disgust with the old ministers and their policies, Olivares, who was only thirty-four at the time of his advent to power, represented the hopes and ideals of the new generation in Castile." ('The Spanish Peninsula 1598-1648', in The New Cambridge Modern History, IV (1970), 457 - 458).

14. For a more detailed examination of this matter see D.L. Shaw, 'Olivares y el Almirante de Castilla (1638)', Hispania, XXVII (1967), 342 - 353 and E.M. Wilson, 'Calderón y Fuenterrabía: el 'Panegírico' al Almirante de Castila', BRAE, XLIX (1969), 253 - 278.

15. For some time I have wondered whether these lines do not conceal a reference to the imagined obstructionist policy pursued by Olivares towards the Admiral and his efforts to wage war on the French: oliuas - Olivares [?]. Cf. the similar play on words as noted below in the Lauro cívico.

16. The full text of this poem is to be found in T.J. Dadson, 'Poesías inéditas de Bocángel', Boletín de la Biblioteca de Menéndez Pelayo, XLVIII (1972), 336 - 342.

17. D.L. Shaw, op. cit., 351.

18. The full text of the Lauro cívico is in T.J. Dadson, op. cit. n.16 above, 331 - 336.

19. The italics are mine.

20. See J.M. Alda Tesán, 'Bocángel y su obra poética', BBMP, XXIII (1947), 10.

21. G. Marañón, El Conde-Duque de Olivares (Madrid 1936), 236 - 240.

22. See, for example, the following document he had drawn up: "En lugar de dicha plaça de Bibliotecario le obligò la junta de su Alteza a contentarse con plaça de contador entretenido ..." (R. Benítez Claros, Vida y poesía de Bocángel (Madrid 1950), 265). My italics.

23. This new tax, along with existing taxation, was designed to raise 500,000 cruzados, which was to be used to equip expeditions for the recovery of Portugal's overseas territories, notably Brazil, lost to the Dutch since the early 1630s.

24. The Lauro cívico was never properly published, which may be because the Duke of Medina-Sidonia attempted to set himself up as King of Andalucía in 1641, in which case Bocángel's poem would not have been welcomed in certain quarters. Medina-Sidonia was pardoned, though losing much of his vast wealth, but the Marquis of Ayamonte (also mentioned in Bocángel's poem) was executed. For details of the plot see R.B. Merriman, Six Contemporaneous Revolutions (Oxford 1938), 135 - 136.

25. This fate is strangely out of tune with the promises made by Philip IV in a letter granting pardon to the towns and cities which had taken part in the riots: "usando de minha costumada clemencia ... Hey por bem de perdoar como desde logo perdoo a todos os que ouuerem intervindo, ajudado, fomentado, e fauorecido por escrito, ou de palaura ... aos promouedores e cabeças das presentes alterações." (Sucesos del año de 1637, BNM MS 2368, fols. 183ff.).

26. The pride and vanity of Portugal in setting up its own King is symbolised by the image of the peacock:

> y Portugal en belico alboroto
> vano Pavon sus circulos deshaze ... (Poesías inéditas, 351)

> El vulgo Portugues, vil Faetonte,
> Sino pauon, que circulos deshaze ... (Ibid., 335)

Bocángel probably had in mind the old topic of the peacock and its proverbially ugly feet, which appear in direct contrast to the beauty of its fan-tail: "deshaz la rueda y mírate los pies". Cf. E.M. Wilson: "The contrast between its magnificence and this ugliness was a commonplace image of pride in sixteenth-century literature ..." ('On Góngora's Angélica y Medoro', BHS, XXX (1953), 90 - 91.

27. The Triunfo de Amor y Marte has no date of publication, but since the marriage it celebrates took place in January 1644, we may assume it to have been written close to that date; the poem was probably intended to be handed round to the guests at the ceremony or at the wedding breakfast afterwards. The full text of the poem is in T.J. Dadson, op. cit., 342 - 354.

28. Bocángel uses this personification in similar circumstances in the Retrato panegírico (RP XXI), the Templo christiano (BOC, II, 98) and El nuevo Olimpo (BOC, II, 163).

29. That war undertaken against rebels was just was a widely-held view at the time: "es una ofensa odiosa contra Dios y contra el

príncipe que el súbdito resista su autoridad ... Se deduce que una
guerra emprendida por un Príncipe contra rebeldes es una de las más
justas, y que todas las medidas permisibles en la guerra pueden uti-
lizarse contra ellos ..." (Quoted by R. del Arco y Garay, La idea de
imperio en la política y la literatura españolas (Madrid 1944), 272,
from Baltasar de Ayala, Tres libros sobre el Derecho de Guerra).

30. BNM MS 3661, fol. 206$^v$. These lines are probably echoes of the
earlier: "Carcel comprada los sepulta vivos; / de subditos apelan a
cautivos." (Poesías inéditas, 350).

31. BOC, II, 98.

32. BOC, II, 94.

33. BNM MS 3661, fol. 206$^v$.

34. Of the long-standing rebellion in the Dutch provinces he wrote
little; he referred briefly to the troubles there in the Templo christiano and commented on the heresies of the Dutch in an academy poem of
the 1630s.

35. For the truth of Bocángel's statements on Isabel, see M. Hume,
The Court of Philip IV. Spain in Decadence (London n.d.), 385 and
Reinas de la antigua España (Madrid n.d.) 319.

36. From the Piedra cándida, BOC. II, 109.

37. BNM MS 18.657$^{14}$, fols. 12$^v$-13$^r$. My italics.

38. BNM MS 18.657$^{14}$, fol. 24$^r$.

39. See, for example, BNM MS 2382, fol. 298$^r$.

40. BOC, II, 163.

41. Antonio Vilanova, 'Fernando de Herrera', in Historia general de
las literaturas hispánicas, II (Barcelona 1968), 742.

42. Cf.: "Eis aqui se descobre a nobre Espanha,
Como cabeça ali de Europa toda ..." (Os Lusíadas, III, 17)

43. Note the following lines by Bocángel's close friend, Salcedo
Coronel, in the Panegírico al Cardenal-Infante:

¡Oh España!, ¡oh, tú, de ilustres atenciones
objeto digno en toda edad luciente
cuya fama envidiosas las naciones
oscurecer presumen ciegamente ... (Cristales de Helicona

(Madrid 1649), fol. 88$^v$.).

44. In El Cortesano español Bocángel expressly warns against taking any
notice of their advice:

Estrañaras los oçiosos
que dan formas al gouierno

        y conjura al arbitrista
        plaga raçional del reyno.  (st. 43 of the autograph copy in

MS Add. 7946 of the University Library, Cambridge).  In the later
Consexos christianos he makes the same point and also adds his support
to the government in these difficult times:

        No te metas à arbitrista,
        no zensures del Govierno,
        donde mas canas cavezas
        rigen el timon de un Reyno.  (R. Benítez Claros, Vida y

poesía de Bocángel (Madrid 1950), 320).

Garcilaso, Albanio, Salicio, Nemoroso, Tirreno, Alcino

Patrick Gallagher (University College, Dublin)

The historical identity of Garcilaso's shepherds has frequently
been asserted. Francisco Sánchez, El Brocense, states that Salicio and
Nemoroso in the First Eclogue are Garcilaso and Boscán, respectively.[1]
Six years later, Herrera accepts the view that Salicio is Garcilaso but
rejects the equation Nemoroso = Boscán, proposing instead that Nemoroso
= Antonio de Fonseca (husband of Isabel Freire).[2] This proposition was
endorsed by Azara in the eighteenth century,[3] but has not gained wider
acceptance, presumably because it is obvious that Herrera advanced it
in the first place only out of a sense of propriety: the right person
to mourn Isabel's death is not Boscán, but her widower.[4] Albanio in
the Second Eclogue is often assumed to be a scion of the House of Alba,
usually Garcilaso's young friend, the fourth Duke, Fernando Alvarez de
Toledo, who is portrayed in the heroic part of the poem as leading the
Emperor's forces to victory against the Turks on the Danube. The
identities of Tirreno and Alcino, the shepherds of the Third Eclogue,
are so seldom discussed as to suggest that an exclusively fictional
existence is deemed adequate for them.

The identification of Salicio as Garcilaso has so far withstood
the test of time, partly because Salicio is an easy anagram of Cilaso
(though imperfect because of its superfluous i) and partly because the
shepherd's jealous recriminations in the First Eclogue have seemed to
represent what might have been the poet's emotions on being rejected by
Isabel Freire. There is now not very much reason to doubt that Salicio
represents Garcilaso, but two false conclusions should be resisted:
(1) that other shepherds do not represent the poet; (2) that Salicio
and the poet sing in unison. Salicio represents Garcilaso at a stage
in his amorous career, a stage from which the poet during his composition of the eclogue finds himself distanced by time and ideology.
Hence, other shepherds, instead of representing, or exclusively
representing, acquaintances of the poet, represent Garcilaso at other
stages. Thus Nemoroso, despite nemus = bosque, could not possibly
represent the happily married Boscán (outlived, as we know, by his
widow), not only because, as Herrera points out, the shepherd talks
about Boscán in the Second Eclogue but because, in the First, he is
mourning the death of his shepherdess. Rather, if Salicio is an imperfect anagram of Cilaso through having one extra letter, Elisa, Nemoroso's
shepherdess, being an imperfect anagram of Isabel through having
one extra letter too, points clearly to the identification of
Nemoroso as Garcilaso. In other words, the shepherds of the First
Eclogue both represent the poet; but their representing him on very
different occasions should suggest some distance between the poet's
implied voice and the explicit bucolic voices which dramatise distinct
circumstances from his past.

To see both shepherds as Garcilaso at different stages is therefore
a critical advance on the view that Salicio was Garcilaso and Nemoroso
someone else. The extravagance of Salicio's effusions, a sly rhetoric
of self-promotion alternating with outbursts of tempestuous recrimi-
nation, alerts attentive readers against supposing that the shepherd
speaks for the poet. Salicio represents what might have been a
younger, immature Garcilaso, a courtly lover, whose self-indulgent
lachrymosity and sentimental excesses should not be given the uncritical
sympathy which, by their artful presentation in song, they aim to win.[5]

Nemoroso's voice in the First Eclogue is closer to Garcilaso's than
is Salicio's: in mourning the death of Elisa Nemoroso's tone is
dignified, and if it is sometimes strenuous in its expression of grief
(e.g. stanzas 23, 24, 25, 27 and 28) it is never intemperate or petulant.
Though he has more reason for tears and does shed them copiously (308-9),
giving his sorrow free rein ("desta manera suelto ya la rienda / a mi
dolor" [338-9]), he does not compete in the production of any more tears
than an unfeigned grief causes him to shed. He is not playing games,
unlike Salicio, whose song rehearses a strategy for the return of
Galatea. Nevertheless, as in Salicio's case, we should avoid the
mistake of an absolute identification of the shepherd with the poet
who, without being coldly remote, keeps his critical distance. This
is evident in Nemoroso's final stanza (the penultimate stanza of the
poem) because the shepherd's ardent prayer for a celestial reunion with
Elisa and consequent immortalisation of their love is couched in a
syntax which undermines his hope, showing underlying doubts, and is
followed by Garcilaso's concluding stanza in which death is symbolically
presented as the ultimate, inescapable and general reality which not
even the time-suspending art of pastoral song can annul:[6]

> Nunca pusieran fin al triste lloro
> los pastores, ni fueran acabadas
> las canciones que solo el monte oýa,
> si mirando las nuves coloradas,
> al tramontar del sol bordadas d'oro,
> no vieran que era ya passado el día;
>  la sombra se veýa
>  venir corriendo apriessa
>  ya por la falda espessa
> del altíssimo monte, y acabando
> el fugitivo sol, de luz escaso
>  su ganado llevando,
> se fueron recogiendo passo a passo.[7]

The difference between Salicio and Nemoroso is one of tone.
Nemoroso's voice is true: an adequate response to the death of Elisa;
Salicio's is false: an extravagant response to being jilted by
Galatea. His art is a covert plea for her return and a campaign for
general sympathy.[8] It is clever, but not quite clever enough to
disguise its strategy. He gives his song away as a ploy by overplaying
his part. Though it is not at first easy to spot this (it is much
easier to be seduced by Salicio's dulce lamentar) sensible students of
the eclogue can keep him at his proper distance. He casts himself for
the part of Orpheus but Garcilaso ironically intends him for a different
rôle: that of Polyphemus. A trained ear should perceive that Salicio
fails in the rôle of Orpheus. Like Polyphemus, he thinks he can sing,
but he is too noisy. His Galatea, like the nymph of the same name in
the ancient myth, is repelled by a cacophony composed to woo her.
Salicio, who argues that her leaving him for another shepherd is monstrous (stanzas 11 and 12), is himself too monstrous for love. This
does not mean that, like the Cyclops, he is physically loathsome but,
rather, signals a mental disability: the cultivated lachrymosity
that places his idea of love in the far-fetched Castilian tradition
represented by the Lamentaciones de amores of Garci Sánchez de Badajoz
and others is a dangerously self-indulgent extravaganza, an irrespon-
sible distortion of a serious subject. Salicio's view that Galatea
has behaved unnaturally by running off with another shepherd is one
that the reader, aware of the poet's Salicio-Polyphemus analogy, will

assess with a certain scepticism.  It is possible for the reader to go
further and share Garcilaso's _ironic_ amusement when a Polyphemus-
figure who usurps the rôle of Orpheus proclaims the monstrosity of
Galatea's new love.

Salicio's association with the immoderate posturing of courtly
love does not allow him a voice that can ring true.  Though he can
aspire to the status of Orpheus (or imply that he has already achieved
it) his art will not have that magic power so long as it is inspired
by the strident pitch and competitively inflated sentiment of _poesía
cancioneril_.

Garcilaso, by censuring courtly love, instead of condemning
Salicio outright, is dramatising an immature phase exacerbated to crisis
by Galatea's violation of a relationship which seemed sanctioned by a
voluntary bond of mutual affection.  Salicio is, therefore, an
apprentice musician, game enough to simulate a skill as yet unmastered,
but falling short of the artistic perfection required of any Orpheus-
figure one could agree to take seriously.

He has a prototype, Albanio, in the Second Eclogue, composed
almost certainly before the First.[10]  Garcilaso studies have not
investigated the two poems in the light of this not-too-recondite
similarity.  Albanio, it is traditionally held, must mean someone
belonging to the house of Alba, and hence not Garcilaso himself.  But,
considered together, the poems themselves show that Salicio's condition
and behaviour in the First Eclogue are a refined version of Albanio's
in the Second.  Albanio's rôle is a rehearsal for the much more cunning
and sophisticated, but otherwise similar, part which Salicio plays in
Eclogue I.  But while the latter shepherd represents an immature though
artful Garcilaso, the former exemplifies the same immature phase in a
highly-esteemed friend.

Verses in the Second Eclogue which must be biographical because
they are otherwise gratuitous establish Albanio's separate identity:
he and Camila are related by blood ("una donzella / de mi sangre y
agüelos decendida" [170-1]).  There being no bond of consanguinity
between Garcilaso and Isabel Freire shows that the poet is not here
bucolicising himself and his Portuguese lady.  Albanio was an admirable
denizen of the Tagus valley and, as a friend, closest to Salicio and
Nemoroso:

SAL.        Estraño enxemplo es ver en qué a parado
            este gentil mancebo, Nemoroso,
            ya a nosotros, que l'emos más tratado,
              manso, cuerdo, agradable, virtüoso,
            sufrido, conversable, buen amigo,
            y con un alto ingenio, gran reposo.    (901-6)

Salicio was far away from the Tagus when Albanio's nervous breakdown
occurred and is told something of the story on his return:

SAL.        Parte de tu trabajo ya m'avía
            contado Galafrón, que fue presente
            en aqueste lugar el mesmo día,
              mas no supo dezir del acidente
            la causa principal, bien que pensava
            que era mal que dezir no se consiente;
              y a la sazón en la ciudad yo estava,
            como tú sabes bien, aparejando
            aquel largo camino que 'sperava,

                    y esto que digo me contaron quando
                    torné a bolver...                    (128-38)

Anxious to help his unfortunate friend, he now asks Albanio to unburden
his grief "que'l mal, comunicándose, mejora" (142). No literary
purpose is served by Salicio's extra-conventional advertence to his
absence from the pastoral community or having to spend some time in the
city to get ready for a long journey. Garcilaso is obviously talking
about himself in order to chronicle a sequence of real events (a real
absence from Toledo, long journey and return to the Tagus valley) in
relation to other events extrinsic to the poem but represented in it by
Albanio's history.

Who, then, is Albanio? A poem that ends with almost 800 lines of
heroic eulogy of the House of Alba cannot begin with an eclogue about
a shepherd called Albanio for no reason at all. Since most of the
eulogy is about Fernando Alvarez de Toledo, the fourth Duke of Alba,
Albanio is more likely to represent him than anyone else.[11] The trouble
with this identification is the unseemliness of the shepherd's conduct.
In casting Fernando for a pastoral part, would Garcilaso not have
baulked at low-style comic moments, lust, lunacy and attempted suicides?
Perhaps; but then an immature Fernando represented by a love-crazed
shepherd would surely have been permissible in a poem in which the
glorious exploits of a mature Fernando are so generously celebrated.
Albanio's being from the Tagus valley instead of Alba de Tormes is
unimportant since the Tagus is Garcilaso's locus amóenus, the setting
for all three eclogues.

Albanio's identity is also unimportant, at least to students of the
eclogue as poetry, because he is a type of lover rather than an exclusively historical individual. His connexion with Fernando is contra-
puntal, the former's descent from nobility to madness and utter
debasement being answered by the latter's rise to worthiness, maturity
and contentment. Albanio is what any lover without guidance is in
danger of becoming; but he can be cured by a strong injection of reason,
the antidote to his madness (1842-54).

Pending such treatment Albanio remains the prototype of Salicio in
Eclogue I; is, in effect, a Salicio silvestre, a wild man and primitive
precursor of the would-be Orpheus in the later poem.

Salicio's opening apostrophe to his absent shepherdess ("¡O más
dura que mármol a mis quexas / y al encendido fuego en que me quemo /
más elada que nieve, Galatea!" [57-9]) is a polished and stylised
version of Albanio's similar exclamation:

                    "  ¡O fiera", dixe, "más que tigre hircana
                    y más sorda a mis quexas que'l rüydo
                    embravecido de la mar insana!"       (563-5) .

Galatea's indifference is more 'aesthetically' presented: she is not
so much a force of nature as a work of art. The comparison is ecphrastic,
statuesque; the images still and inanimate; she is a marble sculpture,
colder than snow; urbanely aloof. Camila is all movement, an untamed
huntress, warm-blooded but indomitable.

Salicio's commendation of himself echoes Polyphemus's song in
considerable detail though he himself implicitly invites comparison
with Orpheus. The importance of this comparison is clear: if we
allow it, Galatea, like the rest of nature, should be softened by his
song and if she is not, is unnatural, hence culpable. This is the
high point of Salicio's argument:

                tú sola contra mí t'endureciste;     (206)

it echoes Camila's obduracy in Albanio's complaint:

                ni tu dureza cruda enterneciste.     (574)

    Salicio's recriminatory rhetorical questions recall those of his
prototype.  Stanza XIV of the First Eclogue begins:

                ¿Cómo te vine en tanto menosprecio?
                ¿Cómo te fuy tan presto aborrecible?
                ¿Cómo te faltó en mí el conocimiento?   (183-5)

Albanio had already made these points:

                ¿Cómo pudiste tan presto olvidarte
                d'aquel tan luengo amor, y de sus ciegos
                ñudos en sola un ora desligarte?     (578-80)

Salicio's lachrymosity, artfully emphasised by the regular end-of-stanza
refrain "Salid, sin duelo, lágrimas, corriendo", is not Garcilaso's only
approximation to the Castilian lamentations of love:  Albanio's vale-
dictory apostrophe to his divinities, beasts, mountains, fields and
rivers is indebted to the same tradition that takes its cue from
Jeremiah's challenge (O vos omnes, que transitis per viam, attendite,
et videte si est dolor sicut dolor meus):

                ¡O dioses,......!
                .....................
                recebid las palabras que la boca
                echa con la doliente ánima fuera

                ¡O náiades,......!
                .....................
                assí, nympha, jamás en tal te veas
                .....................

                ¡O hermosas oreadas......!
                .....................
                dexad de perseguir las alimañas
                venid a ver un hombre perseguido,
                a quien no valen fuerças ya ni mañas.

                ¡O dryades......!
                .....................
                parad mientes un rato a mis querellas.
                                                  (602-28)

The tearfulness of Albanio's lamentations is established from the
moment Camila runs away for the first time:  "que hize de mis lágrimas
un río" (490); "el largo llanto, el desvanecimiento" (495); "antes, con
mi llorar, hazía espantados / todos quantos a verme allí venían" (516-7);
"ninguna otra repuesta dar sabía, / rompiendo con solloços mi gemido"
(525-6); "... solté la rienda al triste llanto" (562); "al affligido
y triste quando llora" (680).

    A difference between Albanio and Salicio seems to arise in
connexion with the classical personae adopted by the shepherds.  Albanio,
for instance, hints that he is a type of Narcissus.[12]  Salicio aspires

to the powers of Orpheus, although we are invited by the poet to see
him as Polyphemus. But Polyphemus of course becomes a grotesque
Narcissus when, in Ovid's version[13], he comments favourably on his
monstrous reflexion, and Salicio follows Polyphemus's song in this (as
in other major details):

> No soy, pues, bien mirado
> tan difforme ni feo,
> que aun agora me veo
> en esta agua que corre clara y pura
> y cierto no trocara mi figura
> con esse que de mí s'está reyendo    (175-80)

Salicio, not being a monster, could be right to consider himself hand-
some or even handsomer than his rival but, ironically, the pleasure he
finds in the contemplation of his image, though reminiscent of the
Narcissus story (and hence linked to Albanio's predicament), recalls
Polyphemus, and thus warns the reader of the shepherd's unsuitability.

What Garcialso condemns in Albanio is an attitude to love dominated by a lust apparently sanctioned by the <u>cancionero</u> exaltation of
desire. Whether Salicio in the First Eclogue is guilty of a similar
offence it is impossible to know. But there are some signs of a rather
tiresome possessiveness in Salicio's attitude to Galatea[14] which
remind us of Albanio's cruder attempt to 'possess' Camila by overpowering her in order to stop her escaping from him a second time
(766-864).

But if Albanio is a 'Salicio silvestre', as this paper argues, it
seems equally true that the other shepherds were once Albanios.
Salicio and Nemoroso in the Second Eclogue both confess that Albanio's
sufferings are not new to them; they are either older or have passed
through Albanio's phase earlier. Garcilaso frequently implies that
this kind of disorder is commonplace, a more-or-less inevitable
occurrence in the life of the pastoral lover. "¿Piensas que tu tormento
como nuevo / escucho?" (347-8) Salicio asks Albanio. Salicio is still
scarred by his experience and begs Albanio to trust him and confide in
him, promising sympathy and understanding:

> Assí que, pues te muestro abiertamente
> que no estoy inocente destos males,
> que aun traygo las señales de las llagas,
> no es bien que tú te hagas tan esquivo,
> que mientras estás bivo, ser podría
> que por alguna vía t'avisasse,
> o contigo llorasse, que no es malo
> tener al pie del palo quien se duela
> del mal, y sin cautela t'aconseje.    (356-64)

The grave and serene Nemoroso was cured of "amor insano" (1093) by the
sage Severo, restored to spiritual good health and freed from enslave-
ment to the senses:

> Tras esto luego se me presentava,
> sin antojos delante, la vileza
> de lo que antes ardiendo desseava.
>   Assí curó mi mal, con tal destreza,
> el sabio viejo, como t'é contado,
> que bolvió el alma a su naturaleza
> y soltó el coraçon aherrojado.    (1122-8)

As the only shepherd who figures in all three eclogues, Nemoroso appears to hold some special importance for Garcilaso. The Nemoroso of Eclogues I and III undoubtedly represents the poet after the death of Isabel Freire, whose pastoral name is Elisa; and while one cannot be certain that the Nemoroso of Eclogue II is the same shepherd, it seems reasonable to suppose that he represents the poet at a different stage: after his recovery from the marriage of Isabel but before her death. In all three eclogues he has passed beyond the extravagant and immoderate immaturity dramatised by Albanio and the apprentice poet-musician Salicio who hopes, in Eclogue I, to fool everyone into believing that he can make the world bend and sway to his art. (It is not just as an anagram of Cilaso that Garcilaso calls this shepherd Salicio, 'willowy'.)

The death of Isabel completes the comparison of Garcilaso and Orpheus. Having lost Isabel twice the poet can, in the pastoral guise of Nemoroso, immortalise Isabel and himself, by composing elegies on the banks of the Tagus, the river whose waters will carry his words from Toledo to Lisbon and, indeed, past the Portuguese lady's birthplace to the Atlantic and the Spanish seaborne empire, the distant Castilian-speaking world which – with the conquest of Mexico (1519-1522) and Peru (1531-1534) – was being established during Garcilaso's lifetime.[15]

Nemoroso, then, after the death of Isabel (1534?) is the poet's bucolic persona in his time of grief. Because her loss gives him a true (rather than strident) elegiac voice, he realises the powers of Orpheus, becoming the man whose tragic love-song enchants the sylvan world (nemus = bosque / vega; Nemoroso = 'del bosque' / 'de la vega' and 'pastor enamorado [amoroso] del nemus'). In the Third Eclogue, Garcilaso shows the theme of tragic love illustrated on the nymphs' tapestries linking Orpheus and Nemoroso, who has already acquired, since the composition of the First Eclogue, some fame on the banks of the Tagus as the grief-stricken singer of Elisa's death. Garcilaso is here claiming that he is already famous and will be remembered as a Spanish Orpheus.

Thyrreno and Alcino, acting on Virgil's amoebaean advice[16] give us alternating stanzas of amatory dialectic. There are no clear biographical hints to help us see through the pastoral disguise and they may therefore be more purely fictional shepherds than Albanio, Salicio and Nemoroso. Yet not entirely, perhaps: as two of the most highly-esteemed shepherds of the Tagus valley, and young men of the same age[17] it is unlikely that they represent nobody.

Thyrreno sings of happy love, Alcino of unhappy. Since (a) Garcilaso in this eclogue asserts his own fame as a poet and that of Fernando in Eclogue II and (b) Fernando's happiness in love is cele-brated in that poem and (c) Thyrreno and Alcino are both famous and around the same age, they could represent Fernando and Garcilaso. Fernando's link with his pastoral name could be his triumphant return to Spain after the defeat of the Turks; the Emperor's armada sailing westwards across the Tyrrhenian Sea, is, after all, evoked in Eclogue II:

> Tras esto blanqueava falda y seno
> con velas, al Tirreno, del armada
> sublime y ensalçada y gloriosa.
> Con la prora espumosa las galeras,
> como nadantes fieras, el mar cortan
> hasta que en fin aportan con corona
> de lauro a Barcelona...            (1692-8)

# N O T E S

1. "Egloga Primera. Salicio es Garci-Lasso. Nemoroso, Boscán:
porque nemus es bosque." _Obras del Excelente Poeta Garci Lasso de la_
_Vega. Con anotaciones y enmiendas del Licenciado Francisco Sanchez,_
_Cathedratico de Rhethorica en Salamanca. Dirigidas al muy ilustre_
_señor Licenciado D. Diego Lopez de Cuniga y Sotomayor. Con Privilegio_.
(Salamanca 1574); commentary reprinted in Antonio Gallego Morell,
_Garcilaso y sus comentaristas_ (Universidad de Granada 1966); see note
B-95, p.255.

2. "Es de doblado título y se introducen en ella dos pastores, uno
celoso, que se queja por ver a otro preferido en su amor; éste se llama
Salicio; y es ya comun opinion que se entiende por G. L. mismo. El
otro, que llora la muerte de su Ninfa, es Nemoroso y no, como piensan
algunos, es Boscan, aludiendo al nombre; porque nemus es bosque. Pues
vemos en la egloga segunda donde refiere Nemoroso a Salicio la historia,
que monstró Tormes a Severo, que el mismo Nemoroso alaba a Boscan. Y
en la tercera lloró Nemoroso la muerte de Elisa:

                entre la verde hierba degollada.

La cual es doña Isabel Freire, que murió de parto; y asi se deja
entender, si no me engaño, que este pastor es su marido Antonio de
Fonseca." _Obras de Garcilaso de la Vega con Anotaciones de Fernando_
_de Herrera_ (Seville 1580); commentary reprinted in Gallego Morell,
op. cit., see note H-423, pp.457-458.

3. "...algunos han sido de parecer que Nemoroso es Boscan, fundados
en que Nemus es bosque; pero Herrera con mejor fundamento cree que
Nemoroso es D. Antonio de Fonseca, marido de Elisa, que es Doña Isabel
Freire, que murió de sobreparto." _Obras de Garcilaso de la Vega_
_ilustradas con notas de Don José Nicolás de Azara_ (Madrid, Imprenta
Real de la Gaceta, 1765); commentary reprinted in Gallego Morell,
op. cit., see note A-63, pp.655-656.

4. I have commented elsewhere on these traditional identifications.
See Patrick Gallagher, 'Hacia una poética de Garcilaso: la subversión
de la armonía en su arte; apuntes sobre la "Egloga primera"', _CuH_,
CVII, No.319 (1977), 113-124; esp. 114, note 5.

5. Salicio's song owes its competitive lachrymosity to the Castilian
_Lamentaciones de amores_ and, particularly, to a poem so entitled by
Garci Sánchez de Badajoz. This fact gives us a clear idea of the type
of courtly lover Garcilaso portrays. The 'distance' between the poet
and Salicio is further discussed in Gallagher, art. cit., 115-121;
for the debt to the Castilian _Lamentaciones_ see Patrick Gallagher,
'Garcilaso's First Eclogue and the Lamentations of Love', _FMLS_, IX,
No.2 (1973), 192-199.

6. See 'Hacia una poética...', 121-124.

7. For all Garcilaso quotations in this article I use _Garcilaso de_
_la Vega; Obras completas_, ed. Elias L. Rivers (Madrid, Castalia, 1964).

8. Salicio's persuasive methods are examined in M.J. Woods, 'Rhetoric
in Garcilaso's First Eclogue', _MLN_, 84 (1969), 143-156.

9. I alluded to the Salicio-Orpheus comparison in 1973 ('Garcilaso's First Eclogue...', 193). A more recent article asserts Salicio's adoption 'by artful connexion' of the rôle of Orpheus; see p.80 of Alan K.G. Paterson's study 'Ecphrasis in Garcilaso's "Egloga Tercera"', _MLR_, 77 (1977), 73-92.

10. Lapesa's dates for those two compositions are as reasonable and secure as the biographical data permit them to be: Eclogue II, 1533 - early 1534; Eclogue I, 1534 - early 1535. Rafael Lapesa, _La trayectoria poética de Garcilaso_ (Madrid 1948), 3 and 186-188.

11. This raises a question: how can Albanio who is still deranged at the end of the poem be Fernando whose example it is hoped he will follow? The answer is, I believe, as follows: Albanio represents the immature Fernando not as he was but as he might have become without the Renaissance indoctrination of Boscán and Severo. The fact that Fernando received this training _implies_ that he needed it, even if Garcilaso cannot say so without belittling him. Severo's power to cure courtly love is frequently praised; hence, Fernando, instructed by him, must also have been put right on this score, like everyone else. Fernando's youthful and ardent impatience is briefly evoked by Garcilaso in the marriage scene: "Apenas tienen fuera a don Fernando, / ardiendo y desseando estar ya echado" (1415-6); and in 1369-78 where, on being shown the sleeping nymph that he will marry, he is immediately impassioned, as Albanio is by the sleeping figure of Camila (755-801). The question is more fully considered in my article 'Garcilaso's Second Eclogue and _Don Quixote_: tradition or polygenesis?', _BzRPh_, XI (1972), 38-49.

12. "Ecco sola me muestra ser piadosa" (598); lines 958-62 paraphrase Ovid's account of the myth; see _Metamorphoses_ (III, 448 ff.) The curious inversion of the story belongs to a courtly love tradition identified in a paper on this subject: Elias L. Rivers, 'Albanio as Narcissus', _HR_, 41 (1973), 297-304.

13. _Metamorphoses_, XIII.

14. Textual evidence of possessiveness is adduced in 'Hacia una poética...', (118-9).

15. That the Third Eclogue implicitly makes such claims and suggests such continuities is argued by Paterson (art. cit.), in detail and at length, and, in my opinion, convincingly.

16. In Eclogue VII, 5: "cantare pares et respondere parati."

17. "... entrambos estimados / y sobre quantos pacen la ribera / del Tajo con sus vacas enseñados; / mancebos de una edad.../"(298-301).

"Estalactite":   a génese do poema

Maria Guterres (University of Liverpool)


    Aos 21 anos Carlos de Oliveira publicou o seu primeiro livro de
poesia, Turismo (1942) livro que se enquadra no movimento Neo-Realista.
(O Neo-Realismo veio impor à arte a problemática do social e dos problemas colectivos e inicia-se com o "Novo-Cancioneiro", colecção poética
publicada a partir de 1941).  Já aí aparecem os temas que vão cbsecar
o autor ao longo da sua carreira poética - o clima, a infância, a
insónia, a cólera, o amor, a morte e sobretudo a solidariedade do poeta
com o seu povo.  O poeta ecoa as dores do povo, principalmente no livro
Mãe Pobre (1945) e tenta acordar a "ama-pátria dormindo" com o som dos
seus "versos plebeus":

                    Tosca e rude poesia,
                    meus versos plebeus
                    são corações fechados,
                    trágico peso de palavras
                    como um descer da noite
                    aos descampados.

                    ... E quanto mais nos gelar a frialdade
                    dos teus inúteis astros,
                    mortos de marfim,
                    mais e mais, génio do povo
                    tu cantarás em mim.[1]

    Contudo a partir do livro Cantata (1960) o poeta começa a afastar-
se dos temas ideológicos do Neo-Realismo e a interessar-se pelo tema
das palavras:

                    As palavras
                    cintilam
                    na floresta do sono
                    e o seu rumor
                    de corças perseguidas
                    ágil e esquivo
                    como o vento
                    fala de amor
                    e solidão:
                    quem vos ferir
                    não fere em vão,
                    palavras.    (153)

    Este vai ser um dos temas mais importantes de Micropaisagem (1968)
de que "Estalactite" é o poema principal.  Eduardo Prado Coelho num
estudo sobre a poesia de Carlos de Oliveira integra toda a poesia deste
autor no Neo-Realismo:

        O pcema dá o exemplo, diz-nos como situar o produto no
    seu processo, como adivinhar na sua nudez final a contribuição
    específica dos materiais, os invisíveis instrumentos, as apa-
    gadas mãos que o construíram.  É este o grande objectivo (cujas
    implicações no plano social permitem que se classifique a mais
    recente poesia de Carlos de Oliveira como "neo-Realista").[2]

Porém Nelson de Matos critica esta posição e insiste - com razão - na impossibilidade duma "leitura de carácter ideológico dos últimos livros do poeta".[3]

Mesmo Eduardo Lourenço, o grande crítico e defensor do Neo-Realismo ao analisar Sobre o lado Esquerdo (1962) admite que "um poema como este participa de uma ideia da realidade poética afastada da tradição neo-realista".[4]

. Em Turismo encontramos dois poemas intitulados respectivamente "Amazónia" (9) e "Gândara" (14) que talvez possam explicar a paisagem do mundo poético de Carlos de Oliveira. Eduardo Lourenço num estudo sobre a poesia Neo-Realista, pensa que as duas regiões tiveram um grande impacto no poeta, sobretudo a segunda:

> É possível que a "Amazónia" de Carlos de Oliveira tenha tido menos presença na sua sensibilidade do que nós o supomos, que essa mesma Amazónia seja um pouco sonhada como era se bem nos lembramos em Turismo e que baste o decisivo encontro com a sua Gândara de pinhais, dunas, águas mortas, lagoas, tão viva nos seus romances, para explicar o capital de imagens líquidas, a obsessão pelas coisas decompostas que nos seus poemas abundam.[5]

Parece-nos ser este o caso, porque o poeta apesar de ter nascido no Brasil (Belém, 1921), regressou a Portugal aos dois anos e foi viver para uma aldeia na Gândara, Nossa Senhora das Fevres:

> Lagoas pantanosas, desolação, calcário, areia. Cresci cercado pela pobreza dos camponeses, por uma mortalidade infantil enorme, por uma emigração espantosa. Natural, portanto que tudo isso me tenha tocado.[6]

O que é certo é que o poeta foi influenciado nos seus últimos livros de poesia - Cantata (1960), Micropaisagem (1965) e Entre duas memórias (1971) - pela poesia brasileira, sobretudo a de Carlos Drummond de Andrade e a de João Cabral de Melo Neto. Esta influência nota-se na preferência do poeta por um vocabulário limitado, uma rigorosa secura, brevidade do discurso poético e pelo exercício do poema sobre o poema. Num poema intitulado "Carlos Drummond de Andrade", Carlos de Oliveira admite a influência deste autor na sua poesia e neste poema refere-se ao seu livro Fazendeiro do ar, publicado em 1953:

> Sabe lavrar
> o vento
> onde prosperam
> o seu milho, o seu gado
> fazendeiro do ar habituado
> no arquétipo escrito
> de lavoura,
> meu orgulho onomástico
> deixado
> na outra margem do mar
> quando parti
> para cuidar das lavras deste lado
> e silàbicamente
> me perdi.[10]

João Cabral de Melo Neto disse numa entrevista que concedeu a Inêz Corrêa da Costa: "confesso que desde o princípio construí minha poesia".[7]

Carlos de Oliveira descreve no seu livro O aprendiz de feiticeiro como construíu Micropaisagem:

> O trabalho oficinal é o fulcro sobre que tudo gira [...]
> Para mim esse trabalho consiste quase sempre em alcançar um
> texto muito despojado e deduzido de si mesmo, o que me obriga
> por vezes a transformá-lo numa meditação sobre o seu próprio
> desenvolvimento e destino. É o caso de "Micropaisagem". Um
> texto diante do espelho vendo-se e pensando-se. (262, 263)

Analisemos detalhadamente "Estalactite" e vejamos como o poeta construiu o poema.
Micropaisagem compõe-se de 82 poemas agrupados em 12 ciclos[8] com títulos diferentes. "Estalactite" o primeiro ciclo deste livro contém 14 estrofes, cada uma delas com o número de 14 versos escritos em verso livre. Os versos são curtos, sincopados e muitas vezes compostos duma só palavra.
Da mesma maneira que "Uma faca só lâmina" tem sido considerado um modelo da poética de João Cabral de Melo Neto,[9] que teria como tema o próprio processo de composição, Micropaisagem segundo Eduardo Prado Coelho também "constitue uma verdadeira arte poética, e uma das mais densas e inteligentes da literatura portuguesa contemporânea".[10]
Em "Estalactite" Carlos de Oliveira usa um número restrito de imagens e palavras tiradas do reino mineral: água, pedra, cristal, cal, terra e estalactite. Também tem a obsessão do viscoso, informe e disforme dos reinos mineral e animal similar à de Pablo Neruda. O poema desenvolve-se à volta do seu próprio centro numa busca incessante, uma tentativa de regresso ao enigma da origem. As palavras das duas estrofes de abertura são analisadas, repetidas, decompostas, ordenadas de maneira diferente e transformadas de estrofe para estrofe:

I

O céu calcário
duma colina oca,
donde morosas gotas
de água ou pedra
hão-de cair
daqui a alguns milénios
e acordar
as ténues flores
nas corolas de cal
tão próximas de mim
que julgo ouvir,
filtrado pelo túnel
do tempo, da colina,
o orvalho num jardim.

II

Imaginar
o som do orvalho,
a lenta contracção
das pétalas,
o peso da água
a tal distância,
registar
nessa memória
ao contrário
o ritmo da pedra

                    dissolvida
                    quando poisa
                    gota a gota
                    nas flores antecipadas.

O poeta elabora novas combinações com estas palavras nas estrofes
que se seguem e pouco a pouco reconstitue a génese do poema. É um
processo infinito que continua de verso em verso, cada verso decifrando
o enigma do verso anterior.

Na primeira estrofe enuncia-se o tema do poema: a formação da
estalactite e da poesia. O poeta situa-se no interior do poema
("corolas de cal tão próximas de mim") e começa a interpretar e identificar o mundo que está a criar: sem a sua interpretação este universo
não existiria. O poeta guardou na memória a imagem duma colina donde
os gandareses extraem a sua cal e é esta memória da estalactite calcária
que o poeta vai recriar. O poema genera-se a partir da "colina oca" em
que se encontram as estalactites formadas de "água ou de pedra" con-
struídas gota a gota durante mais milénios e de tal maneira vivas para
o poeta que ele julga ouvir o seu gotejar. As gotas, paradoxicalmente,
de água ou de pedra caindo do tecto da colina formam no chão a estalactite que depois voltará ao seu lugar de origem. O poeta está aqui a
desmistificar a concepção lírica da poesia. As coisas formam-se duma
maneira lógica, objectiva e científica.

Os dois primeiros versos da segunda estrofe vão iniciar a estrofe
IX; subsequentemente e de forma fortemente estruturada, os versos 3 e 4
iniciam a estrofe X, os versos 5 e 6 iniciam a estrofe XI (embora
escritos em três versos nos dois casos); os versos 7, 8 e 9 iniciam a
estrofe XII, enquanto que os versos 10 e 14 encerram a estrofe XIII.
A segunda estrofe continua a descrever a formação da estalactite através
duma relação estreita entre o som e o sentido das palavras. O poeta
busca o centro da terra, o momento inicial onde tudo começa, o ponto
obscuro da memória onde os objectos permanecem idênticos: "registar
nessa memória ao contrário o ritmo da pedra". Nestas duas estrofes as
palavras são os signos que descrevem e representam os objectos. As palavras
são usadas para descrever e interpretar os objectos. Mas a partir da estrofe
III o poeta começa a pôr em causa a possibilidade da linguagem ser incapaz
de representar as coisas. Se as palavras pudessem 'nascer' do interior dos
objectos então o poema poderia achar "o seu micro-rigor". (33) O micro-rigor que
Carlos de Oliveira quer atingir corresponde à "realidade prima" de João Cabral:

                    por fim à realidade
                    prima e tão violenta
                    que ao tentar a apreendê-la
                    tôda imagem rebenta.[11]

Nas estrofes IV e V através das coordenadas do espaço-tempo o poeta
aprofunda "o micro-rigor" e "o ponto-morto" do poema. A espessura, a
densidade e o peso das palavras transformam-se lentamente "nesta
caligrafia de pétalas e letras" (35). A combinação metafórica "de
pétalas e letras" forma as flores calcárias (estalactites). A escrita,
"caligrafia" emana da relação entre a cal e a água.

Na estrofe VI o poeta tenta alcançar um universo meta-linguístico.
As palavras são inadequadas e o "signo" (36) não consegue representar o
objecto. É assim que "o poema sonha o arquétipo do voo" (51) quer dizer
que há interpretações que as palavras não podem reflectir. O voo que
representa o limite da consciência ou da plenitude é impossível de
atingir. Nas estrofes seguintes (VII e VIII) o poeta reflecte sobre a
linguagem e frustrado com a pobreza das palavras, coloca-as no lugar

dos objectos. É o lento gotejar das palavras "o pulsar das palavras"
(37) caindo do "céu calcário" (38), povoado de "estrelas" (37) sobre a
página branca do texto que vai construindo pouco a pouco a estalactite.
João Cabral também se refere frequentemente à folha branca nos seus
poemas, como por exemplo "A lição de poesia":

> Toda manhã consumida
> como um sol imóvel
> diante da folha em branco:
> princípio do mundo, lua nova.[12]

O poeta continua a descrever o mundo subterrâneo de que ele faz
parte e que só existe porque o está descrevendo: "Como se nascesse
apenas por ser escrito" (39). A palavra aqui não representa o objecto:
é o próprio objecto. Cal + grafia = caligrafia: a grafia da cal.

Nas estrofes X e XI a elaboração ou construção da estalactite faz-
se gradualmente através da "contracção de algo mais denso" (40). O
infinitamente grande do "mar" (40) num "microscópio" (40), o infinitamente pequeno, mostra-nos a antítese entre os milénios dum macrocosmos
em evolução e o rigor dum microcosmos tal a estalactite ou o poema.
A estalactite começa a tomar uma forma concreta porque a palavra "pesa,
paira, poisa no papel":

> O peso
> da água
> a tal distância
> é quase
> imperceptível
> porém pesa,
> paira,
> poisa no papel
> um passado
> de pedra
> [cal ← colina]
> que queima
> quando
> cai. (41)

A seguir (estrofes XII a XV) as palavras reflectidas no papel "como
imagens num espelho" (43) tornam-se "de novo compreensíveis" (43).
O significante e o significado, a imagem da coisa e a própria coisa
são outra vez separadas e o poeta vai dar uma ordem às palavras que é
arbitrária porque:

> O poema
> atinge
> tal concentração
> que transforma
> a própria
> lucidez
> em energia
> e explode
> para sair
> de si. (45)

A força de linguagem é tal que a palavra se transforma no objecto e a
linguagem torna-se independente do poeta. Encontramos a mesma imagem
na quadra final de Uma faca só lâmina de João Cabral.

Nas estrofes XVI, XVII e XVIII o poeta aprofunda a ideia da
explosão do poema. Carlos de Oliveira usa imagens científicas para
descrever a explosão do poema. Fá-lo como se descrevesse a explosão
dum motor: "a força comprimida age ao inverso do excesso em que se
contraiu" (46) e o poema finalmente "rebenta incapaz de conter a sua
forma" (47), depois de:

> transpor
> a linha do horizonte
> interior
> o momento
> em que a dilatação
> se ultrapassa
> a si mesma
> e transgride
> o limite
> da estabilidade
> o equilíbrio
> que torna as coisas
> coesas. (48, 49)

A estrofe XIX repete e retoma sob formas diferentes versos da
estrofe V, mas o sentido não é o mesmo. A substituição das palavras
não é gratuita, ao contrário mostra a estrutura rigorosa do poema. Na
estrofe XIX a transformação "numa caligrafia de letras vagueando no
ar" (49, 50) é feita duma maneira violenta e brutal. O poeta usa os
vocábulos "bruscos acidentes" e "pulverizar" (49) em vez de "suaves
acidentes" e "florir" (35). As estrofes seguintes (XX a XXII) descrevem as transformações que sucedem à explosão. "O poema sonha ainda
o arquétipo do voo" (51), mas não pode alcançar a liberdade ou a
plenitude e "cai e localiza na cal o ponto morto" (51) e a estalactite
regressa ao seu ponto de origem, "dentro da colina povoada outra vez
por colunas morosas". (52)

Na estrofe XXIII é a linguagem que vai construir e pensar o poema
e é ela que vai encaminhar a mão que escreve:

> encaminhando-a
> entre a pouca luz
> do texto
> à sílaba crucial
> da única palavra
> que é
> ao mesmo tempo
> água e pedra: sombra,
> som ... (53)

As palavras construíram a harmoniosa estalactite, gotas de orvalho
sobre as flores calcárias. O que fica é a sombra da estalactite na
página branca existindo "apenas por ser escrita" (54). A memória é
uma estalactite - o poeta buscou através da memória dum céu calcário
duma colina oca a formação da estalactite na natureza e no poema. O
poema é a recriação do mundo de obsessões e fantasmas de Carlos de
Oliveira.

O poeta aplicou neste poema a sua teoria poética exemplificada num
poema intitulado "Lavoisier":

> Na poesia
> natureza variável

das palavras
nada se perde
ou cria,
tudo se transforma:
cada poema
no seu perfil
incerto
e caligráfico,
ja sonha
outra forma. (23)

O poeta tenta fazer na poesia o que Lavoisier fez na ciência. Usa os métodos da dedução e não da indução. As palavras exactas e rigorosas são transformadas e recriadas de verso em verso para antingir o microrigor do poema. O poeta também procurou transgredir os limites da palavra-signo. "Estalactite" é um poema rigorosamente construído, com um vocabulário limitado tirado do reino mineral fossilisado construindose e vendo-se construir. "Estalactite" é na verdade "o poema que as palavras construíram".[13]

# N O T A S

1. Carlos de Oliveira, Trabalho Poético, Volume I (Lisboa, Sá da Costa, 1976), 25. Todas as citações das poesias de Carlos de Oliveira reportam-se aos dois volumes desta edição.

2. Eduardo Prado Coelho, A palavra sobre a palavra (Porto, Portucalense Editora, 1972), 122.

3. Nelson de Matos, A leitura e a crítica (Lisboa, Editorial Estampa, 1971), 123.

4. Eduardo Lourenço, Sentido e Forma da Poesia Neo-Realista (Lisboa, Editora Ulisseia, 1968), 247.

5. Ibid., 184.

6. Carlos de Oliveira, O Aprendiz de Feiticeiro, 2ª edição (Lisboa, Seara Nova, 1973), 260.

7. Entrevista a Maria Inêz Corrêa da Costa 'Um poeta só João', Jornal do Brasil (6 de Abril de 1968).

8. Gastão Cruz na sua crítica sobre Micropaisagem que escreveu para o Diário de Lisboa (19 de Dezembro de 1968) considerou este poema de natureza cíclica, dividindo-o em 12 ciclos.

9. Benedito Nunes, João Cabral de Melo Neto (Petrópolis, Vozes, 1971).

10. Eduardo Prado Coelho, op. cit., 119.

11. João Cabral de Melo Neto, Antologia Poética (Rio, Editora Sabiá, 1967), 172.

12. Ibid., 265.

13. Nelson de Matos, op. cit., 107.

# The artist as subject : a study of Martín Adán's La casa de cartón

J.M. Kinsella (The Queen's University of Belfast)

La casa de cartón[1] was first published from Lima in the Amauta
magazine at the beginning of 1926. After this earlier fragmented publication the first edition came out in 1928 with some five hundred
copies which were handed out personally by the author. Then for thirty
years the book remained out of print until the editor, Juan Mejía Baca,
published it again in 1958, following this with a third and fourth
edition of the work in 1961 and 1971. All of these editions included
an introduction by Luis Alberto Sánchez and a colophon by José Carlos
Mariátegui.

Sánchez views the work as Adán's affirmation of his literary affi-
liations in the face of society and in relation to politics. In his
essay he remarks that "La casa de cartón la levantó Martín en el limbo,
en las nubes, en cualquier parte, adonde sólo le alcance el rumor de
sus aficiones literarias..."[2] For the marxist critic, Mariátegui, the
novel is a statement of outright heresy on the part of an adolescent of
aristocratic background whose literary intentions coincide with his wish
to criticize the bourgeoisie of the Barranco of the nineteen twenties.
Thus Mariátegui concentrates on the author's disrespectful attitudes
towards representatives of the more privileged classes of society. He
summarizes the novel as "un esquema de biografía de Barranco, o mejor,
de sus veraneantes".[3] This earlier critical appraisal illustrates how
from its first appearance La casa de cartón was recognized as an important work written by one of the most promising writers of the generation.
Sánchez speaks of the author's "auténtico sentido artístico"[4] whilst
Mariátegui claims that the success of this publication by an "escritor
y artista de raza"[5] is already fully assured.

Later critical attention has after a long silence endorsed and
elaborated upon this earlier favourable appreciation. Estuardo Núñez,
a classmate of Adán's in the Deutsche Schule in Lima, views the work as
"el libro que abre una etapa nueva en la prosa peruana de este siglo".[6]
The Argentinian critic Juan Carlos Ghiano confirms the freshness of the
work by describing it as "una novela inesperada frente a las estructuras
dominantes en la narrativa de entonces..."[7] He believes that the praise
it has received from two younger writers of the calibre of Mario Vargas
Llosa and Eduardo Bryce Echenique adds substance to his own judgement.
Sebastián Salazar Bondy has summarized the critical recognition given
to La casa de cartón as follows: "La crítica señaló, en síntesis, que
los valores de ese libro se mantenían intactos y que, a pesar de su
inserción dentro de las corrientes vanguardistas, se sustentaba - y, por
ello perduraba tan actual, tan vivo - en una inspiración sincera, en
una intuición aguda, en un estilo rico y original".[8]

If critics have been quick to recognize the merits of the book they
have been much slower to examine it in any real depth. After 1958 there
appeared a series of interesting critical essays on the work. One of
the themes of this more recent criticism has been that of the earlier
categorisation of the book as a novel. Vargas Llosa feels that
Mariátegui was wrong to label it quite simply as a novel, arguing that
"La casa de cartón no es una reproducción de la realidad exterior sino
el testimonio poético, sensorial, intuitivo, no racional de ésta".[9]
Likewise Luis Loayza feels that the work cannot simply be classified as
a novel. He points out that "La casa de cartón no es una novela precisamente porque su autor no pudo 'dejarse de poesías', ni tampoco un
libro de poemas porque esta vez Martín Adán estuvo demasiado próximo

a la realidad".[10]  In his essay on the work, Hubert Weller begins by
claiming that Adán "construye su propia casa de cartón, alejándose de
la realidad, hacia un mundo propio, poético".[11] He later apologises
for his vagueness in defining the genre of the work, remarking that
"se podría considerar La casa de cartón como un poema en prosa, aunque
pequemos de extrema vaguedad, pues ¿cuál es la línea divisoria entre
prosa y verso?"[12]  Mirko Lauer detects a narrative intention in La casa
de cartón but argues that it is neither a novel nor simply a collection
of texts. He outlines the poetic mechanisms employed in the book and
suggests that the sequence of irrational and extremely poetic images[13]
are coherently ordered to produce an overall effect of poetic ambiguity.
This is further underlined by the indefinite nature of the text, the
protean substance of the characters and their inner worlds, and by the
play on identity between the narrator and Ramón.  After a fairly
detailed discussion of these elements Lauer concludes:  "Leer La casa
de cartón como novela, narración o memoria barranquina sería cometer
aquello que Adán se negó a hacer:  restarle al libro sus más luminosas
opciones a la realidad poética".[14]

Without attempting to enter into the theoretical implications of
this debate on the genre of La casa de cartón, there can be no doubt
that discussion of the question of the poetic quality of the work has
had healthy implications for its critical evaluation.  It has meant
that arguments have been centred more on internal than on external
evidence.  It has prevented it from being crudely reduced to a form of
realism which prefers to see literature as documentary reflection of
society or of a given class of society.  The work does contain obvious
social documentation in its ironic portrayal of the middle-classes of
Barranco, both foreign and national, and their hollow lives in what was
a fashionable seaside resort during the nineteen twenties.  However,
Mariátegui's earlier appraisal overemphasizes that aspect of the book
alluding to the town's bourgeoisie.  His summary of the work as essentially "un esquema de biografía de Barranco, o mejor, de sus veraneantes"[15]
is based largely on particular socio-economic premisses.  However,
Adán's work transcends the limits of this more objective realism and
allows more freedom for the attempt to give expression to the perceptions
of the artistic mind itself.  This in its turn calls for the employment
of a flexible verbal medium capable of dealing with the fantasies and
inalienably private moments of the narrator's consciousness.  The final
result is a work of aesthetic impressionism rather than a photographic
analysis of Barranco society.  The style, sometimes lyrical and other
times surrealist, suits the theme in the way the novel is an attempt
to portray the feelings and perceptions of the state of mind of the
narrator, who is the artist himself.

More recent criticism has of course widened the perspectives and
examined the sort of premisses involved in the depiction of reality as
this is grasped by the author's consciousness.  Thus Vargas Llosa,
accepting the poetic premisses on which the novel is established, considers the more intangible and subjective focussing of reality as it is
found in this book.  He remarks that "Martín Adán no se propuso redactar
un documento objetivo de la vida del balneario de Barranco de 1925,
sino transmitir las impresiones, sensaciones y emociones que este barrio
de nueve mil almas significó para él en su infancia y juventud".[16]  He
carries on to assert that the surprising feature of Adán's attempt to
unveil the status of reality as he is presenting it lies precisely in
the manner he chooses to do this, namely by means of the most evasive
literary procedure he could successfully employ.  Vargas Llosa detects
in this the influence of José María Eguren but argues that whereas the
latter uses "el exotismo, el cosmopolitismo, la obsesión del color, el

adjetivo inusitado"[17] in order to create a magical, make-believe world,
Adán employs the same techniques to portray the world around him as it
is reflected in his own consciousness.

The whole novel centres around the consciousness of the narrator
as he recalls a long school vacation during the summer in Barranco.
This could be seen as one particular vacation, and since it is a novel
about adolescence the vacation could respond to a period of awakening
to adult life. In any case, it clearly represents a crucial phase in
the narrator's life. During this phase the author attempts to define
the narrator's own perceptions in relation to the external reality
surrounding him. This might be suitably considered as the central theme
of the novel. The main action is confined to the amorous exploits of
a certain Ramón, his relationship with a prostitute named Catita,
followed by his untimely death. However, the key to the novel is to be
found not so much in these actions per se as in the actual relationship
between Ramón and the narrator and their shared adolescent experiences.
For throughout the novel the reader cannot but be in doubt about the
continual overlapping of experience between the two characters and
wonder about the identity of Ramón. One of the clearest examples of this
overlap of experience occurs in the passage where the narrator is reading to himself from Ramón's diary which has come into the possession of
a German lady, la señorita Muler. The notes concern the possible
reality or unreality of a man. The narrator is not sure whether the
image of the man as portrayed in the diary is a result of Ramón's
fantasies or whether it is in point of fact a true image based on
observation. In an internal monologue he asks himself:

> ¿Habrá existido alguna vez aquel hombre? ¿Habremos
> soñado Ramón y yo? ¿Lo habremos creado Ramón y yo
> con facciones ajenas, con gestos propios? ¿Nos habrá
> llevado el aburrimiento a hacer un hombre? (47)

Within the stricter confines of the narrative itself we would logically
suppose that Ramón is a separate character, whilst on another level, the
fusing of a joint experience into one, the doubts as to the validity of
the man's image, lead us to suspect that the author is presenting us
with the dramatic explicitation of a single state of mind. This is a
problem that can only be worked out within the general context of the
whole novel.

Throughout the book Ramón appears as the man of action, engaged to
the full in living life, whilst the narrator is an observer, a spectator
who participates vicariously in the actions of Ramón. At one point in
the novel the narrator suggests his willingness to play the role of
Ramón and take over his place as the lover of Catita:

> - Tú cataste a Ramón, y él no te supo mal. Pues bien,
> yo seré Ramón. Yo hago mío el deber de él de besarte
> en las muñecas y el de mirarte con los ojos estúpidos,
> dignos de todas las dichas que tenía Ramón. Tonto y
> aludo deber, aceptado en una hora insular, celeste,
> ventosa, abierta, desolada. Yo seré Ramón un mes, dos
> meses, todo el tiempo que tú puedas amar a Ramón. (68)

This passage voiced by the narrator is addressed to Catita after Ramón's
death. The apparent dialogue is, however, another example of the use of
internal monologue reflecting the state of mind of the narrator himself
at this particular moment in time. It expresses his desire to take over
Ramón's role as Catita's lover, once again indicating a further area of

experience in which Ramón and himself coincide. What seems to be implicit in this is that Ramón is an alter ego. This is certainly a view
shared by a number of critics. As Hubert Weller points out: "Podría
ser que este Ramón represente al mismo narrador en su inocencia".[18]
Mirko Lauer elaborates upon this point, observing that "Ramón y el
'narrador' comparten, además de un estilo, una amante, y por lo tanto
un mundo de experiencias que en el libro se presentan provenientes de
una sola voz indiferenciada".[19] Emilio Adolfo Westphalen speaks of
Adán's "proclividad por las dobles y triples identidades".[20] Behind this
tendency to assume more than one identity there can be detected a cleavage
that lies in the soul of the author himself, a dichotomy between action
and contemplation.

This cleavage is made clear throughout the book and can be illustrated by contrasting two passages expressing two attitudes to love on
the part of the narrator and Ramón. The first is taken from a section
of the novel which was originally entitled Paseo de noche when it was
first published in Amauta.[21] The narrator is describing his feelings
towards an unnamed, imaginary beloved:

> ... Ahora yo puedo ser un héroe con el pecho convexo
> y ensangrentado. Si ahora te raptara yo, tú me arran-
> carías mechones de cabellos y clamarías a las cosas
> indiferentes. Tú no lo harás. Yo no te raptaré por
> nada del mundo. Te necesito para ir a tu lado deseando
> raptarte. ¡Ay del que realiza su deseo! (62)

This passage contains elements both of irony and of more serious adolescent fantasy. The proclamation of his desire to be at the side of his
beloved in order to gaze at her and possess her only in his imagination
is placed somewhat ambiguously after the more ironic assertion concerning
his heroism. This juxtaposition allows us to assent more easily to the
writer's expression of his state of sensibility without accusing him of
pompousness. This ironic tone that saturates the work redeems the
limitations of the adolescent intellect, the immaturity of youth portrayed. What is presented to us is the picture of a boy for whom the
tantalising but pleasing experience of aesthetic contemplation is more
important than the consummation of fleshly lusts. His attitude to the
beloved is static, far removed from the idea of sexual arousal; his
attitude to sensual reality is that of contemplation. The narrator's
consciousness is engaged in observing and watching things, in speculating
about his dreams rather than surrendering all the time to immediate
reality, in striving to keep desire always at boiling point. Hence,
the final exclamation in the passage expresses his feeling of pity for
anyone who consummates desire and thus forfeits the pleasures of the
striving and chasing it entails. This anticipates a poetic attitude
and an important theme which are to become fairly central in Adán's
poetry. In particular, it is echoed in a number of sonnets employing
the symbol of the rose in the major work Travesía de extramares.

Later in the same passage the narrator confesses that he loves the
beloved quite simply because she does not love him:

> - Yo te amo porque tú no me amas. Tu pequeñez me
> orienta la esperanza en la búsqueda de la dicha.
> Si tú crecieras como los árboles, yo no sabría qué
> desear. Tú eres la medida de mi gozo. Tú eres la
> medida de mi deseo. (63)

Love is seen here to be stimulated by the impossibility of its attaining its object. It is depicted in terms of freedom and desire, ecstasy and contemplation. For the narrator is someone for whom fantasies of his mind are more real and satisfying than reality as it is actively lived.

In contrast to this more static, deliberate, effortless gazing we discover that Ramón's amorous attentions follow the path of sexual gratification. This is borne out in the episode describing his encounter with Catita:

> Ramón se arrojó en Catita como un nadador en el
> mar - de abajo arriba, primero las manos; después, la
> cabeza; por fin, los pies, flexionados, destalonados.
> En el palo del mes de enero, ensebado todavía con
> sucias nubes frías, quedó Ramón en cielo, en aire, en
> medio, en equilibrio, en ropa de baño, a la punta, con
> cien muchachos trémulos detrás que le apuraban, sobre
> Catita, mar. Ramón cayó mal - de barriga, de bruces,
> asperjándonos a todos nosotros, desprevenidos,
> observadores. (74)

Whereas before the narrator was concerned to focus on his own personal state of mind, he is here recounting a scene full of action. The images he employs denote the idea of movement, of intense physical activity. In the beginning of the passage an impression of the violence of passion is conveyed by the verb "se arrojó" and the comparison with a swimmer plunging headlong into the sea. The likening of Catita to the sea suggests the idea of a girl of overpowering sexual vigour and fertility. The sexual act is represented through the image of the boy climbing a greased pole. On the other hand, the narrator might be recalling an episode in which Ramón did climb a greased pole and another incident when he made love to Catita and then superimposing the two events which both affirm the idea of Ramón's manhood. Ramón takes the centre of the stage in a scene of what appears to be essentially a diversion for his companions who urge him on to climb the pole, to copulate with Catita. This spurring on by his companions constitutes an important ingredient in the adolescent period in which the adolescent shows off in order to prove himself to his companions. Ramón's sexual escapades can be seen as part of this desire to prove to others that he is a man. The boy's sense of passion and urgency and the overwhelming attractiveness of the girl emphasize the idea of sheer adventure and vigorous excitement. Catita is later described as a "mar con olas", which indicates a girl who is both generous and has a tremendous sexual capacity.

After this more playful episode there is a change of tone when Ramón suddenly falls off the pole, catching the onlookers unawares. An atmosphere of shock replaces the previous amusement. The bad fall suffered by Ramón might be symbolic not only of his withdrawal from the sexual act but also of his accidental death. It is at this point that the narrator introduces himself onto the scene, including himself amongst the group of onlookers who are described as "observadores". This word stands in marked contrast to the words which were employed earlier in the passage to denote intense physical activity, and further underlines the opposition between the contemplative immobility of the narrator and the more unrestricted, active behaviour of Ramón.

Throughout the novel the reader cannot help but be confused by the ambivalent way in which the author plays with identity. He may feel entitled to accept two levels of logical validity on which the book may be read. The first, which would presumably view Ramón and the narrator quite simply as two separate characters does tend, however, to underplay if not fully ignore the ambiguity so apparent in the text. The sharing

of the same prose style, evident in the similarity of Ramón's diary and
the narrator's story, the coincidence in their feelings towards Catita,
and the constant overlapping of whole areas of experience throughout
the novel leads one to feel that Adán is attempting to describe a single
state of mind.  On this level, the blurring of identities would lead us
to recognize Ramón and the narrator as the same person in a symbolic
sense.  Ramón might then be regarded as the narrator as he used to be
during the phase when he plunged into an active life like Ramón, a
phase which has since been overtaken by his conscious decision to for-
sake the life of action in favour of a life of comtemplation.  Equally
the accident on the pole and the incident with Catita could then refer
to the symbolic death of the narrator.  They could then be interpreted
as symbolizing a traumatic sexual experience in which a previously
outgoing boy forsakes the active life, is put off sex, and opts for the
life of the spectator.

Another theme that illustrates the idea of the narrator as basically
an observer of life rather than a participant in it is that of middle-
class society in Barranco as it is seen through the eyes of the narrator.
Both foreigners and Peruvians are portrayed with a gentle irony which
results in a humorous sketch of the society of the day.  He creates a
panorama of absurdity not just to entertain the reader but also to open
his eyes to the contrasts and contradictions of life in this sleepy
seaside resort during the nineteen twenties.  Mirko Lauer remarks that
"los puntos más alegres de La casa de cartón tienen un eco que parece
pugnar por convertir el texto en una especie de comentario juicioso a
la realidad barranquina".[22]  What spreads out before us is an indolent
and indifferent town of 'respectable' people.  This is not brought out
in a very explicit way; it is rather conveyed by the ironic social
allusions that recur in the book.  The superficiality and shallowness
of the townsfolk are humorously highlighted in their show of indignation
on learning that a film entitled "Divino Amor" is not to be screened at
the local cinema.  The narrator first of all mocks the content of the
film itself:

> Valentino ... Paisajes de ensueño ... Pasión,
> sacrificio, celos, lujoso vestuario, la vida del gran
> mundo... Y, de pronto,nada! (44)

The mockery continues as he recounts the reaction of the townsfolk to
the cancellation of the film:

> La respetable concurrencia se retiró pataleando
> bravamente, correctamente, como cumplía a ella, gente
> sabidora de sus derechos, gente seria, gente honorable. (44)

The irony is mild; these good people show their more serious side when
their cheap illusions are threatened.  Behind the writer's humour lies
the reality that such honourable people do not have any more serious
preoccupations than the quality of the latest cheap movie.

The banality of the characters' lives is suggested by the narrator's
stressing of seemingly unimportant details.  He concentrates on the
bathing habits of Ramón's aunt and informs us that she was a person who
never read newspapers.  The general implication of this is that she had
no more serious interest; she was a professional holidaymaker who "venía
con el primer calor y se iba con el último". (51)  In particular, there
are numerous allusions to the members of the foreign community living
in the town.  Their ubiquitous influence is treated at times in a joking
fashion as when Lala's mother treads on a "gringo submarino" when she

is bathing in the sea. It is indicated by the sign near the beach -
"Se suplica a los bañistas no hablar en inglés". (31) The characters
themselves are humorously drawn, bearing something of a resemblance to
Dickensian caricatures though cast in a surrealist mould. Behind the
external seriousness and stuffiness of these characters the reader can
detect the hollow and almost farcical quality of their lives. The
narrator concentrates on the eccentricities of these people, spies on
them, reveals hidden corners in their lives, but always with humour.
One illustration of this is to be found in the description of the
English agent of Dawson and Brothers who is a keen angler:

> Este era un inglés que pescaba con caña ... Sin
> duda, era este inglés como todo pescador, un idiota,
> pero no balanceaba las piernas, antes bien, afirmaba
> los pies en el riel de soporte, resbaloso como una loza
> de puro musgoso... ¿Poeta?... Nada de eso: agente
> viajero de la casa Dawson & Brothers, pero pescaba con
> caña. (21)

The character is introduced as the Englishman who went angling as if
this were a summary of his major function in life. For the narrator is
unimpressed by his professional status and prefers to underline the
angling interest by including a wealth of detail concerning the movement
of his legs as he is engaged in this activity and by repeating the
phrase "pescaba con caña" immediately after mentioning the angler's
occupation and the firm he works for. The implication is that it is
only by unveiling the social mask of position or status that a true
picture of his personal function can be revealed. In this case, what
is revealed is the impression of an ineffectual, empty sort of person
hiding behind the illusion that his job and firm give him respectability.
Without passing judgement, Adán is able to depict a ridiculous figure
unaware of the hollowness of his true self.

The German lady, la señorita Muler, is portrayed as a sentimental
and romantic woman who has never really awoken to the concrete meaning
of womanhood but has fashioned for herself in her dreams a fantastic
world populated by figures such as Napoleon and Santa Rosa de Lima.
Though ten years his senior she fell in love with Ramón. However, the
sterility of her life comes through clearly in the image of the sea
that lies behind everything, representing the expansive dullness of her
own life:

> Y detrás de todo el mar inútil y absurdo como un
> quiosko en la mañana que sigue a la tarde de gimkana. (35)

There is a sympathetic portrayal of another German, Herr Oswald Teller,
who was never quite able to leave Germany behind him and speaks of "las
mañanas de Hannover" (36) and keeps a portrait of Bismarck in his room
along with dozens of old German magazines. Here once again the author
spies on the character, painting an amusing but sympathetic picture of
the man.

This ironic sketch of society in Barranco is always played off
against the inner world of the narrator himself. In a style reminiscent
of surrealism in its obvious irrationality and incoherence and its often
outrageous combination of incongruous images, the writer focuses to a
large extent on his own personal experience. He views external reality
as essentially something which remains dependent on the perceptions of
the writer, the narrator himself. This is clearly illustrated in the
image of the pool:

Porque la vida de uno es un charco, pero la
vida de los otros son caras que vienen a mirarse
en él. Sí, Catita. Pero algunas vidas no son un
charco, sino un lago, un mar, un océano donde sólo
se miran el cielo y las montañas, las nubes, grandes
barcos. (69)

This image of the pool in which other people's faces are reflected
suggests an attempt by the authorial mind to capture and reflect its
own perceptions and to communicate them.

This unusual novel represents an innovation in Peruvian literature
this century and has deservedly become something of a masterpiece in
its own right. As an account of the rejection of a life of action in
favour of a life of contemplation it did much in the way of providing
a fluid medium for the further definition of the myriad of perceptions
of the artistic mind in a country where the influence of James Joyce
had not yet established itself.

## N O T A S

1. Martín Adán, La casa de cartón (Lima, Librería-Editorial Juan Mejía
Baca, 1971). All references are to this edition.

2. Luis Alberto Sánchez, 'Prólogo' to La casa de cartón (Lima 1971),
9 - 14.

3. José Carlos Mariátegui, 'Colofón', ibid., 91 -95.

4. Luis Alberto Sánchez, op. cit., 13 - 14.

5. José Carlos Mariátegui, op. cit., 93 -94.

6. Estuardo Núñez, 'Martín Adán y su creación poética', Letras
Peruanas, I, no.4 (Lima, Dec.1951), 98, 127 - 131.

7. Juan Carlos Ghiano, 'Martín Adán, Navegante de Extramares',
La Nación, Buenos Aires, 6 Feb. 1971.

8. Sebastián Salazar Bondy, 'El conflicto vital de Martín Adán',
Obra Poética (Lima 1971), 257 - 262.

9. Mario Vargas Llosa, 'La casa de cartón', Cultura Peruana, XIX,
nos.135 - 136, 137  (Lima 1959).

10. Luis Loayza, 'Martín Adán en La casa de cartón', Proceso, no.0
(Lima 1964), 4 - 5.

11. Hubert P. Weller, 'La casa de cartón de Martín Adán y el mar como
elemento metafórico', Letras, nos. 66 - 67 (Lima 1961), 142 - 153.

12. Hubert P. Weller, art. cit., 143.

13. Lauer uses the term "image" in the sense Ezra Pound gives it:  "An
Image is that which presents an intellectual and emotional complex in

an instant of time". <u>The Art of Poetry</u> (London, Faber and Faber, 1960), 4.

14. Mirko Lauer, <u>Un ensayo sobre la obra poética de Martín Adán</u> (Lima 1972), 17.

15. José Carlos Mariátegui, op. cit., 93 - 94.

16. Mario Vargas Llosa, art. cit., 9.

17. Ibid., 9.

18. Hubert P. Weller, art. cit., 142.

19. Mirko Lauer, op. cit., 14.

20. Emilio Adolfo Westphalen, 'Homenaje a Martín Adán', <u>Amaru</u>, no.9 (Lima, March 1969), 42 - 43.

21. Martín Adán, 'Paseo de Noche', <u>Amauta</u>, no.11 (Lima 1928), 4.

22. Mirko Lauer, op. cit., 74.

# Myth and meaning in Pérez de Ayala's Prometeo

J.J. Macklin (University of Hull)

One of the most fundamental features of Pérez de Ayala's fiction is his use of traditional and well-known literary motifs and situations. The titles of many of his works - Prometeo, Bajo el signo de Artemisa, El curandero de su honra, Los trabajos de Urbano y Simona - reflect this, and show that while Classical literature provides him with some material a great diversity of literary borrowings is involved: Longus, Heliodorus, Cervantes, Calderón, Shakespeare, the Bible and even fairy-tales. This is, of course, a consequence of Ayala's humanistic learning and wide reading, but it also responds to an attitude of mind that understands culture, and literature, as a developing process in which the legacy of the past interacts with the sensibility of the present. Such an attitude results in a type of fiction which, on the surface, is devoid of actuality as it is generally understood but which, in fact, is strikingly modern in that it shares the self-consciousness charac-teristic of much twentieth-century art. Ayala's novels ultimately explore the whole meaning of the creative act, the relationship of art to life, the rôle and function of literature in human experience.

Prometeo (1916) is Pérez de Ayala's first work in which these concerns are brought fully into focus. His earlier novels, in their own way, dealt with the relationship of life to literature, though not in so sustained a manner as to inform the whole nature of the work. In Tinieblas en las cumbres (1907), for example, mythological references and literary allusions abound, but they do not form a consistent or recognisable pattern. In a way, they offer a contrast to the more naturalistic aspects of the novel. Similarly, quotations and epigraphs are extensively used and related to basic themes in the work, much as the title of La pata de la raposa (1910), taken from Alfred de Musset, prefigures Alberto's efforts to shake off the past and establish positive values for life. At the same time, the impregnation of this work with literature underlines Alberto's inability to experience reality directly, so immersed is he in aestheticism. Troteras y danzaderas (1913) is a 'novela-clave' which describes the literary and artistic life of Madrid at the turn of the century and, as one would expect, literary works and theories figure prominently in it. However, it is not until Prometeo that Ayala attempts a full version of an ancient work. In fact, what one finds here is a linking of two myths, that of Prometheus which embodies the principal character's aspiration towards the superhuman, and of Odysseus which provides most of the material for the plot.

Since its appearance in 1916, Prometeo has been published in the company of Luz de domingo and La caída de los Limones with the subtitle 'Novelas poemáticas de la vida española'. These three works naturally group together because of the use of short poems to head each chapter, their date of publication, the fact that they are of similar length and, as we shall see, because of a fundamental similarity of theme. As it happens, they were not originally conceived as a unit or trilogy until their publication in one volume.[1] Luz de domingo had already been published in La novela corta and La caída de los Limones in Los con-temporáneos. In neither case were there any introductory poems to the texts before the first edition. There is, therefore, justification for examining Prometeo in isolation from the other two works, especially since it is the only work in which Ayala attempts a modern version of a Classical myth.

The purpose of this article is not so much to offer a new interpretation of the work as to examine the effects of the particular
narrative method Ayala has chosen, firstly to show how it relates to
Ayala's evolution and concerns as a novelist and secondly as a contribution to what has come to be known as myth criticism. In this respect,
I am less concerned with the history and treatment of the Prometheus
and Odysseus figures in a comparative sense, though naturally one must
be aware of the associations of these myths for the work to be fully
appreciated. From the point of view of narrative technique, however,
what is important is the use of the classical analogy for the purposes
of authorial commentary, for it would appear not to be mere coincidence
that the use of mythological motifs in fiction emerges at a historical
point in the development of the genre when the use of direct comment
begins to be regarded with disapproval by theorists and novelists alike.
The mythological parallel, then, is usually the key to the interpretation
of the work and the means whereby the author imparts his values to the
reader.

In addition to Homer's Odyssey, other literary antecedents have
been suggested for Prometeo. One of Ayala's earliest critics,
Francisco Agustín, takes up Salvador de Madariaga's idea of the kinship
between Prometeo and El conde Lucanor,[2] suggesting that the short novel
is an 'enxiemplo' after the style of Don Juan Manuel in which an exotic
element (in this case Greek) is adapted to contemporary Spanish life.[3]
More recently, Julio Matas has suggested a close connection between
Ayala's 'novelas poemáticas' and Cervantes' 'novelas ejemplares'. Both
give artistic expression to complex truths. Marco acts against the
natural order and his punishment is implicit in his act: his attempt
to create a genius results in the birth of a deformed son. Marco
deviates from the norm of moderation which Ayala regards as an underlying law of nature with the inevitable tragic consequences. Matas
then extends his argument by adding that "Marco sintetiza, en lo
individual, el embotamiento físico y espiritual de la España de su
tiempo".[4] This ideological interpretation, in conformity with the
general outlook of the Generation of 1898, has formed the basis of the
majority of approaches to the work, taking as their point of departure
the subtitle of the trilogy. For example, Donald L. Fabian speculates
that in Prometeo "Ayala means to suggest that the recovery of Spain
will require intelligent, sustained co-operative action rather than
ambitious individual efforts".[5] In similar vein, Norma Urrutia argues
that the work is "un nuevo intento de formular un esquema del español
ideal".[6] Esperanza Rodríguez Monescillo considers that Ayala's fusion
of the myths of Odysseus and Prometheus "tiene su raíz en el propósito
de ejemplificar y aleccionar a sus compatriotas más o menos responsables
del momento histórico desgraciado que España está viviendo, con miras
a lograr de ellos un poco de reflexión sobre los males de la Patria y
un mucho de voluntad de superación y sacrificio".[7] F.W. Weber sees
Prometeo not so much as a work of generational ideology as a "thesis
novel that admonishes against prideful attempts to subjugate life to
the systems of reason",[8] and A. Amorós sees it as a demonstration of
the "fracaso del superhombre nietzscheano".[9]

All of these studies have contributed to a greater understanding
of Ayala's short novel which, because of its nature, has eluded any
one definition. Myths offer a multiplicity of possibilities to a writer
and the Prometheus myth in particular has undergone a considerable
number of interpretations. The most common explanation of why Ayala
has recourse to myth is that by providing analogies between past and
present he demonstrates that there is 'nihil novum sub sole', that basic
human situations have remained identical throughout the ages. All the

strivings of mankind can be discerned behind the archetypal patterns
of antiquity. Such a view exposes Ayala to the criticism that in his
need to repeat, to imitate, he reveals himself to be lacking in real
imagination. Moreover, there is the further criticism that the use of
mythology and other Classical allusions can sound pretentious and
irrelevant in a modern novel. Consequently, there is a tendency to
view a novel like _Prometeo_ as a literary curiosity, "un pequeño juguete
literario", as M. Salgues de Cargill terms it,[10] in which Ayala derives
pleasure from anachronism for its own sake. This tends to concentrate
attention more on the model than the new work, but much more important
in this type of novel than the identification of the source, which is
nearly always made explicit by the author anyway, is the evaluation of
the function of the analogy: how is our reading of a novel with a more
or less realistic theme and modern setting enriched or enhanced by its
being paralleled by some well-known myth? There is a problem here
insofar as readers have differing degrees of mythological knowledge and
some may be unaware of the significance of the allusions. Historically,
the use of mythology has been considered to have the effect of ennobling
modern works, as for example in the cases of Góngora or Camões, but in
more modern times the use of mythology is more complex. Basically a
myth, or mythological title, sets up certain expectations in the reader
which the author is able to exploit. The reader is invited to guess
whether the traditional pattern or outcome of events will be respected.
Thus the myth of Prometheus will arouse certain expectations based on
the various treatments of the story of the Titan. The broad outlines
of the Prometheus tradition are relevant here. Originally the etymology
of Prometheus was thought to be _pramantha_ which meant a stick used to
cause fire by generating sparks through friction. The word also
suggested the snatching away of the divine fire. Nowadays this etymology is rejected in favour of _mantha nein_ meaning forethought and
knowledge. Hesiod, who inaugurated the written tradition, opposed
Prometheus the Provident to Epimetheus the Improvident. In popular
mythology, Prometheus was the creator of man. In Ovid's _Metamorphosis I_,
Pausanius says he saw in Phocea pieces of clay which Prometheus used to
mould human bodies. This idea gives rise to the image of Prometheus as
a symbol of man's emancipation, the _homo creator_ as opposed to the _homo
creatus_, Adam. In the work of Hesiod, Prometheus appears as the
protector of man: he stole fire from Zeus and, as a reprisal, the god
created Pandora (woman) destined to bring man unending misery. With
Aeschylus, the Titan's story is given moral significance and his punishment is closely linked with the problem of suffering. Prometheus in
chains is a noble figure who is treated harshly by Zeus for showing
sympathy for man. Not surprisingly, the early Christians saw Prometheus
as a prefiguration of the Cross, but in general Prometheus is conceived
largely as a symbol of defiance against the divinity who exercises
tyranny over man. This is certainly true in the case of Goethe, whose
Prometheus (1774) is the direct ancestor of modern Promethean man leading straight to Nietzsche and the glorification of the superman, one
who has exceptional talents and raises himself above the common level
of humanity. Shelley's _Prometheus_ (1818) begins with the tyrant Zeus
lying vanquished and is an expression of man's liberation from the idea
of God. The _Sturm und Drang_ take up the notion of Prometheus as creator
in the sense of poet and creative artist. Most nineteenth-century
French versions of the myth (Ménard, Péladan, Dumas) present the Titan
as man's liberator; André Gide's _Le Prométhée mal enchaîné_ (1899) is a
humanist interpretation of the myth. Therefore, through the various
transformations and adaptions to changing circumstances and to new
conceptions of man and the universe, certain traits have been repeatedly

emphasised: the creative artist, the man who thirsts after knowledge, the man of suffering who symbolises the human condition, the redeemer of mankind, the humanist champion of freedom and individualism.[11] The title of Prometeo, then, could be expected to conjure up associations of this sort in a cultured reader.

From an author's point of view, the use of myth offers a short-cut to unfolding the plot and introducing themes: the reader begins with certain existing information and a basic set of assumptions. In addition, myths are stories which have stood the test of time and which embody basic principles of story-telling. Not only that, in a genre now dominated by the influence of Realism, the use of myth to some extent frees the author from the need for plausibility. Myths are only stories after all. Mythology creates a distance between reader and contemporary reality. It also creates distance of a different sort: it deflects attention away from the characters and their lives and towards concern for the completion of a pattern, the perfection of a form. The pleasure in this type of fiction is largely aesthetic in nature. Finally, the use of myth has repercussions for the structure of a work in another way. It prefigures events in the narrative so that the title of a work, the naming of mythological characters, the use of well-known quotations and, in the case of Prometeo, the intro-ductory poems all perform a broadly similar function, in that they anticipate what will or what may happen in the novel. These last two points - the aesthetic function and the thematic function of the myth - are linked. The reader has a certain set of expectations, a number of possibilities are opened up, and as the narrative develops a pattern emerges. This pattern parallels the development of the novel's theme.

The idea of creating the perfect being has led to the frequent comparison of Prometeo with Unamuno's Amor y pedagogía.[12] The compari-son is a fair one in that the fathers in both novels aim at creating a genius and in both cases the children commit suicide by hanging themselves. Both fathers profess to choose their spouses on the basis of genetic selection yet in reality choose them because of physical attraction. But the tone and concerns of the two novels are ultimately very different. Unamuno explores the relationship between father and son, whereas Ayala is more concerned with the aspirations of Marco him-self. Ayala's denouement is inexplicable in terms of the motivation of the plot, whereas that of Amor y pedagogía is capable of explanation in terms of the pressures brought to bear on the boy Apolodoro. In Ayala's novel the use of myth greatly widens the implications of the work. Despite the title of Prometeo, it is Ulysses who dominates for most of the work and the reader is left to speculate on the possible connection between the two myths. In fact, a mythological title does no more than indicate that the theme or events of the work have some, as yet unde-fined, connection with the myth.

Prometeo spans five chapters of unequal length. Initially, the Homeric parallel is rigorously pursued but increasingly the tone of the work becomes more sombre and the language used more direct. Thus the whole movement of the novel represents an undermining of the character's heroic ideal. Often in mythological novels the parallel is a private affair between reader and author and the character may be totally unaware of it. It must be said that this is not the case here. The novel works on the principle of mythical identification and the whole technique of the novel is justified internally by the fact that Marco is a professional Classical scholar. At the same time, however, there is a difference between our awareness of the myth and the character's awareness of it. The exploitation of this difference is the key to the novel's success. One could summarise the development of the novel as

involving a decreasing number of possibilities both in terms of the
choices open to Marco and the shape given to the mythological material.
The reader's hypotheses are gradually narrowed by the revelation of new
material until the completed pattern has emerged.

The first chapter of <u>Prometeo</u> is recounted in mock-heroic style in
which the ancient and modern are juxtaposed. The epic mood is evoked
in the application of the term 'rapsodia' to the prologue and the
indication that this will be a modern version of the myth is implied in
the title of the initial poem. There are two levels of prefiguration
present from the outset. The overall pattern is dictated by the well-
known story of Odysseus while the detail and, more importantly, the
significance of the story are foreshadowed by the poem. What interests
Ayala above all are the associations of Odysseus the traveller (the
whole novel takes the form of a quest), since the motif of the journey
is easily related to the theme of self-realisation. This is the
essential meaning of the poem: man must shake off the legacy of the
past and start life afresh. Linked to this are the themes of exile and
separation which culminate in the final exhortation to self-sufficiency:

> Sé tú mismo tu dueño, sé isleño.
> Haz de tu vida prodigioso sueño
> renovándose sin cesar.
> Abrázate al flotante leño.
> Echate a navegar por la mar.[13]

This sets up limitless and unknown possibilities by creating a
vision of man full of latent potentialities which should not be stifled
by routine or convention. This poem, then, strikes a heroic note by
glorifying the exceptional man. This spiritual journey finds its
correlative in Marco's journey from Italy to Spain in search of fulfilment, and in his escape by raft from the modern Calypso. Dualities
of this kind are a prominent feature of the first chapter and are seen
most particularly in the blending of high and low styles, the counter-
pointing of the heroic and the mundane, both of which give rise to a
whole series of anachronisms. The mythical is juxtaposed to the every-
day as the 'fábula antigua' is adapted to modern times. The story is
no longer taking place in a heroic age; it is told not by a bard but by
a novelist:

> Así, lo que en las edades épicas fue canto
> heroico al son de la cítara, es ahora voz muda
> y gráfica, esto es, palabra escrita, sin otro
> acompañamiento que la estridencia lánguida de la
> pluma metálica sobre el papel deleznable. El
> aeda ha degenerado en novelador (594)

The Muse invoked, the Muse of fiction, is the goddess of gossip, and in
the summary of the <u>Odyssey</u> which follows this dual perspective is
highlighted: "canta" / "cuenta"; Florence under the aegis of Ares and
then John the Baptist (a direct borrowing from Dante); Herod and Pilate
as the proverbial equivalents of Scylla and Charybdis; "brebajes
ambrosianos" / "bebidas alcohólicas" (594-95). Later he refers to the
"rojo néctar y cristalina ambrosía, que el tabernero, hombre lego en
asuntos de mitología, denominaba vino y aguardiente" (597). In this
way Ayala calls attention to the fact that two very different ages are
being evoked and the inevitable question which the reader must ask is
whether heroic ideals have any place in modern circumstances. Ayala's
humour is, of course, highly ambiguous, as is the whole prefiguration.

These pages could be read as an attack on the vulgarity of modern life and as nostalgia for a more noble and heroic past. Equally, there is more than a suggestion that literature itself has become degenerate. After the evocation of Odysseus' wanderings, Ayala concentrates on one adventure, the encounter with Nausicaa, and then interrupts his preliminary rhapsody to comment to the reader on its strangeness. It is at this point that the story proper begins and the mythological allusions are clarified.

Ayala's short novel is based primarily on Books V, VI and VII of Homer's Odyssey, and the summary of Marco's life (594-95 and 607-09) uses the main details of Odysseus' story to King Alcinous (Books IX-XII). But Ayala does not merely use the broad outlines but quotes almost directly from the original. The repeated use of the epic epithet, "Nausicaa de los brazos blancos", for example, adds to the epic tone of his novel, but much more extensive quotations are also incorporated into it. The description of Calypso's cave is very reminiscent of Homer:

> Crecían allí el sauce, el álamo y el odífero ciprés,
> en donde los pájaros que despliegan sus alas fabrican
> el nido; el gavilán y la gárrula corneja marina,
> que se inquieta siempre con el runrún del oleaje.
> Cuatro arroyos discurrían, apartándose y juntándose,
> a modo de red, con aguas límpidas verdecían los
> blandos prados y nacían violetas y copia diversa
> de otras flores. Por el frente de la casa subía
> temblando una parra virgen, con racimos agraces. (596)[14]

Similarly Marco's shipwreck and the storm at sea: "Ahora el Euros se la cedía a Zéfiros para que este la arrastrase, ahora el Notos se la cedía a Bóreas" (597).[15] Nausicaa's dream is taken directly from Homer, in particular the exhortation to look to her appearance "porque la hora de tus desposorios se acerca, y ya no serás doncella por mucho más tiempo" (599). Marco addresses Nausicaa with the exact words used by Odysseus in the epic: "Si eres diosa, de las que habitan el dilatado Ouranos, me pareces Artemisa, hija del gran Zeus, por la belleza, la estatura y la gracia. Si eres mortal de las que habitan en la tierra tres veces dichosos tus padre y madre venerables; tres veces dichosos tus hermanos; pero, más feliz que todos, el que colmándote con los presentes del Himeneo, te conduzca a su hogar" (600).[16] All these examples of near-quotation add to the literary-imitative nature of the work, and call attention to the act of writing itself. From an aesthetic point of view they have the twin effect of achieving both familiarity and novelty. The old quotation is blended into the new work and yet retains a sort of independence from it. It retains its original significance and is modified by its new context. Herman Meyer uses the terms 'assimilation' and 'dissimilation':

> In general it might be maintained that the charm
> of a quotation emanates from a unique tension
> between assimilation and dissimilation: it links
> itself closely with its new environment but at the
> same time detaches itself from it, thus permitting
> another world to radiate into the self-contained
> world of the novel.[17]

There is a more general question of adaption involved here. Just as the old material has to be adapted to the new work, so too has the reader to adapt himself to a type of fiction which is unfamiliar. The myth helps create this sense of strangeness, of remoteness.

The poem which opens the second chapter is concerned with individuality, expressed through the image of Odysseus' bow. This represents each man's capacity for achievement, his unique ability which others do not possess. Failure to realise this ability is equivalent to destroying one's full potential.

> Tú, como yo, todos, hermano,
> todos somos como Odysseus,
> todos poseemos un arco,
> para los demás imposible,
> para uno mismo ágil y blando.
> Todos apuntamos al cielo.
> Si alguno no apunta..., ¡menguado! (601)

Chapter II explains Marco's mythical identification with his hero Odysseus which is so complete that even the narrator is affected to such a degree that he recounts a "verídica historia en un estilo alegórico, épico y desaforado" (601). This is a further illustration of the ambivalence of Ayala's treatment of the character. On the one hand, the myth is brought down to earth and treated irreverently by a technique of ironic juxtaposition. On the other, Marco attracts by the uniqueness of his vision and the strength of his personality. The principle of imitation works on two levels: the character imitates a mythical hero while the author imitates an older work. In fact, those very qualities which Marco admires in Odysseus - "la mezcla de lo heroico con lo humorístico" (602) - are precisely those which determine the novel's mood. In his nostalgia for the past, and in his monomania, Marco senses his incompatibility with the modern world. Thus the second chapter makes increasing reference to contemporary circumstances as the various allusions of Chapter I are explained. Ayala had begun his work using the epic device of in medias res and now he adopts a retrospective viewpoint and reveals those aspects of Marco's life which are relevant to his present theme: both his parents were dead by the time he had reached sixteen; he was independent; endowed with physical and intellectual prowess; precocious and introverted; solitary and with a febrile imagination; confident that man holds the key to his destiny in his own hands: "libre por entero y dueño de sí mismo y de lo porvenir" (603). His uncle's remarks, though intended quite differently, are interpreted by Marco in the same light: "Tienes en tu favor cuanto un hombre puede apetecer al comenzar la vida. Si fracasas, tuya será la culpa" (603). Marco has a sense of the infinite and his ambition, though ill-defined, is grandiose. It is concerned with the fullest possible expression of his essential self:

> Quería ser él, él mismo, pero en forma que no
> acertaba todavía a definir; quería su propia
> exaltación hasta un grado máximo, a modo de gran
> dique levantado en mitad del caudal de las edades,
> que detiene y recoge todas las aguas del pasado en
> un ancho y profundo remanso, y luego las va vertiendo
> al futuro en eminente e impetuosa cascada. (603)

Just as in the novel the world of myth is counterpointed with the real world, so too are Marco's aspirations and ideas set against the common sense of his uncle. Marco seeks fulfilment through wisdom which for him involves an alliance of thought and action. For his uncle, wisdom does not lead to success since it leads to deliberation and vacillation and is therefore an impediment to action. The uncle's ethics are based on personal experience, instinct and will-power. This form of antithetic dialogue is characteristic of the novel of the Generation of 1898 as are some of the ideas being discussed, especially the conflict between intellectualism and vitalism. In fact, the chapter is reminiscent of Part IV of Baroja's El árbol de la ciencia (1911) in which Andrés engages in dialogue with his uncle Iturrioz, who warns his nephew: "este intelectualismo no te llevará a nada bueno".[18] Here, though, what Marco seeks is a sense of continuity, of communion with the past so that the present is a kind of culmination of all human culture. He wants to imbibe "los jugos más quintaesenciados, rancios y generosos del corazón e intelectos humanos a través de los siglos" (605). Marco believes in a sort of cultural exclusivism, in which everything contributes to the "realización cabal del propio destino" (606). This elusive objective becomes the goal of Marco's quest to solve "el gran problema: el de ponerse de acuerdo consigo mismo, el de descubrir el ideal que a uno le conviene" (606). In a sense, it is a quest for integration, an attempt to harmonise his thoughts, feelings and actions. The quest for this ideal is a difficult one but now for the first time it is identified as an aspiration towards the superhuman, the Promethean: "El aspiraba al tipo semidivino, al Prometeo, y si a no serlo él mismo, cuando menos a concebirlo, a comprenderlo, a adivinarlo, a ayudar a su gestación" (607).

Increasingly the ideal conflicts with experience. The perfect trinity of 'fuerza', 'gracia' and 'astucia' is nowhere to be found; happiness for the intellectual is illusory. The quest for the ideal forms a large part of the explanation of the Homeric allusions of Chapter I. The "tierra de los lotófagos" is Seville where Marco had slipped into a temporary state of oblivion. Circe becomes a Seville prostitute who helps him dissipate his inheritance. The reference to the "morada de Aides" appears as an allusion to one of the Castilian towns, probably Salamanca, which would make the reference to "Teiresias, que era un sabio y tenía cara de búho" mean almost certainly Unamuno. This would be in keeping with the reference to the hero's loss of humanity through his excessive dedication to intellectual pursuits. The city of the sun (Helios) turns out to be Madrid. The journey through Spain mirrors Marco's quest for values and the theme of the futility of life and the theme of Spain, now "el país de las imposibilidades", are linked to make Chapter II the most markedly generational in the short novel.

By a process of education Marco realises that happiness does indeed reside in action but that this action must be conceived by the man of thought who is a frustrated man of action. The man of thought will only find fulfilment through engendering the real man of action, the man who will be the redeemer of mankind. Although there is no indication of what the new Prometheus will offer to humanity, Marco's new ideal has all the aura of a sacred mission. Another, and more fundamental, divergence of opinion now arises between nephew and uncle. For Marco the superhuman man enables the species to develop on to a higher level whereas for the uncle it is the species which, through its own development, creates the conditions whereby the superhuman man can emerge. This more cautious and more humble view contains within it a note of warning: Prometheus is the culmination of a process of evolution, a symbol of man's potential, that cannot be realised too soon or too quickly. Marco, however, adheres to his conviction that he is the "instrumento providencial y dilecto del genio de la especie" (611). While in the first chapter ambiguity was created by a double-edged attitude to the mythological material, in the second chapter the ambivalence is continued by the internal argumentation in which conflicting views are given more or less equal weight. Although Marco has come up against a series of obstacles in the pursuit of his dream he has, if not overcome them, at least circumvented them by channelling his energies into "la obsesión de la paternidad heroica" (612). His field of action has been restricted but it still exists.

The third chapter, dedicated to Nausicaa, is relatively short. Again the initial poem prefigures the chapter and crystallises its essence. It links together the themes of nakedness (the idea of coming into the world with nothing, seen precisely in Marco being washed up naked on the shore, thereby echoing the first poem on the need to shake off the trappings of the past), of destiny, of the superhuman, of conjugal union and eternity. These themes are now taken up and projected onto the future line of the narrative and, in fact, this chapter marks a change in emphasis from past to future. Given her role in the work, Nausicaa is treated with less attention than Odysseus. The process of demythification is continued in the ridiculous surname, Meana, which undermines any suggestion of the eternal woman contained in her first name, Perpetua. Certain traits are given relief - grace, prettiness and freshness - and one peculiar characteristic is doubly stressed - her trace of masculinity: "un poco varonil por el carácter y la expresión" and "cierto aire... poco feminino, un sí era no era hombruno" (614). Some attention is devoted to her family background to show how they are an agreeable and well-liked family and make the point that the father is something of a womaniser. By a careful progression, the next chapter title and poem foreshadow the union of Marco and Perpetua. The story now becomes increasingly straightforward as the mythological parallel is kept distinctly out of sight. For example, the bringing of the news of the shipwreck could not be more down-to-earth. Perpetua's mistress is not spinning (as in the original epic) but having her hair done. Any possible significance Marco's nakedness might have is reduced to "es seguro que habrá cogido un catarro" (618). Humour of this type is an essential ingredient of the novel. There is the humour of anachronism: Nausicaa plays badminton on the beach, for example, and of the blend of high and low styles. The playful mention of "un pollino llamado Agamemnón" (599) fits in with the work's mythological aura. Ayala delights in simple word-plays, for example, "y con el estío el hastío de Marco" (612) and the novel contains short humorous scenes: the dinner-table discussion of Greek (622) or about possible clothes for Marco (619). Overall, there are two effects here: on one level the ideal and pretensions are made to seem incompatible with the mood in which his adventure is recounted, and on another the important point to the story is masked by an atmosphere of fun. Because of the short comic scenes Chapter IV initially marks a delay in the narrative, but it is enlivened by flashes of social comment: the pretensions of the new nobility, the low esteem in which learning is held and eventually the conflict between the individual and his social self.

The Promethean idea is reintroduced as marriage is discussed. For Marco, marriage must be "una obra sabia de selección de la especie" (626), a genetic process on the part of an elite-producing group. But the potential failure of such an ideal is hinted at as a prophetic and ominous note is quietly introduced: "Un filósofo de la antigüedad quería que no se verificasen uniones sino entre individuos perfectos y adecuados el uno al otro. Y quería más: que el fruto de estas uniones, si por accidente naciera defectuoso, no se la consintiese vivir" (626). Marco's ideas perplex Perpetua and one senses a gulf between them, as one also sensed between Marco and the other characters: his uncle did not understand him (605), nor does Don Tesifonte (628) and indeed he does not understand himself. None of this, of course, undermines Marco's self-confidence and Chapter IV ends with his resounding laughter, an expression of his pride, his sense of well-being and intrinsic feeling of superiority.

It is the collapse of all this which is prefigured in the poem of Chapter V, ironically entitled 'Prometeo'. The promise of the temple falls in ruins and the reason why this should be so is only alluded to. There is a suggestion that the spiritual side has been neglected, that the body has taken precedence over the soul, that its cult has proved false and the gods have not been satisfied. Equally there is a hint of some divine retribution which would be in keeping with the ancient myth of gods and men locked in feud and would especially apply to the revolt of the Titan, Prometheus. This new note casts a shadow over the optimism of the early part of the chapter. Indeed, this is one of the effects of the use of myth in the first place: a touch of fatalism is added to the plot as soon as it is set in motion for we await the inexorable working-out of some preordained pattern.

The expectations raised in the previous four chapters are close to fulfilment as the birth of the long-awaited hero approaches. One of the achievements of this short novel is that in a comparatively few pages Ayala has created the impression that a lot has taken place and that the birth of Prometheus is the end of a long period of preparation on Marco's part. Right until the end Marco fails to read the signs. The sinister flashes of lightning over the cemetery have quite different connotations from the normal for Marco. He thinks again of "Prometeo, que arrebató la lumbre viva del hogar de los Inmortales y la puso al servicio de los hombres" (630). But the "confianza en el Destino" which he has masks an insidious fear of the child being born abnormal. This weakness, this ultimate lack of confidence in the critical moment reveals man's continuing dependence on the divinity to whom Marco now directs an anguished prayer. The peace which ensues contrasts sharply with the pains of childbirth. Marco's prayer is unanswered and the child turns out to be "una criatura repugnante, enclenque, el cráneo dilatado, la espalda sinuosa. Prometeo." (631). The juxtaposition of the description with the heroic name reinforces the irony of the novel's denouement. Marco falls back no longer "dueño de sí" and the reader cannot but recall his earlier self-confidence: "libre por entero y dueño de sí mismo". The background noises are the solitary barking of a dog and the tolling of the death knell. A whole series of ironies follow. The redeemer of mankind is totally alienated from his fellow men. Engendered through an intellectual conception of reproduction he is precocious in his own sexual awareness, a trait presumably inherited from his grandfather. This inheritance, by virtue of the arbitrary laws of genetics, causes the final tragedy. A further irony, noted by E.A. Johnson,[19] is that Prometeo, son of the sailor Odysseus, hides his deformity in a little sailor suit. The use of 'Prometeo' becomes increasingly frequent and in fact we never hear his real, only his mythological, name. There is no need, for it is obvious that this is no Prometheus. As Marco turns in on himself the novel focusses more and more on the son. The tone of the work becomes more sombre and the language more direct until it attains a maximum of objectivity in the final paragraph. The stark realism with which the novel ends contrasts brutally with the high-flown style of its opening. For the milkmaid, Prometeo is not a god, but the devil. He is an exceptional being by virtue of his abnormality: not superhuman but subhuman. Homeric prose and literary imitation give way to detached reporting and present dialogue. The process of demythification is also carried out on a linguistic level.

No clear explanation is offered for the failure of Marco's ideal, for there is no logical explanation why things should have turned out the way they did. One might suspect that Nausicaa was chosen at random and was not the perfect woman. Because of his lifestyle, Marco may have been undergoing a process of bodily decline induced perhaps by alcohol, a fact to which Ayala repeatedly alludes. Ernest A. Johnson tries to explain the outcome by arguing that Marco "has dared to play at being a Pagan Greek centuries after Christ's visit to earth" and adds that "there can be no doubt that Pérez de Ayala expected Marco to turn to Christ".[20] He suggests that when writing _Prometeo_ Ayala had in mind Dante's _Inferno_ XXVI, especially lines 112-20 and 141-46 with their exhortation to the 'feeling' life. The implication is that only God can deliver man from the limitations and corruption of this world. In fact, Johnson's textual parallels are not proven, though the broad humanist background to the work, which also includes Socrates, Aeschylus, the Bible and Cervantes, is apparent. Moreover, these echoes of the concerns of previous writers are not motivated in any way within the structure of the plot as those from the _Odyssey_ clearly are. They do underline, however, the essential nature of Ayala's fiction as it endeavours to transcend the immediate present by extracting from it what is permanent and eternal in human experience. The fact is that Marco does turn to Christ and his prayer is answered in the form of his hunchback son. One could argue that Marco has not yet attained Promethean stature and liberated himself from the tyranny of the gods. The ultimate failure of Marco's ideal would not seem to be due to any lack of foresight on his part, but rather to a strange quirk of fate, manifest in the random workings of the laws of genetics. Ayala's novel, if it demonstrates anything, demonstrates the arbitrariness of human life and the inability of the will to control it.

From an aesthetic point of view, _Prometeo_ is based on a fundamental and curiously anachronistic principle of Ayala's art, the principle of literary imitation, which is not to be understood as mere reproduction, but rather as the evocation of familiar topoi, situations and patterns. This is the meaning of originality for Ayala. In _Las Máscaras_ he wrote: "El autor es más original - y no hay paradoja - cuanto más remotas son las resonancias que en él se concentran; como si dijéramos que sus raíces beben la sustancia de las tradiciones literarias primordiales".[21] This principle of imitation applies to the two other 'novelas poemáticas'.

_Luz de domingo_ is, in essence, a modern ballad, which uses a verse epigraph from the _Poema de Mio Cid_ to prefigure the theme and tone of the work. The poems which begin each chapter are themselves in ballad metre and, of course, ballads are by nature narrative in structure and objective in tone. Although they deal with a variety of subjects, the most characteristic ballad themes are the tragedy of life, and the themes of justice and revenge. These are precisely the themes of _Luz de domingo_ and would suggest themselves to any cultured reader. At the same time, the novel deals with a contemporary social reality in which individual vulnerability in the face of political power and corruption is exposed. Ayala exploits the traditional themes of honour and nobility and shows the hollowness of these values in a modern society. This is naturally a point of contact with _Prometeo_ but more important is the fact that Ayala, by his use of poetry and ballad literature, demonstrates his interest in the role of literature itself. In _Luz de domingo_ he uses literature as a sort of escape from reality by creating a literary world not unlike the real world but made more bearable by the imposition of a final harmony and peace. The real and the ideal are again shown to be incompatible.

In an article in El Sol, E. Gómez de Baquero writes of these poematic introductions to these novels: "Cada una de estas poesías liminares es la condensación sentimental del tema de la novela; su expresión cuasi musical, íntima, sentimiento antes que forma concreta, mientras que la narración de la novela es la expresión plástica, el desarrollo histórico del asunto..."[22] Our attitude to the story is shaped before we begin reading. This technique is continued in La caída de los Limones where the illusion of the fictional world acts as a mirror of the world Arias inhabits, a world of his own making, fashioned to his own needs. Thus the theme of all three 'novelas poemáticas' is the striving after some unattainable reality. In each novel life and literature are interwoven to create a strange feeling of ambivalence in the reader. In Luz de domingo the ideal is found in some unreal world; in La caída de los Limones the illusion of the unreal world is shattered by the intrusion of the real; in Prometeo, the myth is rewritten to show the futility of pursuing a heroic ideal. Theme and technique go hand in hand: the world of myth is submitted to the test of reality. In a sense, there are three levels of narration in Prometeo: the real world where the tragedy unfolds, the mythological world which parallels it, and the vantage-point of the author, and reader, which defines the relationship between the two. The prefiguration is doubly ironic in that its real significance is lost on the character.

Although short, Prometeo is thematically a very rich work. There are in it elements of social criticism. It is, like Belarmino y Apolonio, an exercise in perspectivism in which reality is modified according to the point of view from which it is seen and described, an illustration both of the limitations of the partial view and the capacity of art for transcending it. Equally, it explores the Cervantine preoccupation of the effect of reading on the mind and looks back to Alberto Díaz de Guzmán and forward to Tigre Juan. Marco, like these characters, enacts a literary role in the real world; he transmutes life into art. As an extension of this, it is tempting to see in Prometeo an image of the creative artist which, as I pointed out earlier, is a prominent feature of the Prometheus tradition. Is Ayala, in Prometeo, dramatising the anguish of the writer who conceives his ideal work, anticipates its effect on his readers and even on the course of the world, carefully and meticulously prepares it and then produces something pitiful, scorned and doomed to failure? Ayala's life was a struggle to come to terms with his art, to overcome "la maldición originaria del artista", as he called it in Belarmino y Apolonio, to create the perfect work. He wrote of this ideal in Principios y finales de la novela: "Quizá el soñado ideal de todo gran novelista ha sido una sola novela universal, en el otoño de su existencia... Pero se escribe antes porque uno no tiene la vida garantizada y el futuro reside en el regazo de los dioses".[23]

If this is so, then Ayala's attitude to Marco is not one of total deflation and Prometeo is more an expression of the author's pessimism thinly disguised by a veil of humour. It contains no small measure of regret at the degeneration of both literature and mankind towards vulgarity and mediocrity and yet is profoundly sceptical of any possibility of redemption. From an early stage in his life Ayala was fascinated by the exceptional being, the man of genius, and his relationship to the rest of humanity. This relationship is discussed in Troteras y danzaderas in characteristically equivocal terms. Nietzsche's assertion that "Un pueblo o una raza es la disipación de energía que la Naturaleza se permite para crear seis grandes hombres y para destruirlos

en seguida" is turned around by Alberto into "Estos seis hombres son
la disipación de energía que de cuando en cuando la Naturaleza se permite para que los pueblos y las razas vivan; esto es, para que tengan
conciencia clara de que viven".[24] This is very similar to the difference
of opinion between Marco and his uncle in Prometeo. Ayala deals with
this problem in his essays on Nietzsche in La Pluma entitled 'Apostillas
y divagaciones: Nietzsche' and published in 1921 and 1922.[25] Ayala
is clearly attracted by Nietzschean vitalism, by the German's "tendencia
a trascender y superar los tipos ya logrados... Nadie como Nietzsche
mostró tanta fe en los destinos terrenos del hombre. Es el precursor
de la Eugenética, la ciencia primordial del porvenir". But at the same
time he is concerned about the implications of "la ansiedad de dominio"
and "la guerra cósmica" in which the whole of Nature is involved in a
constant struggle within itself for the survival of the fittest. Ayala
resists the universal application of biological laws, and argues that
man is also governed by rational and emotional laws unknown in the rest
of Nature. Moreover, Ayala sees Nature not as competitive but as
cooperative. This idea of cooperation is central to Ayala's world-
view and informs his thinking on the concept of the Superman. In the
first place, he says, the Superman is an ideal which will perhaps be
realised "en el futuro futurísimo". The whole concept is nothing more
than a symbol, and as a symbol cannot have an objectively real existence: "Por muy fiel y escrupuloso que sea el arte en la copia de las
cosas materiales, sensibles e históricas, el producto de su esfuerzo,
así que está concluso y nace a la vida, ya no pertenece al fuero de la
realidad ideal; es un símbolo. He aquí, en suma, el doble postulado
del símbolo: la no existencia real y la pura existencia como ideal".
The creation of superman now is a refutation of the symbol. Prometeo
exposes not so much the failure of the concept of the Superman as a
misunderstanding of it. The use of the myth becomes clear: myths and
symbols take man beyond his immediate situation and enable him to see
life in terms of what is possible and as such they are aspirations which
can never be realised. On a more straightforward level, Prometeo is a
lesson in humility. Myth is the patrimony of the whole of humanity and
not of one individual: the self can only be realised in and through
others. As Ayala writes in his essay on Nietzsche: "el hombre
desapoderadamente aquejado de la ansiedad de dominio, como dice Nietzsche,
o, como se dio en el Renacimiento italiano, deseoso de realizar la
plenitud de su personalidad, percibe, si es inteligente, que sus medios
son limitados, que necesita de los demás hombres". Prometeo is an
expression of Ayala's humanist ethic.

Prometeo, then, does more than use a mythological parallel: it
explores the whole significance of myth itself. The myth is used on
one level to provide a commentary on Marco's action, but for most of the
narrative it is highly ambiguous so that the reader is constantly
speculating on its possible meaning. While it prefigures the action,
the myth is only useful retrospectively in interpreting that action. In
fact, this function partly recedes behind the aesthetic purpose of the
myth which is to shape in advance the narrative material so that the
reader anticipates the completion of a pattern. The possibilities set
up by the mythical prefiguration are gradually diminished as the
narrative develops until the completed form emerges. The reader's
attention would seem to be diverted away from any involvement with the
character towards more formal considerations. Finally, Ayala counter-
points the worlds of myth and reality and evaluates the distinctive
attributes of each by showing Marco's failure to equate the two. A
myth is a collective, ideal truth which, if realised, would no longer be
myth. Approached in this way, Prometeo can be seen to offer another

perspective on a dilemma characteristic of early twentieth-century art: the relationship of life to art, of the subjective, created world to objective reality. Far from asserting the superiority of art over life, or vice versa, Ayala proclaims the distinctiveness of both. By making literature rather than life the prime raw material of his fiction and by his self-conscious handling of that material, Ayala creates an autonomous, self-contained world in which the thematic is subordinated to the aesthetic: any ultimate discoveries the reader might make are concerned with the nature and meaning of myth itself.

N O T E S

1. Imprenta Clásica Española (Madrid 1916).

2. Salvador de Madariaga, Semblanzas literarias contemporáneas (Barcelona 1924).

3. F. Agustín, Ramón Pérez de Ayala. Su vida y obras (Madrid 1927), 162 - 164.

4. Julio Matas, Contra el honor. Las novelas normativas de Ramón Pérez de Ayala (Madrid 1974), 46.

5. D.L. Fabian, 'Action and Idea in Amor y pedagogía and Prometeo', Hispania, XLI (1958), 32.

6. N. Urrutia, De Troteras a Tigre Juan (Madrid 1960), 44.

7. Esperanza Rodríguez Monescillo, 'El mundo helénico de Ramón Pérez de Ayala', Actas del Segundo Congreso Español de Estudios Clásicos (Madrid 1961), 512.

8. F.W. Weber, The Literary Perspectivism of Ramón Pérez de Ayala (Chapel Hill 1966), 41.

9. A. Amorós, La novela intelectual de Ramón Pérez de Ayala (Madrid 1972), 258.

10. M. Salgues de Cargill, Los mitos clásicos y modernos en la novela de Pérez de Ayala (Jaén 1971), 52.

11. See R. Trousson, Le mythe de Prométhée dans la littérature européenne (Geneva 1964), and Luis Díez del Corral, La función del mito clásico en la literatura contemporánea (Madrid 1957), especially 246 - 251.

12. D.L. Fabian, art. cit.

13. Ramón Pérez de Ayala, Otras completas, Vol.II (Madrid 1963), 593. All references are to this edition and are incorporated in the text.

14. Cf. Homer, The Odyssey: "The cave was sheltered by a verdant copse of alders, aspens, and fragrant cypresses, which was the roosting-place of feathered creatures, horned owls and falcons and garrulous choughs,

birds of the coast, whose daily business takes them down to the sea. Trailing round the very mouth of the cavern, a garden vine ran riot, with great bunches of ripe grapes; while from four separate but neighbouring springs four crystal rivulets were trained to run this way and that, and in soft meadows on either side the iris and parsley flourished". Trans. E.V. Rieu (London, Penguin, 1970), 89 - 90.

15. "Now the South wind would toss it to the North to play with, now the East would leave it for the West to chase". Ibid., 96.

16. "If you are one of the gods who live in the sky, it is of Artemis, the Daughter of almighty Zeus, that your beauty, grace and stature most remind me. But if you are one of his mortals who live on earth, then lucky are your father and your gentle mother; lucky your brothers too... But he is the happiest of them all who with his wedding gifts can win you for his love". Ibid., 106.

17. Herman Meyer, The Poetics of Quotation in the European Novel (Princeton 1968), 6.

18. Pío Baroja, El árbol de la ciencia (Madrid 1969), 125.

19. E.A. Johnson, 'The Humanities and the Prometeo of Ramón Pérez de Ayala', Hispania, XXVIII (Sept. 1955), 379.

20. Johnson, 279.

21. Las Máscaras, in Obras completas, Vol.III, 161.

22. E. Gómez de Baquero ('Andrenio'), 'Las nuevas novelas ejemplares', El Sol, 20th May 1924.

23. Principios y finales de la novela (Madrid 1958), 15.

24. Obras completas, Vol.I, 629.

25. La Pluma, No. 19 (Dec. 1921), 321 - 336; No. 20 (Jan. 1922), 1 - 18; No. 21 (Feb. 1922), 65 - 67. These are reproduced in Más divagaciones literarias, in Obras completas, Vol.IV, 1089 - 1134.

De la influencia de Unamuno en El tragaluz, de Antonio Buero Vallejo

Guadalupe Martínez Lacalle (The Queen's University of Belfast)

El tragaluz, un buen ejemplo del mejor teatro español contemporáneo, del mejor arte dramático de Buero Vallejo, ha sido objeto de atención crítica desde su estreno en Madrid, en 1967. Opiniones divididas, pero en conjunto favorables, estudios sobre su originalidad y significado, sus dimensiones socio-políticas y humanas, sus implicaciones filosóficas, etc., hacen de esta tragedia una fuente inagotable. En los estrechos límites del presente artículo, vamos a concentrarnos en los puntos principales de la obra, vistos a la luz de coincidencias con Unamuno o posible influencia del mismo, influencia reconocida por Buero en varias ocasiones.[1] Estos puntos son: el significado de la tragedia en su estructura, es decir, un estudio de los investigadores del futuro; la figura del Padre, y el cainismo de los personajes Mario y Vicente; la integración dramática entre individualidad y colectividad.

Buero, que define El tragaluz como "una investigación sobre el individuo como enigma ontológico", concentra en unos pocos personajes el tema básico de su obra en general: la dualidad básica del ser humano en sus diversos aspectos; el individuo, ser metafísico y psicológico, y el individuo como miembro de la colectividad social, y, en ambos casos, la adquisición de conciencia, el deber moral del hombre - individuo y colectividad - de contribuir al progreso histórico: la dualidad de Caín y Abel hechas una.

Bien es sabido que Buero Vallejo experimenta con el pasado en sus llamadas obras históricas. En la obra que nos ocupa, el experimento realizado es muy similar, puesto que la meta en ambos casos es la misma: mostrar un pasado que podría haber sido mejor; conocer las causas por las que ese pasado no fue mejor; llegar a una visión del futuro en que historia e intra-historia hayan logrado unirse posiblemente. Descubrir los errores históricos, promover el valor intrahistórico, es decir, ahondar en la superficie histórica del mar, - usando la conocida metáfora unamuniana -, así como encontrar la esencia de la tradición eterna formada, como en la familia de El tragaluz, de gentes anónimas, pero cuya "importancia infinita" y singular es enorme para la colectividad. La familia del siglo XX, tan insignificante aparentemente, tiene tanta importancia para Buero, como la tendría para Unamuno, como los héroes y sus hazañas recogidos en la historia. Esta visión refleja la de Unamuno en En torno al casticismo:[2]

> Esa vida intra-histórica, silenciosa y continua como
> el fondo mismo del mar, es la sustancia del progreso,
> la verdadera tradición, la tradición eterna, no la
> tradición mentida que se suele ir a buscar al pasado
> enterrado en libros y papeles y monumentos y piedras.
> (OC III, 1960, 185)

En esta ocasión, el dramaturgo Buero, en su búsqueda de nuevos medios de expresión, presenta una gran tragedia en forma de un proceso, como ocurre con otras obras, pero con la particularidad de que el juicio de la sociedad actual - la de los años 60 - es el de las generaciones futuras; el juicio de la sociedad española como la juzga la generación actual, el espectador del siglo actual, una vez que ha adquirido conciencia de su situación.

El tragaluz se subtitula "experimento en dos partes" y es así, como experimento con el tiempo (un juicio dentro de otro juicio) como Él y

Ella, jóvenes de un siglo futuro,[3] reviven para el espectador contemporáneo la tragedia de una familia intrahistórica, eterna dentro de su temporalidad, humilde y destruida como resultado de la guerra civil (1936-1939). El público contemporáneo alcanzará una doble identidad temporal, ya que se le insta a que viva conscientemente algunas escenas de la vida de una familia del siglo XX, su tiempo 'real'; como gentes del tiempo actual, se les ofrece conciencia de que sus acciones serán juzgadas (de hecho ya lo están siendo) por generaciones futuras. Es decir, al público se le ruega que actúe como espectador o participador de su propio tiempo, de su propia historia, proyectando su personalidad en la historia. Buero presenta una continuidad individual; "una visión del hombre dominando su propia historia". Es decir, que al dirigirse a los espectadores actuales Él y Ella, como personas de un siglo futuro, les están pidiendo que participen en el experimento con ellos. Sobre el problema de la participación Buero ha expresado lo siguiente:

> Para mí, el problema [de la participación] es más delicado y profundo: consiste en arrastrar suavemente al público y sin que éste repare en ello a su <u>transmutación</u> en un público diferente. Los investigadores de <u>El tragaluz</u> pretenden futurizarlo; aumentar su conciencia histórica y con ello, su conciencia del presente.[4]

El público se hace, pues, sujeto y objeto del drama.[5]

Estos investigadores presentan la acción en sus dos partes. Al comienzo de la misma explican los medios de que se han valido para reproducir a lo vivo una historia de un tiempo muy lejano para ellos – así como para los espectadores –. La ciencia ha adquirido tal estado de perfección que se han podido recobrar del pasado, por medio de proyectores espaciales y cerebros electrónicos, acciones y palabras cuyas huellas han quedado fijas en el espacio, así como sentimientos y pensamientos que se han convertido en imágenes. Como Ella dice: "¿Dónde está la barrera entre las cosas y la mente?" (238)[6] Él, por su parte, añade: "Estáis presenciando una experiencia de realidad total: sucesos y pensamientos en mezcla inseparable" (ibid.). De acuerdo con la intensidad de la luz de los 'proyectores espaciales', los personajes están en el escenario, bien parados, bien moviéndose a diversas velocidades. Cuando un personaje piensa en otro, la luz mueve la acción a un plano diferente del escenario. De este modo, a los espectadores se les somete a una experiencia en que los límites entre el mundo subjetivo y el objetivo (el mundo de ilusión y realidad) son invisibles, no existen. Este proceso da a la obra un elemento de ciencia ficción.[7]

Aunque los investigadores del futuro no estén directamente conectados con la historia de la familia del siglo XX, Buero apunta que ellos son la justificación entera del drama.[8]

A través de los diálogos de esta pareja se dan las implicaciones filosófico-sociales de la tragedia. Él explica que "la historia que hemos logrado rescatar del pasado nos da, explícita ya en aquel lejano tiempo, la <u>pregunta</u>" (212). Se refiere a la identidad del hombre, tema básico existencial y unamuniano que no ha sido solucionado en el siglo en que se hace la investigación. Los investigadores continúan preguntándose: "El tiempo... la pregunta" (309). (El tiempo, para el Unamuno de <u>En torno al casticismo</u>, es forma de la eternidad.) Con esta pregunta Buero llega a la esencia del individuo y, por tanto, a la esencia de la colectividad. En la obra de Buero, la pregunta que reitera una y otra vez, casi siempre el Padre, "¿quién es ése?", se traduce en una posible solución a los problemas del ser humano. Al correr de la obra, se hace más y más patente que el Padre y la pareja de investigadores intentan alcanzar una meta similar. El Padre, con su afición de recortar personas individuales de postales y revistas, y los narradores del futuro, al plasmar imágenes y pensamientos del pasado, están trabajando para destacar la validez del individuo. Recordando las palabras de Ella, de que "Ése eres tú, y tú y tú. Yo soy tú, y tú eres yo", y que "Todos hemos vivido, y viviremos, todas las vidas" (291), el hombre podrá vencer su ineficacia y crueldad. De la conciencia individual se llega a la conciencia colectiva. Buero dramáticamente intenta aclarar la psicología colectiva partiendo de una concepción de la psicología individual. Las palabras de Unamuno en su ensayo "Quijotismo y Cervantismo" expresan una idea similar:

> Penétrate de que el mundo eres tú, y esfuérzate en
> salvarlo, para salvarte. El mundo es tu mundo, tu
> mundo eres tú, pero no el yo egoísta, sino el hombre.
> Dentro del mundo, de mi mundo, que soy yo, yo soy
> uno de tantos prójimos. (OC V, ed. 1952, 594)

Somos responsables moralmente de los otros y la solidaridad humana será el único medio, juntamente con la conciencia, de lograr un mundo nuevo y pacífico: "Nos sabemos ya solidarios, no sólo de quienes viven, sino del pasado entero. Inocentes con quienes lo fueron; culpables con quienes lo fueron" (290), añade Ella. Así, en el siglo futuro de los investigadores se habrá llegado a un estado superior de conocimiento en que la injusticia, las guerras, los terrores de la sociedad del siglo XX se habrán superado. Como Él afirma: "Hoy ya no caemos en aquellos errores. Un ojo implacable nos mira, y es nuestro propio ojo" (308), y también, "El presente nos vigila; el porvenir nos conocerá, como nosotros a quienes nos precedieron" (308-309); la propia conciencia individual de nuestra responsabilidad para con los otros (conciencia colectiva), el hecho de que el presente histórico nos vigila y juzga, todo esto hace que no cometamos las mismas faltas de nuestros antepasados. De lo anteriormente expuesto se deduce que los investigadores son parte esencial del drama: la "historia oscura y singular" podría remplazarse por otra similar, pero los investigadores del futuro no. Son indispensables, y esto se ve de nuevo cuando la tragedia está a punto de terminar y Él, dirigiéndose a un público de su siglo futuro arguye:

> Si no os habéis sentido en algún instante verdaderos
> seres del siglo veinte, pero observados y juzgados
> por una especie de conciencia futura; si no os habéis
> sentido en algún otro momento como seres de un futuro
> hecho ya presente que juzgan, con rigor y piedad, a
> gentes muy antiguas y acaso iguales a vosotros, el
> experimento ha fracasado. (309)

Incluso los seres del siglo XX son juzgados con "rigor y piedad" por las generaciones futuras, por la misma generación que está ahora viva, la presente generación. Así que, a unos espectadores de mediados del siglo XX se les hace no solamente que piensen y juzguen (racionalmente), sino también que sientan y teman (emocionalmente) sus propios errores, los fallos de la sociedad de su tiempo, de su siglo. Si no consiguen su objetivo "el experimento habrá fracasado". La noción de catarsis aristotélica todavía está vigente, aunque Buero explore nuevas técnicas.

La visión del futuro que nos ofrece Buero a través de los investigadores es una vez más optimista. A través de una posible solución ética y social a los problemas del mundo de hoy, Buero intenta

"sobrecoger al público universal". Vemos las aspiraciones del pasado
realizadas. Sin embargo, Buero ha manifestado:

> La tragedia no se escamotea; para llegar a ese estadio
> superior del futuro (que, en rigor, no se da por seguro,
> pues la obra pertenece a nuestro presente y patentiza
> su carácter, entre irónico y grave, de advertencia) no
> se oculta que aún tendremos que pasar por tremendas
> "mentiras y catástrofes" colectivas. Pero el coro de
> los investigadores es la esperanza, como lo fue, a
> menudo, el coro griego.[9]

Así pues, al igual que Unamuno en En torno al casticismo y Del
sentimiento trágico de la vida: "Tiene el mundo temporal raíces en la
eternidad, y allí está junto el ayer con el hoy y el mañana" (OC XVI,
1964, 328), Buero trata de relacionar pasado, presente y futuro. En
El tragaluz hay una convergencia y síntesis de historia e intrahistoria:
esta unión realizada a través de una toma de conciencia, hará que el
género humano alcance un máximo de civilización, de desarrollo histórico,
ético, social, etc.

El y Ella presentan la historia diciendo que "Cuando estos fantasmas
vivieron solía decirse que la mirada a los árboles impedía ver el bosque"
(213).[10] Sin embargo, debemos mirar a cada "árbol [...] para que
nuestra visión del bosque [...] no se deshumanice" (ibid.). El hombre
permanece humano sólo cuando no olvida el valor del individuo.

En la historia del siglo XX hay una condena implícita de la sociedad
injusta, materialista y deshumanizada, con la ética de devorar y ser
devorado;[11] de una sociedad en que los seres humanos casi necesariamente
son víctimas o verdugos o ambas cosas, en que triunfan los desaprensivos
y no los íntegros.

La familia objeto del experimento de la pareja del futuro, vive en
un sótano cuyo único contacto con el mundo exterior, al nivel de la
calle, lo constituye un tragaluz. La componen el Padre, la Madre y
Mario, el hijo menor. Vicente, el mayor, ha prosperado y vive independientemente. En tiempos pasados, a finales de la guerra civil,
tenían una hija de dos años, Elvirita, que murió de hambre. En parte
murió por las circunstancias del momento histórico, en parte como
consecuencia del egoísmo de su hermano mayor, que, en aquella estación
de ferrocarril en que estaban todos dispuestos a volver a Madrid en el
año 1939, tomó el tren, olvidándose de los que quedaban atrás, y
llevándose las escasas provisiones con que contaba la familia. Como
reacción, el Padre se refugió en la locura. La mente del Padre se
detuvo en el tiempo poco después de los acontecimientos citados, cuando
los primeros síntomas de su enfermedad se declararon. Si el tren para
Vicente simbólicamente representa su iniciación en la carrera de la
vida, para su padre, que lo perdió, fue el final.

El Padre, "un ser oscuro y enfermo" (213), símbolo de la conciencia
en la obra (para Unamuno la conciencia del universo es Dios), es una
figura mucho más enigmática de lo que parece a primera vista, es uno de
los personajes anormales que se dan con frecuencia en las obras de Buero,
un personaje anormal, pero visionario, que adquiere una perspectiva
vital más amplia que el resto de los personajes que integran la obra.[12]
Al principio aparece como un viejo loco; vive en un mundo en que locura
y razón se confunden. Destroza a silletazos, según se nos cuenta, el
televisor que le regaló Vicente. Se pone furioso cuando la trasmisión
de "El Misterio de Elche" la interrumpen con una serie de anuncios de
lavadoras, detergentes, etc. Es la protesta de un loco-lúcido contra
la sociedad enajenante que 'rompe' la 'realidad'. (Don Quijote

destroza el retablo de Maese Pedro (II, xxvi) cuando el recitador
falsea la 'realidad' de la historia de Don Gaiferos y su esposa Mali-
sendra.) Este enfermo de arterioesclerosis ha perdido la memoria y la
capacidad cognoscitiva; de hecho no reconoce a ningún miembro de su
familia y padece de confusión de identidad, lo que es apreciable cuando
alguien nombra a su hijo y homónimo Vicente.[13] Tampoco se reconoce a
sí mismo cuando se ve reflejado en un espejo, pues lo que en éste se ve
es una simple imagen del Padre tal como los otros le ven, y no un reflejo del conflicto de su realidad íntima. La metáfora del espejo como
signo de desdoblamiento de la personalidad se da en Unamuno.

En una de las primeras escenas juega al tren (el tren que constituye su mayor obsesión) con su mujer;[14] es un viejo divertido a causa
de sus aparentes incongruencias, pero que, en realidad sufre hondamente.[15]
Identifica a su mujer con su madre: recuérdese que para Unamuno toda
mujer es una madre en potencia, tanto espiritual como biológicamente, y
que el amor maternal es compasión.[16] En su ensayo "A una aspirante a
escritora", Unamuno opina: "La mujer es madre ante todo [...] Quiere
al amante o al marido con amor maternal y, su amor crece cuando le
siente débil, cuando siente que es preciso defenderle por muy fuerte que
en otros respectos parezca" (OC IV, 1960, 717-718).

La Madre[17] de El tragaluz se ve obligada a tratar a su marido como
a un niño. Los niños mueren metafóricamente cuando crecen; pierden su
inocencia y se convierten en adultos culpables y responsables. Unamuno
en su Cancionero, habla de "Nuestro íntimo ser, el que nos entona el
canto de pureza de la niñez lejana" (OC II, ed. 1951, 748). Esta pureza
es algo innato que constituye el estrato básico de la personalidad,
antes que la conciencia se le imponga. "Todos estamos muertos" (253),
Mario le dice a su madre en una de las escenas más líricas de la obra.
Vicente, como veremos después, quiere volver a la niñez perdida.
Quiere volver al sueño de la vida, por miedo a ser absorbido en el
abismo de la nada, para des-nacer en la eternidad del olvido donde todo
duerme. En Unamuno es frecuente la imagen de la madre y el niño. Muchos
personajes quieren volver a la niñez y parece que la encuentran en el
lecho de muerte.[18] Como apunta R.L. Predmore: "In the mother-child
images [Unamuno] may have found a way to turn his back at times on the
chill prospect of everlasting death, but at bottom they satisfied his
yearning no more than did the substitute immortality of posthumous
literary fame".[19]

Sin embargo, el Padre ve en Encarna la encarnación de su hija
Elvirita. Cuando Encarna, echándose a llorar revela que está esperando
un hijo de Vicente, el Padre, contento, le pregunta: "¿He oído bien?
¿Vas a ser madre? ¡Claro, has crecido tanto! ¡No llores, nena! ¡Tener
un hijo es lo más bonito del mundo!" (299-300), y luego, dándole un
muñeco de papel, le aconseja: "Cuídalo mucho y vivirá" (302). A Vicente
le ofrece un consejo similar en una ocasión: "Hay que tener hijos y
velar por ellos" (266).

La idea de que el Padre no reconozca a sus hijos, de que ellos no
ocupen lugar en la mente del Padre (de Dios), la estudiaremos a través
de la interpretación unamuniana del mito bíblico de Caín y Abel, leyenda
que preocupó a Unamuno toda su vida y que asocia con el tema de España.[20]

Ser inmortal es sobrevivir en la memoria de los otros, según se
afirma en Del sentimiento trágico de la vida; es triunfar sobre la
tendencia natural al olvido:

> La memoria es la base de la personalidad individual,
> así como la tradición lo es de la personalidad colectiva
> de un pueblo. Se vive en el recuerdo y por el recuerdo,
> y nuestra vida espiritual no es, en el fondo, sino el

> esfuerzo de nuestro recuerdo por perseverar, por
> hacerse esperanza, el esfuerzo de nuestro pasado
> por hacerse porvenir. (<u>OC</u> XVI, 1964, 135)

Así, la muerte de Abel a manos de Caín fue por sobrevivir en la memoria
de Dios. La lucha fue de carácter espiritual, no material, pues las
ofrendas de ambos hermanos eran igualmente buenas. "La envidia es mil
veces más terrible que el hambre, porque es hambre espiritual", añade
Unamuno (ibid., 182-183).

El Padre intenta proteger al género humano. Por su gran compromiso
con el ser humano, el Padre recorta figuras humanas de tarjetas postales
y revistas para preservarlas, para librarlas de todo mal en su archivo
particular. El Padre, como Don Quijote, ha perdido la razón y sus
actos, a los ojos de los demás, son locuras. Al recortar figuras, una
a una, les está concediendo valor de individuales, y, por tanto, de
universales: a su manera, medio loca, medio lúcida, está llevando a
cabo el mismo empeño que los investigadores del futuro. Unamuno en el
Comentario a <u>Cómo se hace una novela</u> afirma que al adquirir conciencia
de lo individual, se adquiere conciencia de lo universal, y, por tanto,
de lo divino o eterno:

> ... lo provisorio es lo eterno, [...] el aquí es el
> centro del espacio infinito, el foco de la infinitud,
> y el ahora el centro del tiempo, el foco de la
> eternidad; [...] lo individual es lo universal – en
> lógica los juicios individuales se asimilan a los
> universales – y por tanto lo eterno, [...] no hay
> otra política que la de salvar en la historia a los
> individuos. (<u>OC</u> X, 1961, 846-847)

Don Quijote reafirma su identidad con las famosas palabras "yo sé
quién soy", busca la inmortalidad, la perduración en la mente de los
otros. El Padre tiene fe absoluta en su empresa de liberador. El
conoce la identidad de las personas retratadas en sus postales y revistas, y, sin embargo, reitera la pregunta "¿Quién es ése?", y si
Vicente le contesta, "uno cualquiera" (230), se irrita, porque él sí
que lo sabe, a él sí le preocupa el ser humano. Si les formula "la
tremenda pregunta", es para probarlos. Vicente sospecha que su padre
se cree Dios (como veremos después). Pero Vicente (y Mario) el adulto,
no ocupa lugar en el archivo de su padre. "Ya le he dicho que no está
en mi archivo" (276), le contesta a Vicente cuando éste le pregunta si
le reconoce. Como el Dios del Antiguo Testamento (<u>Génesis</u>, IV, 2-7),
el Dios de Caín y Abel, el Padre no reconoce a sus hijos. Pero, por
otra parte, el Padre busca ansiosamente a su niño perdido, a Vicente,
a un recién nacido a quien, incluso, oye llorar: "¡Tengo que buscar
a mi hijo!" (251), dice angustiado; pero cuando lo encuentra lo mata.

Al estar en continuo contacto con el mundo de su padre, en el que
razón y locura se confunden, a Mario se le despierta la curiosidad por
saber lo que encierra su gran interés por las postales. Observando sus
rarezas, el gran conocimiento de lo real que posee el Padre, llega al
fondo de la cuestión sobre su enfermedad y la culpabilidad de Vicente.[21]
Para Mario, "un hombre capaz de preguntar lo que él pregunta ... tiene
que ser mucho más que un viejo imbécil" (257). Como al Padre, a Mario
– a quien su hermano tacha de Quijote en varias ocasiones – le preocupan
problemas sobre la identidad humana, la condición humana con sus problemas existenciales. Por el contrario, para Vicente las personas
retratadas en las postales están simplemente muertas, con lo que denota
su profunda indiferencia por el ser humano. "¿Quién era? A los activos

como tú no les importa. Pero yo me lo tropiezo ahí, en la postal, inmóvil..." (259), le dice Mario, a lo que él replica: "O sea, muerto" (ibid.). La falta de solidaridad, de interés en el ser humano que muestra Vicente contrasta con su hermano y padre y con la tarea similar que están desarrollando los experimentadores del futuro, como ya hemos señalado. "Pienso si no fue retratado para que yo, muchos años después, me preguntase quién era. Sí, sí; y también pienso a veces si se podría [...]emprender una investigación" (259-260). Para Vicente la naturaleza de la realidad, el enigma del individuo, su relación con el otro o con los otros son asuntos incomprensibles: Mario, conociendo las dificultades que estos problemas entrañan, le arguye: "Es como querer saber el comportamiento de un electrón en una galaxia lejanísima" (260), que, de acuerdo con Vicente, es "¡El punto de vista de Dios!" (ibid.). Mario, al igual que tantos personajes buerianos, va en busca de lo inalcanzable: "Que nunca tendremos, pero que anhelamos" (ibid.). Es decir, que la naturaleza humana es limitada y la condición humana, algo que el hombre sueña con trascender.[22]

Mario no ha prosperado en la vida, desempeña "mil trabajillos fugaces" y corrige pruebas de imprenta que le proporciona su hermano. Como el resto de la familia 'que no tomó el tren', vive marginado de la sociedad, en parte por su propia falta, viviendo en un pasado muerto, pero aparentando exceso de escrúpulos, sin integrarse en la sociedad por carencia de iniciativa: es pasivo, pensador e idealista a primera vista. Vicente, muy al contrario, es activo, enérgico, realista, que tiene un puesto lucrativo en una editorial, está completamente integrado en la sociedad capitalista y materialista que le rodea. Ayuda a mantener a su familia con dinero y regalos propios de la sociedad de consumo.

Mario, aunque más íntegro que su hermano, se niega a luchar por la vida. Vicente, que carece de principios morales, tiene razón al aconsejar a su hermano: "¡No harás nada útil si no actúas! Y no conocerás a los hombres sin tratarlos, ni a ti mismo, si no te mezclas con ellos" (258). Vicente rechaza a los que no han prosperado en la sociedad. Sus padres y hermano "No han sabido salir de aquel pozo" (221). Esta referencia al sótano como pozo se da con frecuencia en la obra. Pero aunque el pozo refleje la vida estancada, reflejo de interioridad, en que Mario ha decidido permanecer (como reflejo quizás de una sociedad podrida, del "marasmo de España", de acuerdo con la terminología unamuniana) el conocimiento que Mario, hombre de interioridad, tiene del hombre, lo ha adquirido observando y meditando. En el Prólogo a La tía Tula (1921) Unamuno se expresa de la siguiente manera:

> En mi novela Abel Sánchez intenté escarbar en ciertos
> sótanos y escondrijos del corazón, en ciertas catacumbas del alma, adonde no gustan descender los más
> de los mortales. Creen que en esas catacumbas hay
> muertos, a los que lo mejor es no visitar, y esos
> muertos, sin embargo, nos gobiernan. Es la herencia
> de Caín. (OC IX, 1961, 527)

No obstante, Vicente volverá más y más al sótano familiar. Como hemos apuntado, las raíces del antagonismo fraternal están en la actitud opuesta que tienen ante la vida.. Vicente intenta abrir los ojos a su hermano a la realidad de la vida como él la entiende: "¡Estás soñando! ¡Despierta!" (258), pero Mario duda de que la actitud vital de su hermano sea más positiva y le pregunta, "¿Quién debe despertar? ¡Veo a mi alrededor muchos activos, pero están dormidos! ¡Llegan a creerse más irreprochables cuanto más se encanallan!" (258-259). Los activos

101

tienen poco tiempo para meditar sobre el enigma de la existencia.
Recordemos las palabras de Ella: "Los activos olvidaban la contemplación; quienes contemplaban no sabían actuar" (308). Vicente es un
hombre social, exterior, que posee un yo público, pero que carece de
vida interior, de yo privado. En términos unamunianos Vicente no tiene
personalidad, sino individualidad.

La rivalidad y envidia de los hermanos va quedando más y más
patente según avanza la tragedia.

Pero la actitud pasiva de Mario puede ser tan perjudicial a la
sociedad y al individuo como el pragmatismo del activo Vicente. La
influencia de Unamuno sigue clara. En Cómo se hace una novela, refiriéndose al proceso histórico - y a la ficción - como proyección y
reflejo, acción y contemplación, dice lo siguiente: "Y aquí entra lo
de la acción y la contemplación, la política y la novela. La acción
es contemplativa, la contemplación es activa; la política es novelesca
y la novela es política" (OC X, 1961, 910). Buero, por otra parte,
ha manifestado que su interés por este tema es antiguo, diciendo:
"... el vasto mundo de la jolosotra oriental me ha preocupado durante
casi toda mi vida. Y es en esas lecturas del Bajarad Gita, del yoga,
etc. [...] donde podrían estar quizás las chispas iniciales de mi
obsesión por armonizar contemplación y acción".[23]

Conforme avanza el drama llegamos a comprender que la aparente
dualidad, la del activo y el pasivo, etc., no es tan clara. Poco a
poco llegamos a la conclusión de que Buero muestra en estos dos hermanos
a dos seres humanos, tales que ni en uno se dan tintes completamente
positivos, ni en el otro tintes completamente negativos. Refiriéndose
a aquellos críticos que se dedicaron a hacer de Mario y Vicente dos
héroes de folletín, Buero afirma que si bien él escogería al hermano
menor por parecerle un tipo más interesante y humano, "El tipo ideal
para una conducta equilibrada hubiera sido un hombre intermedio entre
los dos hermanos ... un 70 por 100 del menor y un 30 del mayor".[24]

Con esta presentación profundamente psicológica de estos personajes,
Buero les ofrece carácter trágico, dándole a la obra una profundidad
extraordinaria, sobre todo en las escenas finales.

De acuerdo con la interpretación de Unamuno de la leyenda de Caín
y Abel, Caín no es necesariamente malo ni su hermano necesariamente
bueno. Unamuno incluso invierte los valores, trasmuta los papeles
bíblicos porque a él le interesan los problemas dialécticos producidos
por la envidia. La bondad y la maldad se implican mutuamente, de
manera que las dos características se dan en la lucha fratricida,
violencia y soledad que produce la envidia. Unamuno ve algo positivo
en Caín el labrador, el fundador de la primera ciudad con sus implicaciones futuras de prosperidad y cultura, siendo así que su acción
fue de carácter social, de valor trascendente de la inmortalidad. El
lado destructor de la naturaleza de Caín podría redimirse, cosa que no
suele ocurrir con los personajes de Unamuno, pero sí ocurre con los de
Buero. Abel es pastor errante, enemigo de la sociedad compacta: no
produce nada. El mito de Caín y Abel representa dos actitudes básicas
en la lucha existencial. Unamuno en Paisajes se expresa de esta manera:
"¡Pueblos pastores que pasan sobre la tierra! ¡Pueblos labradores que
se agrupan en torno a las ciudades! ¡Entera dualidad de la historia
humana!" (OC I, 1959, 60).

Al comienzo de El tragaluz el deseo de Mario por establecer su yo
por un proceso continuo de proyección, reflexión y recreación, su
deseo de aclarar el pasado, que no recuerda bien, es sincero. Comparte
los ideales de Eugenio Beltrán - el novelista cuya carrera destroza
Vicente - acerca de la sociedad y actúa de manera similar. Por eso
rechaza Mario la ayuda que le brinda su hermano para que trabaje

con él en la editora.  Le dice:

> Me repugna vuestro mundo.  Todos piensan que en él no
> cabe sino comerte a los demás o ser comido.  Y
> encima, todos te dicen: ¡devora antes de que te
> devoren! Te daremos bellas teorías para tu tran-
> quilidad.  La lucha por la vida... El mal inevitable
> para llegar al bien necesario... La caridad bien
> entendida... (257),

y luego echa en cara a su hermano su oportunismo, su carencia de
principios morales, el seguir el juego de la sociedad.  Mario no está
de acuerdo con las teorías utilitarias del mundo que le rodea.  Pero
en el fondo, dentro de sus acusaciones hay envidia.  Vicente, por otra
parte, se alegra de que Mario no haya aceptado su propuesta: "No
sabe él lo generosa que era mi oferta.  Porque le he mentido: no me
agradaría tenerle aquí.  Con sus rarezas resultaría bastante incómodo"
(250).

A lo largo de la obra, Mario intenta que su hermano reconozca la
parte que tuvo en la tragedia familiar.  Lo va atrayendo al "pozo".
Pero como él llega a reconocer, su subconsciente trabaja en sus sueños
y le indica que él va a ser indirectamente responsable de la muerte de
Vicente.  En un sueño de anticipación profética, que tiene un significado
primario, Mario, sentado en uno de los lados de un precipicio, corrige
pruebas tranquilamente mientras da tironcitos a una cuerda que ata su
muñeca a la cintura de un desconocido que corre por la otra ladera.
Lo acerca al abismo y, de un tirón repentino, lo despeña.  Como le dice
a Encarna al final de la obra, "Yo le incité a volver.  ¡Me creía
pasivo, y estaba actuando tremendamente!" (310).  Como resultado de la
actuación de Mario, las visitas de Vicente a su familia se hacen más
asiduas: está procurando que su padre lo reconozca; vuelve al lugar
inicial como si quisiera sufrir un proceso de arrepentimiento y puri-
ficación para obtener perdón por su culpa.[25]

En dos escenas - una en cada parte del drama y con similar propósito -, Vicente juega a adivinar la identidad de las personas que
pasan por delante del tragaluz, que se revelan súbitamente a través
de unas palabras o unas piernas.  Es el juego cervantino de la ficción
y la realidad que conduce a vías de conocimiento profundas.  Era un
pasatiempo para los hermanos cuando eran niños, y un juego ahora para
Mario y su padre.  Como afirma Buero Vallejo, la realidad parcial del
tragaluz

> es cosa que va moldeando la psique de Vicente y
> enfrentándole con su autorreconocimiento hasta
> llevarlo a la culminación de su destino.  Bueno,
> por eso doy yo tanta importancia a este aspecto de
> la capacidad de crear conexiones con lo que nos
> rodea en función de nuestros propios problemas;
> porque la coincidencia es algo que creamos nosotros,
> claro está".[26]

Mario, que está acostumbrado a vivir una realidad parcial como la del
Padre, encuentra significado en esa realidad incompleta (y en la
realidad incompleta de piernas y palabras a través del tragaluz) que
es capaz de darle a Vicente (que no acepta la realidad fragmentaria
del mundo como se proyecta en el tragaluz) una visión de la vida que
finalmente resulta ser más verdadera que la de su hermano realista.
Por este medio, Mario lleva a su hermano a aceptar su realidad de

hombre culpable que ha hecho y ccntinúa haciendo víctimas, víctimas que
le obliga a reconocer entre los transeúntes que pasan ante el tragaluz.
Uno de ellos es Eugenio Beltrán; otro, Encarna, una campesina cuya
única preocupación en la vida es la prostitución, y que, irónicamente,
está prostituida siendo la amante de Vicente.  En el choque de pasiones
de los hermanos Encarna hace un papel muy importante.  También en
conexión con ella se descubre la rivalidad y la envidia de los hermanos y
su similaridad de carácter.  Cuando en la escena que constituye el
clímax de la obra Encarna descubre ante toda la familia sus relaciones
con Vicente y su embarazo, Mario (que parecía el novio bueno, pero que
en realidad su intuición de que su hermano era rival en amores le hacía
pretenderla) la trata con desprecio al igual que Vicente que la despide
de secretaria.  Pero Mario, incluso reprochándole a su hermano el ser
un "pequeño dictadorzuelo", no se compadece de ella:  de hecho la ha
estado usando en sus maquinaciones contra Vicente.  Encarna ha temido
siempre a Vicente: "Al principio creí que le quería... Y, sobre todo,
tenía miedo... Tenía miedo, Mario.  También ahora lo tengo.  Ten piedad
de mi miedo, Mario" (289).  Pero Mario la trata con la misma crueldad
que su hermano.  (Al final de la tragedia Mario le pide a Encarna que
se compadezca de él, y ella acaba aceptando.)  Mario vive del odio a
su hermano.  Es la misma pasión de  Joaquín Monegro por Abel Sánchez
en la novela de Unamuno Abel Sánchez.  Los dos hermanos de El tragaluz
no pueden comunicar; el contacto directo sólo produce odio y soledad.
La lucha por sobrevivir es inevitable.  Si bien Unamuno sabe que la
envidia posee un enorme potencial destructivo - como expresa en el
ensayo "Ni envidiado ni envidioso": "La triste envidia, avaricia
espiritual de las almas pobres, fructifica sin florecer, como la higuera,
en estos tristes páramos del espíritu" (OC IV, 1960, 1160) -, sabe
también que puede abocar a la "más alta conciencia espiritual", esta
conciencia que ambos hermanos adquieren en El tragaluz.  La envidia de
Mario, como la de Joaquín, es trágica, con rasgos positivos además de
negativos.  Mario en su lucha intenta autoafirmarse, exaltar su yo;
intenta también perjudicar a Vicente.  La envidia de Vicente, como la
de Abel (y con él la envidia colectiva), se basa en una falta de
adecuación espiritual:  como hemos apuntado, es indiferente a los otros
y a su sufrimiento, es, por tanto, egoísta y dominante: su envidia
rebaja el yo de los otros a su propio nivel.

     La rivalidad de los hermanos, y la envidia que hace presa de
Mario, se hace más evidente en conexión con la Madre, a quien Mario
acusa de preferir a su hermano.  La Madre le ruega que se case con
Encarna.  Mario le increpa: "¿No es a mi hermano a quien se lo tenías
que proponer?" (293), "También le disculparás lo de Encarna, claro
[...]  ¡Vamos a olvidarlo, como otras cosas!  ¡Es tan bueno!" (ibid.).
Poco después le dice resentido:

          ¡No es mala chica Encarna, no!  ¡Y además se comprende
          su flaqueza!  ¡El demonio de Vicente es tan simpático!
          Pero nn es mujer para él; él merece otra cosa.  ¡Mario,
          sí!  ¡Mario puede cargar con ella!"  (293-294)

     En esta contienda envidiosa no solamente está Encarna (como en el
caso de Joaquín y Abel respecto de Helena), sino el éxito social de
Vicente.  Quizás Mario anhele una seguridad ontológica que cree que le
ha robado Vicente y está luchando por que se la devuelva.  En el caso
de Abel Sánchez, la leyenda de Caín-Joaquín es el enlace entre la
envidia y la seguridad ontológica.  El conflicto de voluntades se
resuelve en El tragaluz con el entendimiento mutuo, con una compasión
en ambos casos, como veremos a continuación.

Pero es en la escena del juicio cuando el pasado se hace presente, cuando se da una trasmutación de papeles, de víctima a torturador, cuando las víctimas de Vicente afloran a la superficie y Mario se declara juez, ya que el verdadero juez, el Padre enajenado no podría dar un veredicto. Mario declara: "Soy un juez. Porque el verdadero juez no puede juzgar. Aunque, ¿quién sabe? ¿Puede usted juzgar, padre?" (298). Mario entonces se remonta a la esencia de la cuestión, a la estación de ferrocarril al final de la guerra, cuando, de hecho, los soldados que ocupaban el retrete del tren, por cuya ventanilla entró Vicente, le empujaban para que se bajara. "Pero el tren arrancó... y se te llevó para siempre. Porque ya nunca has bajado de él" (303). Tuvo un mal comienzo en la vida y después continuó 'viajando' de la misma manera. Sin embargo, Mario comprende la actuación de Vicente dadas las circunstancias de su niñez:

> ¡Les estorbabas! Y nosotros también te estorbábamos.
> La guerra había sido atroz para todos, el futuro era
> incierto y, de pronto, comprendiste que el saco era tu
> primer botín. No te culpo del todo; sólo eras un
> muchacho hambriento y asustado. Nos tocó crecer en
> años difíciles... (304-305)

Las palabras de Mario describen la cruda realidad de las miserias de la guerra civil y el futuro incierto que del momento histórico resultó. Pero la inclinación egoísta del Vicente niño podría haberla refrenado él después, en una sociedad mejor. Vicente es un producto auténtico de las condiciones sociales que apunta Buero, a diferencia de Unamuno en su novela citada. Pero la intención de Mario al aclarar las cosas en el juicio es condenar a su hermano como adulto y sus atropellos de adulto, porque,

> ¡... ahora, hombre ya, sí eres culpable! Has hecho
> pocas víctimas, desde luego; hay innumerables canallas
> que las han hecho por miles, por millones. ¡Pero tú
> eres como ellos! Dale tiempo al tiempo y verás crecer
> el número de las tuyas... Y tu botín. (305)

Él, Mario, un niño sensible, en aquella época aprendió de pronto la injusticia del mundo, de donde se deduce la reacción pasiva posterior.

La apreciación que hace Mario de su hermano como ser humano es correcta. Las palabras citadas arriba muestran lo que era Vicente, lo que es, y lo que habría sido si hubiera vivido más tiempo.

Finalmente, Vicente descarga su conciencia en su padre, como si estuviera rogando a Dios que le perdonara por sus crímenes, con las siguientes palabras:[27] "Le hablo como quien habla a Dios sin creer en Dios, porque quisiera que Él estuviese ahí... Pero no está, y nadie es castigado, y la vida sigue" (306). Más tarde, en el mismo diálogo, añade: "Quisiera que me entendiese y me castigase, como cuando era un niño, para poder perdonarme luego" (307). Vicente está añorando los días lejanos de la niñez; está buscando su yo concreto y esencial. Aparece más que nunca como figura trágica. Pero, al mismo tiempo, una vez más expresa su indiferencia por el ser humano, por la muerte de su hermana, así como por los 'individuos' de papel que su padre está tan ansioso de 'salvar'. La muerte era un suceso diario en la guerra: bombas, hambre, la crueldad del hombre para con el hombre: "Cuando me enteré de su muerte pensé: un niño más" (306), afirma sacando de su bolsillo un muñeco de papel que su padre le había dado. "¡Elvirita murió por mi culpa, padre!" (307), declara mientras juega con el muñeco.

Pero, aunque está dispuesto a que le castigue su padre y le perdone, descarta la posibilidad de empezar de nuevo, de cambiar las estructuras de la sociedad a la que pertenece: volverá y continuará pisoteando a los otros como algo inevitable, porque, "¿quién puede terminar con las canalladas en un mundo canalla?" (306). Pero a esta pregunta Vicente encuentra una respuesta inesperada: "Yo", pronunciada por el Padre con toda claridad. A continuación se oyen los golpecitos en el cristal del tragaluz (que, como hemos observado, el Padre asocia con el tren) que dan los niños a quienes toma por sus hijos; las palabras de Vicente, "Ahora hay que volver ahí arriba... y seguir pisoteando a los demás" (307) al tiempo que le devuelve el muñeco de papel arrugado (símbolo de la falta de preocupación que tiene Vicente por el individuo); el fragor de la máquina del tren (un pensamiento, el recuerdo de la estación al final de la guerra) que aumenta. Todos estos factores hacen que el Padre vuelva al pasado y recobre a su hijo perdido para apuñalarlo con las tijeras con que solía 'cuidar' la vida de los individuos. Al asestarle los tijeratazos le ordena: "No subas al tren" [...] "Tú no subirás al tren" [...] "¡No!"... "¡No!" [...] "¡Elvirita!" (307, 308).

Vicente confiesa su culpa de la que tiene conciencia, pero no llega a redimirse al no rechazar su egoísmo, al no cambiar para realizarse como ser humano, no llega a alcanzar la salvación a través de otro, como veremos que le ocurre a Mario.

Tan pronto como el Padre reconoce a su hijo, él, el Dios creador de Vicente, destruye su creación. En su momento 'lúcido' el Padre castiga a su hijo como adulto una vez que le ha reconocido de joven. Recordemos de nuevo, que en Unamuno, los personajes que quieren recobrar la niñez perdida, la encuentran en la muerte. En El tragaluz, Vicente está cansado de ser hombre y expresa su deseo de volver a ser niño.[28]

El Padre, pues, tiene un doble valor en la obra. Veamos las siguientes palabras de Unamuno en Cómo se hace una novela: "Estar loco.se dice que es haber perdido la razón. La razón, pero no la verdad, porque hay locos que dicen las verdades que los demás callan por no ser ni racional ni razonable decirlas, y por eso se dice que están locos" (OC X, 1961, 873). Tiene el valor real y el simbólico, ambos con profundo poder sugestivo.[29]

A Vicente lo mata su padre, no por las víctimas del pasado ni por las del presente; no por haber causado la muerte de su hermana o por haber influido en la vida de su hermano, que se ha convertido en un resentido al margen de la sociedad; no por haber sido la causa de la enfermedad del Padre o de la infelicidad oculta de la Madre; no por haber sido la causa de la desgracia de Encarna o por haber destrozado la carrera del novelista Beltrán. Es castigado, porque a pesar de confesarse culpable, de su deseo de comprensión, perdón y castigo a la vez, él, como individuo, no hace el esfuerzo necesario para romper con el presente e iniciar una nueva vida. Él ha hecho frente a su realidad, pero no cambiará su presente y continuará viajando en aquel tren simbólico "que nunca para" sin dejar de hacer víctimas. Vicente está luchando entre la afirmación de su individualidad y la responsabilidad para con la sociedad colectiva de su tiempo, de la cual, él es también una víctima.

En Del sentimiento trágico de la vida Unamuno opina lo siguiente acerca de la culpa (palabras que podrían aplicarse a Vicente):

> Y el que la culpa es colectiva no ha de servir para
> sacudirme de ella sobre los demás, sino para cargar
> sobre mí las culpas de los otros, las de todos, no
> para difundir mi culpa y anegarla en la culpa total,
> sino para hacer la culpa total mía; no para enajenar

mi culpa, sino para ensimismarme, y apropiarme,
adentrándomela, la de todos. Y cada uno debe
contribuir a curarla, por lo que otros no hacen.
El que la sociedad sea culpable agrava la culpa
de cada uno. (OC XVI, 1964, 413)

En la escena final del drama, Mario admite su parte de culpa en la
tragedia. Le confiesa a Encarna: "Lo fui atrayendo ... hasta que cayó
en el precipicio" (310, véase 242). Pero las intenciones de ambos quedan
claras, ya que: "Él quería engañarse... y ver claro; yo quería salvarlo
... y matarlo. ¿Qué queríamos en realidad?" (310). Ninguno de los dos
por lo tanto, representa maldad o bondad a ultranza; son psicológica-
mente seres humanos. El Mario de Buero (con Unamuno) niega la interpretación tradicional de Abel como víctima: "Yo no soy bueno; mi hermano
no era malo. Por eso volvió. A su modo, quiso pagar" (ibid.). Y a
continuación revela la lucha por Encarna a quien usaron como comodín en
su contienda: "¿Y qué hemos hecho nosotros contigo? [...] ¿No te hemos
usado los dos para herirnos con más violencia?" (ibid.). Mario añade:
"¿Quién soy yo? ¿Quién ha sido víctima de quién?" (ibid.). En la tragedia de Unamuno El Otro, los dos hermanos terminan por hacerse uno mismo.
El Otro se pregunta: "¿Yo? ¿Asesino yo? Pero ¿quién soy yo? ¿Quién
es el asesino? ¿Quién el asesinado? ¿Quién el verdugo? ¿Quién la víctima?" (OC XII, 1961, 824). Unamuno sentía la dramática dualidad que
existe siempre en el alma humana. En el Prólogo a Tres novelas ejemplares
y un prólogo define al ser humano desde un punto de vista existencial:
"Y es que todo hombre humano lleva dentro de sí las siete virtudes y sus
siete opuestos vicios capitales [...] Y saca de sí mismo lo mismo al
tirano que al esclavo, al criminal que al santo, a Caín que a Abel" (OC
IX, 1961, 421). El hombre es verdugo y víctima de sí mismo.
Ambos personajes confiesan su culpa al final de la tragedia (lo
mismo hace Joaquín Monegro a lo largo de la novela): los dos son libres
y culpables. La consecuencia del odio fraternal ha sido la autodestruc-
ción para afirmar su personalidad. Los dos han luchado por redimirse,
pero sus aspiraciones han chocado.
La tragedia de Caín-Joaquín-Mario es la de la imposibilidad de ser
por la presencia del otro, de Abel-Vicente, al igual que la posibilidad
de ser ha sido disminuida por la presencia de Mario-Abel. Los dos
hermanos llegan a conocerse en función de lo que comparten.
La unión de antagonistas transforma su autoafirmación en fuerza
creadora de la sociedad. Caín trasmite como herencia su conflicto trágico, de acuerdo con el Antiguo Testamento; pero redención se da en el
Nuevo Testamento. En el caso de Mario su redención la consigue por
Encarna, a quien acepta, haciendo suyo el hijo de Vicente. (En Unamuno
el tema del amor está ligado al de la personalidad, pero a Joaquín
Monegro no le redime el amor de Antonia.) En El tragaluz la esperanza
en el futuro está, pues, patente; esperanza de una sociedad más justa,
de un hombre más feliz y sin temores. Esperanza de las generaciones
futuras a través del niño que va a nacer (de lo individual a lo colectivo);
esperanza que lleva la Madre cuando al final abre el tragaluz y mira a
los transeúntes "con los ojos llenos de recuerdos" (311). La "esperanza
trágica", como la denomina Buero, se da también en el público, en
nosotros que hemos presenciado la tragedia, que hemos sufrido una emoción catártica, que hemos adquirido conciencia de los males que aquejan
a la humanidad del siglo XX, que hemos experimentado la esperanza de un
siglo futuro en que los problemas actuales han sido superados, que hemos
sido jueces de nuestro propio tiempo.
En su lucha, pues, Mario y Vicente llegan a una mayor conciencia.
Pero, como afirma Buero Vallejo, "El tragaluz es un drama de conciencia

no sólo individual sino histórico y social, pues nuestros conflictos individuales tienen siempre bases histórico-sociales".[30] De aquí la diferencia de actitudes entre Buero y Unamuno. Éste plantea sus problemas filosóficos de una manera más abstracta y personal; Buero parte de lo concreto hacia lo colectivo social en un contexto histórico. A ambos autores les preocupan los mismos problemas.

En El tragaluz, al igual que en todos los dramas de Buero, existe una esperanza de solución o síntesis a los problemas enfocados. La concepción de lo trágico en Buero es más abierta y conciliadora que en Unamuno. Siendo la concepción de lo trágico unamuniana más cerrada, más radicalmente existencialista, en ella el hombre se debate en una lucha continua entre opuestos, una lucha infinita y sin síntesis. La actitud de Buero, como él afirma, se aproximaría más a la concepción dialéctica hegeliana (a una "corrección hegeliana"), es decir, que mediante el posible juego dialéctico de la historia,"un juego dialéctico que nos permite esperanzas - aunque no sean seguras - y que no se ejerce con un rigor verdaderamente hegeliano sino mediante la acción, también, relativamente libre de los hombres"[31] se aliviará el carácter trágico de los conflictos, se afrontarán esperanzadoramente los aspectos concretos de los problemas sociales.


# N O T A S

1. Buero ha apuntado también la influencia de Pérez Galdós, Ortega y Gasset, de los clásicos españoles. Entre los autores extranjeros, Ibsen, Pirandello, Artaud, Brecht y Becket.

2. Las citas de Unamuno, a no ser que se indique lo contrario, son de las Obras Completas, ed. Manuel García Blanco (Madrid, Afrodisio Aguado, 1959-1964), 16 vols. (En el texto se darán como OC, volumen y año.) Las referencias a El tragaluz están tomadas de El concierto de San Ovidio y El tragaluz, ed. Ricardo Doménech (Madrid, Clásicos Castalia, 1971).

3. "El remoto siglo futuro en que los sitúo [...] bien podría ser el XXV o el XXX", escribe Buero a Ida Molina (18.8.1970), correspondencia que puede encontrarse como apéndice a su tesis, Search for Truth in the Plays of Buero Vallejo in the Light of his multi-faceted Concept of Tragedy (Doc. Diss. University of Cincinnati, 1973). Mic A/516. Main Library, QUB.

4. Ibid.

5. Véase John W. Kronik, 'El tragaluz and Man's Existence in History', HR, XLI (1973), 371-396.

6. Estas palabras encierran el problema filosófico esencial de la verdad. Ideas similares pueden encontrarse en otras obras de Buero, como, por ejemplo, en Aventura en lo gris.

7. A raíz del estreno de El tragaluz hubo crítica adversa de la intervención de estos investigadores del futuro. Véase Ángel Fernández Santos, 'Una entrevista con Buero Vallejo sobre El tragaluz', El mirlo blanco, 10 (Madrid, Taurus, 1968), 64-78. (Este artículo fue publicado

primero en <u>Primer Acto</u>, XC (Noviembre 1967), 7-15.)

8. "Para mí, <u>El tragaluz</u> sería inconcebible sin estos personajes. No entiendo esta obra, me resultaría incomprensible despojada de los 'investigadores'", ibid., 68.

9. Carta de Buero a Ida Molina, loc. cit., op. cit. nota 3 arriba.

10. Esta metáfora del mundo como bosque puede verse a través del existencialismo austríaco de Martín Buber en la escuela psicológica alemana del "Gestalt".

11. Cf. las palabras de Paulus en <u>La doble historia del Doctor Valmy</u>: "Entre devorar y ser devorado, escojo lo primero".

12. Véase Kenneth Brown, 'The Significance of Insanity in four Plays by Antonio Buero Vallejo', <u>REH</u>, VIII (1974), 247-260.

13. En <u>El tragaluz</u> Buero admite la influencia de la tragédia unamuniana <u>El Otro</u>, como también la influencia del Borges de <u>Los teólogos</u> y del <u>Enrique IV</u> de Pirandello, sobre todo en la figura del Padre, así como la de <u>Don Quijote</u>. Véase Ida Molina, 'Note on the Dialectics of the Search for Truth in <u>El Otro</u> and in <u>El tragaluz</u>', <u>RN</u>, XIV (1972), 1-4.

14. El tragaluz, que él toma por la ventana de un tren, el sótano y el tren son los símbolos más prominentes de la obra. El ruido del tren expresa un pensamiento y será muy importante en el desenlace de la obra. Véase John Kronik, op. cit.

15. La última escena de la primera parte denota el gran sufrimiento que padece: Dos niños y una niña, a quienes el Padre toma por sus hijos, golpean el cristal del tragaluz y le instan a que se vaya con ellos a jugar a la glorieta. El Padre les aconseja lleno de congoja: "¡Ten tú cuidado en la glorieta, Elvirita! ¡Eres tan pequeña! [...] ¡Mario! ¡Vicente! ¡Cuidad de Elvirita!" (269), y al decir el nombre de la niña solloza desesperadamente. Los golpes en el cristal del tragaluz ocurren de nuevo en la escena crítica, en que Vicente se enfrenta con la muerte.

16. Véase Sánchez Barbudo, 'La formación del pensamiento de Unamuno. Una experiencia decisiva: la crisis de 1897', <u>HR</u>, XVIII (1950), 218-243; R.L. Prèdmore, 'Flesh and Spirit in the Works of Unamuno', <u>PMLA</u>, LXX (1955), 587-605.

17. La Madre, víctima silenciosa, sufre continuamente al recordar a su hija muerta. Ella es la única persona que recuerda la verdad de la enfermedad de su marido, de lo ocurrido al final de la guerra, pero oculta sus sentimientos esperando que todos olviden y sean felices. "Hay que vivir" (frase que pronuncian muchos personajes de Unamuno; frase que dirá Encarna al final de <u>El tragaluz</u>) y para ello hay que olvidar el pasado. Compárese con las palabras de Él y Ella: "Durante siglos tuvimos que olvidar para que el pasado no nos paralizase; ahora debemos recordar incesantemente para que el pasado no nos envenene" (290). Véase Carlos Blanco Aguinaga, 'La madre, su regazo y el "sueño de dormir" en la obra de Unamuno', <u>Cuadernos de la Cátedra Miguel de Unamuno</u>, VII (1956), 69-84.

18. Véase <u>Soledad</u>, <u>La esfinge</u>, <u>El pasado que vuelve</u>, <u>Sombras de sueño</u>, entre sus dramas.

19. Op. cit., 597-598.

20. Véase Carlos Clavería, 'Sobre el tema de Caín y Abel en la obra de Unamuno', Temas de Unamuno (Madrid, Gredos, 1970); Paul Ilic, 'The Cain Myth', An Existential View of Self and Society (Madison and London, The University of Wisconsin Press, 1967); Nicholas G. Round, Unamuno. Abel Sánchez (London, Critical Guides to Spanish Texts, Tamesis Books, 1974); Eduardo Francolí, 'El tema de Caín y Abel en Unamuno y Buero Vallejo', RN, XIV, 224-251; Minako Nonoyama, 'La personalidad en los dramas de Buero Vallejo y de Unamuno', Hispanófila, XLIX (1973), 69-78.

21. Véase Gabriela Chambordon, 'El conocimiento poético en el teatro de Antonio Buero Vallejo', CHA, 253-254 (1971), 52-98.

22. Véase José Luis Abellán, 'El tema del misterio en Buero Vallejo. (Un teatro de la realidad trascendente.)', Ínsula, 174 (Mayo 1961), 15.

23. Carta de Buero a Ida Molina (4.10.1972), op. cit.

24. Ángel Fernández Santos, op. cit. nota 7 arriba, p.73.

25. Véase Frank P. Casa, 'The Problem of National Reconciliation in Buero Vallejo's El tragaluz', RHM, XXXV (1969), 285-294. La interpretación de Casa acerca de la lucha fratricida como reflejo de la contienda civil, 1936-39, es un tanto excesiva. Esta opinión nuestra fue corroborada en su día por Buero Vallejo en una entrevista.

26. Véase Armando Carlos Isasi Angulo, 'El teatro de Antonio Buero Vallejo (entrevista con el autor)', PSA, LXVII (1972), 281-320.

27. En Hoy es fiesta hay una escena muy parecida. En ella, Silverio trata de confesar su culpa a su esposa sorda, aunque sabe que ella no podrá oirle.

28. Véase, para interpretaciones distintas, Ricardo Doménech, El teatro de Buero Vallejo. (Una meditación española.) (Madrid, Gredos, 1973); Robert L. Nicholas, The Tragic Stages of Antonio Buero Vallejo (Chapel Hill, Estudios de Hispanófila 23, University of Carolina Press, 1972).

29. Buero, en una discusión sobre el valor de la alucinación dice lo siguiente: "Aunque [....] sabemos qué es una alucinación, en el fondo lo ignoramos; pues sabemos también que las formas de captación de la realidad son, en el hombre, a veces muy extrañas. El loco de El tragaluz captaba a veces, mediante sus delirios cosas formidablemente ciertas. El aprovechamiento dramático de estos enigmas es, por ello, coherente con una dramatización en profundidad de lo real". Ángel Fernández Santos, 'Sobre El sueño de la razón. Una conversación con Antonio Buero Vallejo', Primer Acto, CXVII (Febrero 1970), 18-27 (p.21, col.1).

30. Carta de Buero a Ida Molina (18.8.1970), op. cit.

31. Carta de Buero a Ida Molina (19.9.1970).

Sobre las reglas del uso del acento y de las letras i y y en Ortografía, edición de la Real Academia Española de 1969

Jacinto Martínez Lacalle (The American School in Paris)


Las Nuevas Normas de Prosodia y Ortografía de la Real Academia Española, de aplicación potestativa desde el 1. de septiembre de 1952, pasaron a ser de aplicación preceptiva el 1. de enero de 1959. Un "nuevo texto definitivo" de las mismas fue publicado en 1958 como apéndice a la Gramática de 1931, sin que hubiera derogación expresa de los preceptos antiguos incompatibles con los nuevos. Para obviar los inconvenientes de tal situación, la Academia preparó un opúsculo cuyas pruebas presentó al V Congreso de Academias de la Lengua Española (Quito, 1968), que sugirió varias enmiendas; estas se recogieron en una Ortografía - "texto definitivo", según se lee en la página 3 - publicada en 1969, que reemplazó al código ortográfico contenido en la Gramática.[1] Nosotros estudiamos el texto de la Ortografía y quedamos sorprendidos por las carencias que observamos en un trabajo publicado por la Academia Española tras el examen y enmiendas de un congreso de las Academias. Escribimos ulteriormente unas consideraciones sobre esa Ortografía, acabadas y mecanografiadas en 1972, que, para consternación nuestra, no llegaron a publicarse (aunque, afortunadamente, guardamos un calco). En 1974 la Academia publicó una segunda edición corregida y aumentada de la Ortografía - también "texto definitivo", según pág. 3 -, donde algunas carencias de la primera edición estaban remediadas.[2] Como creemos que en 1978 seguirá siendo aleccionador el exhibir la situación de la Ortografía española de 1969 a 1974, hemos redactado el presente trabajo, extraído de nuestras inéditas consideraciones, limitándonos, por estarnos medido el espacio, a las reglas del uso del acento y de las letras i y y.[3]

I. Las reglas o normas del acento.

1. Las reglas generales.

Las normas o reglas de la acentuación establecidas con base en la división de las palabras tónicas simples en agudas, llanas y esdrújulas[4] están contenidas en OR 34; esas reglas, harto conocidas, están consideradas como las generales del acento, ya que, según el párrafo primero de OR 35, las demás son, "respecto de las reglas ya sentadas" en OR 34, "excepciones y explicaciones", necesitadas por la existencia de hiatos y sinéresis con elementos tónicos, homófonos átonos y tónicos, y palabras compuestas. Esto no obstante, en el párrafo segundo de OR 35 se encuentra la sorprendente declaración de que el acento de vahído, búho y cuatro grafías más, está puesto "por virtud de la regla general", cuando es evidente que lo está por virtud de una regla excepcional, todavía no sentada, y necesitada por la existencia de hiatos con elemento tónico.

La paradoja procede de un defecto de compilación de la Ortografía. El párrafo segundo de OR 35 procede de las Nuevas Normas (con excepción de los tres últimos ejemplos está tomado literalmente de NN 25); como en ese opúsculo se le da al término 'regla general' o 'norma general' uh sentido muy amplio al preceptuarse en NN 12 que la norma del diptongo y la del hiato - a las que habremos de volver - "se establecerán como normas generales de acentuación", es pertinente emplearlo en NN 25 para declarar que el acento de vahído y las grafías siguientes está puesto por virtud de la regla general. Ahora bien, para la compilación de la Ortografía se ha prescindido del citado enunciado de NN 12 y, no obstante, se ha hecho uso del texto completo de NN 25 sin pensar en el desajuste así producido.[5]

2. La regla del hiato o azeuxis.

Según OR 36 [a], "cuando una vocal extrema tónica va delante o detrás de una vocal intermedia átona, no hay diptongo, sino hiato, y la vocal tónica llevará acento ortográfico". Ese texto, donde está contenida la regla excepcional del acento en la representación de palabras con hiato con elemento tónico (más arriba llamada 'norma del hiato'), es redundante. Si, según DIC 56 átono, el adjetivo 'átono' "aplícase a la vocal, sílaba o palabra que se pronuncia sin acento prosódico", y, según DIC 56 tónico, el adjetivo 'tónico' "aplícase a la vocal o sílaba que recibe el impulso del acento prosódico", un sonido tónico y un sonido átono no pueden formar parte de la misma sílaba, salvo si se admite que una misma sílaba puede ser átona y tónica a la vez; al no formar parte de la misma sílaba, habrán de formar parte de sílabas distintas; al formar parte de sílabas distintas, habrá hiato por definición.

Aunque la redundancia no daña ni enmascara la norma contenida en el texto (que está tomado de NN 12 b, también redundante), hubiera sido deseable una factura diferente.[6]

3. La regla del diptongo.

Según OR 37 [a], "cuando una vocal intermedia tónica va delante o detrás de vocal extrema átona, forman siempre diptongo, y la acentuación gráfica de éste, cuando sea necesaria, irá sobre la vocal intermedia, o sobre la segunda, si las dos son extremas". Ese texto, donde parece contenerse la regla complementaria del acento en la representación de palabras con diptongo tónico (más arriba llamada 'norma del diptongo'), es contradictorio en la primera parte y absurdo en la última. La contradicción es evidente: si uno de esos sonidos vocales es tónico y el otro es átono, pertenece cada uno a sílaba distinta; si cada uno pertenece a sílaba distinta, están en hiato; pero está prescrito que forman diptongo; luego pertenece cada uno a sílaba distinta y a la misma sílaba al mismo tiempo. Ahora bien, esa contradicción puede soslayarse si el hermeneuta consigue averiguar lo que verosímilmente quiso escribir la Academia en lugar de lo que realmente escribió: es verosímil que haya querido significar una regla ortológica (idéntica a la contenida en el texto, también contradictorio, de NN 12 a) por la que se prescribe la realización de diptongo en todos los casos en que el núcleo silábico de la sílaba tónica es un fonema vocal intermedio precedido o seguido de un fonema vocal extremo. Y, una vez soslayada esa contradicción, el enunciado de la regla ortográfica del acento en la representación de tales diptongos es inteligible.

El absurdo se contiene en la última parte de OR 37 [a], donde se intenta regular el acento en la representación del diptongo resultante del encuentro de los dos fonemas vocales extremos: es tal la factura, que el texto viene a ser equivalente a 'si un diptongo resultante del encuentro de fonema vocal intermedio y fonema vocal extremo resulta del encuentro de dos fonemas vocales extremos, entonces el acento, cuando haya de ponerse, se pondrá sobre la grafía del segundo elemento del diptongo'; ese texto, que no tiene precedente en las Nuevas Normas, es un puro desatino, desprovisto de significado, o, si se quiere, es un enunciado significativo pero vacío por carecer de denotación, ya que la clase de los fonemas vocales que son intermedios y extremos a la vez es una clase vacía.[7]

Según GR 539 e, "si hay diptongo en la sílaba de dicciones agudas, llanas o esdrújulas que, según lo prescrito, se deba acentuar, el signo ortográfico irá sobre la vocal fuerte, o sobre la segunda si las dos son débiles". Gracias a ese texto antiguo, ni contradictorio ni absurdo, es posible descubrir cómo trabajó el redactor de la Ortografía, quien tomó de la Gramática la expresión "o sobre la segunda, si las dos son débiles", modernizó la terminología, y puso la expresión modernizada en un texto procedente de NN 12 a[8] sin ocuparse del absurdo resultante del aglomerado.[9] Afortunadamente, el texto citado de GR 539 e le permite al hermeneuta descubrir que era intención de la Academia significar una regla del acento en la representación de diptongos tónicos formados por dos fonemas vocales extremos.

4. Consecuencias de la regla ortológica del diptongo.

Antes de la promulgación de las Nuevas Normas la Academia se limitaba a enseñar en la Gramática que no siempre que hay encuentro de fonemas vocales susceptibles de reducirse a diptongo se realiza diptongo; después, impone en ciertos casos al hispanohablante una pronunciación oficialmente correcta.[10] Con ello, palabras de uso diario como 'criada', 'piano', 'diario', que son realizadas ordinariamente como trisílabas, deberán por precepto realizarse como bisílabas, y palabras ordinariamente bisílabas como 'cruel', 'prior', 'fiar', 'Sión', 'guión' deberán realizarse como monosílabas. Es más: cuando el fonema vocal intermedio tónico es el primero del grupo, la norma puede resultar absolutamente inadecuada. Así, por ejemplo, las palabras 'Zeus' y 'Reus' habrán de ser monosílabas, y, análogamente, la palabra 'tedéum' deberá realizarse como bisílaba aguda y no como trisílaba llana. Y así también, ciertas palabras americanas como 'cháhuar', 'nahua', 'náhuatle', 'queltehue', en todas las cuales hay un fonema vocal intermedio tónico seguido por el fonema vocal extremo posterior seguido a su vez por un fonema vocal intermedio, deberán realizarse con reducción de los dos primeros de esos tres fonemas vocales a diptongo en hiato con el tercer sonido; y para la realización de esos diptongo y azeuxis habrá de intercalarse una oclusión global, ajena a la pronunciación española.[11]

Estas innovaciones ortológicas afectan notablemente a ciertas formas de los verbos de la primera conjugación en los que la radical de la primera persona de singular del presente de indicativo acaba en sonido vocal extremo tónico en hiato con la desinencia (como 'envío' y 'actúo'), y a todas las formas irregulares con desinencia tónica de los verbos de la tercera conjugación (como 'sonreír') cuya radical del infinitivo termina en el fonema vocal intermedio anterior (todos los cuales son irregulares, según GR 110). Y cuando la radical del infinitivo de los verbos de esos dos grupos es monosílaba, entonces se ven afectadas la representación de las personas primera y tercera de singular del pretérito indefinido de los verbos, preceptivamente monosílabos, del grupo de la primera conjugación (como 'criar', 'fiar', 'liar', 'piar', 'puar'), y la representación de la tercera persona de singular del pretérito indefinido de los verbos con infinitivo bisílabo del grupo de la tercera conjugación ('freír' y 'reír'), por haber de realizarse diptongo en la forma verbal correspondiente, con lo que esta se realizará como monosílaba, y no se pondrá acento en su representación de acuerdo con la norma general de la omisión del acento en la grafía de los monosílabos tónicos (norma contenida en OR 38 a y OR 34 1ª. a).

A pesar de lo que antecede, en OR 51 3ª. se encuentra el texto siguiente: "Convendría también usar la diéresis en aquellas palabras que, de no puntuarse con ella, se pudieran pronunciar indebidamente, como, por ejemplo, pié, pretérito indefinido del verbo piar, que de este modo se diferenciaría con toda claridad del imperativo o subjuntivo del mismo verbo, píe, y del nombre pie". Del citado texto se deduce que, según la Academia, la pronunciación correcta de la primera persona de singular del pretérito indefinido del verbo 'piar' y la pronunciación correcta del nombre 'pie' son diferentes; al ser diferentes, en el encuentro de fonema vocal extremo con fonema vocal intermedio tónico no es obligatoria al menos una vez la realización de diptongo; al no realizarse diptongo, se contradice el precepto contenido en OR 36 [a], según el cual en tales casos se forma siempre diptongo.[12]

Si se admite la primacía de OR 37 [a], entonces, con la impresión de la grafía pié en OR 51 3.° - y en DIC 70 diéresis -, la Academia ha violado la regla del acento en la representación de los monosílabos, pues, por precepto, la forma verbal 'pié' es monosílaba, y su representación gráfica ha de estar inacentuada. Esa norma está violada por la Academia en diferentes ocasiones: así, el nombre del signo ortográfico cuyo uso se regula en OR 53 está allí representado por medio de la grafía guión; así, en el Diccionario de 1970 se encuentran las grafías duán, mué, pión, ruán, trué y truhán.[13]

Además, según OR 41 b, el nombre de cierta ciudad francesa puede representarse en español por medio de las grafías Lyon o Lyón; con arreglo a la norma de OR 37 [a], solo es correcta la primera de esas dos grafías, porque al adaptarse la palabra francesa a la pronunciación española ha de realizarse diptongo, con lo que esa palabra se realizará como monosílaba.

También está en contradicción con la norma del diptongo la conservación del acento en DIC 70 tedéum: según OR 41 [a], la representación del tono de los términos latinos usados en español está regulada por las normas castellanas; por consiguiente, en la representación gráfica de palabras como 'tedéum', que es aguda por precepto académico, no debe ponerse acento, con arreglo a la norma general.[14]

Para concluir: Si las consecuencias de la existencia de la regla ortológica del diptongo le suscitaren problemas al hispanoescribiente, le aconsejaremos que siga el ejemplo dado por la propia Academia, la cual prescindió de esa norma en la Ortografía y en el Diccionario de 1970 cada vez que de su aplicación hubiera de resultar la supresión de acentos prescritos en las normas generales de la acentuación de las grafías de las palabras agudas y llanas.

5. La regla del acento en la grafía ui.

Según OR 37 b, "la combinación ui se considera, para la práctica de la escritura, como diptongo en todos los casos. Sólo llevará acento cuando lo pida el número 37 [a]; y el acento se marcará en la segunda vocal, es decir, en la i: casuístico, benjuí; pero casuista, voz llana, se escribirá sin tilde; construí, atribuí". Con la norma contenida en ese texto se le da una solución práctica y expeditiva al problema ortográfico suscitado por la fluctuación de diptongo a hiato en el encuentro de los dos fonemas vocales extremos, en el orden mencionado.

La Academia no previó tampoco las consecuencias de esta nueva norma. Así, en OR 24 a está impresa la grafía acentuada huí como ejemplo ilustrativo de la norma allí contenida. Con la posición del acento en esa grafía se viola de nuevo la norma de la acentuación de los monosílabos tónicos: si, "para la práctica de la escritura", el encuentro de los citados fonemas en el orden citado ha de considerarse como diptongo en todos los casos, entonces la primera persona de singular del pretérito indefinido del verbo 'huir' ha de considerarse como diptongo "para la práctica de la escritura"; al haber de considerarse como diptongo, habrá de considerarse como monosílaba; al haber de considerarse como monosílaba, en su representación no deberá ponerse acento, y ello, aunque la Academia haya hecho imprimir la grafía huí. (Análogamente, la primera persona de singular del pretérito indefinido y la segunda persona de plural del presente de indicativo de verbos bisílabos como 'fluir', 'luir', 'fruir' deberán representarse con grafía inacentuada.)

Para concluir: De la impresión por la Academia de la grafía huí puede inducirse que, en la representación de las formas verbales citadas, la norma de OR 37 b no se aplicará si de su aplicación hubiere de resultar la omisión de acentos que, según GR 95 c (Ejemplo de la tercera conjugación: PARTIR), deban ponerse regularmente; así, verbigracia, en la grafía huís, por analogía con el modelo de GR 95 c "partís", habrá de conservarse el acento. Esa norma se aplicará solamente para impedir la posición de acentos que, según la regla del hiato de OR 36 [a], deben ponerse en la representación de ciertas formas de los verbos de la tercera conjugación cuya radical del infinitivo termina en fonema vocal intermedio; así, ni en la grafía huid ni en la grafía fruid ha de ponerse acento aunque lo haya en embaíd, reíd y oíd, ya que no lo hay en partid.[15]

6. El acento en la representación de ciertos monosílabos.

Según OR 38 a, "los monosílabos nunca necesitarían llevar el acento escrito [...]: no obstante, se escribe el acento cuando existen dos monosílabos iguales en su forma, pero con distinta función gramatical, en una de las cuales lleva acento fonético y en otra es átono; v.gr.: el, artículo, y él, pronombre; mi, tu, pronombres posesivos, y mí, tú, pronombres personales; mas, conjunción adversativa, y más, adverbio de comparación; si, conjunción condicional, y sí, pronombre y adverbio de afirmación; de, preposición, y dé, tiempo del verbo dar; se, pronombre átono, y sé, persona de los verbos ser y saber". Cabe preguntarse si la enumeración es completa.

La expresión 'función gramatical de las palabras' parece sinónima de 'oficio que desempeñan las palabras'; según el oficio que las palabras desempeñan, están clasificadas en GR 7 en "nueve clases, llamadas partes de la oración; a saber: nombre substantivo, nombre adjetivo, pronombre, artículo, verbo, adverbio, preposición, conjunción e interjección", subclasificada cada una a su vez en diversos números de la Gramática. De ser acertada esa interpretación, en el texto de OR 38 a viene a decirse que, si hay dos palabras monosílabas homófonas, si la una es átona y la otra es tónica, si la una y la otra pertenecen a diferente clase de las llamadas 'partes de la oración' o, de pertenecer a la misma, pertenecen a diferente subclase, y si la representación de la una y de la otra está formada por los mismos signos alfabéticos en el mismo orden, entonces en la representación de la monosílaba tónica ha de ponerse acento.

Ahora bien, en la impresión del Diccionario de 1970 no está seguida esa interpretación de la norma. Así, los nombres substantivos definidos como "primera voz", "tercera voz", "sexta voz" y "séptima voz de la escala música" en DIC 70 do[1], mi[1], la[2], si[2], respectivamente, están representados con grafías inacentuadas, aunque son tónicos y homófonos de palabras átonas cuya función gramatical no es la del nombre substantivo, a saber, el adverbio de lugar 'do', el posesivo 'mi', el artículo 'la' y el pronombre 'la', y la conjunción condicional 'si'; así, en DIC 70 mas[1], mas[2] se encuentran grafías inacentuadas con las que se representan dos substantivos tónicos homófonos entre sí y, además, homófonos de la conjunción adversativa átona 'mas'; así, en DIC 70 lo[2] se encuentra la grafía inacentuada de un substantivo tónico, homófono del artículo átono 'lo' y del pronombre personal átono 'lo'; y así, en DIC 70 tan[1], tan[2] se encuentran grafías inacentuadas con las que se representan dos substantivos tónicos homófonos entre sí y, además, homófonos del adverbio de cantidad átono 'tan'.

A causa de las omisiones del acento en representaciones gráficas que, según la interpretación propuesta de la norma, deberían tenerlo, cabe pensar que esa interpretación no es acertada, y que, en realidad, en el citado texto de la norma están enumerados completamente todos los nueve casos en que se aplica. Ahora bien, en DIC 70 té, donde se define un substantivo monosílabo tónico, se representa este con grafía acentuada, y en DIC 70 te, donde se define un pronombre personal monosílabo átono, se representa este con grafía inacentuada, lo que invalida esa segunda interpretación.

En la práctica, y sin contar los casos de palabras anticuadas como 'ál', 'hí', 'dél', la norma solo tiene aplicación en los nueve y uno ya citados.[16]

Para terminar: Podría objetársenos que el texto citado procede de uno antiguo, pues está tomado casi literalmente de GR 540 a, y no de las Nuevas Normas; responderíamos que, por lo menos, no hubiera sido difícil incluir los monosílabos 'té' y 'te' en la enumeración de OR 38 a. Por otra parte, ni a los autores del proyecto de la Ortografía ni a los congresistas del V Congreso de Quito les vino a la mente el que no hay en el código ortográfico español una norma reguladora de la posición u omisión del acento en la grafía del plural del substantivo 'té'; nosotros creemos que deberá representarse sin acento por no haber una palabra átona homófona de ese substantivo en plural.

7. El acento en la representación de ciertos pronombres, adjetivos y adverbios tónicos.

Según OR 38 e, "los relativos que, cual, quien, cuyo, y los adverbios cuando, cuan, cuanto, como y donde llevarán tilde en las oraciones interrogativas y exclamativas". De todos los de la nueva Ortografía, en el citado texto se contiene el ejemplo quizá más aleccionador de distinción entre lo que se preceptúa y lo que hubiera querido preceptuarse.

En el citado texto está empleado el término 'relativo' en plural. Según DIC 56 relativo, ese término equivale en Gramática a 'pronombre relativo'; luego una parte del texto de OR 38 e es equivalente al que sigue: 'los pronombres relativos 'que', 'cual', 'quien', 'cuyo' se representarán con acento cuando estén en oraciones interrogativas y exclamativas'. Ahora bien, en GR 72 a se contiene una división de los pronombres en tres clases, a saber, la de los interrogativos, la de los demostrativos y la de los relativos, y en GR 72 b están enumerados los miembros de cada una de esas tres clases; según esa lista, los pronombres interrogativos son '¿quién?', '¿qué?', '¿cuál?', '¿cúyo?'y '¿cuánto?' y los pronombres relativos son 'quien', 'que', 'cual', 'cuyo' y 'cuanto'.[17] Partiendo de la citada lista puede concluirse que la clase de los pronombres relativos y la clase de los pronombres interrogativos no solo no son iguales sino que, además, se excluyen mutuamente, lo cual está plenamente confirmado en GR 73: los pronombres interrogativos "tienen [...] la misma forma, y también los mismos accidentes gramaticales que los relativos, de los que se distinguen por el acento en la escritura y por la entonación en el habla". Esto no obstante, en la primera parte del texto de OR 38 e se contiene una norma regulativa de la posición del acento en la representación de ciertos pronombres relativos en ciertos casos, y está omitida toda norma de la posición del acento en la representación de los pronombres interrogativos: si el hispanoescribiente se sujetare a OR 38 e, en las frases (sirvan de ejemplo) '¿qué estudia el muchacho que ganó el premio?' y '¿quién puede amar a un hombre a quien todos odian?', deberá representar con acento los relativos 'que' y 'quien', y sin él, con arreglo a la norma general de los monosílabos tónicos, los interrogativos 'qué' y 'quién'.

Según la última parte del texto de OR 38 e, "los adverbios cuando cuan, cuanto, como y donde llevarán tilde en las oraciones interrogativas y exclamativas". De acuerdo con ese enunciado, en la representación gráfica de los adverbios átonos 'cuan' (por ejemplo, '¿no será el castigo tan grande, cuan grande fue la falta?'), 'cuanto' (p. ej., '¿no están tan sobrados de fantasía cuanto escasos de conocimiento?'), 'como' (p. ej.,'¿por qué no lo haces como te dije') y 'donde' (p. ej., '¿no es esta la calle donde naciste?') que se encuentren en oraciones interrogativas o exclamativas, ha de ponerse acento.

Según GR 168 a, "ha de tenerse en cuenta que para clasificar una palabra se ha de atender, antes que a su estructura material, al oficio que desempeña en la oración. Así, cuanto y tanto, por ejemplo, son adjetivos en cuantos hombres, tantos enemigos; son pronombres en tiene tanto cuanto quiere, y adverbios, en cuanto más me adula tanto más lo desprecio": al emplear el término 'adverbio' (en plural), el redactor

de OR 38 e ha dejado excluidas del código ortográfico las normas de la
posición del acento en las representaciones gráficas del adjetivo
'cuanto' y del pronombre 'cuanto' (y sus variantes respectivas en género
y número) cuando son tónicos.[18]

Conviene añadir, para terminar, que en el texto correspondiente de
GR 540 d (defectuoso por otros conceptos) no se contiene disparidad entre
lo realmente preceptuado y lo que se intentó preceptuar.[19]

II. Las reglas o normas del uso de las letras i y y.

8. Declaración introductoria.

Según OR 24, "las letras i, y representan algunos valores fonéticos
comunes que a menudo se interfieren entre sí". Esos valores fonéticos
constituyen un conjunto de sonidos al que pertenecen las varientes de
un fonema consonante palatal sonoro y unos sonidos vocales, semivocal y
semiconsonante, variantes del fonema vocal extremo anterior.[20]

9. La representación de sonido consonante. La letra y.

También según OR 24, "usamos la y [...] cuando es consonante: rayo,
haya, cónyuge, yema, yo, yunque. Exceptúanse algunas palabras que
ofrecen la combinación hia, hie, como hiato, hierro (metal), hiendo
(de hender), hiel, hiena, hialino, enhiesto. Hiedra y hierba pueden
escribirse así, o bien yedra, yerba". Aunque el sujeto de 'es consonante' no está expreso, es muy probable que lo sea 'la y', con lo que
el enunciado inicial del texto citado viene a ser equivalente a 'usamos
la letra y cuando la letra y es consonante', enunciado de inteligibilidad no inmediata que es preciso interpretar. Es muy probable que sea
equivalente a 'usamos la y cuanto la y representa sonido consonante' o,
mejor, 'usamos la y cuando con la y se representa sonido consonante';
en todo caso, en tal enunciado no se contiene norma ninguna, pues es obvio
que también usamos la letra y cuando con la letra y se representa sonido
no consonante, como en Juan y María, ¡ay!, etc.[21] Una vez más resulta
necesario descubrir lo que la Academia quiso significar, a saber: que
los sonidos consonantes del conjunto mencionado se representan por medio
de la letra y, excepto en ciertos casos en que se emplea la grafía hi.

Siguiendo esa interpretación, si para representar esos sonidos
consonantes hay que emplear la letra y o la grafía hi (con exclusión
recíproca, excepto en dos casos), entonces, por contraposición, cuando
para representar un sonido no se emplean ni la letra y ni la grafía hi,
el sonido representado no será de los consonantes pertenecientes al
susodicho conjunto. Así, aun ignorándolo el redactor, en el texto citado
se contiene una regla de ortología. La aplicación de esa regla, junta
con la del diptongo contenida en OR 37 [a], puede resultar en una
pronunciación artificial o ardua para el hispanohablante; así, por
ejemplo, en la pronunciación de las palabras 'ion' y 'iota' no deberá
realizarse sonido consonante inicial sino semiconsonante, al haber diptongo preceptivamente; y así, por ejemplo, en la pronunciación de las
palabras 'iatrogénico', 'ionizante', 'iotización' habrá de evitarse la
realización de sonido consonante inicial, aunque puede elegirse entre
la realización de dos sílabas o bien de un diptongo por ser átonos los
dos fonemas iniciales. Y en las palabras 'paranoia' y 'pereion', el
sonido representado por la letra i no ha de formar sílaba con el sonido
vocal átono que le sigue inmediatamente, sino con el sonido vocal tónico
que inmediatamente le precede: el hablante se verá forzado a realizar
un sonido semivocal seguido de un sonido vocal, para lo que tendrá que
intercalar una oclusión glotal.

10. La representación de sonido consonante. La grafía hi.

El enunciado de la regla de la grafía hi "exceptúanse [de representarse con y] algunas palabras que ofrecen la combinación hia, hie"
es anfibológico. Si la oración relativa 'que ofrecen la combinación
hia, hie' ha de entenderse como especificativa o determinativa (lo que

117

parece ser el caso según la doctrina de GR 350 a, ya que no hay coma
entre las representaciones gráficas de 'algunas palabras' y 'que ofrecen la combinación hia, hie'), entonces en el texto viene a decirse que
solo en algunos casos con la grafía hi seguida inmediatamente de las
letras a o e se representa sonido consonante; pero si esa oración
relativa ha de entenderse como explicativa o incidental, entonces en el
texto viene a decirse que en cualquier caso con la grafía hi seguida
inmediatamente de las letras a o e se representa sonido consonante, pues
el texto así entendido es equivalente a 'exceptúanse algunas palabras,
que ofrecen la combinación hia, hie', equivalente a 'exceptúanse algunas
palabras, que son todas las que ofrecen la combinación hia, hie'.

Si debe prevalecer la primera inteligencia del texto, es conveniente
que el hablante sepa en qué palabras habrá de realizar, según la Academia,
sonido consonante, y en qué palabras no habrá de realizarlo. De todos
modos, cualquiera de las dos que sea la inteligencia prevaleciente, es
preceptivo que el tecnicismo 'hiato' suene con consonante inicial;[22]
así mismo, la palabra 'enhiesto' - y con ella quizá también 'inhiesto',
'lomienhiesto', 'lominhiesto', y ciertas formas del verbo 'enhestar' o
'inhestar', que es irregular según la Gramática (Tabla, pág. 113) - ha
de realizarse con sonido consonante del susodicho conjunto. Y si debe
prevalecer la segunda inteligencia del texto, entonces la forma verbal
'adhiero' (y como ella otras del verbo 'adherir') ha de sonar también
con sonido consonante del mismo conjunto.

11. La representación de sonido no consonante.

Según OR 24, "usamos la y [...] cuando, precedida de una vocal,
termina palabra: ¡ay!, [...] buey, [...] convoy, [...] muy, Ruy, etc."
A pesar de las deficiencias del texto (que se dan por descubiertas y
criticadas, y que se soslayan), es evidente que a la norma ahí contenida
no están sujetas las representaciones de las sinéresis terminales de
sílaba sin serlo de palabra. Como ese caso no está previsto en los
textos de las normas del uso de la letra y, en la representación de esas
sinéresis se hará uso de la letra i, con arreglo a la última norma de
OR 24, a saber: "usamos la i [...] en todos los casos no previstos en
las reglas anteriores". Sin embargo, en el Suplemento del Diccionario
de 1970 están impresas las grafías guaycurú, guaymense y guaymeño. Es
innegable que la aceptación oficial de la grafía usual de ciertos
americanismos puede suscitar problemas de no fácil solución. Con todo,
sería prudente que la Academia adecuara con urgencia las normas a la
realidad pluricontinental de la lengua española para evitar en lo sucesivo
un caso semejante a este, en que la norma ortográfica, solemnemente
confirmada en 1969, ha sido subrepticiamente violada por la Academia en
1970, con ocasión de la impresión del Diccionario.

12. La representación de cinco formas verbales seguidas de pronombre enclítico.

Esas formas son 'doy', 'estoy', 'soy', 'voy' y 'hay'. Cuando están
seguidas de pronombre enclítico, es laborioso averiguar si ha de hacerse
uso de la letra i o de la letra y para representar el sonido semivocal
del susodicho conjunto.

Según DIC 56 enclítico, "[enclítico] dícese de la partícula o parte
de la oración que se liga con el vocablo precedente, formando con él
una sola palabra. En la lengua española son partículas los pronombres
pospuestos al verbo". Según lo citado, el sonido semivocal de esas
formas verbales seguidas de enclíticos no es final de palabra sino solamente final de sílaba, por lo que habrá de representarse con la letra
i. Pero esa interpretación no está de acuerdo con la práctica de la
Academia, que hizo imprimir en GR 252 las grafías le voy a buscar,
voyle a buscar; la impresión de voyle ha de obedecer a una norma ortográfica, la cual no está explícitamente contenida en la Ortografía.

Para intentar hallarle solución al problema conviene someter la definición de <u>DIC 56</u> <u>enclítico</u> a juicio crítico basado en las definiciones y normas de la <u>Gramática</u>. Se afirma en ese artículo que el verbo y los pronombres enclíticos forman una palabra; ahora bien, según <u>GR 36</u>, 38, toda palabra española es primitiva[23] o derivada o compuesta o parasintética; con apoyo en <u>GR 177-186</u>, 189 es fácil llegar a la conclusión de que un verbo con enclítico no es una palabra ni primitiva ni derivada ni parasintética, por lo que, de ser una palabra, habrá de serlo compuesta; según <u>GR 187</u>, "para que un vocablo sea compuesto ha de reunir dos condiciones, una lógica y otra gráfica, o sea: que se fundan en la mente dos ideas para designar una nueva, y que se junten en la escritura las voces que designan dichas ideas para expresar la nueva", de donde se deduce que ningún verbo con pronombre enclítico es una palabra compuesta, pues, aunque la grafía del verbo y la del enclítico están ligadas como si con ellas se representara una palabra simple, la denotación de un verbo con pronombre enclítico sigue siendo idéntica a la denotación de ese verbo con ese pronombre cuando proclítico; pero una palabra que no es ni primitiva ni derivada ni compuesta ni parasintética, simplemente, no es una palabra; luego, a pesar de la definición de <u>DC 56</u> <u>enclítico</u>, un verbo con enclítico no es una palabra sino un grupo tónico cada uno de cuyos miembros conserva su identidad propia. Por estas razones, tan conforme a la norma ortográfica es la grafía <u>le</u> <u>voy</u> como la grafía <u>voyle</u>.[24]

    III. Nota conclusiva.

Con la publicación de la <u>Ortografía</u>, la Academia, en lugar de una obra que, independientemente de su valor normativo, tenía que haber sido modelo de rigor y claridad, divulgó algo así como una antología de los errores que deben evitar los que quieran preparar correctamente un trabajo. En las páginas precedentes se han discutido el absurdo, la anfibología, la contradicción, la redundancia, la enumeración incompleta, el enunciado inextricable, el texto puesto sin orden, el texto sintetizado sin coherencia, la distinción entre lo significado y lo que se quiso significar, la imprevisión de las consecuencias de lo establecido. Si las Academias de la Lengua Española han de poseer una autoridad indiscutida, imprescindible para llevar adelante tantos y tales trabajos cuantos y cuales de ellas esperamos, habrán de guardarse en lo venidero de incurrir en tamaño yerro.

<u>Apéndice</u>

Como ejemplos de la incuria con que está hecha la <u>Ortografía</u>, mostraremos finalmente un caso de confusión patente entre la lengua hablada y la escritura, y dos casos de inhábil manejo de los tipos de letra de imprenta.

Se lee en <u>OR 10</u> (y <u>ORSE 10</u>) que, por acuerdo de la Academia, la letra <u>w</u> habrá de definirse en el <u>Diccionario</u> como "letra llamada <u>v</u> <u>doble</u>"; es evidente que el compilador no ha tenido consciencia de que, en ese texto, con la grafía <u>v</u> <u>doble</u> no se representa el nombre de la letra <u>w</u> ni nada en absoluto, porque, como con el signo gráfico <u>v</u>, primera parte de esa grafía, solo puede representarse el signo gráfico mismo, o sea, la letra <u>v</u> (salvo si se admite que con la grafía <u>v</u> puede representarse una palabra de la lengua española), mientras que con el signo gráfico <u>doble</u> se representa un fenómeno sonoro, a saber, la palabra española 'doble', la grafía <u>v</u> <u>doble</u> es una aglomeración de letras que no tiene representación significativa ninguna. (Es verosímil que haya querido hacerse del pseudonombre '<u>v</u> <u>doble</u>' una abreviatura de '<u>ve</u> <u>doble</u> o uve <u>doble</u>'. Conviene advertir que en <u>DIC 70</u> <u>w</u> la Academia reincide, y dice de esa letra que "su nombre es <u>v</u> <u>doble</u>".

En la Ortografía tanto las letras del abecedario como los nombres de ellas están representados con letra bastardilla, elección a la que no hay que oponer reparo siempre que no haya inconsistencia ni mengua de la inteligibilidad. Ahora bien, según OR 28 c (y ORSE 28 c), "el sonido de r múltiple se representa con r doble (rr)"; si tal es el caso, entonces, por individualización universal, la palabra 'parra' podrá representarse con las grafías par doblea y parra. (Es verosímil que con la grafía r doble haya querido representarse un nombre de la letra doble rr, letra ni incluida ni nominada en el abecedario de OR 1 c – ni en el de ORSE 1 d.)

De nuevo según OR 10 (mas no ORSE 10), "en palabras [de procedencia extranjera] totalmente incorporadas al idioma es frecuente que la grafía w haya sido reemplazada por v simple"; si tal es el caso, entonces, por individualización universal, como cierta palabra que procede de la alemana 'Walzer' (a saber, 'vals') está totalmente incorporada al idioma, y como en la representación de ella ha sido reemplazada la grafía w, esa palabra podrá representarse con la grafía v simpleals. (No le encontramos ninguna circunstancia atenuante a la impresión de tal grafía. Tal vez sea errata de imprenta, aunque no parece creerlo así Rosenblat, en cuyas Actuales normas – mencionadas en nuestra nota número 1, y en las que está reproducido íntegramente el texto de la Ortografía de 1969–, página 101, se encuentra "por v simple". En todo caso, en ORSE 10 y en DIC 70 w está impreso "por v simple".)


N O T A S

1. Para el detalle de los trabajos y ediciones académicos tocantes a las innovaciones ortográficas entre 1952 y 1973, consúltese Ángel Rosenblat, Actuales normas ortográficas y prosódicas de la Academia Española (Barcelona 1974), Introducción.

2. Los preliminares de ambas ediciones (pág. 3) son equiformes – con una sola excepción: "reunido en Quito el año pasado" (ed. de 1969); "reunido en Quito el año 1968" (ed. de 1974) – lo que puede inducir a la creencia errónea de que el "texto definitivo" de la segunda edición fue resultado del examen y enmiendas propuestas en la reunión de Quito. En realidad, de aquel V Congreso salió el "texto definitivo" de la primera, es decir, el de las carencias que tanto nos sorprendieron.

3. Al hacer referencia a la Ortografía de 1969 empleamos la abreviatura 'OR' (p. ej., 'OR 35', 'OR 38 a', 'OR 51 3.', cuya suplencia respectiva juzgamos evidente); a las Nuevas Normas de 1958, la abreviatura 'NN' (p. ej., 'NN 25', 'NN 12 a'); a la Gramática, 'GR'; a la decimonona edición del Diccionario de la Lengua Española (1970), 'DIC 70' (p. ej., 'DIC 70 diéresis', 'DIC 70 do¹'); a la decimoctava edición del Diccionario (1956), 'DIC 56'. Al hacer referencia a la Ortografía. Segunda edición corregida y aumentada de 1974, 'ORSE'.

4. Esa división está mencionada en OR 33 a, donde, además, se menciona la clase de las palabras sobresdrújulas. No obstante, en OR 34 no está contenida la conocida norma de la posición del acento en las grafías de todas las sobresdrújulas, la cual el estudioso puede descubrir por sus propios medios en el enunciado final de OR 39. (En la frase final de ORSE 34 se remite al estudioso a ORSE 39; OR 39 y ORSE 39 son equiformes.)

5. El párrafo correspondiente de ORSE 35 está tomado literalmente del texto discutido de OR 35.

6. El texto de ORSE 36 [a] y el de OR 36 [a] son equiformes.

7. La forma lógica del texto académico es casi idéntica a la del que sigue: 'Cuando un célibe varón mayor de dieciséis años cohabita con célibe hembra mayor de catorce años, forman siempre legítimo matrimonio, y la administración de los bienes de este, cuando los haya, estará a cargo del célibe varón, o a cargo del de más edad si los dos son hembras'.

8. A saber: "El encuentro de vocal fuerte tónica con débil átona, o de débil átona con fuerte tónica, forma siempre diptongo, y la acentuación gráfica de éste, cuando sea necesaria, se hará con arreglo a lo dispuesto en el número 539, letra e, de la Gramática".

9. En ORSE 37 a, b no se contiene el absurdo de OR 37 [a].

10. En ORSE 37 a, también contradictorio, y ORSE 37 b no se contiene la norma ortológica del diptongo.

11. No hay exageración en valerse de tales americanismos: según OR 35, "la h muda colocada entre dos vocales no impide que éstas formen diptongo", y, según OR 22, "esta letra [...] no tiene hoy sonido alguno en nuestro idioma"; luego sigue siendo preceptiva la realización de diptongo en esas palabras al ser tónicos los fonemas vocales intermedios seguidos por fonema vocal extremo que en ellas se encuentran.

12. En la Ortografía de 1974 no se encuentra ningún texto donde se aconseje el empleo facultativo de la diéresis a manera de OR 51 3º.

13. Cf. ORSE 37 b: "Cuando una vocal intermedia tónica va detrás de vocal extrema átona sin formar con ella diptongo fonético, la tónica llevará acento gráfico en las condiciones señaladas por las reglas 1ª a) y d) del § 34 [reglas del acento de ciertas palabras agudas]; así en deslié, situó, etc., y en bisílabos como los pretéritos cié, ció, crié, crió, fié, fió, frió, guié, guió, lié, lió, pié [N.B.], pió, pué, pué, rió, rué, ruó, trié, trió, los substantivos guión, Sión, truhán, el adjetivo pión, etc." (Una vez que la Academia ha renunciado a la norma ortológica del diptongo, la especificación de las reglas ahí contenidas no es absolutamente necesaria.)

14. Nótese que a los ejemplos de términos latinos usados en español que se encuentran en OR 41 [a] se les ha yuxtapuesto 'tedéum' (N.B.) y 'réquiem' en ORSE 41 [a].

15. Cf. ORSE 37 c: "La combinación ui sólo llevará acento gráfico, que irá sobre la i, cuando lo pidan las reglas 1ª a) y 3ª del § 34 [reglas del acento de ciertas palabras agudas y las esdrújulas]: así en huí [N.B.], fluí (ambos bisílabos y agudos), construí, atribuí, benjuí, casuístico, jesuítico, etc.; pero huid, huir, fluid, fluir, construir, atribuir, casuista, jesuita no llevarán tilde [...]".

16. Conviene advertir que la norma del acento en la grafía de los monosílabos 'cuál', 'cuán', 'qué' y 'quién' se contiene en OR 38 e, mientras que la norma del acento en la grafía del adverbio interrogativo 'dó' no se contiene en la Ortografía.

17. Ambas enumeraciones son incompletas por faltar las formas femeninas y plurales de los pronombres enumerados que las tienen. La de los relativos está completada en GR 75, y la de los interrogativos lo está indirectamente en GR 73.

18. Nótese que en OR 38 e tampoco se contienen las normas de la posición del acento en las grafías de los pronombres indefinidos 'cuál', 'quién' y 'quiénes', ni en las de los adverbios exclamativos 'qué', 'cuál', ni en la del adverbio distributivo 'cuándo' en oraciones aseverativas. Ni tampoco la norma de la interjección 'qué'.

19. El texto de ORSE 38 e y el de OR 38 son equiformes.

20. No todos los lingüistas juzgan que los dos últimos sonidos sean realizaciones del fonema vocal extremo anterior. Consúltese Real Academia Española (Comisión de Gramática), Esbozo de una nueva Gramática de la Lengua Española (Madrid 1973), § 1.3.3b.

21. Análogo es el caso de la norma del uso de la letra c. Según OR 12 (y ORSE 12), "se escriben con c: 1º. Las dicciones en que precede con sonido de k a las vocales a, o, u o a cualquier consonante, sea o no líquida, o en que termina sílaba [...]. 2º. Las dicciones en que precede con sonido de z a las vocales e, i [...]"; ese texto, siguiendo la interpretación más probable, es equivalente a 'se escriben con la letra c las dicciones en que la letra c precede con sonido de k a las vocales a, o, u o a cualquier consonante, sea o no líquida, o en que la letra c con sonido de k termina sílaba, y las dicciones en que la letra c precede con sonido de z a las vocales e, i', el cual es una simple tautología – por no emplear el término familiar 'perogrullada', pues,. cualquiera que sea el sonido representado con la letra c, si en la representación de una palabra se emplea la letra c, en la representación de esa palabra se emplea la letra c. (Análogo es el caso de la norma del uso de la letra g; cf. OR 19 y ORSE 19.)

22. Emplee 'azeuxis', sinónimo de 'hiato' según DIC 70 Suplemento azeuxis, el que, como nosotros, no quisiere escribir, por ejemplo, 'diptongo y hiato'.

23. Nos parece que los términos 'palabra simple' y 'palabra primitiva' tienen idéntica denotación: hemos prescindido completamente del primero.

24. El texto de ORSE 24 y el de OR 24 son casi equiformes; hay entre ellos diferencias sin importancia ni cuantitativa ni cualitativa que no afectan ni a la factura desmañada del uno y del otro ni a su contenido normativo.

# Epic, ballad, drama:  the Mocedades del Cid

S.J. McMullan (The Queen's University of Belfast)

The exploits of Rodrigo de Vivar first appear in extant vernacular poetry in the late twelfth- or early thirteenth-century Poema de Mio Cid; Ximena has an important part to play in the poem, and yet the story of her marriage is never mentioned: when the tale begins, the hero is already a husband and a father.  The poet directs all interest towards the most memorable events of the Cid's life:  his exile, his triumphs in battle, his conquest of Valencia; we learn virtually nothing of the hero's background and youth.

In this regard, the Poema de Mio Cid is characteristic of the early epic; as A.D. Deyermond reminds us:  "The earliest poems to deal with an epic hero normally and naturally present him at the height of his powers.  It is only at a fairly late stage in the development of an epic tradition that attention is focussed on the hero's birth, childhood and youth:  when an epic hero is known, curiosity about his origins is to be expected, as is a desire to hear of further exploits".[1]  The poet must needs invent fresh details of the hero's career, and the tendency is therefore away from 'historicity' and towards 'novelization', in the terms of Menéndez Pidal.

It is this process which lies behind the Gesta de las mocedades de Rodrigo.  This epic has been ascribed to the late thirteenth or early fourteenth century; although the text itself has not survived, most of the poem's narrative, and even some of its verse, can be reconstructed from the detailed prose rendering absorbed by the Crónica de los reyes de Castilla and various derivative histories.[2]  The Gesta is intimately related to an extant epic, the Mocedades de Rodrigo, or Refundición: although the evidence is meagre and it is difficult to establish a precise relationship, Menéndez Pidal argues convincingly that the lost Gesta prosified by the chronicles gave rise to an intermediate version, and that it is from this lost intermediate version that the extant Refundición and the ballads descend.[3]  The important point here is that the ballads concerning the Cid's youth derive from an epic source other than the Refundición.

It is well known that Guillén de Castro utilized traditional ballads as source material for his Mocedades del Cid;[4] but the extent of his verbal debts, together with the light that his treatment of ballad material throws on his own dramatic skill and literary style, has never been fully analysed.  It is to this subject, with reference to Guillén's Comedia primera, that the present article is directed.

The first scene of this play, which depicts the knighting of the hero, is the amplification of a theme to be found in two of the traditional ballads.  The first treats King Fernando's siege of Coimbra and consequent victory over the Moors; the consecration of a mosque as a church ensues:  "Nombróse Santa María / La mezquita que han hallado",[5] and it is in this converted mosque that the poet localizes the ceremony of Rodrigo's knighting:

> Y en ella se habia armado
> Caballero Don Rodrigo
> De Vivar, el afamado.

The ceremony itself is granted only a few lines of swift narrative:

<pre>
                    El Rey le ciño la espada;
                    ........................
                    Y por hacerle mas honra
                    La Reina le dió el caballo,
                    Y Doña Urraca la infanta,
                    Las espuelas le ha calzado.
</pre>

The second of the source ballads, Doña Urraca's taunt "Afuera, afuera,
Rodrigo" (Durán 774), omits the locality of the church, but does give
the name of the saint to whom the altar is dedicated; the outline of the
scene remains unchanged:

<pre>
                    Cuando fuiste caballero
                    En el altar de Santiago,
                    Cuando el Rey fué tu padrino,
                    Tú, Rodrigo, el afijado:
                    Mi padre te dió las armas,
                    Mi madre te dió el caballo,
                    Yo te calcé las espuelas
                    Porque fueras mas honrado.
</pre>

In Guillén de Castro's version, we find that the scene is set, once
more, before the altar of Santiago, where the King presents him with his
arms, the Queen equips him with a horse, and the Infanta fastens on his
spurs. But while in the ballads the scene is narrated briefly and con-
cisely, the traditional material is used by Guillén as the basis upon
which he erects the whole pomp and magnificence of a court occasion.
The purpose of Guillén's extensive elaboration would appear to be at
least threefold: first, it affords a sumptuous opening to his drama,
firing the audience's historical imagination, and thereby capturing their
interest in the plot; secondly, it introduces with one sweep the central
characters of the action, and rapidly but effectively sketches the
salient traits of their personality: the proud and impetuous nature of
Sancho, the Cid's dignified air of responsibility; and thirdly, and
perhaps most important of all, it hints at the motivation of these characters throughout the ensuing events of the drama - the asides by Urraca
and Ximena are highly indicative of their part in the action.

The attraction of Urraca towards the Cid had, of course, been
expressed quite openly in the ballad, where she states: "Pensé de casar
contigo". The Urraca of Guillén de Castro is granted a far more complex
psychology - she never publicly admits her love for the Cid; her line
"pensé casarme con él" (1862), is directed, in confidence, to her tutor.
Her intuition apprehends the love between the hero and Ximena, and honour
prevents any approach on her part.[6]

At the very outset of the play, Ximena's asides reveal her love for
Rodrigo: when asked by Urraca for her opinion of the young man, she
replies: "Que es galán", and adds, to the audience, "y que sus ojos le
dan / al alma sabrosa pena" (17-19). These, the first words she speaks,
immediately establish a motivation unprecedented in epic and ballad
tradition.

The extant <u>Mocedades</u> epic had depicted Ximena retracting her plea
for vengeance, since she has decided that she wants to marry Rodrigo;
she does not, however, appear to love him: she claims to be doing this
as an example to Fernando:

<pre>
    mostrarvos he assosegar a Castilla,   e a los reynos otro tal;
    datme a Rodrigo por marido,   aquel que mató a mi padre. (375-376)[7]
</pre>

And in the epic, the marriage is plainly contrary to Rodrigo's will:
he is summoned to court, and before he even has time to realize what
is happening, the perfunctory betrothal has already been effected; his
reaction is one of anger:

> Rodrigo respondió muy sañudo    contra el rey don Fernando:
> "Señor, vos me despossastes,    más a mi pessar que de grado [...]
> (437-438)

In the extant epic, then, Rodrigo is overtly hostile to the king's
will regarding the marriage with Ximena; his attitude in this case is
typical of his characterization throughout the Mocedades. Deyermond
writes: "... we find that he insults his father in public, insults
and threatens his king, treats his bride with extreme abruptness ...
From the time that he vows to win five battles until the expedition to
France, Rodrigo seizes almost every opportunity of humiliating King
Fernando and asserting his own superiority" (p.19). Deyermond does not,
however, lay the entire responsibility for the deterioration in Rodrigo's
character upon the Mocedades poet: he cites Menéndez Pidal's conclusion that the epic (later than the Gesta but earlier than the
Mocedades) from which the ballads descend already presents evidence of
this deterioration, and continues: "Lack of intermediate texts prevents us from deciding how many of the changes found in MR when we
compare it with the Gesta are really the work of the MR poet, but it
is fair to assume that he merely exaggerated a pre-existing tradition"
(p.18). Far though they may be, in their portrayal of Rodrigo, from
the tradition of the Poema de Mio Cid, the ballads do not share the
extreme characteristics of the extant Mocedades.
    The ballads continue the anti-romantic attitude of epic tradition:
they never give any hint that Rodrigo and Ximena feel the slightest
affection for one another; the marriage is a matter of expediency, an
attempt to bring to an end the family feud. The fifteenth ballad of
the Romancero del Cid (Durán 738) depicts the proposal of marriage as
originating with Ximena herself; however, it is not romantic love
which prompts her to so direct a procedure: her motives are of the
most materialistic nature:

> Y es que aquese Don Rodrigo
> Por marido yo os pedia.
> Ternéme por bien casada,
> Honrada me contaria,
> Que soy cierta que su hacienda
> Ha de ir en mejoría,
> Y él mayor en el estado
> Que en la vuestra tierra habia.

Rodrigo, for his part, agrees to the marriage not because of any
personal feelings in the matter, but because such is the king's will;
Fernando states: "Yo vos ruego que lo hagais", and Rodrigo replies:

> - Pláceme, Rey mi señor,
> .......................
> En esto y en todo aquello
> Que tu voluntad sería. -

Here, then, the rebel vassal attitude is totally absent, and Rodrigo
submits to the marriage as an act of obedience.

But Guillén radically departs from ballad tradition: in his version Ximena is at the outset attracted towards the hero, and the Cid is similarly enamoured before he undertakes the retribution. And in this version, it is the conflict between love and honour in the hearts of both protagonists which forms the very essence of the plot.[8]

The ceremony is concluded and all withdraw save the king, who recalls his four counsellors. He informs them of his choice of Diego Laínez as guardian of his son; Count Lozano reveals his jealousy at the suggestion, and when reproved by the king, strikes Diego.

None of the surviving ballads agrees with this explanation of the reason behind the Count's blow. For the action following on this insult, Guillén uses the second and third _romances_ of the Cid; the second (Durán 725), depicting Diego as he entrusts the act of revenge to Rodrigo, merely states: "Contóle su agravio"; no indication is given of the events leading up to the insult. The third ballad (Durán 726) does attempt to provide some motivation: the reason given here is a theft perpetrated by Diego Laínez against the Count:

> - Hijos, mirad por la honra,
> Que yo vivo deshonrado.
> Porque les quité una liebre
> A unos galgos que cazando
> Hallé del Conde famoso,
> Conde Lozano llamado:
> Palabras suyas y viles
> Me ha dicho y me ha ultrajado.

This is a detail understandably omitted by Guillén since the light it throws on Diego Laínez's character can hardly be considered favourable; we can feel little distress at the dishonour of a man who has, after all, been punished no more than he deserved. In fact, the ballad appears, somewhat inexplicably, to have diverted the responsibility for forging the first link in the chain of revenge and counter-revenge away from the Count and towards Diego Laínez. The extant epic of the _Mocedades_ had seen the root cause as a theft on the part of the Count:

> El conde don Gómez de Gormaz    a Diego Laynez fizo daño:
> ferióle los pastores    et robóle el ganado (294-295)

and this unprovoked attack by the Count is, we feel, a valid reason for Rodrigo's act of revenge. The ballads distort this sense of justification; their example is rejected by Guillén, who attempts to achieve a greater consistency of character portrayal. In his version, both Diego Laínez and the Count preserve their honesty intact and the conflict now arises through ambitious rivalry; as the first cause behind the action of the whole _comedia_, the personality clash between two proud characters carries a far greater conviction than frivolous escapades of petty theft.[9]

In the following scene, Rodrigo, in conversation with his two brothers, renews his vow of winning five pitched battles, a vow first made in the presence of the king during the knighting ceremony. The five battles in Guillén's play reflect, of course, the "cinco lides campales" of epic tradition: in the _Refundición_, the only extant example of this tradition, the vow had been that Rodrigo, betrothed against his will by the king, would not approach Ximena:

> nin me vea con ella    en yermo nin en poblado,
> fasta que venza çinco lides    en buena lid en canpo. (440-441)

The traditional motif of the five pitched battles is elaborated also in the ballads: in the fifteenth (Durán 738), the Cid, immediately after the betrothal ceremony, takes his bride to his home, where he entrusts her to his mother's keeping. He swears that before he consummates the marriage, he will defeat five Moorish armies:

> Prometió como quien era
> Que á ella no llegaria
> Hasta que las cinco huestes
> De los moros no vencia.

Guillén no longer has the motif of forced betrothal open to him and, if he is to retain the familiar characteristics of the Cid's career, he must needs seek an alternative object for the vow; and this object he finds in the king's own sword with which Rodrigo has been entrusted:

> otra vez juro y prometo
> de no ceñirme su espada,
> ......................
> hasta que llegue a vencer
> cinco batallas campales. (325-326; 330-331)

Diego enters; since his advanced years prevent him from making any attempt to vindicate his honour, he determines to entrust the act of revenge to his sons, and calls in the youngest. And here, as we have seen, the sources of Guillén are ballads two and three of the Romancero del Cid. Verbal parallels are stronger with the second ballad: conclusive in this regard is the Cid's reaction to the test, which in the ballad was depicted:

> - Soltedes, padre, en mal hora,
> Soltedes, en hora mala,
> Que á no ser padre, no hiciera
> Satisfaccion de palabras.

And in Guillén we find the Cid exclaiming:

> ¡Padre! ¡Soltad en mal hora!
> ¡Soltad, padre, en hora mala!
> ¡Si no fuérades mi padre
> diéraos una bofetada!... (468-471)

However, as far as the action is concerned, the second ballad alone cannot have provided Guillén's source material; in this ballad the test consists of a squeezing of the hand, and this version is retained by Guillén with regard to the Cid's younger brothers: to each in turn Diego "Tómale la mano a su hijo, y apriétasela lo más fuerte que pudiere". But when the Cid is brought in, "Muérdele un dedo de la mano fuertemente". It is from the third ballad alone that Guillén could have derived this detail, for it is only in the third ballad that the testing of the sons is described in the terms: "Tomóle el dedo en la boca, / Fuertemente le ha apretado". Guillén is thus combining the two versions, reserving for Rodrigo the more arduous test.

We are informed at this point in the third ballad that the Cid is illegitimate; here Diego Laínez is credited with four sons:

> Los tres son de su mujer,
> Pero el otro era bastardo,

Y aquel que bastardo era,<br>
Era el buen Cid castellano.

The poet insists upon this point: when Diego calls in his sons, one
by one, to test their valour, the Cid is summoned last because: "era
el más chico, y bastardo". This detail is typical of the late epic:
when an audience has become familiar with all the major events of a
hero's life, the demand for new material arises; the poet is forced
to invent incidents by which to retain the audience's interest, and
scandalous stories were always well received. In the Mocedades text
we are told that Fernán González's mother "andava mala mugier con los
moros" (p.258), and given the story behind Pero Mudo's chance conception (882).[10] The detail of the Cid's illegitimacy is absent from the
extant Mocedades text, but in all probability some allusion to it
figured in the text from which the ballads derive: Armistead has shown
that the motif existed before the Gesta, for in his reconstruction of the
lost poem he tells us that it gives details of the hero's ancestry,
possibly refuting the tradition that he was illegitimate.[11]

Emphasis on sexual scandal is thus a characteristic of the late
epic, and it has, in this case, been taken up and continued by ballad
tradition. Guillén de Castro, on the other hand, had no interest in
whetting the audience's appetite by means of scurrilous tales. The
Cid he presents is, rather than the hero of decadent epic, the polished
and refined nobleman; the questionable detail of illegitimate birth is
thus omitted by him.[12]

Rodrigo's reaction to the testing of his valour satisfies his
father, and he is entrusted with the act of revenge. He remains alone
on stage, and expresses all the conflict between his honour and his
love, repeating nearly word for word the greater part of the fourth
ballad (Durán 727). The main difference between the original ballad
and Guillén's adaptation of it lies, naturally enough, in the presentation: the framework of the ballad had been a narrative in the third
person which incorporated a monologue by Rodrigo. In Guillén's version
Rodrigo's speech absorbs both narrative and monologue, reflecting the
entire ballad very closely. We may take as indicative the following
lines:

| Romance IV | Comedia (542-549) |
|---|---|
| Pensativo estaba el Cid | ¿Qué imagino? Pues que tengo |
| Viéndose de pocos años, | más valor que pocos años, |
| Para vengar a su padre | para vengar a mi padre |
| Matando al conde Lozano. | matando al Conde Loçano |
| Miraba el bando temido | ¿qué importa el bando temido |
| Del poderoso contrario, | del poderoso contrario, |
| Que tenia en las montañas | aunque tenga en las montañas |
| Mil amigos asturianos. | mil amigos Asturianos? |

We may notice here some attempt on the part of Guillén to enliven what
might otherwise prove on the stage to be an excessive use of monologue
(another thirty-five lines are to follow); Guillén's major concession
to dramatic requirements is the introduction of the rhetorical question
as a means of emphasizing the psychological tension. Rodrigo's reso-
lution is finally made, and the action moves to the residence of Count
Lozano.

The fifth and sixth ballads present the Cid's challenge: in the
fifth, this challenge consists entirely of a monologue, as the Cid
lists his grievances against the Count; the sixth allows the Count

one retort. Guillén's skill in dramatic technique is obvious in his
transformation of this material: instead of adopting the main structure of a monologue, which would become tedious on a stage, he adapts
the challenge to form a short and lively dialogue between Rodrigo and
the Count, a device which clearly has a far greater dramatic impact.
Notice the sense of urgency imparted by the broken lines:

      RODRIGO.  ....................
                        ¿Conde?
      CONDE.            ¿Quién es?
      RODRIGO.                      A esta parte
                quiero dezirte quién soy.
                ....................
      CONDE.    ¿Qué me quieres?
      RODRIGO.                    Quiero hablarte.- (758-759; 761) -

and so on.

Guillén's second major innovation in his use of the traditional
ballad concerns the psychological motivation of his characters: there
is no hesitation in the _romances_ in Rodrigo's resolve to kill the
Count: he hears the call of duty and has no qualms as to his action.
The love-duty conflict, which is, as we have seen, absent from epic
and ballad tradition, is given its most forceful expression in this
scene. Witness Rodrigo's thrice repeated lament, which assumes the
proportions of a funeral chant: "¡Que he de verter / sangre del alma!
¡Ay, Ximena!" (684-685, 712-713 and 732-733).

The idea of allowing Ximena to be present at the dispute between
her father and her lover is a further innovation of Guillén, and provides the most effective means for heightening the dramatic conflict
inherent in the situation: Rodrigo's honour forces him to take the
desperate step of inciting the father of his beloved to a duel even
as she watches from her window, and the girl is compelled to witness
the act which, through her own highly developed sense of honour, is to
make her lover her mortal enemy. In this scene, then, Guillén is
utilizing to the full the resources of dramatic technique.

A further divergence from the source ballads is to be noted in
the presentation of the Count's death. The _romances_ are rather brutal
and primitive: they briefly describe Rodrigo as he cuts off the
Count's head and presents it to his father. Guillén discards this
barbarous detail; in his version the Count is killed off-stage and we
do not witness any affront to the corpse: we are simply _told_ later
that Diego Laínez washes his cheek in the blood of the offender.

In spite of these multiple divergences, the parallels between the
_romances_ and Guillén's _comedia_ are strong enough to suggest that the
ballads did in fact provide the source material here: the Count of
the sixth ballad mocks the extreme youth of the Cid, just as he does
in the _comedia_, and the insult _rapaz_ is the same, as also is the threat
of ignominious beating. Compare the ballad: "Vete, rapaz, non te
faga / Azotar cual paje niño", with the _comedia_:

                Quita, rapaz; [...]
                Vete, novel Cavallero,
                .....................
                [...]        quien
                tiene la leche en los labios.
                .....................
                Vete, vete, si no quiés
                que [...]
                te dé a tí mil puntapiés. (774-775; 784-785; 810-813)

Act II opens with the entry to the king of Ximena and Diego, who plead their causes at some length. There are several extant ballads relating Ximena's demands for justice from the king, and reflections of them are to be found throughout Guillén's play. The ninth ballad (Durán 732) describes the confusion which breaks out after the act of revenge:

> Grande rumor se levanta
> De gritos, armas y voces
> En el palacio del Rey
> Donde son los ricos-homes.

In the drama, this is adapted to form the king's opening speech:

> ¿Qué rüido, grita y lloro,
> que hasta las nuves abrasa,
> rompe el silencio en mi casa,
> y en mi respeto el decoro? (866-869)

The ballad presents Ximena entering with the words: "Justicia, buen Rey, te pido", while in the drama her opening words are: "¡Justicia, justicia pido!" (890). In all other details, however, the ballad has been greatly elaborated, and in a way which clearly reveals Guillén's knowledge of stage-craft. He increases the dramatic impact by adding to the presence of Ximena that of Diego Laínez; significantly, they enter through opposite doors, and both bear some mark of blood: "ella con un pañuelo lleno de sangre y él teñido en sangre el carrillo". They both prostrate themselves in identical attitudes before the king:

> XIMENA.   ¡Rey, a tus pies he llegado!
> DIEGO L.  Rey, a tus pies he venido. (892-893)

But while their actions and attitudes are identical, their mental states are in absolute opposition. While one bewails her misfortune, the other exults in his triumph; the speeches are closely parallel in form but express diametrically opposed emotions. Ximena urges: "¡Justicia, justicia pido!", while Diego proclaims: "Justa vengança he tomado" (891). Their rival cases are presented:

> XIMENA.   ¡Señor, a mi padre han muerto!
> DIEGO L.  Señor, matóle mi hijo;
>           fué obligación sin malicia.
> XIMENA.   Fué malicia y confiança.
> DIEGO L.  Hay en los hombres vengança.
> XIMENA.   ¡Y havrá en los Reyes justicia! (896-901)

The opposition is evoked most forcefully with the lines:

> XIMENA.   ¡Señor, mi padre he perdido!
> DIEGO L.  ¡Señor, mi honor he cobrado! (906-907)

The sharply contrasting reactions to the vengeance scene, the joy of Diego Laínez and the despair of Ximena, are thus placed in vivid tension by the dramatist.

The verbal parallelism but emotional conflict of the ensuing speeches has been noted by Joaquín Casalduero:[13] Ximena sees in the fatal wound a cause for suffering:

Yo vi con mis propios ojos
teñido el luziente azero:
mira si con causa muero
entre tan justos enojos. (918-921)

But Diego sees in the wound the restoration of his honour:

Yo vi, Señor,
que en aquel pecho enemigo
la espada de mi Rodrigo
entrava a buscar mi honor. (938-941)

Ximena approaches to sympathize and mourn:

Yo llegué casi sin vida,
y sin alma ¡triste yo!
a mi padre, que me habló
por la boca de la herida. (922-925)

Whereas Diego approaches to perfect his revenge:

Llegué, y halléle sin vida,
y puse con alma esenta
el coraçón en mi afrenta
y los dedos en su herida. (942-945)

Moreover, apart from this verbal parallelism, there is, as Casalduero
points out, "en el parlamento de ambos el motivo de la cabeza", for
Ximena concludes her speech with the words:  "costar tiene una cabeça
/ cada gota desta sangre" (936-937), and Diego takes up the idea:
"Con mi cabeça cortada / quede Ximena contenta" (970-971).  And
Casalduero concludes:  "este paralelismo al comienzo del acto hace
resaltar el contraste:  dolor por la muerte del padre, alegría por
haber recobrado el honor".
      The technique of verbal parallelism, like that of verbal anti-
thesis, for the purpose of evoking or emphasizing emotional states is
one of Guillén's most frequent stylistic devices.  It is employed with
great effect in a later scene, where Rodrigo and Ximena come face to
face for the first time after the act of revenge; Ximena is forced to
affect hostility, yet for one brief moment we realize the basic
harmony of their feelings, a harmony suggested by the parallelism:

RODRIGO.   ¡Ay, Ximena!  ¿Quién dixera ...
XIMENA.    ¡Ay, Rodrigo!  ¿Quién pensara ...
RODRIGO.   ... que mi dicha se acabara?
XIMENA.    ... y que mi bien feneciera? (1200-1203)

The antithesis which follows appears all the more striking:

XIMENA.    ¡Vete, y déxame penando!
RODRIGO.   ¡Quédate, iréme muriendo! (1207-1208)

The momentary harmony is shattered.
      This entire scene, with Rodrigo offering himself as the willing
victim of Ximena's honour code, is, of course, totally unparalleled
in ballad tradition;[14] there he had merely turned a deaf ear to her
pleas for vengeance.  The ninth ballad (Durán 732) is typical in this
respect:

> En esto, viendo Jimena,
> Que Rodrigo no responde,
> Y que tomando las riendas
> En su caballo se pone [...]

In the play there follows an extremely moving scene, again without parallel in the ballads, where Diego anxiously awaits his son,
fearing at every moment that some misfortune has overtaken him.  When
Rodrigo eventually appears, the old man relates the invasion of Castile
by the Moors and suggests that Rodrigo attempt to regain the king's
favour by victory in battle.

The fourteenth ballad (Durán 737) had described the invasion of
Castile by the Moors, the Cid's battle with them in the Montes de Oca,
and the capture of five Moorish kings:

> Gran salto diera en los moros:
> En Montes-d'Oca, el castillo,
> Venciera todos los moros
> Y prendió los reyes cinco.

To overcome the problem of staging a full-scale battle, in his dramatization of this narrative account, Guillén introduces an additional
character, one of whose functions is that of describing the events for
us:  the scene opens with a shepherd fleeing before the Moors; he
escapes pursuit, and from the top of a rock where the enemy cannot
reach him he hurls abuse at them and informs the audience of the
battle's progress.

Here the ballads had permitted of no diversion in their sober and
dignified narration.  The dramatic instinct of Guillén, however,
supported by the ever-powerful precedent of Lope, grasped the potential
of combining with the glorious deeds of battle the comic facetiousness
of its rustic participants.  The crudity of the shepherd's humour may
be gauged from the following extract:

> REY MORO.    ....................
>              porque, después de Mahoma,
>              ninguno mayor que yo!
> PASTOR.      Si es mayor el que es más alto,
>              yo lo soy entre estos cerros. (1451-1454)

The comic interlude comes as a welcome relief after the dramatic
tension of the preceding scenes.

The Cid returns to court, on the crest of triumph, and is being
congratulated by the king when Ximena enters in mourning.  She pleads
her case against Rodrigo in a speech adapted from the thirteenth ballad
(Durán 736).

This had begun with a short piece of narrative in the third person whose object was to situate the action; in the drama, this description is put into the mouths of the characters themselves.  It is
an escudero who recites, word for word, the first two lines:  "Sentado
está el Señor Rey / en su silla de respaldo" (1713-1714), while
Ximena herself paraphrases lines four to eight:

| Romance | Comedia |
|---------|---------|
| Dadivoso y justiciero | Si es Magno, si es justiciero, |
| Premia al bueno y pena al malo; | premie al bueno y pene al malo; |
| Que castigos y mercedes | que castigos y mercedes |
| Hacen seguros vasallos. | hazen seguros vasallos.[15] |

Then follow eight lines spoken by Diego (1721-1728). With reference
to these lines Robert R. La Du has remarked: "The first thing that
calls attention to these lines is the sharp break in dialog which they
occasion". The whole preceding scene is presented to the audience
entirely by means of dialogue, just as is the rest of this final scene
of Act II; the eight lines of Diego, on the other hand, are addressed
not to any of the characters but directly to the audience. The lines
have no functional value; the information which they impart - comment
on the entry of the escuderos and description of their dress, details
of Ximena's parentage, reaction of the characters present, Ximena's
attitude before the king - all this is already known by, or now
apparent to, the audience. These lines are also set apart from the
rest of the scene by the introduction of the preterite tense ("entraron
de quatro en quatro / escuderos de Ximena" (1722-1723); "suspenso
quedó Palacio (1726) ); this contrasts with the present tense of the
opening eight lines of the scene ("Sentado está el Señor Rey" (1713) ),
which would seem to be the proper tense for the description of the
action now going on. Furthermore, there is an apparent contradiction
between the number of attendants accompanying Ximena mentioned in the
stage directions at the beginning of the scene ("Sale Ximena [...]
con quatro escuderos"), and the number mentioned by Diego ("entraron
de quatro en quatro / escuderos [...] ").[16]
    The incongruities here are clearly the result of Guillén's desire
to preserve as far as possible the traditional form of his material.
La Du concludes: "Because Guillén de Castro knew that he could anticipate a favorable reception for this romance because of the people's
great love for their ballads, he did not hesitate to have Diego turn
directly to the audience to remind them, in the declamation of his
solemn lines, that the poetry of the romancero was being used in this
portion of Las mocedades del Cid" (p.49).
    However, it seems unlikely that Guillén was consciously adopting
this technique as a way of informing his audience of his sources, as
La Du suggests; rather than a deliberate desire to isolate the ballad
from the dramatic action, what we have here is, on the contrary, simply
a failure to incorporate the ballad successfully within it. The
problem with which Guillén was faced is a familiar one: how can an
independent unit of narrative verse, whether descriptive, emotive or
merely informative, be harmoniously integrated within a swift, dramatic structure? This section is, admittedly, one of Guillén's least
successful attempts at adapting the source material to his own dramatic requirements; hence the incongruities in his presentation.[17]
    Ximena's monologue ensues, preserving in the main the pattern of
the original ballad; the opening lines of the traditional version:

> - Señor, hoy hace seis meses
> Que murió mi padre á manos
> De un muchacho, que las tuyas
> Para matador criaron

become with Guillén:

> Señor, hoy haze tres meses
> que murió mi padre a manos
> de un rapaz, a quien las tuyas
> para matador criaron. (1729-1732)

In the ballad, Ximena voices the complaint that "Cuatro veces he
venido / A tus piés [...] "; this statement is obviously omitted by

Guillén since it does not pertain to Ximena's case in the drama.
Guillén returns to a faithful rendering of the ballad with his next
lines:

> Don Rodrigo de Bivar,
> sobervio, orgulloso y bravo,
> profanó tus leyes justas,
> y tú le amparas ufano,

which closely reflect the original:

> Don Rodrigo de Vivar,
> Rapaz orgulloso y vano,
> Profana tus justas leyes,
> Y tú amparas un profano.

Nevertheless, we find an interesting deviation in lines 1737-1740:
the corresponding section in the ballad had been:

> Tú le celas, tú le encubres,
> Y despues de puesto en salvo
> Castigas á tus merinos,
> Porque no pueden prendallo.

These lines are rejected by Guillén, and in their place he offers a
series of carefully balanced phrases:

> Son tus ojos sus espías,
> tu retrete su sagrado,
> tu favor sus alas libres,
> y su libertad mis daños.

Once more, then, Guillén's love of verbal patterns overrules the
influence of his model. The following section is transcribed by
Guillén practically word for word (the two points at which Guillén
diverges are indicated, with the original ballad rendering in brackets):

> Si de Dios los Reyes justos     (los buenos reyes)
> la semejança y el cargo
> representan en la tierra
> con los humildes humanos,
> no deviera de ser Rey
> bien temido, y bien amado,
> quien desmaya la justicia     (fallesce en la
> y esfuerça los desacatos.               justicia)

Guillén's divergences here are of minimal significance. He does,
however, introduce an image not found in the original ballad:

> A tu justicia, Señor,
> que es árbol de nuestro amparo,
> no se arrimen malhechores,
> indignos de ver sus ramos,

an image which is not, perhaps, strikingly original, but which nevertheless is not totally lacking in poetic effect. The next four lines
are closely paraphrased:

| Romance | Comedia |
|---|---|
| ¡Mal lo miras! mal lo piensas! | Mal lo miras, mal lo sientes, |
| Perdona si mal te fablo, | y perdona si mal hablo; |
| Que la injuria en la mujer | que en boca de una muger |
| Vuelve el respeto en agravio. | tiene licencia un agravio. |

After these lines of close imitation, we meet an interesting
development in the section 1757-1772, for which there is no precedent
in the ballad; when Ximena contrasts her own situation with that of
Rodrigo, we encounter again a technique that Guillén de Castro has
used previously:

> él ofensor, yo ofendida;
> yo gimiendo y él triunfando;
> él arrastrando banderas,
> . y yo lutos arrastrando;
> él levantando trofeos,
> y yo padeciendo agravios;
> él soberbio, yo encogida,
> yo agraviada, y él honrado,
> yo afligida, y él contento,
> él riendo, y yo llorando. (1763-1772)

Conflicting emotional states are thus once more expressed by means of
perfectly balanced antithesis. The words preceding this section, like
Fernando's speech which follows it, are closely modelled on the
traditional pattern; if the audience was familiar with the ballad, as
we must suppose, Guillén's interruption of it in order to introduce
his passage of antithetical concepts would be all the more striking
and thus gain considerably in dramatic effect.

Act II ends with the lines:

```
DIEGO L.   ....................
            ¡Ay, hijo del alma mía!
 XIMENA.   -¡Ay, enemigo adorado!-
 RODRIGO.  -¡Oh, amor, en tu Sol me yelo!-
 URRACA.   -¡Oh, amor, en celos me abraso!-  (1817-1820)
```

Casalduero has drawn attention to: "los cuatro versos unidos de dos
en dos (Ay - Oh), la primera pareja con la antítesis en el centro
(hijo - enemigo), la segunda al final (yelo - abraso); además, en el
tercer verso el oxymoron (sol - yelo)" (Estudios, 63). The Act thus
closes with a supreme example of verbal parallelism in vivid opposition to emotional conflict.

Act III presents us with the delivery to King Fernando of a
letter claiming the right of Aragon to the town of Calahorra. The
question of the possession of this town derives ultimately from epic
tradition: in the extant Refundición, the King of Aragon sends Don
Martín to Fernando's court to demand Calahorra in person, and to offer
himself as the champion of the Aragonese cause. None of Fernando's
knights accepts the challenge, but Rodrigo returns at this moment from
battle with the Moors, and takes upon himself the cause of Castile.
He asks for a delay, however, so that he may go on a pilgrimage to
Santiago, and a plazo of thirty days is granted; the action immediately
turns to the events of his journey to Galicia.

The ballads also appear to follow this pattern: numbers nineteen
and twenty of the Romancero (Durán 742-743), recounting the incidents

of the pilgrimage, conclude with the words that Rodrigo, immediately
on his return, fights the duel with Don Martín; we can thus presume
that in this tradition also the Calahorra question would have first
arisen immediately prior to Rodrigo's departure.

Guillén de Castro retains in his version the motifs of the
Calahorra question and the Cid's pilgrimage to Santiago, but he
interrupts the action for the insertion of two elements: the first
concerns the stratagem effected by the king in an attempt to test
the validity of certain rumours concerning Ximena's love for Rodrigo;
the second relates to Ximena's protests to the king against the hero's
misdemeanours. In the ballad tradition, both these elements would be
incongruous here: it is precisely at this point in the popular
versions that the wedding between hero and heroine is celebrated.
The twentieth ballad (Durán 743) is most specific in this regard:

> Celebradas ya las bodas,
> A do la corte yacia
> De Rodrigo con Jimena,
> A quien tanto el Rey queria,
> El Cid pide al Rey licencia
> Para ir en romería
> Al apóstol Santiago.

Guillén rejects this idea of early marriage presumably because of the
problem it poses with regard to psychological motivation. The ballads
present us with the sudden, unexplained and apparently inexplicable
reconciliation between deadly enemies; whereas Guillén attempts to
portray a union of gradual and logical development, a union which his
hero and heroine can finally consummate and yet still reveal complete
psychological consistency.

It is primarily in order to facilitate this conclusion that
Guillén introduces the episode of the king's subterfuge, an episode
of his own invention; Arias informs the king: "el tratar el casamiento
/ de Rodrigo con Ximena / será alivio de su pena"; to which the king
replies that the idea had, in fact, crossed his mind, but that he
feared Ximena's displeasure: "Yo estuve en tu pensamiento, / pero no
lo osé intentar / por no crecer su disgusto" (1953-1958). Clearly,
once Fernando has reassured himself of Ximena's true feelings - and
this he admirably succeeds in doing by proclaiming a false report of
Rodrigo's death - he is in an ideal position for imposing the only
satisfactory conclusion.

The second element introduced into the traditional sequence here
is a practically verbatim reproduction of part of the eleventh ballad:
this is a variant of Ximena's pleas for justice from the king, and had
obviously figured at a far earlier stage in the time scheme of the
ballads. Guillén adds to Ximena's speech a few details of his own
invention, but nevertheless retains the Romancero version almost intact.
Interesting from the point of view of Guillén's elaboration is the
following section (Ximena has been speaking of Rodrigo's gavilán):

| Romance | Comedia |
|---|---|
| Por facerme mas despecho | y por hazerme despecho |
| Cébalo en mi palomare, | dispara a mi palomar |
| Mátame mis palomillas | flechas, que a los vientos tira, |
| Criadas y por criare; | y en el corazón me dan; |
| La sangre que sale d'ellas | mátame mis palomicas |
| Teñido me ha mi briale. | criadas, y por criar; |

la sangre que sale de ellas
me ha salpicado el brial.
(1981-1988)

The sexual symbolism is already quite blatant in the original
ballad: the medieval lyric offers numerous examples of the sparrow-
hawk in his representative role of the aggressive male; the dove, for
her part, is a constant symbol of the chastity, or fidelity, of the
female. Here Rodrigo's sparrow-hawk attacks and wounds Ximena's doves;
the blood which issues from the encounter bespatters the girl's skirt.
We apparently have here a dream fantasy on the part of Ximena, a fantasy
which reveals her own subconscious desire to submit her virginity to
the Cid.

Guillén, as though afraid that his audience might miss the point,
clarifies the significance of the episode; he retains the allusion to
the sparrow-hawk: "cavallero en un cavallo, / y en su mano un gavilán"
(1975-1976), but he continues by introducing the idea of the arrow
which, apart from possessing a symbolism of its own, allows Ximena, by
a subtle double-entendre, to commit what we should call today a Freudian
slip: the arrows dispatched by Rodrigo supposedly wound her because
they kill her doves and cause her grief. The audience, however, knows
better: the arrows are in fact those of love, which have pierced her
to the heart.

Moreover, Casalduero justly points out the hazy, dream-like
quality which, in Guillén's version, Ximena's experience assumes:
"El sueño ("sospecho que lo soñáis", "lo habréis soñado esta noche"),
la locura ("que estoy loca sólo falta que digáis"), el trastrueque
temporal ("cada día", "Rodrigo ha muchos días, señora, que ausente
está", "ante que se fuese ha sido") cobran un significado profundo"
(Estudios, 68).

Ximena's words reveal all the desires and torments of her subconscious mind;[18] the audience, who can see through the surface meaning
of these words and penetrate their hidden significance, is more fully
prepared to accept the psychological validity of the dénouement.

The two innovations added here to the framework of the original
romances, the king's subterfuge and Ximena's fantasy, thus reveal
themselves to be primarily the result of Guillén's desire to invest
his heroine with a greater psychological consistency, and to establish,
thereby, the basis for a convincing and satisfying conclusion.

The play now returns to the narrative sequence of the ballads:
Diego disproves the truth of Ximena's accusations concerning the Cid's
misdemeanours by stating that he is, in fact, performing a pilgrimage
to Santiago; it is to this pilgrimage that the action now moves, and
we are presented with the incident of the Cid's meeting with Saint
Lazarus in the form of a leper.

This legend is a late addition to the Cidian cycle; according to
Armistead's reconstruction, it figured in the lost Gesta ('Structure',
342); it reappears, with minor modifications, in the extant Refundición,[19]
and it is from epic stock that it becomes part of the Romancero.
Dealing with this incident we find ballads nineteen and twenty (Durán
742-743), which Guillén follows closely as far as the action is concerned, though verbal parallels are limited to the line "¡San Lázaro
soy, Rodrigo!" (2331).

To the schematic narrative of the ballad, however, Guillén has
introduced a new element - that of comic incident: a gracioso is
provided, again in the shape of the pastor, who this time arouses
laughter through his greed. Once more, then, Guillén reveals his
desire to give some comic relief to his main dramatic theme, and the

contrast is extremely marked here: the _gracioso_ gambols in the very
scene which presents us with the saint in disguise.

As well as providing an element of humour, this character also
gives Guillén an opportunity to emphasize the true religious devotion
of the hero. The Cid's severe Christianity is mocked by the shepherd:

> Con todo, en esta jornada,
> da risa tu devoción
> con dorada guarnición,
> y con espuela dorada,
>   con plumas en el sombrero,
> a cavallo, y en la mano
> un rosario. (2159-2165)

The Cid's religious zeal is now about to be put to the test. The
voice of the leper is heard, telling the Cid that fighting against
the Moors is not, in itself, the way to heaven: "¡No con sólo pelear
/ se gana el cielo, Rodrigo!" (2197-2198). And Rodrigo reveals
immediately that his piety is not reserved for feats of arms alone; he
proves that he can not only kill the enemies of Christ, but also - of
equal if not of greater importance - aid his fellow Christians in
their suffering. And this he does by stretching out his hand to the
poor leper. The complementary nature of these two aspects of
Christianity, the militant and the compassionate, is further emphasized by the words of the leper:

> Todo es menester, Rodrigo:
> matar allá al enemigo,
> y valer aquí al hermano. (2209-2211)

The Cid is thus depicted here as the perfect Christian: his faith
is militant in that he constantly exerts himself in battle against the
infidel; and yet his military prowess is in no way detrimental to his
capacity for experiencing a truly Christian compassion. The moral
excellence of the hero, which had been implicit in the ballads, is
explicitly emphasized by Guillén de Castro.[20]

The action returns to the Castilian court, where the Aragonese
giant, Don Martín, is insolently defying the Castilian knights and
claiming the disputed territory. Concerning the matter of Calahorra,
Guillén's use of traditional material leads him into incongruity:
he has already presented us with the letter from the Aragonese king,
with Fernando's decision to resolve the question by means of single
combat, and with his choice of the Cid as his champion:

> Remitir quiero a la espada
> esta justicia que sigo,
> y al Mió Cid, al mi Rodrigo,
> encargalle esta jornada. (1925-1928)

This corresponds to the ballad: "Fernando nombró á Rodrigo / De
Vivar, el muy nombrado" (Durán 744). Now, however, Guillén turns away
from the ballad account, and contradicts himself: the king asks for
a volunteer among the Castilian knights, who will accept the challenge,
and is disillusioned to find that the volunteer is not forthcoming.
But the Cid returns at this moment from Santiago and eagerly steps
forward. Guillén's departure from the source ballad in the interval
between his introduction of the Calahorra question and his development

of this theme has clearly caused him to forget that he was utilizing the traditional account for his presentation. The Cid is now depicted as willingly offering his own life in the cause of king and country, and the sympathetic light this throws on the hero would appear to be the reason behind the sudden contradiction.

Into the development of the Calahorra episode, Guillén introduces a scene which is intended to link the two plays that form his Mocedades del Cid: the division by Fernando of his composite kingdom. For this account, and the consequent aggression on the part of Sancho, the ultimate source is an epic poem, the Cantar de Sancho II y cerco de Zamora. No poetic text of this epic is extant, but the Cantar was prosified in the Primera Crónica General and can be reconstructed by means of the chronicle version.[21] This epic gave rise to the ballads, and these, once more, provided Guillén's source material for the historical events of his drama: towards the end of the first play we have the division of the kingdom, while the major part of the second play concerns Sancho's hostilities against his brothers and sisters, his siege of the city of Zamora, and his murder at the hands of a traitor.

The Calahorra question now, finally, reaches its conclusion in the duel between the Cid and Don Martín. Contrary to the example of the ballads, in the drama the Aragonese knight is not merely championing his king's cause for the possession of Calahorra: Guillén also links this character to the theme of Ximena's vengeance in such a way as to precipitate the conclusion. Ximena has offered her hand to the man who will bring her the Cid's head, and Don Martín takes this task upon himself. The Calahorra question thus comes to play an integrated part in the plot structure of Guillén's drama, in contrast to its episodic nature in the ballad tradition.[22] When Rodrigo returns triumphant from the field of combat, he has not merely asserted Fernando's legal right to Calahorra: as John G. Weiger points out, in Castro's version the combat between the two rivals assumes the proportions of a "jugement de Dieu". Rodrigo's victory is a public declaration that God favours his claim to Ximena's hand, and the king, as God's representative on Earth, pronounces judgement: "yo pronuncio la sentencia / en su favor" (2988-2989). Ximena is able to accept the marriage as God's will: "Haré lo que el cielo ordena" (2994); her love for Rodrigo may be consummated without detriment to her honour.[23] The marriage, far from being the unaccountable union of opposites which it had appeared in ballad tradition, becomes a reconciliation fully justified through Guillén's deepening of psychological motivation and his structural changes.[24]

# NOTES

1. _Epic Poetry and the Clergy: Studies on the Mocedades de Rodrigo_ (London, Colección Támesis, 1969), 9.

2. Samuel G. Armistead, 'The Structure of the _Refundición de las Mocedades de Rodrigo_', _Romance Philology_, XVII (1963-1964), 338-345, at p. 341. See also his "_La Gesta de las Mocedades de Rodrigo_": Reflections of a Lost Epic Poem in the "_Crónica de los reyes de Castilla_" and the "_Crónica general de 1344_" (doctoral thesis, Princeton 1955; abstract in _Dissertation Abstracts_, XV (1955), 2198-2199).

3. _Romancero hispánico (Hispano-portugués, americano y sefardí). Teoría e historia_ (Madrid 1953), I, 219-220. For an alternative view, see 'Structure', 342, where Armistead suggests that the _Gesta_ and the _Refundición_ derive from a common source.

4. Some account is given by G.W. Umphrey, whose edition _Las mocedades del Cid por Guillén de Castro_ (New York 1939), includes nine of the source ballads. The edition by Víctor Said Armesto (Madrid, Clásicos Castellanos, 1962 reprint) also contains helpful information. (All references are to this edition.) Ballad material is reproduced in W.E. Wilson's _Guillén de Castro_ (New York, Twayne, 1973). Guillén's reinterpretation of traditional material with reference to the presentation of his hero has been discussed in two articles: W.C. McCrary views Castro's Rodrigo as "an accommodation of the medieval legends to the universal hero myth" in 'Guillén de Castro and the _Mocedades_ of Rodrigo: A Study of Tradition and Innovation', _Romance Studies in Memory of Edward B. Ham_ (Hayward-California, California State College Publications, no. 2, 1967), 89-102; while Russell P. Sebold examines Rodrigo as an exemplary Christian figure in 'Un David español, o "Galán Divino": el Cid Contrarreformista de Guillén de Castro', _Homage to John M. Hill. In Memoriam_ (Madrid 1968), 217-242.

5. Agustín Durán, _Romancero general_ (B.A.E., X, 1849-1851), no. 749.

6. Interesting in this context is the article by Samuel G. Armistead, '"The Enamored Doña Urraca" in Chronicles and Balladry', _Romance Philology_, XI (1957-1958), 26-29. Armistead traces the account of Doña Urraca's role in Rodrigo's upbringing to an early tradition, already present in the _Cantar del Cerco de Zamora_, which states that Rodrigo's youth was spent with Urraca at Zamora. The 14th-century chronicles, however, mention a strong bond of affection between the two, an element not even implied in earlier texts. And this affection, with possible suggestions of scandal, had its origin, Armistead believes, in some manifestation of the popular epic. The chroniclers, while utilizing epic accounts, nevertheless saw fit to omit any incidents which might reflect badly on members of the royal household, and thus Urraca's reputation emerged unscathed in works for learned consumption. Armistead concludes: "the enamored princess of the 16th-century ballad ... very probably represents the late fruit of a 200 year old epic tradition".

7. Ed. R. Menéndez Pidal, _Reliquias de la poesía épica española_ (Madrid 1951).

8. Barbara Matulka has investigated Guillén's source for elements in his plot which are absent from the ballads. In _The Cid as a Courtly Hero:_

From the Amadís to Corneille (New York 1928), she indicates as one of
the principal differences between traditional accounts and Guillén's
version the love of Rodrigo and Ximena prior to the vengeance scene,
and Matulka attributes this motif to the influence of the prose romances.
Matulka reiterates her point in 'The Courtly Cid Theme in the Primaleón',
Romanic Review, XXV (1934),298-313, where it is her purpose to demonstrate that the Cid-Ximena story "gradually drew into its compass and
texture all the chivalric motives which constitute the framework of the
Primaleón and other romances of chivalry" (p.300). The vehicle by which
these chivalric motives were conveyed to Guillén de Castro is, Matulka
tells us, an epic poem by Diego Jiménez de Ayllón, published in Antwerp
in 1568, which contained, among other modifications to tradition, the
idea that the love of Rodrigo and Ximena existed before the fatal duel.
However, Matulka does go on to admit that the parallel is not close,
she offers no evidence of verbal borrowings, and remarks, when speaking
of Ayllón's epic and the Florisel romance: "Nor is it proven that Castro
drew directly upon them" (Cid as Courtly Hero, 40). In fact, there are
several worrying features which may cause some hesitation about the
wholesale acceptance of her argument (see below).

9. Matulka observes that in the epic by Ayllón the motivation behind
the challenge and duel is the Count's jealousy; there, however, the
jealousy is directed against the Cid himself, rather than against his
father, and this involves a considerable distortion of the traditional
account of subsequent events - Diego's testing of his sons is obviously
inapplicable. Guillén remains far closer to the ballad presentation
of the episode.

10. For the erotic interest of the Mocedades de Rodrigo see Deyermond,
Epic Poetry, 52-53.

11. Armistead's reconstruction of the lost poem is given in La Gesta,
20-58; a summary may be found in 'Structure', 342.

12. The rejection of this traditional motif appears all the more
interesting in the light of Matulka's research: she speaks of the
"telescoping of the national hero with those other revered heroes of the
Primaleón and the Amadís" ('Courtly Cid', 313). The mystery which
surrounds the birth of so many heroes of chivalresque romances - of
Amadís himself, even - is a well-known motif. If Guillén is refashioning
his hero on the model of the chivalresque protagonists, and if the motif
of mysterious origin, be it through illegitimacy or other causes, is
present in that model, why then should Guillén reject it here?

13. Estudios sobre el teatro español (Madrid 1962), 58.

14. This is a further motif which Matulka attributes to the influence
of the chivalresque romance: "Florisel, while living in the palace of
Queen Sidonia, felt his old love for the Queen reviving. Finally,
unable to stand the torment any longer, he handed his sword to Sidonia
asking her to kill him, just as did Rodrigo in both the Mocedades and
Corneille" (Cid as Courtly Hero, 24).

15. For the implications of the change of mood, see I.T. Agheana,
'Guillén de Castro's creative use of the Romancero: one instance in
Las Mocedades del Cid', Bulletin of the "Comediantes", 27 (1975), 79-80.

'Eight lines from <u>Las Mocedades del Cid</u>', <u>Romance Notes</u>, I (1959–1960), 46–49, at p. 47. For a contrary view, see Luciano García Lorenzo, <u>El teatro de Guillén de Castro</u> (Barcelona 1976), 114–115.

17. G.W. Umphrey remarked: "In his adaptation of the ballad to the first part of the scene, Castro shows a notable lack of his usual skill in handling his ballad sources, and the contradictions and inconsistencies can hardly be explained away. The ballad is clumsily distributed among the various personages, and some of the lines interpolated by the dramatist, lines 1715 and 1716 for example, are quite inane" (p.155).

18. G.W. Umphrey is clearly unhappy with this section: "The inconsistency of Jimena's speech is due to the introduction of a ballad that does not harmonize with the central theme of the play" (pp.158–159). And Paul Bénichou ('El casamiento del Cid', <u>NRFH</u>, VII (1953), 316–336), reveals similar misgivings: " ... Guillén de Castro no quiso sacrificar las conocidas quejas, y las incluyó en su comedia (vs. 1973 y sigs.) suponiendo <u>con graciosa inverosimilitud</u> que, al pintar a Rodrigo tan cruel e insolente con ella, Jimena <u>miente</u> para conseguir que lo castiguen (vs. 1999 y sigs.)" (p.331, n.36, italics mine). The point is, surely, that Ximena is not deliberately lying; although her accusations are false, they are the result of a fantasy which, for the girl herself, has a very real significance. The speech, then, harmonizes perfectly with Ximena's characterization throughout the play.

19. For a discussion of the episode's significance, see Deyermond, pp.113–115.

20. The importance of the leper episode for an understanding of Castro's portrayal of his hero is treated in detail by Russell P. Sebold, 'Un David español ...', art. cit. note 4 above.

21. See Carola Reig, <u>El Cantar de Sancho II y cerco de Zamora</u> (Madrid, <u>RFE</u> Anejo XXXVII, 1947).

22. Matulka has observed: "Before Castro, the encounter [between Rodrigo and Don Martín] was only an additional exploit of the Cid ... it was in no way connected with his love for Jimena. Moreover, it took place <u>after</u> the marriage ..." (<u>Cid as Courtly Hero</u>, 15). She asks the reason for the change, and replies: "It is manifestly a contamination from the <u>Florisel de Niquea</u> story, in which the defenders of the Queen's honor successively attacked the man whose head she had requested". We have had ample evidence of the radical divergences from ballad tradition which Guillén is obliged to make in his dramatization of a narrative. May we not see the new significance attached to the Don Martín episode as a conscious attempt to impose some sense of dramatic unity upon the disparate ballad elements, rather than as a passive submission to fictional themes?

23. 'Sobre la originalidad e independencia de Guillén de Castro', <u>Hispanófila</u>, XXXI (1967), 1–15.

24. Matulka has described the love theme in Ayllón's epic as "retaining the main elements of the <u>Romancero</u>" (<u>Cid as Courtly Hero</u>, 40), and Bénichou ('Sobre el casamiento del Cid', <u>NRFH</u>, VIII (1954), 79) emphasizes that in this epic, Ximena "de acuerdo con la tradición, acaba pidiéndolo ella misma por marido". Even though we must acknowledge the possibility of Guillén's indebtedness to Ayllón for his theme of the protagonists'

love prior to the vengeance scene, nevertheless, Guillén's logical
development of this theme and his psychologically convincing conclusion
to it are clearly original.

I should like to take this opportunity to express my thanks to
A.D. Deyermond, who read this article in typescript, and whose comments
were most helpful.

Paul Valéry and Jorge Guillén 1919-1936:  a case of logique imaginative?

Terence McMullan (The Queen's University of Belfast)

> Il n'est pas de mot qui vienne plus aisément
> ni plus souvent sous la plume de la critique que
> le mot d'_influence_, et il n'est point de notion
> plus vague parmi les vagues notions qui composent
> l'armement illusoire de l'esthétique.  Rien
> toutefois dans l'examen de nos productions qui
> intéresse plus philosophiquement l'intellect et
> le doive plus exciter à l'analyse que cette
> modification progressive d'un esprit par l'oeuvre
> d'un autre [...] cette activité dérivée est
> essentielle à la production dans tous les genres.

PAUL VALERY[1]

> Literariamente no hay libro nuevo sin libros
> anteriores.

JORGE GUILLEN[2]

On 17th May 1924 the most eminent French poet of the time addressed a meeting at the Residencia de Estudiantes in Madrid.  His subject was Baudelaire, and printed invitations to the lecture began by introducing the distinguished speaker as follows:  'La crítica más autorizada ve hoy en Paul Valéry al representante ejemplar de la pura poesía francesa. Se discute su norma - y su labor - pero su prestigio no'.[3]  Despite the hint of polemic here, during the 1920s the dominant attitude to Valéry in Spain was one of adulation.[4]  He was 'el primer poeta de França';[5] one of his finest verse-compositions 'Le Cimetière marin' was regarded in serious critical circles as 'la obra fundamental de la poesía francesa de este decenio';[6] his prose-writings were those of 'L'assaigista més lúcid, agut i encisadorament desencisat del nostre temps'.[7]  In the Residencia de Estudiantes that May one of his most enthusiastic and intelligent Spanish readers listened avidly as Valéry recited the famous sonnet from _Les fleurs du mal_ that starts 'Sois sage, oh ma douleur...'[8]. That attentive listener who shortly afterwards accompanied the French visitor on an excursion to Aranjuez was the rising Spanish poet Jorge Guillén.  The two were already well acquainted.  Guillén had lived for six years in Paris (1918-23) working as a lector at the Sorbonne. Mathilde Pomès had introduced them at Adrienne Monnier's bookshop in the rue de l'Odéon[9] 'hacia 1921 o 22',[10] and the Spaniard became a regular caller at Valéry's house at 40 rue de Villejust where their topics of conversation included literature and literary theory.[11]  This personal contact was maintained throughout the 1920s on Guillén's frequent return trips to Paris when he made a point of going to see the French writer.  Undoubtedly, external factors such as their friendship, the Spaniard's translations of Valéry, and his choice of epigraphs from the latter's poems[12] have contributed to the opinion that works like _Charmes_ had an important influence on the future author of _Cántico_.  But is there any textual substance to this notion?[13]

Although literary critics have expended considerable energy scrutinising the relationship between Valéry's work and that of Guillén, it could be argued that the exact nature of the French writer's impact on the author of _Cántico_ has still to be fully elucidated.  The clumsiness of some approaches to the subject, by provoking a critical backlash,[14] produced an atmosphere in which the study of influence became regarded as at best distracting and at worst destructive.[15] To a noticeable extent this hostility has inhibited investigation of what is, by any standards, a delicate and complex topic.[16] The present examination is undertaken in the belief that when aesthetic debts are dispassionately dissected the genuinely creative artist emerges, not diminished, but with his originality defined more sharply than by any other process.

A survey of published opinion suggests at least four reasons why the established critical view should be revised. First, the picture that has been built up is, with a few exceptions,[17] emphatically one of differentiation as opposed to comparison. Thus while space and effort are lavished on what separates the author of Charmes from Guillén, points of close contact between the two are either ignored or minimised.[18] Consequently this reassessment will seek not to challenge the irrefutable distinctions demonstrated by others,[19] but rather to shed light on possible sources of stimulus neglected previously and so achieve a more accurate distribution in the balance of evidence. A second weakness in current criticism is its occasional element of superficiality: some of the relatively meagre positive data already available involve broad similarities, not to say coincidental commonplaces, unrefined by textual analysis or illustration and hence unlikely to strike the reader as decisive or even significant.[20] Thirdly, inadequate attention has been focussed on how influence is connected to development in the Spanish poet's early work. Despite the lip service paid now and then to this crucial feature,[21] for the most part students of Valéry's impact have treated Cántico monolithically in the complete edition, with inevitably misleading results.[22] But J.M. Blecua's annotated Cántico (1936) now provides an indispensable basis for any discussion of chronological evolution since it offers details of variant versions as well as dates of composition and first publication for every collected pre-Civil War poem.[23] This vital information will be supplemented here by an equally essential first-hand knowledge of Guillén's uncollected prose and verse.[24] A fourth cause of dissatisfaction with the critical status quo is that the precise instances of probable borrowing identified to date are widely dispersed in the bibliography. What better starting-point, therefore, than the evaluation and synthesis of this scattered material in favour of Valéry's effect on the Spanish poet.

Three years after his arrival in Paris, Guillén had still very few publications to his credit.[25] On the other hand, during that same period, Valéry's reputation as a poet soared with the appearance of La Jeune Parque (1917), and Album de vers anciens 1890-1900 (1920).[26] Moreover, although Charmes was not issued as a book until two years later, by the summer of 1920 the majority of its poems were familiar to the literati thanks to the literary magazines.[27] How did the future author of Cántico react to these verse texts?[28] According to his own retrospective account, one of the qualities that would most inspire him in Valéry's work was 'el rigor de la forma'.[29] Contemporary evidence corroborates this since both the 1928 and 1936 editions of Cántico show a sustained preference for strict prosody. Regularly-patterned poems are three times commoner than those exhibiting some disregard of rhyme or metre.[30] Given the collection's remarkable range of stanza-type,[31] Guillén's formal control is all the more impressive. Indeed it presupposes a conscious disciplining of artistic creativity that has wider ramifications in the technique of these two writers. Thus Ciplijauskaité notes in each of them 'El aspecto laborioso de la obra' (269) meaning that they invest a good deal of deliberate effort

in forging their poetry. The endless revision that Valéry wryly calls
'ce goût pervers de la reprise indéfinie' (I 1497) is matched in
Cántico by a protracted process of reworking and elaboration stretching
over a thirty-year span. If, as seems likely, Ciplijauskaité is correct
in asserting that 'El afán por la forma más perfecta explica el gran
número de variantes de cada poema en ambos autores' (270) then the
exemplary standards set by Valéry must take some of the credit. But,
equally, one cannot help admiring the productive tenacity with which
the Spanish poet successfully cultivated a stylistic rigour that
severely curtailed the volume of its French originator's verse.[32] Not
that Valéry himself viewed conventions of form as stifling constraints.
He thought of them rather as a stimulating and stabilising framework
for the creative act: 'je trouve progressivement mon ouvrage à partir
de pures conditions de forme' (I 1504). Blanch senses an identical
approach in Guillén, when he speculates that by tracing the evolution
of certain poems through successive editions of Cántico 'Vemos, en
efecto, que lo que queda no es siempre la idea, sino un ritmo pre-
determinado o algunas rimas elegidas' (294).[33] Blecua's edition tends
to support such a conclusion on the evidence of the complete variant
versions it reproduces for thirty or so poems, less than half-a-dozen
of which deviate noticeably from the original verse-structure when
revised.[34] Finally, in addition to nurturing such broad attitudes to
form as those listed above, the precedents set by Valéry might also be
said to have affected Guillén's choice of stanza-pattern. As several
critics have realized[35] the Spanish poet favours the French décima
(ababccdeed) used in Charmes, as an alternative to the home-grown
espinela variety (abbaaccddc). Nevertheless it has so far escaped
critical attention that while up until 1928 the French version is pre-
ferred (10 : 7), the trend is reversed from 1928 to 1936 (4 : 9), and
overall the espinela just outnumbers its foreign rival by 14 to 16.
Clearly here is an aspect of Valéry's appeal that the author of Cántico
soon outgrew.[36]

Features of content also reinforce the argument for influence.
The celebrated label poésie pure, which Valéry invented virtually by
accident, designated a desire common to a series of French poets from
Baudelaire onwards to rid verse of non-poetic elements.[37] An effect on
subject-matter was to increase the importance of poetry as a theme in its
own right. Charmes contains a number of poems that can be interpreted
as art reflecting on itself, on its own first principles. 'Palme'
(I 153-6), a striking illustration of the tendency,[38] has been compared
by Macrí (25-6) to Guillén's 'Pino' (No.110 1923-8) since in both the
tree symbolises a poetry that grows towards enlightenment nourished by
what it extracts from the physical reality in which it is rooted.[39]
Of course the theme of poetry is a well established motif in Cántico
(1928) as a whole, inspiring, at a conservative estimate, almost a
dozen verse-texts.[40] However, its total absence from the fifty new
poems of the 1936 edition shows that here too the French writer's
impact was relatively short-lived. Yet, while it lasted, some of
Valéry's other preoccupations appear to have rubbed off on Guillén.
For example, the most crucial thing that 'Cantique des colonnes' (I
116-8, pub. 1919) contributed to 'Ciudad de los estíos' (No.29 1920-8)
was not its temporary epigraph (in the 1928 edition only), nor its play
of sunlight on architecture (be it Classical Greek or modern urban),
but rather its enthusiasm for a clarity of vision capable of sublimating
human instinct.[41] This entailed the exercise of an analytical intelligence that finds parallel metaphorical expression elsewhere: for the
French poet, in the bursting plenitude of overripe pomegranates ('Les
Grenades' I 146); for the Spaniard, in a mental alertness stripped to

its essentials like the branch of a tree in Autumn: 'Árbol ágil, / Mundo terso, mente monda, guante en mano al aire. // ¡Cómo aguzan / Su pormenor tranquilo las nuevas nervaduras!' (No.91 'Rama del otoño' 1923-8, 3-6).[42] By thus articulating his identical commitment to lucidity from a diametrically opposite angle the future author of Cántico reveals his independent and creative treatment of source material. But those who cultivate such a contemplative approach must brave the attractions of passive quiescence, as evoked in 'Ebauche d'un serpent' (I 138-146). There the seductive snake of the Eden myth, having cynically declared that 'l'univers n'est qu'un défaut / Dans la pureté du Non-être!' (29-30), has his paralysing pessimism rejected by Valéry in the closing lines (308-310).[43] In an uncollected lyrical prose composition entitled 'Demonios' (1923), reproduced below for the first time since its original publication (see Appendix B), Guillén likewise survives the temptation represented by that absolute but static Perfection prefigured in Charmes:

> -¡Ah, la ruindad negativa del acto! - me susurra la voz de mi
> Demonio -.   Acto: Dios en la mente del incrédulo.
>     Y la voz de la Perfección me susurra: - Actos: fatales erratas
> al editar en conclusiones la potencia pura, la pura posibilidad.
> ¡Demoníaca Perfección!

Moreover, the tension between inertia and action just mentioned is explored at greater depth in one of Valéry's finest achievements, 'Le Cimetière marin' (I 147-151, pub.1920). Certain of its details anticipate Cántico with uncanny accuracy (e.g. 'Je m'abandonne à ce brillant espace' 39), and its six-line stanzas (aabccb) may well have provided the rhyme-scheme for No.100 'La Florida' (1923-8).[44] Nevertheless, again, the French poem's fundamental lesson for Guillén lies partly in its susceptibility to the ascetic lure of an Absolute depicted in stanzas twelve to fourteen as the zenith of mental clarity ('l'esprit clair' 72), the supreme detachment from the vicissitudes of existence, a self-sufficient state of contemplative repose.[45] At the same time the text's significance also resides partly in Valéry's realisation (lines 78-81) that his restless consciousness cannot be absorbed but only annihilated within a universe thus reduced to its immutable essence by his mind. So in stanzas twenty-two to twenty-four he forsakes the sterility of abstract speculation to plunge into physical reality. 'Le Cimetière marin', having thus portrayed the speaker's momentary withdrawal into a rarefied realm of meditation isolated from life, culminates with his re-immersion in bodily experience:

> Courons à l'onde en rejaillir vivant! (132).[46]

Guillén's sensitivty to this passage is obvious from 'Valéry en el recuerdo' (op. cit. 70) where he specifically comments on 'Ese esfuerzo hacia la vida, reanimada por la frescura del mar'. In Cántico itself a still more extraordinary illustration of his response is provided by No.113 'La salida' (1927-8) whose composition coincided exactly with the period when the Spanish poet had been asked by Valéry to undertake a translation of 'Le Cimetière marin'.[47] Needless to say, it would be unfair to describe 'La salida' as simply a gloss on the line of French verse quoted above. Clearly, however, Guillén develops here, in a manner consistent with his own creative personality, the expressive potential latent in a Valéry image that propounds the restorative value of direct contact with the material world. Central to 'Le Cimetière marin', then, there is a polarity between immobility and dynamism whose impact can be felt in <u>Cántico</u>, with poems like No.19 'Perfección del círculo' (1926) at one extreme, and examples such as No.113 'La salida' (1927-8) at the other.

Valéry was undoubtedly an outstanding poet though not a particularly prolific one. On the other hand he did produce a vast body of theoretical writings which, moreover, contain some of his best work. The Spanish journals of the 1920s indicate that his prose attracted nearly as much attention as his verse (see Appendix A). This interest in the essays was shared by Guillén too. On 8th July 1926, for instance, writing to a friend, he remarked enthusiastically of Valéry: 'Cada día me embarga más - cada día más - su prosa' (Blanch 288). But his acquaintance with the theoretical writings probably dates from much earlier. Indeed, when in 1924 the French author sent him a copy of <u>Variété</u> (ibid.) it is likely that he was already familiar with those of its essays that had been appearing individually since 1919. Certain common critical assumptions about what Guillén assimilated from Valéry presuppose the influence of the latter's prose works.[48] Furthermore, Ciplijauskaité has noted astutely: 'Si Guillén trata de incluir al mundo entero en su mundo poético, Valéry divide el suyo en facetas distintas, y examinar sólo una de ellas significaría enfocarlo de manera muy parcial' (293). And yet her analysis of the essays, like Zardoya's, has yielded somewhat negative results. Ironically, it is possible that the systematic and comprehensive balance of their approach is to blame. Since at a high literary level borrowing tends to be unpredictably eclectic rather than methodical, it is surely unwise to expect an indebted text to mirror only the most representative characteristics of a source. Therefore, in considering how the Spanish poet reacted to Valéry's prose[49] the aim here will be to simply let the inner pattern of the evidence emerge.

One of Paul Valéry's most important theoretical writings, the <u>Introduction à la Méthode de Léonard de Vinci</u>, dating partly from 1894 but reissued somewhat amplified in 1919,[50] depicts the archetypal creative intelligence, exemplified by Leonardo, thus:

> Et lui se devait considérer comme un modèle de bel
> animal pensant, absolument souple et délié; doué de
> plusieurs modes de mouvement; sachant, sous la
> moindre intention du cavalier, sans défenses et sans
> retards, passer d'une allure à une autre. Esprit de
> finesse, esprit de géométrie, on les épouse, on les
> abandonne, comme fait le cheval accompli ses
> rythmes successifs...
> [...] Léonard, de recherche en recherche, se fait
> très simplement toujours plus admirable écuyer de
> sa propre nature.                                    (I 1210-2)

Just as the rider must direct and channel the turbulent vitality of his horse, so too the inventive mind should control and discipline its own creative energies. In 1924 Guillén published two versions of a <u>décima</u> entitled 'Estatua ecuestre' (No.57).[51] When it was revised, prior to its inclusion in <u>Cántico</u> (1928), a significant change occurred. What had previously been a third-person singular description had shifted into the first-person:

> Permanece el trote aquí,
> Entre su arranque y mi mano:
> Bien ceñida queda así
> Su intención de ser lejano.
> Porque voy en un corcel

A la maravilla fiel:
Inmóvil con todo brío.
¡Y a fuerza de cuánta calma
Tengo en bronce toda el alma,
Clara en el cielo del frío!

Consequently the text now ressembled much more closely an indirect
definition of his own poetry ('Inmóvil con todo brío'). Like Leonardo
he bridles his impetuous imagination to achieve a result that is both
durable and lucid (11.9-10). This echo of Valéry clarifies the final
stanza of another Cántico poem, 'El otoño: isla' (No.21), reworked
in 1928 from material first used in a longer composition six years
earlier. Here the parallel between the effects of Autumn, and the
vibrant, stripped-down quality of Guillén's own verse is obvious enough:

¡Amor a la línea!
La vid se desnuda
De una vestidura
Demasiado rica. [...]

Estilo en la dicha,
Sapiencia en el pasmo [...]

Y todo el espacio,
Tan continuo, vibra.  (11. 5-8, 13-14, 27-28).

However, the ascetic, autumnal overtones culminate rather unexpectedly
in an image of dynamic vigour:

—¡Pronto, pronto, ensilla
Mi mejor caballo!
¡El camino es ancho
Para mi porfía!  (11. 33-36)

To interpret Guillén's steed as a symbol of his creative powers is both
to reaffirm this text's organic unity as an oblique arte poética, and
to sense another trace of the French author's Leonardo.
    Elsewhere in the same prose work Valéry also seems to anticipate
certain early Cántico poems when he considers how this contained verve
should be applied to the understanding of objective reality. Accurate
observation of physical phenomena, an initial stage in this empirical
process, is, he claims, mostly thwarted by the tendency of language
towards abstraction:

La plupart des gens y voient par l'intellect bien plus
souvent que par les yeux. Au lieu d'espaces colorés,.
ils prennent connaissance de concepts. Une forme
cubique, blanchâtre, en hauteur, et trouée de reflets
de vitres est immédiatement une maison pour eux:  la
Maison! Idée complexe, accord de qualités abstraites.  (I 1165).

Two points are worth noting here. The significance of the material
world as a focus of attention is acknowledged, and the importance of
analysing exactly what we see is stressed. It is as if, in the first
instance, the reliability with which our eyes register the concrete
world depends on slowing down (in other words magnifying) the act of
perception itself, and so prolonging the transition from percept to
concept, the better to behold the external environment on its own
terms. One might deduce from the instance given that a technique of

delayed verbal recognition could restore the freshness of visual
experience advocated by Valéry. Some pre-Civil War poems by Guillén
appear to be based on the same principle. Cántico (No.108) was first
published, untitled, in 1927 by the literary magazine Litoral (No.1
dated November 1926), as follows:

> Blancos, rosas... Azules casi en veta,
> Retraídos, mentales.
> Puntos de luz dirigen sus señales
> Hacia ninguna meta.
>
> Pero el color, infiel a la penumbra,
> Se consolida en masa.
> Yacente en el verano de la casa,
> Una forma se alumbra.
>
> Claridad aguzada entre perfiles
> De tan puros tranquilos,
> Que cortan y aniquilan con sus filos
> Las confusiones viles.
>
> Desnuda está la carne. Su evidencia
> Se resuelve en reposo.
> Cabal monotonía: prodigioso
> Colmo de la presencia.
>
> ¡Plenitud inmediata, sin ambiente,
> Del cuerpo femenino!
> Ningún primor: ni voz ni flor. ¿Destino?
> ¡Oh absoluto presente!

A haze of colour and form is gradually focussed for virtually the entire
length of the text (11.1-18) into a definible object, namely, the nude
body of a reclining woman. In this slowly unfolding act of perception,
Guillén reveals, with almost clinical precision, his sensitivity to
the material realm.[52]

Similarly heightened responses to concrete reality, extending even
to some of its most elusive features, are evident moreover in Leonardo's
sketches, which can render visible 'l'épaisseur du cristal vague de
l'espace' (I 1177), an achievement equalled by the author of Cántico
in such poems as 'Presencia del aire' (No.5), 'El horizonte' (No.98),
and 'Los aires' (No.120). Indeed, where physical awareness is concerned,
there is nothing in Leonardo's experience of his environment too trivial
or too disquieting to escape the watchful eye and reflective consciousness
of his creative mind. Hence Valéry's remark: 'Il guette la chute
légère du pied que se pose, le squelette silencieux dans les chairs'
(I 1179). Cántico encompasses a range of reactions reminiscent of the
phrase just quoted but Guillén uses these sensations in his own individual way to plumb extremes of the human condition. For him: '[...]
el pie caminante siente / La integridad del planeta' ('Perfección'
No.82, 11.9-10, begun 1926 and published 1934), implies a confidence in
life which is counterbalanced by sober though comparably palpable
intimations of mortality in 'La cabeza' (No.74 1923-1926):

> ¡Tierno canto de la frente,
> Batido por tanta onda!
> La palma presume monda
> La calavera inminente.
> Si la tez dice que miente
> El tacto en ese barrunto,

> Porque a un gran primor en punto
> —Ápice de su matiz—
> Conduce la piel feliz,
> Palpa el hueso ya difunto.

Nevertheless in their shared susceptibility to the two images indicated
(the footstep, and the skeleton concealed in the flesh), both Valéry's
Leonardo and the Spanish poet adhere to keen and direct observation as
a key to comprehending the structure of the concrete world.

However, as is plain from another prose work, Eupalinos ou l'architecte (1921),[53] Valéry, speaking through the character Phèdre, believed
that, generally, the full cognitive potential of sense perceptions was
not properly appreciated:

> Ce corps est un instrument admirable, dont je m'assure
> que les vivants, qui l'ont tous à leur service, n'usent
> pas dans sa plénitude [...] ils ignorent quelles
> liaisons universelles ils contiennent, et de quelle
> substance prodigieuse ils sont faits.  Par elle cependant
> ils participent de ce qu'ils voient et de ce qu'ils
> touchent:  ils sont pierres, ils sont arbres; ils
> échangent des contacts et des souffles avec la matière
> qui les englobe.  Ils touchent, ils sont touchés [...];
> et quand ils tombent dans la rêverie, ou dans le sommeil
> indéfini, ils reproduisent la nature des eaux, ils se
> font sables et nuées ...  Dans d'autres occasions ils
> accumulent et projettent la foudre! ...[54]
> [...] Instrument vivant de la vie, vous êtes à chacun
> de nous l'unique objet qui se compare à l'univers.  La
> sphère tout entière vous a toujours pour centre; ô chose
> réciproque de l'attention de tout le ciel étoilé!  Vous
> êtes bien la mesure du monde, dont mon âme ne me présente
> que le dehors.   (II 98-99)

Offering a new slant on the Classical notion of the microcosm and the
macrocosm, Phèdre's eulogy postulates a universal network of material
and metaphorical relationships converging on the human body.  There is
the suggestion that Man is an integral part of the cosmos primarily by
virtue of his physical nature:  'ils ignorent [...] de quelle substance
prodigieuse ils sont faits.  Par elle cependant ils participent de ce
qu'ils voient et de ce qu'ils touchent'.  And this in turn confers on
the individual the capacity to evaluate and define external reality:
'Ce corps est un instrument admirable [...]  Vous êtes bien la mesure
du monde'.

Undoubtedly, for the student of Valéry's influence on Guillén, the
most striking detail in the passage reproduced above is the phrase:
'La sphère tout entière vous a toujours pour centre'.  The French writer
enlarges on it very effectively in his essay 'Au sujet d'Eurêka' (1921):[55]

> Une première forme d'univers m'est offerte par l'ensemble
> des choses que je vois.  Mes yeux entraînent ma vision de
> place en place, et trouvent des affections de toute part.
> Ma vision excite la mobilité de mes yeux à l'agrandir, à
> l'élargir, à la creuser sans cesse.  Il n'est pas de
> mouvement de ces yeux qui rencontre une région d'invisibilité;
> il n'en est point qui n'engendre des effets colorés; et par
> le groupe de ces mouvements qui s'enchaînent entre eux, qui
> se prolongent, qui s'absorbent ou se correspondent l'un

l'autre, je suis comme enfermé dans ma propriété de
percevoir. Toute la diversité de mes vues se compose
dans l'unité de ma conscience motrice.
    J'acquiers l'impression générale et constante d'une
sphère de simultanéité qui est attachée à ma présence.
Elle se transporte avec moi, son contenu est indéfini-
ment variable, mais elle conserve sa plénitude par
toutes les substitutions qu'elle peut subir. Si je me
déplace, ou si les corps qui m'environnent se modifient,
l'unité de ma représentation totale, la propriété qu'elle
possède de m'enclore, n'en est pas altérée. J'ai beau
me fuir, m'agiter de toute manière, je suis toujours
enveloppé de tous les <u>mouvements-voyants</u> de mon corps,
qui se transforment les uns dans les autres et me
reconduisent invinciblement à la même situation centrale.
    Je vois donc un <u>tout</u>. Je dis que c'est un Tout, car il
épuise en quelque sorte ma capacité de voir. Je ne puis
rien voir que dans cette forme d'un seul tenant, et dans
cette juxtaposition qui m'environne. Toutes mes autres
sensations se réfèrent à quelque lieu de cette enceinte,
dont le centre pense et se parle. (I 864-5)[56]

The orb enclosing the speaker is, therefore, the literal boundary of
his field of vision. It constitutes an actual area of visibility. In
other words, through a process of sensory perception that Valéry calls
'la connaissance par les yeux' (I 865), a definition of his physical
surroundings takes shape. Moreover, at the same time, the curving
circumferences of this encircling universe encapsulate the observer's
awareness, forming, so to speak, a 'sphere' of consciousness, as he
explains in the <u>Introduction à la Méthode de Léonard de Vinci</u>:

    L'observateur est pris dans une sphère que ne se brise
    jamais; où il y a des différences qui seront les mouve-
    ments et les objets, et dont la surface se conserve close,
    bien que toutes les portions s'en renouvellent et s'y
    déplacent. L'observateur n'est d'abord que la condition
    de cet espace fini: à chaque instant il est cet espace
    fini. Nul souvenir, aucun pouvoir ne le trouble tant qu'il
    s'égale à ce qu'il regarde. (I 1167)

    Many of the overtones which the 'sphere of simultaneity' carries
for Valéry the prose theorist (its perceptual origins, its convergence
on the observer, its structuring of consciousness, its associations of
plenitude, totality, and harmony) are also characteristic of the early
<u>Cántico</u>, where situations circumscribed by curves and circles, or
encompassed within concave limits, are frequently portrayed. Guillén
apparently finds the tendency to describe things as being <u>around</u> him
virtually irresistible: 'Se ofrece, se extiende, / Cunde en torno el
día / Tangible.' (No.7 'Tiempo perdido en la orilla' 1932 11.1-3).[57]
Aspects of Nature supply the concrete basis for this visual phenomenon,
whether it be the sweep of the surrounding landscape: 'Valles / Rondan
por los tejados.' (No.41 'Temprano cristal' 1931 11.15-16);[58] the ring
of the horizon: 'Horizontes en círculo / Se abren.' (No.119 'Meseta'
1927 11.13-14); birds wheeling in flight: '¡Oh altura envolvente! /
Rondan los vencejos' (No.18 'Relieves' 1927-28 version 11.17-18);[59] or
the curvature of a dome-shaped sky:

```
                Queda curvo el firmamento,
                Compacto azul, sobre el día.
                Es el redondeamiento
                Del esplendor:  mediodía.
                Todo es cúpula.
                (No.82 'Perfección' 1926-34 11.1-5)60
```

Like the French writer, Guillén confirms that the impression of
rotundity created by the heavens marks the outward limits of his power
of sight:

```
                Con misterio acaban
                En filos de cima,
                Sujeta a la línea
                Fiel a la mirada,

                Los claros, amables
                Muros de un misterio,
                Invisible dentro
                Del bloque del aire.
                (No.19 'Perfección del círculo' 1926 11.1-8)
```

But the observer whose gaze embraces his environment, inescapably
becomes, as a corollary, the focal point of this sphere of perceived
reality:

```
                ¿Dónde extraviarse, dónde?
                Mi centro es este punto:
                Cualquiera.  ¡Tan plenario
                Siempre me aguarda el mundo!
                (No.2 'Más allá' 1935 11.173-176)
```

It is hard not to recall here the field of vision that Valéry depicts
('elle conserve sa plénitude par toutes les substitutions qu'elle peut
subir' I 865), one to which he also is inextricably bound ('J'ai beau
me fuir, m'agiter de toute manière, je suis toujours enveloppé de tous
les mouvements-voyants de mon corps, qui se transforment les uns dans
les autres et me reconduisent invinciblement à la même situation
centrale' (ibid.). Interestingly, experience of convergence for the
author of Cántico extends to less cosmically grandiose and more domestic
contexts:  'Hacia mi compañía / La habitación converge. / ¡Qué de
objetos!' (No.2 'Más allá' 1935 11.89-91).61  Of course, neither Valéry
nor Guillén considers the seeing eye to be simply an impassive instrument registering sense-data.  According to a previously cited passage
from the essay on Leonardo:  'L'observateur n'est d'abord que la
condition de cet espace fini:  à chaque instant il est cet espace fini'.
If he is synonymous with his sphere of perception then it presumably
is the receptacle or mould that defines the state of his consciousness.
Hence perhaps the fact that in Cántico roundness itself acquires human
connotations:  'el día al fin logra / Rotundidad humana' (No.2 'Más
allá' 1935 11.161-162).  Personal moods and states of mind are delineated
in circular or spherical terms:  '¡Simultáneos / Apremios me conducen /
Por círculos de rapto!', 'Un encanto es un orbe. / Obsesión repentina /
Se centra, se recoge' (No. 27 'Salvación de la primavera' 1932 11.74-76,
90-92).62  So too are individual moments of heightened awareness:
'¡Redondo Ahora!' (No.83 'Ahora' 1926 1.2), 'Rodea el tiempo' (No.2
'Más allá' 1935 1.6).  The lines just quoted from the Introduction à
la Méthode de Léonard de Vinci continue:  'Nul souvenir, aucun pouvoir
ne le trouble tant qu'il s'égale à ce qu'il regarde'.  Nowhere is this

subtle fusion between perception and consciousness, with its concomitant aura of wholeness and fulfilment, more effectively demonstrated than in 'Las doce en el reloj' (No.118, 1935) in which the characteristic image of the circle is obliquely suggested, partly by a hint of surrounding panoramic landscape, and partly by the circuit of the clock-face completed at noon:

> Dije: ¡Todo ya pleno!
> Un álamo vibró.
> Las hojas plateadas
> Sonaron con amor.
> Los verdes eran grises,
> El amor era sol.
> Entonces, mediodía,
> Un pájaro sumió
> Su cantar en el viento
> Con tal adoración
> Que se sintió cantada
> Bajo el viento la flor
> Crecida entre las mieses,
> Más altas. Era yo,
> Centro en aquel instante
> De tanto alrededor,
> Quien lo veía todo
> Completo para un dios.
> Dije: Todo completo.
> ¡Las doce en el reloj![63]

'Las doce en el reloj' sketches the situation of encirclement by a fluent use of impressionistic understatement that shows just how far Guillén has transcended Valéry's 'sphère de simultanéité'.

A final aspect of the French writer's epistemological theories, and possibly the most important one, remains to be examined. It is summed up towards the end of 'Au sujet d'Eurêka' as follows: having successfully employed sense-perceptions to define its own consciousness, how can the creative mind then proceed to formulate the underlying structure of the physical universe in an objectively valid way? Or, to pose the question in his own words: 'Comment passer de l'univers restreint et instantané à l'univers complet et absolu?' (I 866). There is a potential solution in the relationship between Leonardo's speculative Méthode, and the sphere, circle and curve whose intricate function now requires further analysis.

Foreshadowing modern scientific technique, Leonardo's hypotheses translate into visual terms natural processes or cosmic relationships whose existence can be inferred from physical observation but which remain invisible. Put at its simplest, this 'psychic experimentation' (I 1193), as Valéry calls it, involves 'l'émission d'une image, d'une relation mentale concrète entre des phénomènes' (ibid.). Guillén's interest in the mechanics of the universe is hinted at in a 1925-26 draft of the then untitled poem No.23 from Cántico, where 11.19-20 refer to 'La esfera, / Tan armilar'.[64] The Spanish poet's recourse to the geometrically interrelated images of the curve, circle, and sphere is, in some respects, symptomatic of his desire to construct such a model in a more animated version. Thus No.2 'Más allá' 1932-35 11.105-112, for instance, evokes, hidden in the world of matter, energies whose presence is manifested in the curved handle[65] of an unidentified object:

                    Material jubiloso
                    Convierte en superficie
                    Manifiesta a sus átomos
                    Tristes, siempre invisibles.

                    Y por un filo escueto,
                    O al amor de una curva
                    De asa, la energía
                    De plenitud actúa.

It is as if the normally unseen cosmic flow had suddenly revealed its
characteristic form. No.27 'Salvación de la primavera' 1932 11.105-108
communicates a comparable impression in a more abstract way:

                    La plenitud en punto
                    De la tan ofrecida
                    Naturaleza salva
                    Su comba de armonía.

Elsewhere the circle also is used to represent the almost electrically-
charged forces of Nature conducted to Man by physical contact: '¡Mis
pies / Sienten la Tierra en una ráfaga / De redondez!' (No.111 'Viento
saltado' 1932 11.26-28). With a shock of recognition, so to speak, he
intuits a broad organic symmetry underlying tangible reality. As for
the sphere, in No.124 'Redondez' 1926-33 11.1-6, it shapes a sky that
radiates cosmic energy:

                    Restituido a su altura
                    Más cóncava, más unida,
                    Sin conversiones de nubes
                    Ni flotación de calina,
                    El firmamento derrama,
                    Ya invasor, una energía.[66]

Nor should another fundamental element in Guillén's geometrical vocabulary[67]
be forgotten, namely, the straight line, with its connotations of trenchant precision:

                    Resbala en su riel
                    La recta. Corre, corre,
                    Corre a su conclusión. [...]

                    Por una red de rumbos,
                    Clarísimos de tarde,
                    Van exactas delicias.

                    Y a los rayos del sol,
                    Evidentes, se ciñe
                    La ciudad esencial.
                    (No.29 'Ciudad de los estíos' 1928 11.7-9, 16-22).[68]

Again the effect is one of an external dynamic power channelled along
pre-existing paths. Furthermore, these rectilinear shafts of light,
traced in the mind's eye, supply the pattern through which the observer
can mentally grasp the urban panorama ('se ciñe / La ciudad') and make
sense of it. There is a parallel here with a passage where the French
author describes an identical interpretation of the sun's rays by
Leonardo:

'L'air, dit-il, est rempli d'infinies lignes droites et
rayonnantes, entrecroisées et tissues sans que l'une emprunte
jamais le parcours d'une autre, et elles représentent pour
chaque objet la vraie FORME de leur raison, (de leur expli-
cation).' [...] Cette phrase paraît contenir le premier
germe de la théorie des ondulations lumineuses [...]
Elle donne l'image du squelette d'un système d'ondes dont
toutes ces lignes seraient les directions de propagation.
(I 1192-1193).

In the nineteenth century Faraday also cultivated 'le prolongement, par
son imagination, des phénomènes observés' (I 1194) thus successfully
defining some of the fundamental laws of physics:

Lui aussi voyait des systèmes de lignes unissant tous les
corps, remplissant tout l'espace, pour expliquer les
phénomènes électriques et même la gravitation; ces lignes
de force, nous les apprécions ici comme celles de la moindre
résistance de compréhension! (I 1194-1195).

Valéry coins the expression logique imaginative (I 1194) to denote the
charting of such latent lines of force.[69] It is clear that the early
Cántico contains geometrical allusions that serve the same purpose. In
addition to examples already outlined, No.114 'Playa (Niños)' 1927-1928
visualises a process by which the beams of a 'sol rectilíneo' (1.8) link
children's outstretched hands to sea shells lying on the shore: 'Los
rayos [...] / Se rinden a las manos / Más pequeñas. / ¡Oh vínculos /
Rubios! Y conchas, conchas. / ¡Accorde, cierre, círculo!' (11.9, 17-20).
With the circuit's completion comes the realisation of a universal network of interdependency like that delineated in No.100 'La Florida'
1928 11.19-24:

(Alrededor - haz de vivaces
Vínculos — vibran los enlaces
En las nervaduras del orbe,
Tan envolventes. ¡Cuántos nudos
Activos, aún más agudos
Dentro de quien tanto se absorbe!).

The principle of logique imaginative might therefore be said to have
facilitated Guillén's explicit depiction of an integrated cosmos,[70]
and to have rendered that concept more accessible to the reader. Indeed
it inevitably colours and enriches our reaction to the whole system of
geometrical references in Cántico (1936).
    In view of the evidence sifted above, the very least that can be
said is that Valéry's essays had as much impact on Guillén as the poems.
What is really extraordinary, though, is the fact that the prose-
influence just examined can be traced back to as few as three texts, all
of which appeared between 1919 and 1921. Furthermore the effects of
these seem to have been fairly durable since the examples quoted divide
more or less evenly between 1919-28 and 1929-36. It would probably be
true to say that they last because the author of the Spanish collection
adapts them to his own needs (as happens with the images of domestic
concentricity quoted earlier). A particularly striking instance of
Guillén breathing new life into borrowed material is the tremendous
fruitfulness for his poetry of the geometrical images proposed by the
French writer, a phenomenon all the more surprising because the author
of La Jeune Parque and Charmes made no attempt to exploit their

expressive capacity in his own verse. Hence the paradox that _Cántico's_
debt to the begetter of _Charmes_ is precisely one of the elements that
most separates the two works. Perhaps the last word here is best left
to Valéry:

> Quand un ouvrage, ou toute une oeuvre, agit sur quelqu'un,
> non par toutes ses qualités, mais par certaine ou certaines
> d'entre elles, c'est alors que l'influence prend ses valeurs
> les plus remarquables. Le développement séparé d'une
> qualité de l'un par toute la puissance de l'autre manque
> rarement d'engendrer des effets d'extrême originalité.
> (I 635)


## APPENDIX A

Paul Valéry and Spanish Periodicals 1918-1936

(*)   Also quoted in Blanch _La Poesía Pura Española_ (op.cit.). Some
      errors of pagination, etc. have been corrected.
 *    References contained in Blanch but unknown to me. They are
      included for the sake of completeness.
All the remaining entries plus those marked (*) have been consulted in
the original periodicals.

'La Novísima Poesía: Antología Lírica' - R(afael). C(ansinos)-
A(ssens). tr. 'Cantique des colonnes' omitting the first three
stanzas. _Cervantes,_ (May 1919), 93-95.

(*)   Andrés Sobejano tr. 'Las granadas' and 'Los pasos'. _La Verdad_
      'Suplemento Literario', 10 (16th March 1924).

(*)   'Paul Valéry en Madrid' - reprints in original French, letter from
      Valéry to Ortega expressing gratitude for the warm welcome on
      his recent visit to Madrid. _Revista de Occidente,_ (May 1924),
      259-260.

 *    'Paul Valéry en Madrid'. _Heraldo de Madrid,_ (17th May 1924).

 *    article on Valéry's visit to Barcelona. _La Revista,_ 205-210
      (April-June 1924).

(*)   'Paul Valéry y su obra' - anon. art. originally printed on the
      invitations to V's Residencia de Estudiantes lecture. _La Verdad_
      'Suplemento Literario', 22 (8th June 1924).

José Bergamín 'La supervivencia de Paul Valéry'. _La Verdad_
'Suplemento Literario', 22 (8th June 1924).

(*)   'Baudelaire y su descendencia' ['Situation de Baudelaire'] - anon.
      tr. of Valéry's French lecture given at the Residencia de
      Estudiantes to the 'Sociedad de Cursos y Conferencias de Madrid'
      17th May 1924. _Revista de Occidente,_ (June 1924), 261-290.

'Paul Valéry' - a portrait by E. Bécat accompanies a short introduction to Valéry's work by C.S., inspired by V's recent visit
to Catalonia. D'Ací d'Allà, 78 (June 1924), 427.

Valéry's recent visit to Catalonia prompts an untitled and
anon. full-page art. discussing his work vis-à-vis that of
Mallarmé. Revista de Catalunya, 1 (July 1924), 82-83.

Antonio Marichalar 'Memoria de Paul Valéry'. Alfar, 42 (August
1924), 3.

'Una Europa' - J.P. discusses Valéry's essay 'Caractères de
l'Esprit Européen' published in Revue Universelle. Revista
de Catalunya, 2 (August 1924), 201-204.

(*)  Gerardo Diego 'Retórica y poesía' - thoughts stimulated by
Valéry's Variété. Revista de Occidente, VI (1924), 280-286.

'Paul Valéry traduit a l'anglès' - pub. of English tr. of 'Le
Serpent' (TLS Jan. 1925), prompts anon. reflections on V's
approach to poetry. Revista de Poesía, 1 (January 1925), 59.

'L'obscuritat' - anon. tr. of Valéry's comments (Revue
Universelle 19th August 1925) on 'La Jeune Parque'. Revista
de Poesía, 3-4 (May-July 1925), 184-185.

J.P. "Paul Valéry a Barcelona" - tr. fragment from F. Lefèvre
Entretiens avec M. Paul Valéry. La Publicitat, (6th Feb.
1926), 1.

anon. art. "El parlament de Paul Valéry" (International PEN
congress). La Publicitat, (16th May 1926), 2.

(*)  "Carta Inédita" - 'Los A. de S.' tr. a letter by Valéry that
had recently appeared in a special hommage issue of Le
Capitole dedicated to him. La Verdad 'Suplemento Literario',
55 (4th July 1926).

(*)  anon. tr. fragment of essay by Valéry "En torno a Verlaine"
["Passage de Verlaine"]. La Verdad 'Suplemento Literario',
59 (10th October 1926).

(*)  Fernando Vela "La Poesía Pura (Información de un debate
literario)". Revista de Occidente, (November 1926), 217-240.

(*)  Jorge Guillén "Carta a Fernando Vela". Verso y Prosa, 2
(February 1927), 2.

(*)  Valéry's poem 'Les Grenades" printed in French with two
successive Spanish versions in prose and verse by Jorge
Guillén. Verso y Prosa, 4 (April 1927).

(*)  tr. Valéry's essay "Notas sobre la grandeza y la decadencia
de Europa". Revista de Occidente, (April 1927), 1-14.

anon. tr. edited version "Del discurs de Paul Valéry a
l'Acadèmia Francesa" first instalment La Publicitat,
(1st July 1927), 4-5; second and final instalment La
Publicitat, (2nd July 1927), 5-6.

\*     S. de Madariaga "La recepción de Paul Valéry". <u>El Sol</u>, (3rd July 1927).

C.C. tr. "Discurs de recepció a l'Acadèmia Francesa de Paul Valéry". <u>Revista de Catalunya</u>, 37 (July 1927), 34-55.

A.R.i V. "L'obscuritat de Paul Valéry" - report on A. Bellessort's art. about Valéry in <u>Le Journal des Débats</u>. <u>Revista de Catalunya</u>, 37 (July 1927), 104-106.

anon. art. "Paul Valéry i 'les capelletes'". <u>Art Novell</u>, 43 (July 1927), 16.

(\*)   Benjamín Jarnés "Los pies, el pie" - art. on Valéry centred on his recent election to the Académie Française. <u>Revista de Occidente</u>, (August 1927), 239-244.

anon. art. "El pensament de Paul Valéry", <u>D'Ací i d'Allà</u>, 116 (August 1927), 241.

Alfons Maseras tr. Valéry's poem "Narcís parla" (complete except for lines 14-17). <u>D'Ací i d'Allà</u>, 120 (December 1927), 385.

anon. tr. of two fragments from Valéry's dialogue "Eupalinos o el Arquitecto". <u>La Gaceta Literaria</u>, 32 (15th April 1928).

anon. tr. Valéry's essay "Stéphane Mallarmé". <u>La Nova Revista</u>, 18 (June 1928), 165-167.

Alfons Maseras tr. Valéry's poem "El vi perdut". <u>D'Ací i d'Allà</u>, 127 (July 1928), 264.

(\*)   A. Marichalar "Introducción al método de Monsieur Teste" - a discussion of Valéry's prose work <u>Monsieur Teste</u>. <u>Revista de Occidente</u>, (October 1928), 28-43.

anon. note "Paul Valéry comenta Poe". <u>L'Amic de les Arts</u>, 29 (31st October 1928), 224.

Tómas Garcés "Valéry - Maragall". <u>La Publicitat</u>, (25th December 1928), 6.

anon. art. "Paul Valéry discuteix de literatura, art i ciència". <u>D'Ací i d'Allà</u>, 133 (January 1929), 14; 34.

(\*)   J. Bergamín "Monóculo de Paul Valéry". <u>Litoral</u>, 8 (May 1929), 26-27.

(\*)   Jorge Guillén tr. "Le Cimetière Marin" - printed as a parallel text with French on the left- and Spanish on the right-hand page. <u>Revista de Occidente</u>, (June 1929), 340-353.

(\*)   (Fernando) V(ela). "Para acompañar a una traducción" - concise commentary on Valéry's "Le Cimetière Marin" prompted by Guillén's tr. of it. <u>Revista de Occidente</u>, (June 1929), 395-397.

A. de Falgairolle reviews Brémond's <u>Racine et Valéry</u>. <u>Mirador</u>, 109 (5th March 1931), 4.

anon. section of 'Varietats' entitled "La poesia francesa segons Paul Valéry" includes two paragraphs from <u>Regards sur le Monde Actuel</u>. <u>Mirador</u>, 133 (20th August 1931), 6.

Carles Soldevila "Davant una edició de les obres de Paul Valéry". <u>D'Ací i d'Allà</u>, 168 (December 1931), 458.

D.P. "Varietats" - three notes on Valéry: 'Traduccions de Valéry'; 'Valéry a Catalunya'; 'De Valéry com a recepta' (which contains a Catalan tr. of "Les Grenades"). <u>Mirador</u>, 155 (21st January 1932), 6.

anon. tr. of fragment of Valéry's essay "A propósito del 'Cementerio Marino'". <u>Hoja Literaria</u>, (April 1933), 8.

\* M. Manent "Conversa amb Paul Valéry". <u>La Veu de Catalunya</u>, (9th May 1933), 16.

(\*) F(élix). R(os). art. on Valéry entitled "Seminario de poesía pura" contains a tr. of "Le Sylphe". <u>Cruz y Raya</u>, 4 (July 1933), 131-134.

anon. tr. Valéry's political views "Els intel·lectuals i Europa". <u>Mirador</u>, 357 (19th December 1935), 3.

\* A. de Falgairolle "Objeciones a P. Valéry". <u>ABC</u> (Madrid), (16th June 1936).

(\*) J. Teixidor "Paul Valéry" - discusses at length Valéry's intro-duction to the <u>Anthologie des Poètes de la NRF</u>, and expresses reservations about his negative definition of 'poetry'. <u>Mirador</u>, 386 (16th July 1936), 6.


# APPENDIX B

Uncollected Early Texts by Jorge Guillén

Macrí reproduces some of these texts in footnotes. Bracketed page references to his <u>Obra poética de Jorge Guillén</u> accompanied by the letter OM will identify the relevant items.

(1) Poems and verse-fragments

⁺Antilógica', <u>España</u>, 271 (10th July 1920), 18 (OM 25).

'Colores de un solo arco', <u>España</u>, 277 (21st August 1920), 11. Also published with minor variants in <u>El Mundo</u> (Madrid), Suplemento Extraordinario (18th September 1920), 11.

<u>Poemas de circunstancias prosaicas</u>: 'Es una factura', <u>La Pluma</u>, 3 (August 1920), 136, (OM 86).

Encarnaciones: 'Igualdad'; 'Canto a la renunciación' (OM 95). [A substantially different version with the same title became number five of the sequence Airecillos in Alfar, 46 (January 1925), 9, (OM 81)]. La Pluma, 15 (August 1921), 110-111.

Poniente de bronce: I 'Bronce negro'; II 'Bronce verde', Indice, 2 (1921), 30-31.

Encarnaciones: 'Falso y cándido incesto';'Para consolarme en la espera', La Pluma, 24 (May 1922), 270-271.

'Aleluyas sentenciosas', La Pluma, 30 (November 1922), 346-347, (OM 166).

'Doctrinal de lebreles', España, 351 (6th January 1923), 8.

La sala pequeña: I (1) 'Don Luis', (OM 65); II 'La niña boba', España, 361 (17th March 1923), 5.

I 'Retumban por todos los cielos', (OM 63). Later published in a longer and rather different form with the title 'La Fe' as first poem in the sequence Airecillos in Alfar, 46 (January 1925), 9, (OM 63); II 'Cementerio entre la bruma', (OM 166); III 'Y se inició el asalto a la inmortalidad', (OM 63); IV 'El niño llora su atroz pena', (OM 166); V 'Las onzas del sol'; VIII '¡Oh sol en el porte del cisne!', (OM 64), La Pluma, 36 (May 1923), 360-362.

Epigramas: I 'Sin caer del corcel cual Saúl'; II '¡Cabrilleo! : alegría de la ola'; III 'Oso y coloso en coso', (OM 69). [This reappeared with some variants and the title 'Fábula deportiva' as third poem in the sequence Airecillos in Alfar, 46 (January 1925), 9, (OM 69)] España, 378 (14th July 1923), 11.

'No bien me atisbe Doña Ella'; 'Goza en las pendencias', España, 401 (22nd December 1923), 7.

'Me dormiré con los ojos', La Verdad 'Suplemento Literario', 12 (30th March 1924).

'Allá a la vuelta de una vez: un mero', (OM 64), Alfar, 42 (August 1924), 2.

Airecillos: 2 'La contradicción jerónima (Claroscuro)', (OM 66); 4 'La prudente amistad', (OM 73); 7 'El bailarín', Alfar, 46 (January 1925), 9.

'La importancia de la familia (Poema poco gongorino)', La Gaceta Literaria, 5 (1st March 1927), 2, (OM 138-139).


(2) Prose

Ventoleras: 'La mujer de viento en el viento', Indice, 3 (1921), 12-13 Reprinted by Díaz Plaja en El poema en prosa en España, (Barcelona 1956).

Cinco Florinatas :  'Demonios'; 'La fuente de Góngora'; 'Globos de risa';
'Galernas de equinoccio'; 'Dios se lamenta de que no puede viajar',
España, 354 (27th January 1923), 9-10.

Florinatas :  I 'Solo para pájaros', (OM 180); II 'Grandeza y decadencia
del Quiquiriquí', (OM 89); III 'Un despertador', (OM 83); IV '¡Milano,
milano!', (OM 85); V 'Margen de río en Julio'; VI 'Cuasi-apodo';
VII 'Ejercicios con la preposición "A"', España, 365 (14th April 1923),
10.  Reprinted by Díaz Plaja, op. cit.

'Aire-Aura', Revista de Occidente (October 1923), 1-8.

Ventolera :  I 'Opereta primaveral'; II 'Fuegos, noches', (OM 85); III
'Invitación al vals (Orgía romántica)'; IV 'Minerales', (OM 86);
V 'En casa', (OM 72,73); VI 'La espera colmada', (OM 96); VII
'Plazuela en su domingo', (OM 72), España, 405 (19-I-1924), 10-11.

'El paraguas en el viento', La Verdad 'Supl.Lit.', 57(Aug.1926), (OM 66).


(3)  Journalism

From 1921 to 1922 Guillén wrote a regular feature called 'Desde
París' for the Madrid newspaper La Libertad.  Some of these articles
are mentioned by Macrí on the pages referred to below:

'Falsa barbarie' (18-1-21), 125; 'El arte anónimo' (28-1-21), 61; 'Una
nación no se enamora nunca' (1-2-21), 68; 'El cañón de papel' (6-2-21),
71; 'Un buen epicúreo llega a Moscú' (22-2-21), 42, 59-60; 'Las repara-
ciones o El cuento de nunca acabar' (27-2-21), 68; 'Vencer no es ganar'
(8-3-21), 68; 'Los modernos presidentes de la Historia' (20-3-21), 70;
'¡Tío barbudo!' (29-3-21), 70; 'El Cementerio de la Estrella' (16-4-21),
68; 'El culto del Gran Hombre' (24-4-21), 67; 'Fresas' (30-4-21), 40;
'Museo de novedades' (7-5-21), 60; 'El desquite del Espíritu' (18-5-21),
62; 'Alegoría de la emoción ordenada' (28-5-21), 139; 'Flaubert y el
académico' (10-7-21), 58; 'Los superlativos patrióticos' (30-7-21), 69;
'El embajador estrecha los lazos' (3-8-21), 61, 71; 'Una tertulia de
Anatole France' (10-1-22), 60, 68; 'La muerte teatral de Molière'
(1-2-22), 26; 'Schnitzler en París' (14-2-22), 60; 'Un pintor nuevo'
(9-3-22), 59; 'Circunloquios.La retirada de Manuel Machado' (28-3-22),
138; 'Circunloquios. El libro blanco' (12-4-22), 138; 'Einstein en París'
(3-5-22), 62; 'Retrato de Einstein' (11-5-22), 59.

Other early articles, not mentioned by any critic, include:

'Desde París' (La Libertad): '1921' (6-1-21); 'Una jugada emocionante'
(23-1-21); 'París vale un Perú' (13-2-21); 'El revolucionario en el
banquillo' (17-3-21); 'París-Babilonia' (9-4-21); 'Negritos' (17-6-21);
'Más negritos' (1-7-21); 'La risa de Flaubert en su centenario' (6-7-21);
'La estación de las modestas ambiciones' (10-8-21); 'Circunloquios. La
poesía nueva' (12-10-21); 'Circunloquios. La Invitación a la soledad'
(25-10-21); 'La vuelta a París' (7-12-21); 'Parisien, parisino, parisiense'
(10-12-21); 'Una causa célebre' (25-12-21); 'El folletín de Landrú'
(29-12-21); 'Anatole France es Anatole Thibault' (18-1-22); 'Los post-
guerreros' (24-3-22); 'Alcestes en 1922' (6-4-22); 'El séptimo arte'
(19-5-22); 'Un "Cocu magnifique" en pequeño' (15-6-22).
'Circunloquios. El gorro, la pipa y la pluma de Flaubert' Indice 4
(1922) 15-17.
'El premio Nobel - Anatole France', España, 303 (14-1-22), 12.

For additional references to some of the texts in this appendix, see:

C.B. Morris, A Generation of Spanish Poets, (Cambridge 1969), 59, 97-101, 119, 132.

K.M. Sibbald, 'The Theme of darkness in Jorge Guillén's early poems and variants to "Cántico (1919-1928)"' in Studies in Modern Spanish Literature and Art presented to Helen F. Grant, (London 1972), 181-189.

K.M. Sibbald, 'Some early versions of the poems of "Cántico (1919-1928)": progress towards claridad'. (BHS, L 1973, 23-44).

A.P. Debicki, La poesía de Jorge Guillén (Madrid 1973), 197-227.

## N O T E S

1.  'Lettre sur Mallarmé' in the Bibliothèque de la Pléiade edition of Paul Valéry Oeuvres I, 634 (Paris 1968).

2.  Jorge Guillén, 'Sobre amistad y poesía', Insula 383, 12.

3.  The note was reprinted as 'Paul Valéry y su obra' in La Verdad 'Suplemento Literario' No.22 (8-6-24).

4.  For an account of hostility to Valéry in Spain see Antonio Blanch La Poesía Pura Española (Madrid 1976), 271-276.

5.  'Paul Valéry', D'Ací d'Allà, 78 (June 1924), 427.

6.  (Fernando) V(ela), 'Para acompañar a una traducción', Revista de Occidente, (June 1929), 396.

7.  This briefest of mentions appeared with a picture of Valéry in D'Ací i d'Allà, 147 (March 1930), 85. For a broader impression of Spanish interest in Valéry see Appendix A.

8.  Note Jorge Guillén's engaging evocation of their meetings in 'Valéry en el recuerdo', Algunos poemas: Paul Valéry (Barcelona 1972), 67-89.

9.  Blanch op. cit., 286.

10.  Jorge Guillén, 'Valéry en el recuerdo', op. cit., 67.

11.  The Spanish poet's discussions with Valéry represent a fundamental point of reference in clarifying the vexed question of poesía pura. See his 'Carta a Fernando Vela' reprinted, among many other places, in Gerardo Diego Poesía Española Contemporánea (Antología) (Madrid 1972, original edition 1932). Note especially phrases like: 'como me decía hace pocas semanas el propio Valéry' (326), and 'El mismo Valéry me lo repetía, una vez más, cierta mañana en la rue de Villejust ...' (327).

12. For an analysis of these translations within a more general comparison of both writers consult Concha Zardoya, 'Jorge Guillén y Paul Valéry' in Poesía Española del Siglo XX (Vol.2) (Madrid 1974), 168-219. As for the epigraphs, 'Cantique des colonnes' (ll.35-36) were used with Guillén's 'Ciudad de los estíos' (1928), while La Jeune Parque (l.370) was attached to 'Muerte a lo lejos' (1930-1935).

13. In addition to the studies by Blanch and Zardoya cited above, the bibliography includes at least three other indispensable contributions to the subject, namely: Claude Vigée, 'Jorge Guillén et les poètes symbolistes français' in Révolte et louanges (Paris 1962), 139-197; Biruté Ciplijauskaité, 'Jorge Guillén y Paul Valéry al despertar' Papeles de Son Armadans No.99, 1964, 267-294; and Oreste Macrí's monumental La obra poética de Jorge Guillén (Barcelona 1976). All of these are essential reading. For convenience, page references to the five basic critical works just listed will be given, where possible, in the body of the text. Hugo Friedrich, Estructura de la lírica moderna (Barcelona 1974) assumes Valéry's influence on the author of Cántico without attempting to explore the phenomenon in its own right.

14. 'Guillén's enthusiasm for Valéry, which he has made no attempt to conceal, has exposed him to the assaults of critics like A. Monterde, whose statement that "Valéry is the master par excellence of Guillén" signals the readiness he shares with others to interpret interest as influence.' C.B. Morris, A Generation of Spanish Poets 1920-36 (Cambridge 1969), 120.

15. As in these two instances: 'Jorge Guillén tradujo a Valéry y es indudable que admiró su poesía. De ahí a ver en Guillén a un discípulo de Valéry hay un paso insalvable, a pesar de lo que hayan podido decir los detractores de Jorge Guillén'. R. Xirau, 'Lectura a Cántico', first published in Cuadernos Americanos año XXI, vol. CXXI marzo-abril 1962, and reproduced in Jorge Guillén ed. Ciplijauskaité (Madrid 1975), 132. 'Recuérdese, a propósito de las relaciones entre Guillén y Valéry, la discusión sobre la 'poesía pura', hoy completamente sobre-pasada. Los desarrollos sucesivos y prodigiosos de Cántico están muy por encima de esa querella inútil. Pero en su época hizo mucho daño a la obra de Guillén y aún continúa alimentando ciertos prejuicios contra'. P. Darmangeat, Antonio Machado. Pedro Salinas. Jorge Guillén, (Madrid 1969), 297, footnote 44.

16. Even A. Blanch, the only critic since 1964 to broach this subject at any length, begins his consideration of features common to the work of Valéry and Guillén with the ominous remark: 'Perderíamos el tiempo buscando analogías en la sustancia poética de estos dos poetas', op. cit. 291.

17. Ciplijauskaité devotes three-and-a-half pages to listing affini-ties between Valéry and Guillén. Blanch's much more extensive study sets aside ten pages for the same purpose. It is harder to decide how much space is involved in Zardoya's case. An eight-page sub-section of her essay, entitled 'Teoría poética', reaches the following ambi-valent conclusion: 'Jorge Guillén, por su parte, aceptaría y repudiaría las fórmulas poéticas valeryanas', op. cit., 215. If this perplexing material were discounted, then the remaining positive data provided by Zardoya could be accommodated in less than two pages.

18. The biggest discrepancy in the proportion of positive to negative evidence can be found in Vigée's blatantly partisan analysis. In over fifty-eight pages of discussion, his grudgingly acknowledged examples of Valéry's impact, if added together, would fit comfortably on half a page.

19. Vigée, Ciplijauskaité, and to some extent Zardoya, taken together, present a broadly valid argument for the author of Cántico having matured into a rather different kind of poet from Valéry. But although this case has been persuasively made there still remains the problem of how the French writer's work affected Guillén during the Spaniard's formative years.

20. Critics have harped on the inadequacy of the case for influence as it is often set out: 'De nombreux critiques ont éffleuré la question. Ils l'ont fait, en général, de façon sommaire.' Vigée op. cit., 139; 'Es curioso notar, sin embargo, que todas las referencias son muy generales y nada más indican este caso sin analizarlo más detenidamente.' Ciplijauskaité op. cit. 267. This has not prevented the continuing formulation of assertions such as: 'También coinciden estos dos poetas en anotar unos temas dominantes: la luz, el aire, el horizonte, el mar, la playa, el cuerpo humano, el desnudo, la noche...'. Blanch op. cit., 298. Needless to say, examination of a subject as controversial as literary cross-fertilisation cannot afford to deal in thematic categories so vague as to be universal. It should also be firmly rooted in specific textual examples.

21. Usually, nothing more precise is forthcoming than: 'ciertas cualidades les aproximan entre sí, sobre todo inicialmente', Zardoya op. cit., 218, or 'Hay que empezar por afirmar una estrecha dependencia de Guillén con relación a Valéry, sobre todo en aquella primera época del poeta castellano', Blanch op. cit., 286.

22. Vigée's quotations take no account of the fact that Cántico was elaborated over a thirty-year period. His references are to the definitive 1950 edition. Similarly, all but two of the poems quoted by Ciplijauskaité were published twenty to thirty years after Valéry's impact.

23. Jorge Guillén: Cántico (1936) ed. J.M. Blecua (Barcelona 1970). For ease of reference, and unless otherwise stated, collected poems by Guillén will be identified in the body of the text by the number assigned to them in the Blecua edition. Where appropriate, dates of publication or composition will also be included. Account has been taken of the corrections to Blecua in K.M. Sibbald's review (BHS L 1973, 101-104). Many of the early versions have been consulted in the original.

24. For full details see Appendix B. Individual items will be identified in the body of the text by title and year of publication.

25. The tally is less than substantial: three uncollected verse-fragments (see Appendix B), and a six-line poem entitled 'La amistad, firme en los mares caóticos' (La Pluma No.5, October 1920), subsequently much revised before its incorporation into Cántico as 'Buque amigo' (No.86). Simultaneously, of course, Guillén was working on unpublished drafts. Blecua's edition indicates that 1919 saw the production of primitive versions of Nos. 13 and 87, while 1920 led to others (Nos. 30, 31, 36, 38). Furthermore, certain texts are described as having been begun

in 1919 (Nos. 48, 53), or in 1920 (Nos. 24, 29, 45, 47, 84). But all
thirteen examples just mentioned have one thing in common: their actual
content is hypothetical. With a single exception (No.31, dated 1921)
no text is forthcoming for any of them prior to 1922 (in most cases
1923 or 1924) and even then it is a revision whose relationship to the
first draft remains highly problematical. Consequently such compositions can only be labelled accurately by date of publication and they
therefore fall outside the chronological scope of the immediate discussion.

26. Valéry's verse and prose works were consulted in the two-volume
Bibliothèque de la Pléiade edition, Oeuvres (Paris 1968). All quotations are identified in the body of the text by volume and page-number.

27. Approximately two-thirds of the collection's twenty-one poems were
individually printed as follows: 'Aurore' (Mercure de France 16-X-1917);
'L'Insinuant' (Les Ecrits Nouveaux VI-1918); 'Au platane' (Les Trois Roses
VIII/IX-1918); 'Le Rameur' (Mercure de France 1-XII-1918); 'La Pythie'
(Les Ecrits Nouveaux II-1919); 'Cantique des colonnes' (Littérature
III-1919); 'Palme' (Nouvelle Revue Française 1-VI-1919); 'Fragments de
Narcisse' consisting mostly of about seventy assorted lines from section I
(La Revue de Paris 5-IX-1919); 'L'Abeille' (Nouvelle Revue Française
1-XII-1919); 'Ode secrète' (Littérature II-1920); 'Les Grenades' (Rythme
et Synthèse V-1920); 'Le Cimetière marin' (Nouvelle Revue Française
1-VI-1920); 'La Dormeuse' (L'Amour de l'Art VI-1920).

28. Guillén was eventually to consider Cántico a 'libro que negativamente
se define como un anti-Charmes'('Una generación' in Lenguaje y poesía
(Madrid 1972), 190 - originally published by Harvard U.P. as Language and
Poetry in 1962.) However, that appraisal should be treated with caution
not only because it was written with hindsight and in the light of the
definitive 1950 edition of Cántico, but also because it need not be
construed as a denial on indebtedness. Where influence is concerned,
contradiction and imitation may represent two sides of the same coin.
Even Vigée, who regards Valéry and the Spanish poet as antithetical
recognises in the very polarity between them a dialectical reaction of
one to the other (146, 151). Moreover, this negative aspect (whose importance as a general literary phenomenon is acknowledged by Valéry, I
634-635) coexists with positive elements suggesting that Guillén's attitude
to Charmes was ambivalent, combining rejection with attraction.

29. J. Guillén 'Valéry en el recuerdo' in Algunos poemas: Paul Valéry
(Barcelona 1972), 78.

30. For the seventy-five poems of Cántico (1928) the proportion of
irregular to regular is 18 : 57. This balance is maintained in the fifty
new poems of Cántico (1936), which divide 11 : 39. Significantly, of
the full one hundred and twenty-five poems in the 1936 edition only three
lack both metrical regularity and rhyme.

31. No less than thirty different permutations are recorded in Blecua's
introduction to Cántico (1936), 57-62.

32. Zardoya (205) rightly draws the essential distinction: whereas
Valéry is captivated by the process of creativity as such (hence,
perhaps, his restricted output); Guillén is more strongly attracted
towards the resultant poem (so his performance is relatively prolific).

33. At times Valéry's mode of composition involved starting with some structural receptacle (a metrical pattern, say) and gradually building up its content (I 1503). J. González Muela finds a reminiscence of the technique in a post-1936 Guillén verse-text 'Hacia el poema' (La Realidad y Jorge Guillén (Madrid 1962), 129), which adds a further dimension to the importance of form highlighted by Blanch. Nevertheless other formal parallels outlined in La Poesía Pura Española prove fairly polemical on closer inspection. For instance, the counterpoint between sentence-rhythm and metrical framework that Blanch detects in Charmes and Cántico (294) is surely of a different order in each case. Even at his most intense Valéry nearly always retains the sonorous smoothness that endows his verse with a sensuously feminine timbre. By contrast, Guillén's usual delivery, elliptically concise, invites dynamic and virile articulation. A second thorny issue raised by the same critic concerns an overlap of diction (297). It is fortunate that his presentation of the material in question deliberately falls short of assuming influence because the coincidences of idiom shared by Valéry and Guillén can be misleading. Typical of the terms he quotes are 'exacto' and 'puro', instantly recognisable as verbal mannerisms of the French writer. However only seven of the seventy-five poems in Cántico (1928) employ 'exacto' and its synonyms. In the fifty new poems of Cántico (1936) there are only four examples, making it a far less pervasive term than might be expected. Statistically, Guillén's recourse to 'puro' and its derivatives yields a higher but ultimately comparable result. Its frequency-rating of about one poem in seven, though surprisingly constant for both early editions of Cántico, is not exceptional when compared with J.R. Jiménez's usage in the Segunda Antolojía Poética 1898-1918 where 'puro' appears in seventy-eight out of five hundred and twenty-two poems (an average ratio of between 1 : 6 and 1 : 7). Valéry's practice differs dramatically, with a frequency at least three times as great: Album de vers anciens (16/21); La Jeune Parque (10); Charmes (11/21). Furthermore, in some of the longer poems 'pur' recurs repeatedly ('Fragments du Narcisse' 10 times; 'Ebauche d'un serpent' 8 times). Quantitative evidence therefore discourages the notion that Guillén and the French writer give the same weight to particular words. But, on a final affinity of diction, what Blanch (300) calls their 'conceptualización de lo sensible' (their peculiar blend of perceptual and abstract vocabulary) may afford a firmer basis for connecting Valéry and Cántico, as will emerge here in another context.

34. Exceptions to the norm are Nos. 11, 50, 101, 104 and 120. Blanch's point holds true as well for the five versions of 'Plaza mayor' given in the introduction to Cántico (1936), 14-23. Notwithstanding such confirmation some prudence is still advisable since the variant versions available certainly represent a mere fraction of those written. Thus although Blecua admits (128) that there were seven drafts of No.27 'Salvación de la primavera' only one is reproduced.

35. Probably the first was E. Díez Canedo in an article for La Nación dated 27-VI-1926: 'La décima, estrofa remozada por los poetas jóvenes - y Apolo sabe si no hay que atribuírselo, en parte al menos, a la décima francesa de Paul Valéry' (reprinted in Estudios de Poesía Española Contemporánea (México 1965), 221). See also C.B. Morris (21), Blanch (295), and especially R.G. Havard 'The early décimas of Jorge Guillén' (BHS XLVIII No.2 1971, 114-115). Valéry favours the (ababccdeed) form in fifty-three out of seventy-two instances (NOT sixty-three out of seventy-three as Havard inexplicably states, though, to be fair, he does get the general emphasis right). The importance of the décimas

in Cántico (1936) is underlined by their arrangement: numerically they make up virtually a quarter of the overall total (a proportion consistent in both the 1928 and 1936 editions) and are grouped together near the middle of the book in a block of espinelas (Nos.63-78) flanked symmetrically on either side by seven décimas francesas (Nos.56-62; 79-85).

36. The attempt to discover additional borrowed stanza-patterns has not produced convincing results. Darmangeat wonders (283) whether the quatrains in No.108 'Desnudo' were suggested by Valéry's 'Au platane' (I 113-115), but the rhyme-scheme is different (G : abba; V : abab) and so are the line-lengths (G : 11/7/11/7; V : 12/6/12/6). No.101 'El cisne' might have been a better candidate for, despite sharing the same line-lengths as 'Desnudo',at least its (abab) rhyme-scheme duplicates that of 'Au platane'.

37. See Valéry (I 609; 1270-1273; 1457), and Guillén 'Poesía pura es todo lo que permanece en el poema después de haber eliminado todo lo que no es poesía' ('Carta a Fernando Vela' in Diego op. cit. 327).

38. Other instances include: 'Aurore' (111-113); 'Poésie' (119-120); 'La Pythie' (130-136); 'Le Sylphe' (136-137); 'Le Rameur' (152-153). All page references are to Valéry, Oeuvres I (Paris 1968).

39. The Spanish poet's initial play on the double-meaning of 'copa' (1-3) may be a teasing allusion to the Symbolist and Modernista idea of the creative artist as high priest of a secular aesthetic cult. By subsequently equating 'obra' (4) with 'amanecer' (7), 'mediodía' (9), and 'sol' (13) all of which are key terms in Cántico, he leaves the reader in no doubt that this is an oblique meditation on the nature of his own verse. An overtly 'purista' note occurs in the closing lines where the sacrificial chalice of poetry (20) is described with proud defiance as 'cristal inútil' embodying the expressly non-utilitarian transparency of form associated with the work of Valéry in particular.

40. Relevant examples include: No.8 'El prólogo' (1924-1926); No.19 'Perfección del círculo' (1926); No.21 'El otoño: isla' (1922-1928); No.22 'Niño' (1924-1928); No.45 'Bosque y bosque' (1920-1926); No.56 'Ruiseñor' (1926); No.57 'Estatua ecuestre' (1924); No.62 'Aridez' (1924-1928); No.100 'La Florida' (1923-1928); No.101 'El cisne' (1923-1927); No.110 'Pino' (1923-1928).

41. It is possible that, on the strength of the 1922 version 'Playera', Macrí (95-96) may overestimate the erotic implications of 'Ciudad de los estíos'. From 1928, the poem's sexual connotations are limited to the opening six lines, being subsequently assimilated within an immense geometrical network whose vertex is the sun and whose radiant light offers the observer a clear-cut image of the city.

42. See also Macrí 23 and 43.

43. Here Man, through his thirst for knowledge, transcends Nothingness to attain Being. Vigée (151-152, 167-168) seriously distorts the overall significance of 'Ebauche d'un serpent'.

44. The two parallels given are new. A few distant echoes of 'Le Cimetière marin' in the early Cántico have also been suggested by critics. Darmangeat (258) finds the effect of 'Où tant de marbre est

tremblant sur tant d'ombres' (line 59) duplicated in No.28 'Primavera delgada' (1926-1928). Macrí (96) surmises that Valéry's reference to Zenon (line 121) inspired the allusion to Euclid in No.29 'Playera' (1920-1922 **version**). And he believes in addition that the 'Stable trésor' in line 13 of the French poem may account for Guillén's choice of the term 'tesoro' in No.27 'Salvación de la primavera' section VII line 180 (1931-1932).

45. For varying perspectives on this consult Vigée (167-168), Ciplijauskaité (270), and Havard 'The early décimas of J. Guillén'(op. cit.,118-119, 125).

46. Darmangeat (296) identifies the line in question as anticipating Guillén but doesn't connect it with any specific Cántico poem.

47. Guillén mentions Valéry's request in a letter to Juan Guerrero Ruiz dated 19-7-27. Blanch (289) reproduces the relevant fragment.

48. A case in point is the geometrical terminology, favoured by both, that critics touch on but rarely analyse: see Vigée (146, 149), Ciplijauskaité (268), Blanch (297). There are occasional literal references to circles and curves in Album de vers anciens and one of its poems, 'Profusion du soir' (I 86-89) actually uses the phrase 'la sphère vidée' (line 10). But that solitary instance is the nearest thing to a geometrical term in Valéry's poetry as a whole.

49. Among the prose works consulted were: Monsieur Teste (1919-1925); Eupalinos ou l'architecte (1921); L'Ame et la danse (1921); Variété (1924 and 1926); Cahier B 1910 (1924 and 1926); Variété II (1929). The publication dates for the two Variété volumes are deceptive. Many of the essays contained in both had been circulating singly in pamphlets or magazines from 1919 onwards. Thus most of the items in Variété II, for example, had appeared by 1926.

50. Also included in Variété (1924 and 1926).

51. According to O. Macrí: 'Se trata de una estatua ecuestre de Felipe III o IV en Madrid'. op. cit., 23, footnote 15.

52. Another good illustration of the same process is provided by No.11 'El manantial' in the 1928 version. A possible reversal of the technique can be observed in No.3 'Naturaleza viva' (1931). Here the object 'mesa', identified in line 1, hardly does justice to the complexity of its material in the natural state. Guillén recaptures that richness through a sense-impression of touch that triggers off a stream of evocations latent in the texture of the wood. It may be worth noting that Valéry's Eupalinos ou l'architecte includes a remarkably similar passage where Socrates states that if a workman: 'construit une table, l'assemblage de ce meuble est un arrangement bien moins complexe que celui de la texture des fibres du bois, et il rapproche grossièrement, dans un certain ordre étranger, les morceaux d'un grand arbre, lesquels s'étaient formés et développés dans d'autres rapports'. (II 124)

53. Also published with L'Ame et la danse, as one volume, in 1923 and twice in 1924.

54. It is curious to note that a number of the details in this para-graph are echoed in poems Guillén completed between 1926 and 1930:

'quelles liaisons universelles ils contiennent' (No.100 'La Florida'
11.19-24, 1928); 'ils sont pierres' (No.93 'Esos cerros' 11.7-10, 1930);
'ils sont arbres' (No.90 'Arbol del otoño' in the 1928 version); 'quand
ils tombent dans la rêverie, ou dans un sommeil indéfini, ils repro-
duisent la nature des eaux, ils se font sables et nuées...' (No.104
'La rendición al sueño' 11. 1, 14, 29 of the 1928 version); 'ils
accumulent et projettent la foudre!...' (No.4 'La tormenta' 1926).

55.  Reprinted in the Revue Européenne (1923), and subsequently
included in Variété (1924 and 1926).

56.  See also Arthur Terry 'Valéry:  escepticismo y poesía', El Urogallo
II, Nos. 11-12, 1971, 27-33.

57.  Other instances occur in No.35 'El distraído' (1931) line 4; No.42
'El desterrado' (1933) line 4; No.109 'El hondo sueño' (1935) lines 3-5.
The use of 'ceñir' (e.g. in Nos. 29, 46, 81, 85) is also relevant.

58.  The same is true of No.89 'Amplitud' (1930) especially 11.6-10.

59.  Another example of this is No.80 'Presencia de la luz' (1926)
11.1-3.

60.  The sky is also curved in No.23 'Esfera terrestre' (1926) 11.3-6;
No.100 'La Florida' (1928) 1.34 and No.124 'Redondez' (1926-1934)
11.1-5, 9-10.

61.  Further illustrations occur earlier in 'Más allá' 11.12-16, and in
No.27 'Salvación de la primavera' (1932) 11.9-11.  If Guillén's images
of encirclement do actually derive from Valéry then their extension
into the domestic context is a clear instance of the Spanish poet's
innovatory handling of source material.

62.  Occasional examples of convergence on an impersonal centre can be
found, and no doubt they are intended to convey a pervasive atmosphere
rather than consolidate an individual consciousness.  See No.16
'Elevación de la claridad' (1924); No.56 'El ruiseñor' (1926); No.82
'Perfección' (1926-1934) and No.87 'Gran silencio' (1919-1923).  This
tendency may well be typical only of an initial phase in Guillén's
development since all the poems concerned had been written by 1926, with
the significant exception of 'Perfección' which, unlike the others,
does contain a human presence, albeit a marginal one (11.8-10).

63.  A commentary on Cántico by its author glosses the poem in question
thus:  'El visible círculo de las horas simboliza el invisible círculo
total', El argumento de la obra (Barcelona 1969), 66.  For an interpretation of such concentric situations, based on Jung's archetypal
mandala symbol, consult R.G. Havard's unpublished Ph.D. thesis
entitled 'Image and theme in Jorge Guillén's Cántico' (University
College Cardiff 1968).

64.  Macrí (op. cit., 20, footnote 10) alludes cryptically to 'una
poesía titulada 'La esfera armilar' de 1926 (Murcia)' which is evidently
a separate treatment of the same theme.  Note too the three-poem
sequence-title 'Mecánica celeste' (Nos.32-34) first used in 1930.

65.  In R. Gullón and J.M. Blecua, La poesía de Jorge Guillén. Dos
ensayos (Zaragoza 1949), 311, the curious 'handle' reference is

traced to an article by Jorge Simmel entitled 'El asa' in the Revista de Occidente No.12 (1924), 294: 'La incorporación del asa a la unidad estética se acentúa otras veces de manera más orgánica; por ejemplo cuando las asas parecen surgir del cuerpo del vaso en tránsito ininterrumpido, formadas por las energías mismas que formaron el vaso'. (Also quoted in Macrí op. cit., 104, footnote 78.) What really matters here, though, is the ease with which this chronologically later borrowing ('Más allá' was not begun until 1932) fits into the broader cosmic pattern projected by Valéry since 1921 and before.

66.  There is a literal evocation of machinery in No.88 'Las máquinas' (1929-1935), which begins: 'Tanta armonía a punto de vibrar / Tiembla' 11.1-2. However, the reverberations generated in Cántico (1936) are almost invariably the expression of a much vaster mechanism. The collection's most disturbing model of Creation is probably the enigmatic gyre in No.87 'Gran silencio' (1919-1928):

> Gran silencio.  Se extiende a la redonda
> La infinitud de un absoluto raso.
> Una sima sin fin horada el centro.
> Y sin cesar girando cae, cae
> Ya invisible y zumbón, celeste Círculo.

No.21 'El otoño: isla' (1922-1928), with its emphasis on the quality of interconnectedness, paints a more reassuring picture:

> ¡Trabazón de brisas
> Entre cielo y álamo!
> Y todo el espacio,
> Tan continuo, vibra. (11.25-28)

In both cases Guillén could be said to act as an antenna receptive to the resonant hum of cosmic energy. These vibrations are a recurring motif as is obvious from No.2 'Más allá' (1932-1935) 1.26; No.15 'Los tres tiempos' (1933) 1.2; No.70 'Jardín que fue de don Pedro' (1934) 1.3; No.119 'Meseta' (1927) 11.4, 14-18 and No.125 'Ardor' (1926-1930) 11.4-5. Furthermore they are complemented by additional poems, too numerous to mention, that shimmer, ripple, seethe and throb to the infinitely subtle rhythms of a pulsating universe.

67.  Even the curves of meandering rivers (e.g. Nos. 28, 35, 56, 71) and similar apparently literal details cannot be excluded a priori here.  The evocation of clear-cut outlines by analogy with architectural plans or artistic draughtsmanship (Nos. 39, and 105 'El nocturno de Chartres') constitutes a related but possibly distinct category.

68.  Comparable instances are provided by No.8 'El prólogo'(1926) 11.1-8, and No.23 'Esfera terrestre' (1924-1928) 11.16-18.

69.  It is a technique fundamental to scientific research but, Valéry claims, equally applicable to artistic creativity generally (I 1196-1197).

70.  It can also be seen operating in No.2 'Más allá' (1932-1935) 11.96-100 and 179-183.

# Legendary material and its elaboration in an idiosyncratic Alphonsine chronicle

D.G. Pattison (University of Oxford)

Manuscript 1277 of the Biblioteca Nacional, Madrid, is an odd version of the chronicles generally called Alphonsine. It is in effect a composite text. Its first part, up to the end of the reign of Ordoño II, is one of four partial manuscripts of the versión regia of the Estoria de Espanna. This version has been carefully described by Diego Catalán, who gave it the name of Crónica fragmentaria.[1] The second part of MS. 1277, from the reign of Alfonso IV to the end of that of Bermudo III, is quite different, representing a late development of that branch of the chronicles known variously as the Vulgata and the Tercera Crónica General, a version of which formed the tercera parte of Ocampo's 1541 edition.[2] Our version, however, has features quite different from Ocampo's text and from other manuscripts of the Vulgata; in short, it is an expanded and interpolated version of this chronicle. It has variously been called the Versión Interpolada (or Refundición) de la Crónica General Vulgata or the Interpolación de la Tercera Crónica General;[3] Versión Interpolada will be used in this article as its short title.

The chronicle is best known for containing a version of the story of the Infantes de Lara which departs substantially from those of most other chronicles and which is generally held to be dependent on a later poetic refundición of the cantar de gesta. I shall return to this subject later; first, though, it should be pointed out that the Versión Interpolada contains a number of other stories based on legendary sources and that a comparison between it and other texts of the Vulgata tradition show that in every case MS. 1277 represents an expansion of its source. The primary purpose of this article is to summarise these expansions and to analyse their nature.

We may consider three relevant stories in addition to that of the Infantes de Lara: those of Fernán González, the Condesa Traidora and the Infant García. In all these cases the Vulgata tells a story similar to that found in the Primera Crónica General: more specifically in the versión vulgar of that chronicle, variants of which are given in Menéndez Pidal's edition. A comparison of these variants with the Vulgata text published by Ocampo shows that the versión vulgar and the Vulgata are not far apart at the points in question. Compared with these (with which we may group the Crónica de Veinte Reyes in the tercera parte) the Versión Interpolada, while similar in narrative structure, shows a constant tendency to amplify and expand. The story of Fernán González provides a good number of examples of this tendency.[4]

Some of the examples are of a specifically religious sententiousness. Although the whole of this story, being based on the clerical Poema de Fernán González, is apt to show this characteristic, the Versión Interpolada contains certain specific instances which go well beyond what is found in the poem or in any other chronicle. Consider, for instance, Fernán González's exhortation to his troops before the battle of Hacinas, when a vision of a fiery serpent has disturbed their sleep. The Vulgata contains a reference to Christ:

> bien deuedes vos saber quel diabro non vos puede
> fazer ningun mal, ca bien sabedes que le tollio
> el poder nuestro sennor Jesu Cristo; e acomende-
> monos a Dios quel fizo todas las cosas del mundo

que es muy poderoso de dar e de toller el bien o
el mal a quien el quisiere ... (Ocampo, fol. 246 r.).[5]

The _Versión Interpolada_ takes this up as follows:

> ... nuestro Redentor Jhesu Cristo, en quien es
> todo el poder; que nos conpro por su sangre peno-
> sa derramada en el arbol de la Santa Vera Cruz
> por salvar el umanal linaje. E pues el murio
> por nosotros, miremos nosotros por el, e pues
> el es poderoso en todas cosas, acomendemonos a el
> e el nos librara de todo poderio e tenpestad mala ...
> (fol. 180 r.-v.).

Sometimes the rhetoric is not so specifically religious. Consider,
for instance, Fernán González's speech to his vassals before the battle
of Lara, answering one of his knights who has advised prudence in the
face of overwhelming odds. In the _Vulgata_ the relevant passage begins:

> Amigos, quiero yo responder a Gonçalo Diaz e con-
> trallar todo quanto el ha dicho ... E dize lo pri-
> mero que escusassemos el lidiar. Mas como ome non
> se puede escusar de la muerte nin foyr della,
> deue morir lo mas honradamente que pudiere. E
> en ganar nos treguas de los moros por pecharles
> algo, de sennores que somos fazernos hemos siervos;
> e en vez de sacar Castiella de la pena e de la
> premia en que esta, doblarsela yamos, ca todos
> los donde nos venimos guardaron lealtad ... (Ocampo,
> fol. 241 r.).[6]

The _Versión Interpolada_ takes up the reference to honourable death and
expands as follows:

> ... ya sabemos que non tenemos cosa mas cierta que
> nos ha de venyr que es la muerte, por la qual
> avemos todos a pasar. E fagovos saber que ay dos
> maneras de muerte: una es trabajada e otra holgada.
> La muerte trabajada es dada a los Reyes, duques,
> condes, caballeros e Ricos omes que trabajan e
> mueren en el servicio de Dios e de la su santa fe,
> e por ganar onrra e pres; e sy muriere el su cuerpo,
> que no muera la su fama e buena nonbradia; e muerte
> folgada es dada a las mugeres, a los ganapanes e a
> los vellacos, que mueren por mal cabo; e por ende no
> quiero que les semejemos nos, mas quiero que digan las
> gentes "Murio el onbre mas no su nonbre"... (fol. 170 r.).

Compare also the Count's homily on the burial of the dead after the
battle of Hacinas. In the _Vulgata_ this is short:

> Amigos, non me paresçe que fazedes bien nin cordura
> en esto que vos queredes embargar de lleuar omes
> muertos a vuestros logares. Ca yo tengo que non
> ganades y nada; e demas non lo tengo por bien, e
> pornedes duelos e grandes roydos en la tierra con
> los muertos a los biuos. Porque los han de embargar
> ca por duelo que fagamos non podremos tornar ninguno
> dellos a nos ... (Ocampo, fol. 247 v.)[7]

while the <u>Versión Interpolada</u> expands:

> Mucho so maravyllado de vos, amygos, de lo que dezides
> como queredes leuar omes muertos a vuestras tierras,
> quanto mas que sabedes que los mas dellos ha tres dias
> que son muertos, e ya vedes quanto les pueden estar para
> andar camyno con ellos. ¿E no vos abasta asaz que tenemos
> aquy llanto e pesar en ver tal perdida, como ante nuestros
> ojos esta? e pues, ¿para que queredes levantar mas llanto
> por la tierra de lo que tenemos, que las nuevas abastan
> asaz que yran dellos a sus tierras? Ca ya sabedes que la
> tierra atan aparejada esta para comer e consumyr las
> carnes de los muertos aquy como en cabo del mundo, que
> tierra somos e en tierra avemos de ser bueltos ... (fol. 183 v.).

It is not only the characters' speech which is treated in this
way. Descriptions of events also become more complex and rhetorical.
When Fernán González is captured and imprisoned by the Leonese king,
the <u>Vulgata</u> comments:

> Quando los castellanos sopieron quel conde Ferran
> Gonçalez era preso, ouieron tan gran pesar e fi-
> zieron tamanno duelo por el como si fuera muerto
> delante dellos. La condesa otrosi quandol oyo
> fue tal como muerta (Ocampo, fol. 252 r.).[8]

The <u>Versión Interpolada</u> begins very similarly. After the Countess
faints, however, reactions become more extreme:

> ... cayo sin espiritu amortecida en tierra, que
> non avia omne que la viera que no ouiera muy gran
> duelo della; e las duennas e donzellas fijas dalgo
> del su palacio que con ella estavan començaron a
> fazer muy grandes llantos, asiendo de sus cabellos,
> Rompiendo sus hazes e pechos, que no tenyan figuras
> de mugeres: tanto que parecia que la cibdad toda se
> sumia con gritos e llanto que por ella andava. E en
> esto estando, tomaron a la condesa apretandole los
> pulsos e echandole agua Rosada a la cara; ovieronla
> ya de tornar, e começo a fazer el mas esquyvo llanto
> que en el mundo podria ser, asiendose de sus cabellos
> que parecian filos de oro luengos a maravilla ...
> (fol. 193 r.-v.).

Finally (and perhaps this is not unconnected with the first example
given above of a preoccupation with religious sententiousness) there
is a tendency towards euphemism or bowdlerisation. Fernán González,
-it will be remembered, is released from his Leonese prison by a ruse
of his wife, who pleads with the King to spend a night with her husband and requests, in the version of the <u>PCG</u>, that

> mandasse sacar al conde de los fierros, diziendol
> que el cauallo trauado nunqua bien podie fazer fijos.
> (<u>PCG</u>, pp.420 b 47 - 421 a 2);

the King's reply is

> "Si Dios me uala, tengo que dize uerdad", et mandol

luego sacar de los fierros et que les fiziessen muy buen
lecho. Et desi yoguieron toda la noche amos en uno
(PCG, p.421 a 3-5 and variants)

It is true that the Vulgata and the Crónica de Veinte Reyes both tone
this down by removing the earthy reference to the horse ("diziendol...
fijos") and replacing it with the phrase "demientra que ella con el
estaua" (Ocampo, fol. 252 v; cf. CVR, MS. N, fol. 24 v.). The Versión
Interpolada, however, alters the whole point by putting a different
motive into the Countess's request:

> que aquellos [fierros] para los robadores e matadores
> convenyan (fol. 194 v.)

and goes on to omit any reference to beds or to the couple sleeping
together.

Similar characteristics, though less widespread, may be seen in
the stories of the Condesa Traidora and the Infant García. An example
from the first concerns the events leading up to the meeting between
the disguised Count Garci-Fernández and doña Sancha, daughter of the
French Count to whose home Garci-Fernández has pursued his erring wife
(PCG, pp.427 b 20 - 428 a 11). It will be recalled that Sancha, after
complaining about the unhappiness brought by her new stepmother, tells
her maid to observe the poor who eat at the castle gates

> e que cates si ay y alguno fijo dalgo e apuesto
> e fermoso, que lo traygas ante mi, e quiero fablar
> con el (Ocampo, fol. 254 r.).

The maid does so, recognises the Castilian Count as a man of quality
by his beautiful hands, and after some cryptic dialogue he reveals his
identity to doña Sancha and offers her marriage if she will aid him in
his revenge. Her motives in giving the above instructions to her maid
are unexpressed, and it may have been with this in mind that the author
of the Versión Interpolada expanded this part of the story, giving to
doña Sancha a pious if not wholly convincing motive:

> Sepas, amiga, que non puedo sofrir mas esta vida atan
> amarga; e pidote yo de gracia que a los proves (sic)
> que aqui en casa de mi padre dan de comer cada dia, que
> tu los quieras visitar e rrequerir mas que fasta aqui
> de aquellas cosas que ayan menester; porque es my volun-
> tad de me adolecer dellos porque el sennor Dios se
> adolezca de mi vida, e me saque desta tribulacion e pena
> en que bivo con my padre e con my madrastra. E rruegote
> yo que los mires bien a todos e veas si entre ellos ay algun
> fidalgo que sea omne apuesto e de buen donayre; e aquel
> que tu vieres que a tus ojos parece bien, que aquel me
> traygas, e fablare con el dos palabras en ffaz de Dios,
> que es mi voluntad de le dar limosna porque rruege (sic) a
> Dios que yo salga desta vida en que bivo (fol. 197 v.).

The same chronicler clearly felt some qualms at a later stage of
the same story about don Sancho's killing of his mother by forcing her
to drink the poisoned cup (cf. PCG, p.454 a 36 - b 15; Ocampo, fol.
268 v.) and inserts the following explanation or apology:

> El conde don Sancho, non pensando que tanto era

el mal que su madre avia de morir, ovo muy gran
pesar e lloro mucho su peccado ... (fol. 220 r.).

As for the story of the Infant García, the interpolations are here
less marked, consisting primarily of expansions of dialogue. When the
Infante visits his betrothed, doña Sancha, she warns him against
going unarmed:

... ca non sabedes quien vos quiere bien o mal
(Ocampo, fol. 273 v.);[10]

in the Versión Interpolada she introduces this with the words:

"Por Dios, amor, syenpre mirad por vos, que non
sabedes ..." (fol. 227 v.).

When the rebellious Vela brothers are about to kill the Infante they
say (as in no other version):

"Tienpo es de pagar las synrazones que vuestro padre
nos fizo" (ibid.);

and doña Sancha again, at his death, throws herself on him with the
words:

"Sennor mio, ¿que ventura fue la mya, que mys ojos vos
viesen matar de vuestros enemygos?" (fol. 228 r.),[11]

once more in this version only.
    A possible explanation for some at least of these additions might
be that the compiler of the Versión Interpolada had at his disposal
later and fuller poetic texts - refundiciones - and incorporated details
from them. There are reasons for doubting this explanation, though.
The additions to the story are most marked in the case of the history
of Fernán González where we untypically do have an extant poetic text,
and one fixed in a written and clerical form early in the thirteenth
century. Though it may be speculated that this poem is itself based
on a popular epic source and that this source may have continued to
evolve in the thirteenth and fourteenth centuries,[12] the rhetorical and
often directly or indirectly religious nature of the additions makes it
hard to reconcile them with any such, presumably popular, tradition.
Nor do the interpolations in any of the three stories discussed above
betray any signs of assonance. It seems more likely that we are dealing
with an idiosyncratic example of what is increasingly to be recognised
as a general tendency on the part of later chronicles to expand and fill
out their material in both stylistic and narrative respects, in line
with their own criteria - criteria to which the word literary may
reasonably be applied.[13] What is idiosyncratic here is the tendency
towards stylistic rather than narrative expansion, as well as the
specifically religious tone given to some at least of the interpolations.
    With these factors in mind, let us return to the Versión Inter-
polada's treatment of the legend of the Infantes de Lara. As I have
already said, it has been generally supposed in this case that the
Versión Interpolada is based on a poetic refundición, the so-called
segundo cantar of the fourteenth century, also postulated as the source
of similar interpolations in the Crónica de 1344. Menéndez Pidal's
conclusion was that both chronicles drew independently on a fourteenth-
century refundición of the cantar de gesta. Writing of the Versión

<u>Interpolada</u> he says:

> ... altera por completo, en la parte relativa a los Infantes,
> el texto de su original en vista de una redacción poética de
> la leyenda, que no es otra sino el 2º Cantar de Gesta ... cuyos
> versos copia a ratos, en tal abundancia y tan fielmente, que
> muchas páginas de esta Cronica aparecen del todo rimadas.[14]

He also admits, however, that some of the additions may be regarded as
"invenciones del cronista" (ibid., note 2), and it may be convenient to
look first at examples of these. We find expansion and clarification,
as when the placing of the Infantes under Ruy Blásquez's tutelage is
expanded to explain that this is for the purpose of punishment (cf.
<u>Reliquias</u>, pp. 186, lines 4-6 and 200); and when the Infantes see the
Moorish standards approach at Almenar (cf. <u>Reliquias</u>, pp. 191, lines 4-9
and 202) Ruy Blásquez's explanation is more complex and more deceitful.[15]
Another tendency of this text is, again, the introduction of pious
motives: so Gonzalo González prays when Almanzor's host appears (cf.
<u>Reliquias</u>, pp. 191, lines 2-3 and 201),[16] and a similar tendency may lie
behind one case of narrative expansion, when Mudarra is offered an escort
by Almanzor on his departure for Castile and requests that it be composed of Christian knights held prisoner (cf. <u>Reliquias</u>, pp. 197, lines
3-4 and 216).

The most striking features of the <u>Versión Interpolada</u>, however,
come towards the end of the story. First, Gonzalo Gustioz's lament over
his sons is expanded from the laconic summary of Ocampo and the <u>PCG</u>[17]
to an extended lament over each head in turn, which has unmistakable
signs of assonance (<u>Reliquias</u>, pp. 205 - 211); second, the final chapter in which Mudarra's revenge is recounted is much expanded and the
sequence of events it contains altered and made more complex. In brief,
Mudarra pursues Ruy Blásquez, defeats him in single combat at Castro
and takes him back to Bilbestre for execution. He then hounds doña
Lambra out of the court and she dies in the Sierra de Mena (<u>Reliquias</u>,
pp. 215 - 236).

It is this material to which Menéndez Pidal was referring in the
quotation from <u>La leyenda</u> reproduced above. The same hypothesis is
maintained by Diego Catalán in <u>Romancero tradicional</u> and it has been
generally accepted until recently.[18] It has however been challenged by
J.G. Cummins, who draws attention to the fact that the <u>Versión Inter-
polada</u> follows the <u>PCG</u> (or, to be more accurate, follows the <u>Vulgata</u>,
which he does not discuss) far more closely than does the <u>Crónica de
1344</u>. He sums up:

> A close examination of the texts suggests that the
> epic version behind most of <u>ITCG</u> [= <u>Versión Interpolada</u>]'
> may have been much closer to the version behind <u>PCG</u>
> than to that behind <u>1344</u>. The <u>1344</u> version includes
> numerous episodes which figure in neither of the other
> accounts, and virtually all the new (i.e. non-<u>PCG</u>)
> elements of the story are in the 1344 account, which
> represents a considerable expansion of the version
> behind <u>PCG</u>. In contrast, the story-line of the <u>ITCG</u>
> version follows almost exactly that of <u>PCG</u>, and prac-
> tically every element of the content of <u>ITCG</u> is already
> present in <u>PCG</u>, in condensed form. The main exception
> is Mudarra's chase of Ruy Velázquez at the end, which
> has all the appearance of being a late appendage borrowed
> from the <u>refundición</u> represented by 1344.[19]

He therefore sees all of what one might call the non-structural innovations of the Versión Interpolada as being due to a difference in
prosifying technique between that chronicle and the PCG. In particular,
the lament of Gonzalo Gustioz may in Cummins' view have formed part of
the original legend but have been drastically condensed in the Alphonsine
prosification.

It will be recalled that the Crónica de 1344 shows signs of being
also based on the hypothetical segundo cantar. Here the evidence is
perhaps stronger, though Pidal's interpretation of it has also been
challenged. A thesis similar to Cummins' had been put forward in 1934
by A. Monteverdi who, basing his findings on a less thorough analysis
than Cummins, wrote of the divergences between the two basic versions
of the chronicle texts.[20] The most recent contribution to the debate
is that of L. Chalon, who criticises Monteverdi's arguments (he seems
not to have been able to take Cummins' into account) and concludes:

> On pourrait, évidemment, penser que le texte de la
> Cr.1344 consacré aux infants de Salas n'est qu'un
> remaniement chronistique des passages correspondants
> de la P.C.G. Un examen attentif de la prose de la
> Cr.1344 révèle qu'elle se fonde sur une base versi-
> fiée pour conter l'histoire des infants, et cela même
> dans les passages qui lui sont particuliers, qui n'ont
> pas de correspondants dans la P.C.G.[21]

Although both Monteverdi and Chalon were discussing the Crónica
de 1344, which is not our direct concern, the argument can be applied
equally to the Versión Interpolada. However, one must proceed with
extreme caution. Only when new narrative elements - like Mudarra's
pursuit of Ruy Blásquez - are combined with unmistakable traces of
assonance may one reasonably postulate a later refundición or segundo
cantar. As Cummins has persuasively argued, the presence of assonance
alone - as in Gonzalo Gustioz's lament - is not a sufficient condition,
since:

> The PCG prosification of the thirteenth-century version is
> characterized by concision and usually by careful concealment
> of epic line-structure. Condensation is achieved partly by
> summarizing in reported speech passages which in the epic
> probably consisted of longer utterances and conversations
> in direct speech ... The most extreme case of this condensation
> of direct speech may well be the lament. (p. 109)

One point of this article has been to show that in a number of
respects the compiler of the Versión Interpolada was doing more than he
had done in the case of other epic legends: that is, to elaborate on
the story to clarify narrative details and characters' motivations.
This liking for narrative expansiveness may well have been what led the
compiler to resurrect the poetic details of Gonzalo Gustioz's lament,
perhaps from some discarded borrador.

To finish, let us return to the refundición and the expanded ending of the story. One detail seems to have struck Diego Catalán as odd
when he wrote, in his additions to his grandfather's La leyenda, having
referred to his dating of the Versión Interpolada to 1512:

> Resulta sorprendente que una mano del siglo XVI
> sea responsable de la transcripción, verso a verso,
> de grandes fragmentos del Cantar de los Infantes
> de hacia 1300.[22]

Indeed the circumstance is suspicious. Cummins has analysed the supposed *segundo cantar* in some detail, showing how the structural innovations have the effect of making the lament "the fulcrum of a see-saw in which Mudarra's weight at one end just about balances that of the seven *Infantes* at the other" (p. 109). He also draws attention to the extension of thematic scope involved in making Ruy Blásquez "not just a wicked uncle, but a rebel against Garcí Fernández" (ibid.), and he analysed the other elements whose purpose seems to be the improvement of overall cohesion (the theme of blood, the idea of Mudarra as a re-incarnation of Gonzalo González, the motif of the hawk) (p. 110). These are literary qualities which some may find it hard to reconcile with an out-and-out neotraditionalist view of epic development. We are increasingly coming to realise that the *Poema de mio cid* with, in C.C. Smith's words

> its high artistry..., its numerous learned
> features, and its written nature[23]

may be quite untypical of the oral tradition. Perhaps one ought to have similar reservations about the so-called *refundición* of the *Cantar de los Infantes de Lara*, which may be neither so early nor so artless as has been assumed.


# N O T E S

1. Diego Catalán, De Alfonso X al Conde de Barcelos (Madrid 1962), 38-42 and note 9, and 176-177. Catalán calls the whole MS. V and distinguishes V¹ (the *Crónica Fragmentaria*) from V², the part under discussion in this article.

2. It is important to distinguish between the *tercera* and *cuarta* partes of Ocampo's chronicle. The first is closely related to the *Crónica de Veinte Reyes*; the second (beginning with the reign of Fernando I and thus better known as containing all the Cidian material) to the *Crónica de Castilla* and the *Primera Crónica General*. See Catalán, De Alfonso X ...., 188-193, and L.F. Lindley Cintra (ed.), *Crónica Geral de Espanha de 1344*, t. I (Lisboa 1951), ccciii.

3. See R. Menéndez Pidal, La leyenda de los infantes de Lara, 3rd ed. (Madrid 1971), 74 and 405-406 (description of the MS.), 559 and 571-572.

4. I have used the edition of the *Poema de Fernán González* by R. Menéndez Pidal in *Reliquias de la poesía épica española* (Madrid 1951) which also contains selections from the text of the *Primera Crónica General* and (in the case of the Infantes de Lara only) from the *Versión Interpolada*. Other texts used are: *Primera Crónica General* (PCG) ed. R. Menéndez Pidal (Madrid 1955); *Crónica de Veinte Reyes* (CVR), MS. N (Escorial Y-I-12); Vulgata: F. D'Ocampo, *Las Quatro Partes Enteras de la Cronica de España ...* (Zamora 1541); *Versión Interpolada*: MS. V² (Madrid, B.N. 1277).

5. Compare PCG, 402 b 10 - 15.

6. Compare PCG, 392 b 24 - 36.

7.   Compare PCG, 405 b 30 - 40.

8.   Compare PCG, 420 a 38 - 44.

9.   Compare PCG, 427 b 30 - 32.

10.  Compare PCG, 470 b 29 - 30.

11.  Compare PCG, 471 and Ocampo fol. 273 v.

12.  See J.B. Avalle Arce, 'El Poema de Fernán González: Clerecía y juglaría', Philological Quarterly, 51 (1972), 60 - 73; and L. Chalon, L'Histoire et l'épopée castillane du moyen âge (Paris 1976), esp. 420-460.

13.  See D. Catalán,'Poesía y Novela en la Historiografía Castellana de los Siglos XIII y XIV', in Mélanges offerts à Rita Lejeune, Vol. I (Gembloux 1969), 423-41; D.G. Pattison, 'The Afrenta de Corpes in Fourteenth-century Historiography', in Mío Cid Studies (London 1977), 129-140, esp. 138-140.

14.  La leyenda de los Infantes de Lara, 74.

15.  In the first instance the Versión Interpolada says "e metieronse los siete ynfantes en mano y poder de don Rodrigo, su tio, que les diese la pena quel mandase" (Reliquias, p. 200); in the second, Ruy Blásquez says "aquellos moros astrosos traen muchas señas por dar a entender que son muchos, e ellos non llegan a mill..." (ibid., 202).

16.  Other cases may be seen in Reliquias, pp. 191, lines 17-18 and 202 (Muño Salido exhorts the Infantes); 192, lines 5-7 and 202 (Diego González's exhortation to his brothers is given a more religious note); and 194, line 24 and 203 (the Infantes' death is marked by the prayer "Dios les aya las almas").

17.  The Vulgata says:  "Desi tomaua las cabeças vna a vna e razonaua con cada vna los buenos fechos que fiziera" (Ocampo, fol. 265 v.); cf. PCG, p. 442 a 14-17.

18.  Diego Catalán (ed.), Romancero Tradicional, II (Madrid 1963), 93. See also, for example, E. von Richthofen, Tradicionalismo épico novelesco (Barcelona 1972), 39-53 and 55-65.

19.  J.G. Cummins, 'The Chronicle Texts of the Legend of the Infantes de Lara', BHS, 53 (1976), 101-116; the quotation is from p. 102.

20.  A. Monteverdi, 'Il cantare degli infanti de Salas', Studi Medievali, Nuova Serie 7 (1934), 113-50.  He sums up: "Le divergenze, che si notano tra la narrazione della prima e quella della seconda Cronica general, non hanno bisogno di essere spiegate con l'esistenza di due distinti cantari.  Potrebbero anche dipendere dal diverso attegiamento dei due cronisti di fronte a un solo cantare". (p. 124)

21.  L'Histoire et l'épopée ..., 509.

22.  La leyenda ..., 559.

23.  Poema de mio Cid, ed. Colin Smith (Oxford 1972), xxxiv.

# Two episodes from the Araucana, Part I : subject and style

Frank Pierce (University of Sheffield)

The _Araucana_ is a poem about war and it is therefore not surprising that any analysis of its style should inevitably draw on passages of combat and of both victory and defeat in arms. Nor should it strike one as strange that such a distinct talent as Ercilla's found its most memorable expression in scenes of violence and carnage.[1] Literature indeed is replete with examples of military prowess, from David, Samson and the Maccabees, Hector, Ulysses and Aeneas, to the heroes of medieval saga and romance, and of the plentiful narratives and dramas of Ercilla's own century. The warrior has been almost as constant a literary type as the lover.

In the _Araucana_ we have a poem which reflects consecrated public habits as one civilisation impinges on another (and one of Ercilla's merits, for long admired, is to have tried to imagine the interplay of values and instincts on both sides of the conflict).[2] In addition the early part of his life as a courtier and soldier of his prince and king, Philip II, illumines his choice of subject and his conscious imitation of ancient poets. The _Araucana_ is a very unusual record of Ercilla's own experiences together with a chronicle-like account of events before he arrived in Chile. With its pervasive first-person manner it has something of an extended memoir, whose striking originality nevertheless recalls both medieval and Renaissance practice and theory.[3] If Ercilla's poem can be said to run counter to certain rules of structure of the genre to which it belongs, the epic, its pseudo-historical presentation recalls both the contemporary histories of the Indies and more than one Spanish so-called historical poem such as those of Sempere (1560), Zapata (1566) and Juan Rufo (1584). The _Araucana_ itself of course set the fashion for yet a new kind of historical poem and inspired a whole series, including its own continuation by Pedro de Oña, on discoveries and conquests in the New World.[4]

Part I embraces accounts of some eight major encounters between the Spaniards (led first by Pedro de Valdivia until his capture and death, and then by his lieutenant, Francisco Villagrán), and the Indians of Arauco, who give their name to the poem. The preparations for the battles and such consequences as rout and celebration form part of the developing pattern, and in these passages Ercilla also personalises the accounts, in Virgilian manner, by giving pride of place to a chosen hero. Some of these battles run into one another or are continuations of the same but interrupted action; for example the three Cantos IV-VI tell first of the fourteen Spanish warriors who came too late to help Valdivia and were themselves attacked and forced to retreat, but then returned to fight the dramatic Battle of Andalicán Hill. This was a heavy Spanish defeat and is followed by massacre and flight, a last stand and a spectacular plunge of Spaniards and their horses over a cliff and into the sea, and a second and degrading flight of those surviving.

These last events, recounted by Ercilla with a consistent use of poetic effects, that is, figures of speech both of syntax and content, are also told in the historical record by Alonso de Góngora Marmolejo, in his _Historia de Chile desde su decubrimiento hasta el año 1575_, Chapters XV and XVI. This prose account was written several years after Part I of the _Araucana_ (published 1569), although Góngora Marmolejo's manuscript was itself not published until 1850, and it is the work of a contemporary of Ercilla in Chile but of whom very little

is known (the available modern edition of his text is to be found in
Vol. 131 of the B.A.E.). The historical account is quite extensive
and coincides with the poem in many details, although not in all, and
it has its own economy, fluency and vigour of style. Nevertheless,
Ercilla, as indicated above, uses his own method of selection and
emphasis to build up a narrative that is essentially poetic.[5]
Let us look at two examples of Ercilla's handling of events.
Firstly and following on from the events (in Cantos IV-VI) alluded to
above, there occurs a passage which might well be called a hymn of
destruction or a poet's fascination with man's genius for pillage and
obliteration. In Canto VII Ercilla concludes his account of the flight
after the defeat at Andalicán, with the retreat by boat over the Biobío
River to Concepción (much of this action is also covered by Góngora
Marmolejo in his Chapter XVI). There then follow the laments of the
townspeople at the Spanish defeat and the subsequent panic and the
decision to abandon Concepción, an act of collective cowardice in the
face of the Indian menace which is stronger than the vain pleas of the
valiant matron, Doña Mencía de Nidos, to the fleeing populace to stay
and fight (this last episode is given special attention by Góngora
Marmolejo, in Chapter XVII). After a necessary rest Lautaro, the
Araucan chief, leads his men to the deserted, silent town:[6]

> A vista de las casas ya la gente
> se reparte por todos los caminos,
> porque el saco del pueblo sea igualmente
> lleno de ropa y falto de vecinos;
> apenas la señal del partir siente,
> cuando cual negra banda de estorninos
> que se abate al montón del blanco trigo,
> baja al pueblo el ejército enemigo.
>
> La ciudad yerma en gran silencio atiende
> el presto asalto y fiera arremetida
> de la bárbara furia, que desciende
> con alto estruendo y con veloz corrida:
> el menos codicioso allí pretende
> la casa más copiosa y bastecida:
> vienen de gran tropel hacia las puertas
> todas de par en par francas y abiertas.
>
> (St. 45-46)

Ercilla captures very vividly the two contrasting actions, flight from
the city by its inhabitants and the descent upon it by the marauders.
This is reinforced by the nature simile involving the swooping of the
black starlings upon the white corn, and the well-chosen and well-
placed adjectives in the second stanza. The city is seen as almost
offering itself as a sacrifice to appease its plunderers and to stand
in for those who have deserted it.
In the following stanza, on the other hand, a series of active
verbs takes along the movement with deliberate speed, as the first to
enter the city search, break open and pull down:

> Corren toda la casa en el momento
> y en un punto escudriñan los rincones,
> muchos por no engañarse por el tiento
> rompen y descerrajan los cajones,
> baten tapices, rimas y ornamento,
> camas de seda y ricos pabellones,

y cuanto descubrir pueden de vista,
que no hay quien los impida ni resista.
(St. 47)

(rima = rimero)

The poet closely observes the thoroughness of the spoliation, which is
vividly suggested by the accumulation of nouns.

This section of Canto VII employs three other similes: the first
immediately following involves a reference to the Greek destruction of
Troy, which is likened to the frenzy of the Araucans and is expressed
by synecdoche:

No con tanto rigor el pueblo griego
entró por el troyano alojamiento,
sembrando frigia sangre y vivo fuego,
talando hasta en el último cimiento;
cuanto de ira, venganza y furor ciego
el bárbaro del robo no contento
arruina, destruye, desperdicia,
y aun no puede cumplir con su malicia.
(St. 48)

This is followed by an impressive distributive statement which with
repetitive insistence enlivens the emerging scene, as it portrays the
Indian greed for unimagined loot and its violent consequences:

Quién sube la escalera, y quién la baja,
quién a la ropa, y quién al cofre aguija,
quién abre, quién desquicia y desencaja,
quién no deja fardel, ni baratija,
quién contiende, quién riñe, quién baraja,
quién alegra, y se mete a la partija:
por las torres, desvanes y tejados
aparecen los bárbaros cargados.
(St. 49)

As this horrendous picture is uncovered, yet another (double)
simile, the first of two from nature, compares the thoroughness of the
sack of Concepción to the diligence of bees:

No en colmenas de abejas la frecuencia,
priesa y solicitud cuando fabrican
en el panal la miel con providencia,
que a los hombres jamás lo comunican;
ni aquel salir, entrar y diligencia
con que las tiernas flores melifican,
se puede comparar, ni ser figura
de lo que aquella gente se apresura.
(St. 50)

This well illustrates that the aptness of a simile in general is to be
sought in the likeness of the action or its result rather than in the
participants or agents, since bees and pillagers are in no other way
similar. Then the poet pursues his analysis of greed and unblinkingly
relates how it can push the restless despoiler to the point where he
obtains nothing rather than much:

Alguno de robar no se contenta
la casa que le da cierta ventura,
que la insaciable voluntad sedienta
otra de mayor presa le figura:
haciendo codiciosa y necia cuenta
busca la incierta y deja la segura,
y llegando el Sol puesto a la posada
se queda, por buscar mucho, sin nada.

(St. 51)

Further, the Indians do not stop here but the robber now robs the robber, and the closest ties are forgotten (in something like the same way that Ercilla had described how panic in the flight of the Spanish soldiers had made each man look to his own safety and ignore the pleas of others):

También se roba entre ellos lo robado,
que poca cuenta y amistad había,
sino se pone en salvo a buen recado,
que allí el mayor ladrón más adquiría:
cuál lo saca arrastrando, cuál cargado
va que del propio hermano no se fía:
más parte a ningún hombre se concede
de aquello que llevar consigo puede.

(St. 52)

The effect is again achieved by the use of a distributive statement.

Once more Ercilla returns to nature for a simile to underline this wholesale looting: he now adds ants to bees as the well-regulated creatures of the instinctive natural scene to describe the single-minded, unnatural and immoral conduct of human beings engaged upon their own form of hoarding. Not the least of our poet's skills is his choice and use of similes:

Como para el invierno se previenen
las guardosas hormigas avisadas,
que a la abundante troje van y vienen,
y andan en acarretos ocupadas,
no se impiden, estorban, ni detienen,
dan las vacías el paso a las cargadas:
así los araucanos codiciosos
entran, salen y vuelven presurosos.

(St. 53)

(acarretos = acarreos)

The Spanish town, however, is not only cleaned out of its treasures. What is left, the houses, are now burned down, and Concepción (Penco) is rased to the ground. Total destruction is now added to the minute and comprehensive pilfering of the town's contents, and once again the keen vision of the poet selects with enthusiasm and his own brand of thoroughness the details of this conflagration which takes over and consumes everything in its path. One also notes the purposeful accumulative statements as the one follows the other:

la codiciosa llama de manera
iba en tanto furor y crecimiento,
que todo el pueblo mísero se abrasa,
corriendo el fuego ya de casa en casa.

(St. 54)

(note in passing the application to the fire of the attribute which had already explained the sacking of the city!)

> Por alto y bajo el fuego se derrama,
> los cielos amenaza el son horrendo,
> de negro humo espeso y viva llama
> la infelice ciudad se va cubriendo:
> treme la tierra entorno, el fuego brama
> de subir a su esfera presumiendo,
> caen de rica labor maderamientos
> resumidos en polvos cenicientos.
>
> (St. 55)
>
> (resumidos = reduced)

After thus describing how the fire takes control of everything it encounters and how it even challenges heaven itself, Ercilla reflects upon the destruction of the rich dwellings of this gold-mining town and their value and on the families and their servants who occupied it (in St. 56-58). He then returns to the incendiaries and their impatience and anger at the tardiness of nature's destructiveness. But this ironic comment on man's perversity is answered as once more the fire stretches up to heaven and as Vulcan himself, not here the blacksmith of the gods but the father of fire, makes his own contribution:

> La grita de los bárbaros se entona,
> no cabe el gozo dentro de sus pechos,
> viendo que el fuego horrible no perdona
> hermosas cuadras, ni labrados techos:
> en tanta multitud no hay tal persona
> que en verlos se duela así deshechos;
> antes suspiran, gimen, y se ofenden,
> porque tanto del fuego se defienden.
>
> Paréceles que es lento y espacioso,
> pues tanto en abrasarlos se tardaba,
> y maldicen al tracio proceloso,
> porque la flaca llama no esforzaba:
> al caer de las casas sonoroso
> un terrible alarido resonaba,
> que junto con el humo y las centellas
> subiendo amenazaba las estrellas.
>
> Crece la fiera llama en tanto grado
> que las más altas nubes encendía;
> tracio con movimiento arrebatado
> sacudiendo los árboles venía,
> y Vulcano al rumor sucio y tiznado
> con los herreros fuelles acudía
> que ayudaron su parte al presto fuego;
> y así se apoderó de todo luego.
>
> (St. 59-61)
>
> (tracio = tracias)

And the crescendo is maintained as the hyperbole of comparison moves, with a certain naturalness, from mythology to a great historical example of pyromania, as Nero sets fire to Rome:

                    Nunca fue de Nerón el gozo tanto
                    de ver en la gran Roma poderosa
                    prendido el fuego ya por cada canto,
                    vista sola a tal hombre deleitosa:
                    ni aquello tan gran gusto le dio, cuanto
                    gusta la gente bárbara dañosa
                    de ver cómo la llama se estendía,
                    y la triste ciudad se consumía.
                                              (St. 62)

     Finally, Ercilla gives us a last definitive sight, steady and yet
amazed, of this annihilation worked by man (once more the use of emphatic adjectives should be noted), who is thus seen at the end as the
vengeful and joyful agent of it all:

                    Era cosa de oir, dura y terrible
                    los estallidos y fornace estruendo,
                    el negro humo espeso e insufrible
                    cual nube en aire así se va imprimiendo:
                    no hay cosa reservada al fuego horrible,
                    todo en sí lo convierte, resumiendo
                    los ricos edificios levantados
                    en antiguos corrales derribados.

                    Llegado al fin el último contento
                    de aquella fiera gente vengativa,
                    aun no parando en esto el mal intento,
                    ni planta en pie, ni cosa dejan viva...
                                              (St. 63-64)
                    (fornace = fornáceo)

There is of course a literary example of the burning of a city surely
known to our poet, namely that of Laurentum, the city of Latinus destroyed by Aeneas, in the Aeneid XII. Ercilla's account of the burning
of Concepción is however very much his own and is clearly a personal
and very vivid poetic record of an historical event. Góngora
Marmolejo in fact gives the shortest account possible (in his Chapter
XVII), and reports that the city's destruction was seen from afar by
one of its citizens who then goes to inform Villagrán and the others at
Santiago: "desde un alto vido andar los indios robando y saqueando lo
que hallaban, quemando las casas" (p.114, col.1). He had however just
before given a few more details of what the fleeing Spaniards had left
behind in Concepción. The comparative coverage of this event by
Ercilla and the historian underlines rather strikingly how the poet
isolated and elaborated something which had for him very clear imaginative appeal, whereas for Góngora Marmolejo it was just one detail in
the abandonment of the city.



                    . . . . . . . . . .



     Much happens in our poem between these last spectacular events
and the next passage chosen for detailed comment, from Canto XIV.
Much of it concerns the bloody encounters of Indians and Spaniards,
with, as before, effective poetic emphasis on individual valour and
endurance. In Canto XIII the poet returns to the point where Villagrán
was hoping to be led secretly across the mountain to Lautaro's fort.

It is here that this hero, a one-time page to Valdivia who returned to
his own people as a youthful warrior (Canto III), and who had been
praised more than once for his warlike virtues, is presented to us in
an unexpectedly human setting. The harsh disciplinarian and the
indomitable warrior are now revealed as a man in love. This interlude
can be said to echo the recent warning given by Ercilla about Fortune
lying in wait for the brave Indians, as Lautaro's beloved, Guacolda,
voices her fearful premonition (just as Andromache had to her lover-
warrior, Hector, in Iliad, VI). The poet, unused, as he says, to
writing of love, with clear rhetorical emphasis ends Canto XIII at this
point, as he tells how Lautaro joins Guacolda in her weeping and as he
declares how his pen is "turbada..." and how "confusa, tarda, y con
temor se mueve" (St. 57). This "hesitation" by the poet in dealing
with a quite un-historical scene does however give increased dramatic
suspension to the equally historical events which Ercilla is at the
moment following through and to the account of which the tender
exchanges between Guacolda and Lautaro are appended: Villagrán crosses
the "fragosa sierra que iguala con las nubes su estatura" (St. 41; note
this much-used poetic hyperbole), and Fortune is to favour him although
the Indians seem safe in their well-protected fort, where they have
been joined by soldiers of other tribes. Before however Ercilla departs
so clearly from his historical material, he adds the telling detail
which gives urgent meaning to the dreams, now described, of both
Lautaro and Guacolda foretelling disaster, and which of course is to
be echoed when, as we shall see in the next canto, Villagrán in fact
penetrated the Indians' defences by avoiding the only path over the
hill:

> Sola una senda este lugar tenía
> de alertas centinelas ocupada,
> otra ni rastro alguno no le había,
> por ser casi la tierra despoblada...
>                    (Canto XIII, St. 43)

When we come to Canto XIV the poet carries forward his unaccus-
tomed subject of love into the opening stanzas, normally reserved in
the Araucana for moralistic reflexions on the action. He now wonders
at how even a savage woman makes such a profession of pure love (he
also portrays some Araucan women as models of constancy and tenderness).
    It is in this gentle setting so reminiscent of the pastoral with
its complaints and professions of affection that Ercilla decides to
introduce once more the contrasting topic of the violence of war. He
does so however by dwelling upon the circumstances surrounding the
lovers' intimacies, namely night with its silence, sleep and rest,
which equally, as it now happens dull and numb the Indians' awareness
of the imminent dangers. The language of this passage with its well-
placed verbs and adjectives powerfully evokes the stillness and the
unhurried pace of night as it gives way to day, and must surely constitute some of Ercilla's finest writing. Firstly, the calm sense of
security as the Indians settle down to rest, the last for many of them:

> los soldados entorno los tizones,
> ya de parlar cansados reposaban,
> teniendo centinelas como digo,
> y el cerro a las espaldas por abrigo.
>                    (St. 3)

The Spaniard's approach is etched in with a well-chosen zeugma:

Villagrán con silencio y paso presto
había el áspero monte atravesado,
....

....
llegado junto al Fuerte, en un buen puesto
viendo que el cielo estaba aun estrellado
paró, esperando el claro y nuevo día
que ya por el oriente descubría.

De ninguno fue visto, ni sentido,
la causa era la noche ser escura,
y haber las centinelas desmentido,
por parte descuidada por segura:
caballo no relincha, ni hay ruido,
que está ya de su parte la ventura,
ésta hace las bestias avisadas,
y a las personas bestias descuidadas.
                                    (St. 4-5)

The syntactically straightforward and leisurely unfolding of this scene
is reinforced by the simple conceit in the last two lines (which adds
up to a new kind of nature comparison!).  The Araucans now unconsciously
complete the preparations for their destruction as the approach of day
ironically sends all of them to sleep, with another telling zeugma
involving a traditional metaphor:

Cuando ya las tinieblas y aire escuro
con la esperada luz se adelgazaban,
las centinelas puestas por el muro
al nuevo día de lejos saludaban:
y pensando tener campo seguro
también a descansar se retiraban,
quedando mudo el fuerte, y los soldados
en vino y dulce sueño sepultados.
                                    (St. 6)

Before the Spaniards pounce on their unsuspecting prey, however, our
poet keeps up the suspense for two more octaves, in the first of which
the oncoming of day and the flight of night are suggested with the aid
of an appropriate floral illustration and one of Ercilla's rare
classical references:

Era llegada al mundo aquella hora
que la escura tiniebla, no pudiendo
sufrir la clara vista de la aurora,
se va en el ocidente retrayendo:
cuando la mustia clicie se mejora
el rostro al rojo oriente revolviendo,
mirando tras las sombras ir la estrella,
y al rubio Apolo Délfico tras ella.
                                    (St. 7)
(clicie, i.e. Clytie = the sunflower)

The course of nature, to which man's life is subject, now forms the
back-cloth and the inevitable agent of man's violence against man:

El español que ve tiempo oportuno
se acerca poco a poco más al fuerte,

> sin estorbo de bárbaro ninguno,
> que sordos los tenía su triste suerte...
>
> (St. 8)

The attack is as sudden as the preparations for it have been shrouded
in silence and carried out with slow deliberation:

> No esperaron los nuestros más, pues viendo
> ser ya tiempo de darles el asalto,
> de súbito levantan un estruendo
> con soberbio alarido, horrendo y alto:
> y en tropel ordenado arremetiendo
> al fuerte van a dar de sobresalto...
>
> (St. 9)

Then in the first of several metaphors and other figures of speech
describing the Indians' unpreparedness, the poet refers to their fort
as "más de sueño bastecido/que al presente peligro apercebido" (St. 9).

The swift Araucan reaction to this unexpected assault is likened,
in the first of two new similes, to that of evildoers who are always
on the alert to any slight sound and immediately spring to their own
defence. Then

> Así medio dormidos y despiertos
> saltan los araucanos alterados,
> y del peligro y sobresalto ciertos
> baten toldos y ranchos levantados:
> por verse de corazas descubiertos,
> no dejan de mostrar pechos airados;
> mas con presteza y ánimo seguro
> acuden al reparo de su muro.
>
> (St. 11)

The reader will of course have noted here the striking conceit involving coraza and pecho, which is to be echoed when we come to the last
moments of Lautaro. Next, in a vigorous stanza of differing metaphors
and yet another crescendo-like figure of distribution, reaching a
challenging hyperbole, Ercilla evokes the details of the Araucan
defence:

> Sacudiendo el pesado y torpe sueño
> y cobrando la furia acostumbrada,
> quién el arco arrebata, quién un leño,
> quién del fuego un tizón, y quién la espada:
> quién aguija al bastón de ajeno dueño,
> quién por salir más presto va sin nada,
> pensando averiguarlo desarmados,
> si no pueden a puños, a bocados.
>
> (St. 12)

Our poet then turns again to Guacolda and Lautaro, the latter reassuring the former, but she admitting no comfort, in a scene reminiscent
of the age-old lyrical theme of love and war ("rompiendo el tierno
punto en sus amores/el duro son de trompas y atambores", St. 13).
Next Ercilla uses the second simile in this passage, recalling the
related obsessive awareness of the miser to any disturbance, but adding
the quite different comparison of the mother rushing to her child's cry
("temiéndole de alguna bestia fiera"), thus enriching the reader's

impression of Lautaro's readiness to protect and his almost instinctive quickness in responding.

Our passage from this battle, which is later to reach Virgilian heights of brutal realism and self-sacrifice and which will stretch into the next canto with the death of all the Indians, now comes to its climax with the four stanzas that tell of the untimely death of their leader. Lautaro, the prototype of the hero, emerges like others almost unarmed but he comes out to his death:

> Revuelto el manto al brazo, en el instante
> con un desnudo estoque, y él desnudo
> corre a la puerta el bárbaro arrogante,
> que armarse así tan súbito no pudo:

(note the double meanings of _desnudo_ ("naked" and "unarmed") and _arrogante_ ("haughty" and "courageous"), as two key adjectives.)

> ¡o pérfida fortuna, o inconstante,
> cómo llevas tu fin por punto crudo
> que el bien de tantos años en un punto
> de un golpe lo arrebatas todo junto!
> (St. 15)

Here Ercilla, in a poet's aside echoing words from Garcilaso's famous Sonnet X, has recalled the earlier fear of Fortune's move against the Araucans, and at the same time has clearly demonstrated his feeling of identity with their cause; this is to be made even more explicit when he laments Lautaro's death.

Ironically the agents of his end are the Indian allies of the Spaniards as they shoot a cloud of arrows. Thus:

> del toldo el hijo de Pillán salía,
> y una flecha a buscarle que venía.
> (St. 16),

in which the fateful nature of the hero's death is vividly suggested by the confluence of the two verbs of action. It is now that Ercilla, as he follows the deadly effect of the arrow, bursts out into a well-remembered lament and praise of Lautaro, that in fact reserved for a champion (and also to be echoed later for Caupolicán):

> Por el siniestro lado (¡o dura suerte!)
> rompe la cruda punta, y tan derecho,
> que pasa el corazón más bravo y fuerte
> que jamás se encerró en humano pecho:
> de tal tiro quedó ufana la muerte
> viendo de un solo golpe tan gran hecho,
> y usurpando la gloria al homicida
> se atribuye a la muerte esta herida.
> (St. 17)

This memorable octave divides easily into two halves: firstly the blow (made, it will be noted, from the left, the sinister side) pierces the fiercest and the stoutest heart (and the two Spanish adjectives combine the same basic meaning) that ever was found in human breast; then an even more daring hyperbole and its personification relate how death arrogates to itself the glory by which one shot brought about such a fateful result.

The poet brings this dramatic interlude to an articulated crescendo as Lautaro's act of dying is set out before us:

> Tanto rigor la aguda flecha trujo
> que el bárbaro tendió sobre la arena,
> abriendo puerta a un abundante flujo
> de negra sangre por copiosa vena:
> del rostro la color se le retrujo,
> los ojos tuerce, y con rabiosa pena
> la alma del mortal cuerpo desatada
> bajó furiosa a la infernal morada.
>
> (St. 18)

The details of death have often been the subject of heroic poetry, and Ercilla in his turn, by simply and baldly listing the stages of the leader's end, achieves his effect of horror and pity, even to the point of sending this savage's soul to hell, which any Christian of his time would believe to be its due (negra however in this context must simply mean "dark" without any moral connotation).[7]

Immediately after this passage, with its own mood and completeness, Ercilla turns his attention to the opening of the general conflict in which the hero will now have no part but which might be said to reflect his own bravery:

> Ganan los nuestros foso y baluarte,
> que nadie los impide, ni embaraza,
> y así por veinte lados la más parte
> pisaba de la fuerza ya la plaza:
> los bárbaros con ánimo y sin arte,
> sin celada, ni escudo, y sin coraza,
> comienzan la batalla peligrosa,
> cruda, fiera, reñida, y sanguinosa.
>
> (St, 19)

This battle is to be as fierce and as sustained as any seen thus far. Ercilla has strikingly turned the reader's vision in the new direction with a vigorous use of zeugma and asyndeton in the second half of this stanza.

These events, namely the advance upon the Indian fort and the subsequent death of Lautaro, are dispatched by Góngora Marmolejo in just a few lines: Villagrán met up with Captain Juan Godíñez, also out after Lautaro, and, led by guides to where the Araucans were, as morning broke they attacked the unsuspecting enemy; the latter fought with great bravery and Lautaro, coming out of his hut, where he had been sleeping, was run through and killed by a soldier who met him and did not recognise him. In the ensuing affray Juan de Villagrán was killed together with three hundred Indians (See Chapter XXII). It is also worth commenting here that this passage from the historical record, like many such, does not resemble that of the Araucana in every detail, and thus it is more than possible that Góngora and Ercilla were using alternative basic sources. There is of course no way of knowing, as for example in this case, whether Ercilla's reference to the false sense of security of the Araucans or the form of Lautaro's death are elaborations of the simple facts common to Góngora and Ercilla or are indeed derived from a more detailed account than that available to the former. What can however be said again with great conviction is that Ercilla used historical material as a poet.

. . . . . . . . . .

It will have been seen that Ercilla's virile and vivid style,
with its relative simplicity, has its own subtleties. The emphasis upon
action brings a constant use of verbs, nouns and adjectives, often in
pairs or bigger units. The hendecasyllable and the octave are exploited
for their flexibilities of syntactical arrangement, both in end-stopped
lines and through enjambement. Other figures of speech exemplify the
needs of narrative verse: for example Ercilla is his own master in the
use of the simile (from nature or human conduct), and of personification,
zeugma, antithesis and synecdoche.[8] Urgency is suggested by distribution, anaphora and asyndeton, as is contemplation or close observation by a more leisurely and expansive manner, including the use of
polysyndeton. Classical or mythological allusions are few but apt and
tend to underline the sparseness and economy of the general style.
Emotional evocation comes through by means of hyperbole and different
kinds of repetition, and this can include lyrical wonder, shock and
pathos. This is the classical Spanish given its much-imitated shape by
Garcilaso, but Ercilla can be seen to have evolved his own peculiar
balance of mellifluousness and detachment. A great admirer, Manuel José
Quintana, in the 1830s, had this to say of the _Araucana_: "Vense allí
las cosas, no se leen".[9]

## N O T E S

1.  Cf. a very recent tribute, by the late E.M. Wilson, to Ercilla's
power as a poet of war: "¿dónde en toda la literatura postrenacentista
hay mejores descripciones de las batallas vistas del punto de vista de
un combatiente en tierras ajenas, de las fuerzas y la valentía de
españoles e italianos de un lado, de los de Arauco de otro? ...Esta
epopeya es de una gran fuerza a pesar de los defectos de la forma".
See _Entre las jarchas y Cernuda. Constantes y variables en la poesía
española_ (Barcelona, Ariel, 1977), 9.

2.  Cf. Ercilla's own statement in the 'Prólogo al Lector' to Pt.II
of his poem (first published 1578): "...pero todo lo merecen los
araucanos, pues ha más de treinta años que sustentan su opinion, sin
jamás habérseles caido las armas de las manos... Y siempre permane-
ciendo en su firme propósito, y entereza, dan materia larga a los
escritores." (_B.A.E._, Vol.XVII, p.61, n.1) For comments on Ercilla's
treatment of the subject throughout the centuries, see the present
writer's _La poesía épica del siglo de oro_, 2nd ed. (Madrid 1968), esp.
Chapters I - V.  Recent comments on the Indians' role in the _Araucana_
can be found in the following studies: Hugo Montes, _Estudios sobre la
'Araucana'_ (Universidad Católica de Valparaíso 1966), 47 - 61;
Augusto Iglesias, _Ercilla y la 'Araucana'_ (Santiago de Chile 1969),
27 - 37, 42 - 45, 56 - 61; Miguel Ángel Vega, _La 'Araucana' de Ercilla_,
2nd ed. (Santiago de Chile 1970), 57 - 67.

3.  Cf. Maxime Chevalier, _L'Arioste en Espagne (1530-1650). Recherches
sur l'influence du 'Roland furieux'_ (Bordeaux 1966), 144 - 158; and,
more recently, J.B. Avalle-Arce, 'El poeta en su poema', _RO_, XXXII
(Segunda Serie) 1971, 155 - 158.

4.   See Pierce, Poesía épica..., 281 - 291; Chevalier, op.cit.,
158 - 164.

5.   Cf. Claude Dumas's revealing comparison of Ercilla's practice
with that of the historians, especially Góngora Marmolejo, 'Réflexions
sur quelques points d'histoire dans "La Araucana" de Ercilla', Travaux
de l'Institut d'Études Latino-Americaines de l'Université de Strasbourg,
II (1964), 735 - 749, which however does not refer to the two episodes
dealt with in this article; see also Julio Caillet-Bois's short but
effective study of the poem and its many topics and devices, Análisis
de la 'Araucana' (Buenos Aires 1967).

6.   The text of the poem used here is a modernised version of that
available in the B.A.E., Vol.XVII, 4 - 157.

7.   It is interesting to note here that the theologically less severe
attitude of a later generation, such as that expressed by Ercilla's
18th-century English translator, William Hayley, renders the last two
lines of this stanza accordingly:

> "His soul, that felt its glorious hopes o'erthrown,
> Retir'd, indignant, to the world unknown".

See F. Pierce, 'Ercilla and England', Hispanic Studies in Honour of
I. González Llubera (Oxford, Dolphin, 1959), 245.

8.   Ercilla's similes recall classical practice, especially in the
preference for those drawn from nature.  Thus bees occur in Homer and
Virgil, ants in Virgil, and starlings in Homer (and Garcilaso),
although in similes of different kinds.  Also, Ercilla echoes Horace,
Seneca and Boethius in his use of comparisons involving misers and
evildoers.  Our poet in this and many other ways of course reflects the
inherited culture of his age.  The variety and originality of the
Araucana's similes have been analysed by Martínez de la Rosa,
Jean Ducamin and José Toribio Medina (see Pierce, Poesía épica...,
132 - 134, 183, and 188, respectively), while G.I. Dale later made a
first systematic study: 'The Homeric simile in the "Araucana" of
Ercilla', Washington University Studies, IX (1921), 233 - 244.

9.   See Pierce, Poesía épica..., 138.

LA REVISTA IBÉRICA : a neglected modernista review

Geoffrey Ribbans (Brown University)

The importance of literary reviews for the study of the modern period in Spain has gradually come to be recognized.[1] Following the early efforts of Guillermo de Torre,[2] Germán Bleiberg[3] and Guillermo Díaz-Plaja,[4] the key reviews Helios and Alma española have been methodically described,[5] but much still remains to be done, especially regarding the smaller and more ephemeral, but still significant, poetic reviews like Arte joven, Electra and Juventud. One of these lesser magazines, La Revista ibérica, has proved particularly elusive. Apart from casual mentions, the only substantial account of the magazine is given, in a rather unsystematic fashion, by Miguel Pérez Ferrero in his biography of the Machado brothers.[6] Indeed, for many years the sequence in the Hemeroteca Municipal of Madrid - the only known copies - was mislaid, apparently irretrievably. However, in the exhibition devoted to Antonio and Manuel Machado at the Biblioteca Nacional in the Summer of 1975, it was on display and I then had the opportunity to examine its contents.

La Revista ibérica came into existence on 15 July 1902, not long after the demise, on 27 March of that year, of Juventud, which in turn had succeeded Electra after a gap of a few months.[7] The new review set out to be wide-ranging in content (it was sub-titled 'Literatura, Pintura, Música, Escultura') as well as in geographical scope, for, as its title implied, it embraced Portugal as well as Spain. It showed no sign however of interest in Catalan literature or even in the exciting modernista revolution in Latin America.

It was to appear twice-monthly, on the 5th and 20th day of each month, and consisted of 32 pages per issue. The organising force behind this venture, as of its two predecessors, was Francisco Villaespesa, who is listed as its director. (Adolfo R. Corvera is the gerente, Ricardo Marín the director artístico and Pedro González Blanco the secretario de redacción.) Its price was 5 pesetas for a three-month subscription within Spain or Portugal. Abroad a year's subscription cost 20 francs. The price of a single issue was one peseta.

Pérez Ferrero[8] speaks of Villaespesa's optimistic insertion of advertisements not commissioned by the business concerned and naturally enough not paid for subsequently. Certainly he did not succeed in attracting sufficient advertisers, since many spaces are left vacant with the tell-tale word 'disponible' across them. It seems probable that its heterogeneity and lack of a coherent sense of direction made it unattractive to any substantial body of readers. At all events, the review's ambitions proved excessive, and only four numbers (15 July, 5 August, 20 August and 15 September 1902) are known. The last number announced that from that issue the magazine would appear on the 15th and 30th of the month (no doubt to explain the ten days' delay in publication), but no further numbers seem to have appeared. Seven months were to elapse before the most sumptuous review of the period, Helios, comes into existence, but Villaespesa is not involved in this new venture, though Pedro González Blanco is. Alma española began to come out later in the year (November 1903) and for several months, almost miraculously, two major literary journals devoted to modern literature and thought existed simultaneously.

Let us now examine the contents of the four issues of the magazine. For the first number Villaespesa succeeds in marshalling a wide range of contributions representing the most diverse points of view.

Perhaps the most interesting prose item is an uncollected review of
Unamuno of a book by Camilo Bargiela. Entitled "El humorismo" it
contains an early mention of Kierkegaard and the three stages of life
from Either/Or. Valle-Inclán has a narrative piece under the title of
"La reina de Delicam". Jacinto Benavente's study on Ibsen comes to
the superficial and disappointing conclusion that "el caviar noruego"
and "la ensalada rusa" are not for the Southern countries with their
"literatura y filosofía claras como el cielo". The institucionista
Manuel B. Cossío gives a foretaste of his great book in "El Greco
(fragmento de un estudio del arte en Toledo)". A study by Edmund
d'Amicis of D'Annunzio completes the prose contributions. In verse,
we find "El lago y la ondina" by Manuel Reina, together with a pencil
sketch of the poet by R. Marín, "La infanta doña María Teresa de
Austria" by Antonio de Zayas,[9] and a pen-portrait ('esbozo impresionista',
it is called) of the American-born symbolist poet Stuart Merrill,
together with a translation of two poems entitled "Poemas de crepúsculo",
by Ramón Pérez de Ayala; the first lines are "En mí habla una nostalgia
de labio y de rosas..." and "Mas ¿eres digno, humano, que bendecirla
quieres...?"[10] Finally, two Portuguese poems are included: "El
cantador" (in Spanish) by Guerra Junqueiro and "Versos da despedida",
by Silvio Rebelo, this time in Portuguese.

The second issue maintains a similar breadth, with prominent
intellectual contributions like the essay by Francisco Giner de los
Ríos "La educación del filisteo",[11] another article, "Idilio pedagógico",
by M.B. Cossío, a study by Pedro González Blanco entitled "Los filósofos
desconocidos: Wladimir Soloviov (muerto en 1900)" and, from abroad,
Paul Bourget, with an essay on Flaubert. Alvaro Xavier de Castro has
a piece of art criticism "Impresiones del Museo del Prado". Benavente
contributes another article, "Intelecto de amor", and there is a
sketch of him by Marín. Camilo Bargiela offers a curious dialogue
between Don Juan and Don Quixote in Buttarelli's inn ("En la hostería
del Laurel"). Juan Ramón Jiménez, still listed as 'Juan R. Jiménez',
is the only Spanish poet to contribute to this number, with "Yo me
moriré...", later collected in Arias tristes (1904). There are again
two Portuguese items: Riveiro de Carvalho's "Lenda portugueza", with
a sketch of the poet by Marín, and "Los siete durmientes", translated
into Spanish, by the well-known symbolist Eugénio de Castro.

Both the artistic and the intellectual concerns of the review
are maintained in the third issue. As regards the first, it contains
Rafael Altamira's "Poesía de las catedrales góticas"[12] and Angelo
Conti's study of "La 'Gioconda'", as well as an essay by 'Angel Guerra'
on Gorki and an excerpt, with a pen-sketch of the novelist, from
Felipe Trigo's La sed de amar, to be published later in the year.
The Portuguese writer Manuel Laranjeira[13] has a substantial article
entitled "Arte nuevo" in which he vehemently denounces symbolism and
religious belief and advocates scientific determination in literature.
In view of the significance of controversies of this type at the time[14]
and of Laranjeira's later development, it is worth quoting his comments
in extenso:

> Basta abrir un libro simbolista para convencernos de que
> ese libro es el producto de un cerebro desordenado - que es
> lo que hay de menos simbólico.
>     Se confunde desgraciadamente el símbolo con el misterio
> y con todo lo que hay de vago y nebuloso.
>     ... La forma en arte debe ser - y lo es en los artistas
> de genio - inseparable de la concepción, su expresión justa,
> su símbolo, en fin.

¿Hizo esto la escuela simbolista? No. El arte debe sugerir, nunca expresar, decían; y, con este principio como escudo, producían un radotage híbrido, desconexo como el humo. Por lo demás, la escuela simbolista lo es verdaderamente, cuando menos pretensiones tiene de serlo.

... Felizmente, hoy hay también quien mira hacia Dios como miraría hacia las ruinas de una cárcel; quien sabe que la vida tiene determinantes naturales, y que las acciones humanas son movidas por un determinismo psíquico. Para éstos, naturalmente, el arte entró por una nueva senda.

Tal es la obra de Zola y de un modo más absoluto las de Ibsen, Strinberg (sic) y Hauptmann, a quienes las muchedumbres no comprenden por el hecho de ignorar éstas los modernos ideales científicos. Y no se diga que el sentido crítico y científico están en desacuerdo con el arte; quien tal afirma, o es un ignorante o un idiota: un ser nocivo de cualquier modo...

El arte nuevo tiene que ser positivo, orientado por un determinismo bisanímico.

Y toda la obra que de otro modo se nortee, será obra muerta, un aborto condenado al olvido, aunque obtenga un éxito momentáneo.

El artista moderno ha de ser educado en las nuevas ideas: es necesario que se las asimile, que las traduzca en sentimientos, y después puede descansar seguro que cumplió su deber, legando a la humanidad una obra fecunda, y no un desahogo lírico y empalagoso, como el que vomitan esos cretinos que se retuercen convulsivamente en su impotencia...

Laranjeira's extreme scientific attitude is hardly in accord with two prose pieces which follow, Manuel Machado's "Solos", a dialogue between Pierrot and Colombine, and Jiménez's gloomy meditations entitled "Cosas tristes".

In verse, the most significant items, undoubtedly, are five poems by Antonio Machado under the title "Del camino".[15] Although none of the poems is unknown, they are the only examples of pre-book publication of poems from "Del camino", the maturest section of his first collection, Soledades (1903). It is significant to note that they are preceded by a line of Berceo's:

Todos sqmos romeros que camino andamos
DE BERCEO

This is the first reference to the medieval poet who clearly had a very marked attraction for Machado;[16] we can now evidently relate the concepts of both the camino and the romero or peregrino, so important in the early Machado, with Berceo.

The poems included are:
I. "Quizás la tarde lenta todavía" (PC XXVII; SGOP, 106[17])
   It offers the same text as S (1903), with its varied first line.[18]
II. "Daba el reloj las doce... y eran doce" (PC XXI; SGOP, 100)
   No variants; in RIb as in S (1903) there is no division into stanzas. One of the finest of Machado's early poems.
III. "¡Oh, figuras del atrio, más humildes" (PC XXVI; SGOP, 105)
   In this case there are substantial variants (omission of two lines, modified last two lines, punctuation changes) so that it is worth reproducing the RIb version:

> ¡Oh, figuras del atrio, más humildes
> cada día y lejanas!
> ¡Mendigos harapientos
> sobre marmóreas gradas!
> ¡Manos que surgen de los mantos viejos
> y de las rotas capas!
> ¿Pasó por vuestro lado
> una ilusión velada
> de la mañana luminosa y fría
> en las horas más plácidas?...
> Era su mano blanca entre las rosas
> como una rosa blanca...

The addition of the lines "miserables ungidos / de eternidades santas" and the revision of the last two lines in S (1903) are clearly improvements.

IV. "Algunos lienzos del recuerdo tienen" (PC XXX; SGOP, 109)

The text is the same as S (1903), without the changes subsequently made to lines 7 and 8.

V. "Tenue rumor de túnicas que pasan" (PC XXV; SGOP, 104)

No variants, except that line 11 reads: "La tarde ha dormido".

For the sake of convenience, it is as well to deal here with the one poem of Machado's which appears in the fourth number of La Revista ibérica. Illustrated by R. Baroja and entitled "Salmodias de abril", it begins:

"La vida hoy tiene ritmo" (PC XLII; SGOP, 130)

Without the title "Campo" given it in S (1903), it has a few variants: line 7 "los blandos junquerales"; line 13 "El campo parpadea"; lines 17, 18 24 with the same text as S (1903); line 28 "marchas". As in most cases where Machado revises his earlier text, an improvement results, with the reiteration of the colour 'verde', the elimination of the exaggerated personified metaphor 'parpadea' and the replacement of 'marchas' by the more natural 'pasas'.

The Revista ibérica poems add six more examples to the very few poems known to have been published before Soledades (1903); with them we now have some thirteen early revisions out of a total of forty-two compositions.

The remaining contents of the fourth issue (15 September) follow the usual varied pattern. In prose, a review by 'Angel Guerra' of Enrico Carradini's Giulio Cesare, an essay by Pedro González Blanco entitled "¿De quién es el Fausto?", a piece by José Jesús García "El señor" and another by Julio de Lemos entitled "Jesús". Manuel Machado has sent from Paris a "Silueta parisiense". Poetry includes, apart from Antonio Machado's poem already described, "Estoy solo" by Juan Ramón Jiménez (later collected in Arias tristes) and "Las grutas de la costa" by Eduardo Marquina. From Portugal come a description of the palace of Cintra by the count of Sabagosa, M. Cardia's "Las opiniones literarias de mi amigo F." and Tomás de Fonseca's "La noche de la miseria", all three in Spanish (for the latter Manuel and Antonio's brother, José Machado, made an illustration). In verse, Eugénio de Castro's "El peregrino" appears in Villaespesa's translation, while Ladislao Patricio has a poem, "Pállida moça", in Portuguese.

The contents of the Revista ibérica are characterized by the eclectic convergence of intellectual historians of the calibre of Giner, Cossío and Altamira, a marked concern with the plastic arts, both by means of articles and illustrations, a considerable interest in modernist poetry and prose by Jiménez, the Machado brothers and Pérez de Ayala (Antonio Machado's contribution being the most

important) and a commendable urge to bring in a substantial Portuguese
contribution which would create a genuine Iberian review. Too wide a
dispersal of interest was no doubt a cause of the magazine's lack of
success. It deserves nonetheless to be accorded a modest place in the
development of modern peninsular literature and to have its contents
assimilated into the literary history of the period.


# N O T E S

1.  See my article written twenty years ago and significantly entitled
'Riqueza inagotada de las revistas literarias modernas', Revista de
literatura, XIII, 25-26 (1958), 30-47.  I then wrote, if I may be
excused the immodesty of quoting myself: "se puede decir que una de las
tareas de investigación más urgentes para los estudios de literatura
moderna es la confección de índices detallados, escrupulosos y completos
de estas revistas" (30).

2.  'La generación española de 1898 en las revistas del tiempo',
Nosotros, 67 (Buenos Aires, 1941), 3-38.

3.  'Algunas publicaciones literarias hacia 1898', Arbor, XI, 36
(1948), 465-480.

4.  'El modernismo a través de las revistas', Modernismo frente a
Noventa y Ocho (Madrid 1951), 20-45.

5.  For Helios, see J.L. Cano, 'Juan Ramón Jiménez y la revista Helios',
Clavileño, VII, 42 (1956), 28-34; D.F. Fogelquist, 'Helios, voz de un
renacimiento hispánico', Revista iberoamericana, XX (1955), 1291-1299;
D. Paniagua, 'Helios (1903-1904)', Punta Europa, 94 and 95 (1964), and
especially Patricia O'Riordan, 'Helios, Revista del modernismo (1903-
1904)', Ábaco, 4 (1973), 57-150.  An index of Alma española (Madrid,
Ediciones Turner, 1978) edited and introduced by Patricia McDermott
(née O'Riordan) has recently appeared.

6.  Vida de Antonio Machado y Manuel (Madrid 1947), 106.

7.  Electra came out between March and May 1901; nine numbers are
known.  Juventud appeared from October 1901 to March 1902 (12 issues).
Arte joven was also published between March and April 1901.

8.  Op. cit., 107.

9.  Collected in Retratos antiguos (Madrid 1902), 143.

10.  I have not succeeded in locating these poems among Stuart Merrill's
publications.

11.  Obras completas, VII, 2nd ed. (1933), 271-274.

12.  Reproduced in De historia y arte (Madrid 1902) and Estudios de
crítica literaria y artística (Madrid 1925).

13. At the time a young medical student. Later, a friend and correspondent of Unamuno's, with an agonized outlook very different from that demonstrated in this article. He committed suicide in 1912. See Julio García Morejón, Unamuno y Portugal, 2nd ed. (Madrid 1971), 441-459.

14. Antonio Machado's gradual rejection of symbolism, for example, dates from about this time. See my essays in Niebla y Soledad (Madrid 1971).

15. Antonio Machado was in Paris during the Spring and Summer of 1902; this may account for his absence from the first two issues. Manuel, who stayed in Paris longer, must have sent his contributions from there.

16. The figure of Berceo, 'poeta y peregrino', is evoked enthusiastically in "Mis poetas" (PC CL), which first appeared in the first edition of PC in 1917.

17. The following abbreviations are used: S (1903): Soledades (1903); SGOP: Soledades, Galerías. Otros poemas (page references are to my edition, Barcelona, Labor, 1975); PC: Poesías completas.

18. For the text of Soledades (1903), see ed. by Rafael Ferreres, (Madrid, Taurus, 1968), and my ed. cit.

Nationalism and the vogue of the historical novel in nineteenth-century Spain

Eamonn Rodgers (Trinity College, Dublin)

It is of some significance for the study of nineteenth-century literature that the major novelists of the period have, with remarkable frequency, described their approach to the writing of novels negatively, by emphasizing what they are not doing. The statement of the Goncourt brothers in the preface to Germinie Lacerteux, "Le public aime les romans faux:  ce roman est un roman vrai", expresses a feeling of alienation from the tastes, assumptions and interests of the vast majority of readers, a feeling which was shared by all writers who sought to convey a message different from what the general public was accustomed to hearing. George Eliot, in the fifth chapter of The Sad Fortunes of the Rev. Amos Barton, warns the reader, with gentle irony, not to expect the heroic deeds and figures commonly found in fiction:

> ... perhaps I am doing a bold thing to bespeak your sympathy on behalf of a man who was so very far from remarkable, - a man whose virtues were not heroic, and who had not the slightest mystery hanging about him, but was palpably and unmistakably commonplace.

When Galdós, in La desheredada, makes Encarnación Guillén say to her vapid and deluded niece, "... tú te has hartado de leer esos librotes que llaman novelas", he is attaching a very specific set of pejorative connotations to the word novela.

These connotations tend to be glossed over in our thinking about the literature of the past. When an undergraduate says he is studying "The Nineteenth-Century Novel", we immediately assume, if he is a student of Spanish, that he is referring to writers like Galdós, Alas, Valera and Pardo Bazán. If, on the other hand, he says he reads a novel on the bus going home, we are likely to assume that he is wasting his time on Jean Plaidy or Micky Spillane. We are, in short, more aware of our own contemporary literature as a large-scale, varied phenomenon, the importance of which is as much sociological as aesthetic, but this awareness fades when we consider the literature of the past. We tend to confine our attention to those writers whose importance resides precisely in the fact that they add to the literary tradition by virtue of their originality and their capacity for innovation. This ability to transcend literary and cultural conventions makes such writers stand out from their contemporaries as far-seeing and therefore unrepresentative figures. Conversely, it may be argued that second-rate literature provides a more reliable guide to the ideals, assumptions and aspirations of a particular society than do major works of original creation.[1] It is the contention of this essay that this is indeed true of the historical novel in nineteenth-century Spain.

By "historical novel" I mean a novel in which history is presented as such, that is as the shared past of author and reader. Such a novel arises in part from the effort to understand and present this past in a certain way. This process is quite distinct from the very common practice of using a historical setting as a convenient source of suitably intricate plots, which minister to the public's desire for excitement, melodrama, suspense and mystery.[2] An extreme example of this practice is provided by Ramón Ortega y Frías's La Casa de Tócame Roque, which can only have merited inclusion in the recent paperback

series <u>La Novela Histórica Española</u> on the tenuous ground that it is
set in the eighteenth century. But it is exclusively a novel of
mystery and intrigue, and offers no interpretation of the past, except
insofar as the past is seen as a time when more exciting things tended
to happen. It is, of course, true that elements of mystery and melodrama occur even in the historical novel properly so called, but this
is simply an index of how novels of all kinds tend to rely on certain
well-tried ingredients of the story-teller's art. The reflection of a
particular interpretation of the past in the historical novel does not
ultimately depend on these ingredients.

The historical novel and the novel of entertainment are not, then,
co-terminous in respect of their content, even if the novel of entertainment frequently used pseudo-historical subject-matter as a source
of melodramatic plots. Neither was the historical novel exclusively
popular in the sense of appealing to a mass reading public. It is true
that the historical novel was the principal beneficiary of the expansion
of the publishing industry after about 1840. The creation of a modest
but substantial reading public for the novel, through the concentration
of population in the major urban centres of Madrid and Barcelona;[3]
changes in printing technology which made it possible both to manufacture
paper and to print large numbers of copies by machine;[4] the resultant
growth of the periodical press: all these factors contributed to the
emergence of popular fiction as a primarily commercial enterprise. In
this enterprise, the profitability of novels with a historical content
was quickly recognized, and it is no accident that the outstanding
example of a successful commercial novelist, Manuel Fernández y González,
is also the major producer of historical or pseudo-historical novels.

It should nevertheless be remembered that the earliest important
examples of the historical genre were written well before the rise of
cheap popular fiction. Rafael Húmara y Salamanca is usually credited
with being the first Spaniard to write a truly historical novel:
<u>Ramiro, Conde de Lucena</u>, published in 1823. One of the most serious
and sophisticated contributions to the genre, Ramón López Soler's <u>Los</u>
<u>bandos de Castilla</u>, appeared in 1830, and between then and 1834 this
author published five more historical novels. In the latter year there
appeared Espronceda's <u>Sancho Saldaña, o el Castellano de Cuéllar</u>, and
Larra's <u>El doncel de don Enrique el Doliente</u>.[5]

Not only is the historical genre well established before the
commercial expansion of the popular novel begins in the eighteen-forties,
but historical novels of a more serious kind, aimed, it would appear,
at a more sophisticated section of the reading public, and sometimes
composed by people who were far from being run-of-the-mill hack-writers,
continued to be written throughout the century, parallel to and independently of the development of the popular novel in the wider sense.
For example, <u>La campana de Huesca</u>, first published in 1852, and reprinted
in 1854 and 1886, comes from the pen of one of the most sober and
scholarly figures of nineteenth-century Spain, Antonio Cánovas del
Castillo.

It should not be supposed from this that the various levels of the
reading public were completely separate and self-contained. Fernández
y González, who so signally managed to turn hack-writing into a way of
life, and who was widely believed to work by dictating two or three
novels simultaneously to different scribes, was invited to contribute
a specially-commissioned serial novel to the middle-class intellectual
review <u>La Revista Contemporánea</u>: this was <u>El privilegio de la Unión</u>,
which ran from March 1880 to August 1881. Although Galdós, in his
<u>Episodios Nacionales</u>, broke radically with the conventions of the
traditional historical novel, and although he often waxed sarcastic

about the deleterious effects of historical romance on popular taste, he confessed once that he had in his youth been an avid reader of Fernández y González's novels.[6] In an obituary written for the Buenos Aires newspaper La Prensa, in January 1888, Galdós paid generous tribute to Fernández y González's verve and inventiveness, and spoke warmly of "el placer indecible de aquellas lecturas sabrosísimas".[7]

Thus while for some purposes we may regard the novel of entertainment and the historical novel as overlapping to a considerable degree, nevertheless the continuing vitality of the historical novel throughout the nineteenth century is to some extent independent of the commercial success of the second-rank novel in general. The reasons why the historical novel proper continued to appeal to various levels of the reading public must be sought in deep-rooted assumptions and aspirations shared by all classes of society. For convenience, we may begin our examination of these aspirations with Galdós's obituary for Fernández y González. What is interesting in this article is that Galdós's criticisms of Fernández y González's glibness and superficiality are tempered by sympathy for the way in which the older writer expressed a certain lyrical elevation, and a characteristically Spanish vitality:

> Fernández y González sentía en su alma, como pocos, la
> tradicional energía del verso castellano y aquella manera
> de decir arrogante y solemne de nuestros dramáticos.
> También produjo composiciones líricas muy notables,
> impregnadas de la propia savia española y romántica de sus
> dramas.[8]

Coming from someone who had said, in his Observaciones sobre la novela contemporánea en España, "el lirismo nos corroe ... como un mal crónico e interno",[9] this statement is indeed remarkable. A clue to the origins of Galdós's admiration for this aspect of Fernández y González's writing is given later in the article. It is regrettable, says Galdós, that Fernández y González turned away from historical subjects after 1870, to concentrate on the exploits of famous criminals, but there is an explanation for this shift:

> ... cuando las naciones gloriosas decaen, dejando de
> intervenir en la política universal, siempre queda en el
> fondo del sentimiento público una aspiración caballeresca
> que se nutre de lo primero que encuentra a mano.[10]

The significance of these two passages is that they encapsulate the dual aspects, military and cultural, of what I have elsewhere called the national inferiority complex of nineteenth-century Spaniards.[11] The crisis of 1898 is important, not as an isolated event, but because military defeat and the disappearance of the last vestiges of Spain's imperial role sharpened a sense of national decadence which had been a chronic preoccupation throughout the century. The literary effects of the crisis of 1898 are well enough known, but it is worth emphasizing that other important military events of the nineteenth century overflowed into literature and the arts in different but comparable ways. The two key episodes in this connexion are the War of Independence and the Moroccan campaign which took place in the winter of 1859-60. In the national consciousness, indeed, these two events were not separate, but part of the same sequence, a sequence which in some minds embraced the whole history of the reconquest of the peninsula from the Moors. As Raymond Carr has pointed out,

A myth of enormous potency, available to radicals and
traditionalists alike, grew out of Spain's unique and
proud resistance [to Napoleon]... defeat was psychologically
disastrous. Exalted patriotism attached itself to victory
over the United States in 1898, to conquest in Morocco,
even to the success of Peral's submarine.[12]

That this intepretation of the recent past was a myth, rather than
history in any sober or objective sense, is underlined by Carr when
he points out that the efficacy of this view as a focus for national
self-esteem was unimpaired by the impact of harsh facts. The essence
of Spain's defiance of Napoleon, for example, was dogged guerrilla
resistance, not military valour or superior strategy. The isolated
victory of Bailén was largely fortuitous, and was due to Napoleon's
belief that Spain represented only a policing problem, which could be
entrusted to untrained troops. The ill-considered euphoria generated
by victory at Bailén obscured the fact that the Spaniards were, in
normal circumstances, bound to fare badly in any further pitched battles
with the French. Their persistence in seeking full-scale engagements
only resulted in a succession of defeats. Similarly, the 1859-60
expedition to Morocco was badly planned and ill-equipped. Two-thirds
of the seven thousand deaths were from cholera. Nevertheless, "behind
a limited police operation ... lay vague notions of an African mission
and a new Crusade against the infidel Moors".[13]

Given this tendency to mythologize historical events, it is hardly
surprising that the myths in question should find expression in literary
form, whether fictional or non-fictional. One of the leading best-
sellers of the nineteenth century was Alarcón's <u>Diario de un testigo
de la Guerra de Africa</u>, the first edition of which sold fifty thousand
copies, and made a profit of ninety thousand <u>duros</u> for the publisher
Gaspar y Roig.[14] One of Ventura Ruiz Aguilera's short stories, <u>Al que
al cielo escupe, en la cara le cae</u>, shows the main character going off
to the Moroccan war, an event which causes the author to declare,

> El laurel de los siete siglos, que había reverdecido con
> lozana pompa en la guerra de la Independencia española, a
> principios del presente, daba ahora coronas para los héroes
> que vengaban en el imperio de Marruecos la funesta memoria
> del Guadalete.[15]

Aguilera sees the War of Independence and the Moroccan campaign as
belonging to a continuum which goes back to the battle in which
Rodrigo, the last Visigothic king, was defeated by Tariq in 711!
Elsewhere in the text, we find confirmation of how acute the preoccupation with national self-respect was at the time the story was written
(1861). Aguilera refers to "las acciones y batallas que tanto
levantaron el nombre español a los ojos de Europa, la cual injustamente
nos consideraba como un pueblo degenerado e incapaz de sostener el brillo
de nuestros antiguos blasones".[16]

There are two further ways in which literature contributes to
the search for national regeneration. As well as specific literary
references which reflect the urge to create a national mythology out of
important historical events, there is a more general tendency to make
the cultivation of literature a patriotic act. The xenophobia, and
specifically gallophobia, which was both the inspiration and the most
enduring result of the War of Independence, entailed in the literary
sphere a conviction that the decadence of Spanish literature, at any
particular moment in the century, was due almost entirely to the

influence of foreign, particularly French models.  Cultural nationalism
was so widespread and so fundamental to Spaniards' thinking about
their national literature in the nineteenth century that it often
united those who were in other respects poles apart.  If the War of
Independence had created, in Carr's words, "a myth ... available to
radicals and traditionalists alike", it was also true that the urge
to cherish and foster the literature of the past was shared by romantics
and neo-classicists, liberals and reactionaries.

Now it is undoubtedly true that the impetus for the revival of
interest in Spanish medieval and Golden Age literature, in the early
nineteenth century, came in large measure from outside the peninsula.
French, English and German romantics seeking to break out of what they
perceived as the strait-jacket of classical rules, readily turned to
Spain in search of literary models, since that country possessed a
long and distinguished tradition of balladry, and of non-classical
drama.  The fact remains that within Spain itself, the issue of the
revival of past literary glories was to a large extent independent of
the polemics about the classical unities.  Writing in 1861, when these
polemics had long been a thing of the past, Amador de los Ríos could
still sum up the eighteenth century in this way:

> Mientras se extendía y dominaba en todas partes la influencia
> galo-clásica, no habían en efecto faltado escritores que,
> alentados por el sentimiento patriótico, tratasen, si no de
> refrenar el movimiento que las letras llevaban, lo cual era
> humanamente imposible, de vindicar al menos el nombre español
> y la gloria de nuestros más ilustres vates, maltratados sin
> consideración ni miramiento por naturales y extranjeros.[17]

Neo-classicism is here equated with things French, and it behoved
all patriotic Spaniards to repudiate the one with the other.  But since
cultural nationalism often produces odd paradoxes, we must also note
that a similar patriotism with regard to the Spanish literary heritage
was expressed by many who would have wished to retain the essential
core of neo-classical theory.  For this latter group, "things French"
means the moral and aesthetic anarchy of romanticism, which Spaniards
are slavishly bent on imitating.  Thus José Joaquín de Mora, while
upholding the authority of the ancients, and drawing frequent support
from Cicero and Quintilian, can still lament national literary decadence
in terms similar to those employed by Amador:

> De tal modo nos hemos acostumbrado a este humillante
> servilismo, que transcurren los años y se multiplican
> las publicaciones, sin que se descubra, en lo que hemos
> querido llamar movimiento literario, una traza de ori-
> ginalidad; un brote espontáneo de ingenio, de imaginación,
> un resto de aquella fecundidad admirable, que nos dio
> nombradía en otros tiempos y que no osaban negarnos los
> más encarnizados enemigos de nuestras glorias.  Parece
> que estamos con la pluma en la mano aguardando a ver por
> dónde despuntan los escritores del reino vecino, para
> apoderarnos inmediatamente del cuadro que trazan, y
> acomodarlo mal o bien a nuestras dimensiones ... olvidamos
> que la nacionalidad es tan esencial a la literatura como
> a la política ...[18]

If those who took up opposing positions in matters of literary
theory could agree to cherish the heritage of the past, it was no less

true that national literature provided a meeting-ground for political
adversaries. Again, we may note two broad tendencies. For writers
like Agustín Durán, the eclipse of Spanish Golden Age drama by neo-
classical literary standards is, in part, the result of modern demo-
cratic philosophies:

> Así fue [Francia] acostumbrándose en medio de la monarquía
> a cierta libertad semirrepublicana, que permitía o toleraba
> a los individuos de ella la censura y discusión de todas
> las opiniones. Introducido ya y generalizado el espíritu
> de análisis, que es tan favorable a las ciencias de hecho
> como perjudicial a las de imaginación y sentimiento íntimo,
> el pueblo francés se separó cada día más del espíritu
> monárquico y del entusiasmo religioso y caballeresco de
> los siglos heroicos de la Edad Media.[19]

For certain political progressives, on the other hand, it was precisely
the monarchical system which produced this result:

> ... el absolutismo monárquico y la intolerancia religiosa
> nos llevaron del florecimiento científico de la Edad Media
> y del florecimiento filosófico y literario de los siglos
> XV y XVI a la triste decadencia de los siglos XVII y XVIII,
> y a convertirnos en un pueblo de copistas e imitadores, que
> es lo que con alguna ligera excepción hemos llegado a ser en
> el siglo XIX.[20]

The ingenuousness of these statements as historical judgements
hardly needs to be emphasized, but this does not invalidate my basic
argument about the pervasiveness of cultural nationalism. The
practical results of this concern for the national literary heritage
are to be seen in the scholarly labour of retrieving and re-editing
medieval and Golden Age works, the beginnings of literary criticism
and literary history in something like their modern forms, and the
writing of new imaginative works in imitation of older genres. Thus
Durán is not only the author of one of the most trenchant expressions
of cultural nationalism, but also a collector and editor of medieval
ballads. Mora, with his Leyendas españolas (1840), inaugurates a
tradition of verse leyendas which was still displaying considerable
vitality more than forty years later: Zorrilla's La leyenda del Cid
dates from 1882. Mora also collected and published, in 1844, the
critical essays of Alberto Lista, who in turn was one of the first to
attempt a serious critical study of Golden Age plays. Amador de los
Ríos is credited by Donald Shaw with being "the first native Spaniard
to write a full-scale Historia crítica de la literatura española
(1861-65) on genuinely scholarly lines".[21] In the field of imitation,
the most significant works are Rivas's Romances históricos (1841), and
various romantic historical dramas such as Bretón de los Herreros's
Vellido Dolfos (1839) and García Gutiérrez's Venganza catalana (1864),
which draw at once on the tradition of verse-drama, and on medieval
ballads and chronicles. Finally, and perhaps most important of all,
the Biblioteca de Autores Españoles, from 1846 on, made large numbers
of medieval and Golden Age works available to a relatively wide
readership, becoming one of the most significant cultural institutions
of the century.

One can summarize the significance for the historical novel of
all this scholarly and creative activity by stating that anyone setting
out to write a historical novel at the end of 1860 need not have gone

outside the peninsula or very far back in time to have available a
body of sources which included the following:

Agustín Durán, Colección de romances castellanos ante·iores al
siglo XVIII (first published in five volumes 1828-1832), reprinted in
two volumes in the B.A.E. 1849-1851, and again in 1851-1854);

José Joaquín de Mora, Leyendas españolas (1840);
Duque de Rivas, Romances históricos (1841);
Crónica de los reyes de Navarra (1843);
Crónica del famoso caballero Cid Rui Diez Campeador (1844);
Poemas épicos, 2 vols. (1851-1854) (B.A.E.);
La gran conquista de ultramar (1858) (B.A.E.);

Crónica de Felipe IV, published by Antonio Benavides in 1860, this
being the first printing since 1554;

Conquista de Córdoba por el Rey San Fernando. Rasgo épico,
dedicado a S.A.R. el Sermo. Príncipe de Asturias (Sevilla 1860).

This leads directly to the second way in which literature
contributes to the quest for national self-confidence. For, as can be
seen from the foregoing list, the bulk of this rediscovered and
revitalized national literature was, in one sense or another, historical
fiction. That is to say that the view of history was mediated through
a literary process of stylization and idealization. This was arguably
true even of chronicles, and still more so of ballads, leyendas and
plays. Thus the nationalism which had led men of every shade of
literary heritage of the past was reinforced when the re-discovered
works themselves turned out to be excellent sources of national myths.
The Cid, the Reconquest, especially the conquest of Granada,[22] the
civil wars of the mid fifteenth century, figures such as the Príncipe
de Viana, Doña Blanca de Navarra, or Alvaro de Luna, figures who could
be either pathetic, wicked, or heroic, but were always sublime: these
were the foci around which patriotic enthusiasm tended to centre.
Once again it is Durán who gives particularly clear expression to this
concern:

> Estamos los españoles con la imaginación muy cercanos a la
> conquista de Granada, para haber olvidado los nobles recuerdos
> de los caballeros árabes y los cristianos que, peleando en el
> campo de honor, se disputaban el premio en generosidad,
> cortesía y amores ... Por mi Dios, por mi rey y por mi dama
> es aún la divisa del noble castellano, y sobre ella han girado
> todas las creaciones poéticas donde brilla el genio nacional,
> desde principios a fines del siglo XVII. Si los extranjeros
> nos llevan algunas ventajas en industria, podemos nosotros
> gloriarnos, a lo menos, de conservar todo el entusiasmo
> patriótico y religioso que no pudo hollar impunemente el que
> dominó a la Europa entera [i.e. Napoleon] y envanecernos de
> conservar ileso y lleno de honor el lema que nos distingue:
> Por mi Dios, por mi rey y por mi dama.[23]

The historical novel, then, could contribute to the rebuilding
of national self-confidence, both by adding to the stock of contemporary Spanish literature, and by celebrating those episodes and figures
from history which fostered the myth of Spanish valour and chivalry.
This is certainly the implication of López Soler's remark, in the
preface to Los bandos de Castilla, that one of the objects of that
novel is to "manifestar que la historia de España ofrece pasajes tan
bellos y propios para despertar la atención de los lectores como las
de Escocia y de Inglaterra".[24] Because the main impetus behind the
writing of historical novels (apart from their obvious entertainment

value and profitability, to which I referred earlier) is the drive
for national self-esteem, we look in vain for any evidence of an
antiquarian or scholarly interest in the past. Galdós's attempt in
the Episodios Nacionales, to study the past in order to understand
the present, by exploring the immediate antecedents of contemporary
political alignments, is an outstanding exception to the general
tendency to view the past simply as a repository of ideals to which
Spaniards should strive to return. One consequence of this emphasis
is a considerable tolerance, perhaps even unconsciousness of anachronism. Thus López Soler is apparently aware of nothing incongruous
when he describes how the impact of a recitation by a fifteenth-century
troubadour communicates itself to his hearers "con velocidad de un
fuego eléctrico", or how those listening "formaban un grupo digno del
vigoroso y sombrío pincel de Salvador Rosa" (p.85). The abbot of a
monastery describes his conversion in terms which reveal a characteristic eighteen-thirties mixture of romantic nature imagery and
religious unction:

> - ... los desengaños y las desgracias hiciéronme dar de mano
> al comercio de los hombres. Como me irritaba su aspecto, me
> separé de sus ciudades; y arrastrado de no sé qué secreto
> impulso, perdíame por los bosques cual si hubiera de hallar
> en ellos alivio a mi saciedad y aburrimiento. Una tarde que
> andaba errando por lo más espeso de la selva, oí de repente
> el eco de una campana; acometióme cierta alegría desconocida,
> y acordéme de las dulces auroras de mi infancia, de los
> cariños de mi buena madre y de la consoladora religión en que
> me habían educado... ¡Ah!, desde aquel momento fui otro hombre:
> lloré y creí ... (p.77)

A similar tolerance of anachronism is to be found in Fernández y
González's El Cid Campeador, which I now want to consider as a paradigm case, illustrating the features of the historical novel we have
been discussing. Thus Rodrigo is made to say, "es necesario salvar
de los moros a esta desventurada España; aún falta por reconquistar
la mitad de ella" (p.108); and after the Cid's death, Alvar Fáñez
describes him as a "buen católico" (p.230). The reason for this
easy-going and unscholarly treatment of concepts which could not have
been current in the Cid's time is made explicit by Fernández y
González when he speaks of Rodrigo as "un mito representante de las
grandezas y del carácter de todo un pueblo representado en un ser
viviente". And he goes on:

> Los actos del Cid todos juntos y cada uno de por sí, forman
> lo que pudiera llamarse una especie de evangelio político
> popular. Es el héroe sin miedo y sin tacha. Por eso era
> adorado en su tiempo. La gloria de su nombre ha llegado
> resplandeciente a nosotros y vivirá mientras viva la inde-
> pendencia española. Y aún en la abyección, si a tal desgracia
> Dios quisiera conducirnos, resonaría como un eco doloroso el
> nombre del Cid. (p.15C)

Fernández y González's treatment of the episode of the Jura de
Santa Gadea is entirely consonant with this view. The Cid has the
moral authority to force Alfonso VI to swear publicly that he had no
hand in the murder of his brother Sancho II, "porque el Cid representaba el principio de la soberanía nacional". Political expediency
and the desire to avoid internal strife in Castile are glossed over:

instead, the emphasis falls on the principles of national independence
and of monarchical authority, which, as we saw earlier, are fundamental
to the sense of national identity, as experienced by writers like
Agustín Durán:

> El principio de la autoridad legítima no puede dispensarse.
> Sin él no hay sociedad posible. Y esto quería el Cid: que
> el rey tuviese autoridad, que nadie pudiese cuestionar sobre
> la legitimidad de su imperio. (p.151)

It is fairly obvious that Fernández y González is using the Cid
as the focus for ideals and aspirations which retained their full
emotional force at the time when he was writing. What is less obvious,
but no less real, is the appeal to his readers of attitudes and values
which at first sight seem alien to a modern sensibility. One of the
central episodes in the novel, the duel between Rodrigo and Gómez de
Gormaz, conde Lozano, owes its interest to the way in which it upholds
the aristocratic military ethic of valour, chivalry, and the exaggerated
sense of personal and family worth. Fernández y González is not, of
course, alone in reflecting such values in a historical novel, but his
treatment is remarkably explicit and emphatic. Vengeance appears to
Rodrigo, not simply as a natural reaction, but as a sacred, inescapable duty imposed on him by the shades of his ancestors. As he
declares to Gimena, just before the duel:

> - ... si yo fuera el hijo oscuro de una pasión desventurada,
> el hijo del ocaso, un hombre sin nombre; si no viniera de la
> noble raza de Nuño Rasura y de Laín Calvo; si comenzado por
> mí un linaje, no fuera fatalmente depositario del honor de
> mis mayores, aunque tu padre me injuriase aleve, aunque me
> soterrase en el polvo, aunque pusiese sobre mi rostro su
> planta y entregase a la infame burla de los villanos mi
> honor, pero solamente el honor mío, yo por tu amor sufriría
> resignado el vencimiento, la vergüenza, la muerte; yo
> arrojaría ante tu padre el roto y mancillado acero. Pero
> no puede ser; no lo quiere Dios: mi triste padre gime doble-
> gado bajo la vergüenza y las sombras de mi estirpe entera
> vagan en torno mío, y ¡venga nuestro honor!, me gritan, con
> muerto, sí, pero terrible labio. (p.72)

Apart from this speech and one further short outburst immediately
following it ("¿Qué más podéis pedirme, irritadas sombras de mis
mayores ... si la pierdo y con ella pierdo el contento, la luz, la
vida de mi alma, el alma de mi ser?"), there is little evidence of
real conflict between Rodrigo's duty to exact vengeance and his love
for Gimena. Even the offer of an apology from Gómez de Gormaz, far
from causing Rodrigo to waver in his resolve, reinforces his steely
determination to refuse all ignoble compromises:

> - ¿No os basta - exclamó haciendo un terrible esfuerzo
> el conde - el que yo declare ante el rey, ante Castilla,
> ante el mundo entero, que en un momento de locura y de
> error ...
> Rodrigo interrumpió de una manera terrible a don Gómez.
> - Si vos hicierais tal infamia - dijo - , que tengo la
> seguridad de que no la haréis, yo despreciaría a Gimena,
> yo os despreciaría a vos: a Gimena, por ser hija del que
> tal hizo y tal dijo, y a vos, porque el que añade una

infamia a otra infamia es más vil que el vil judío que
vendió a Jesucristo Nuestro Señor. (p.74)

Such single-minded dedication to the ideals of chivalry enables
the opponents, by a strange paradox, to rise magnanimously above their
quarrel, not indeed to abandon it, which would be unthinkable, but to
arrive at a kind of reconciliation through each recognizing the valour
and nobility of the other. When the Conde announces to his followers
that if he is killed, Rodrigo is to be given a safe-conduct out of his
lands, the narrator remarks:

No podía ser esto más noble ni más caballeresco. Rodrigo
se conmovió. Sintió todo el amargor de su desdicha al verse
obligado a matar a aquel caballero, tan digno de ser su padre. (p.77)

The duel ends with the following emotionally-charged dialogue:

- ... guardad mi espada, que en su limpio acero vea [limpia?]
su faz de vergüenza vuestro anciano padre...
- Yo guardaré, señor, vuestra invencible espada para
morir con ella desesperado en el combate. Dios sabe
cuánto me pesa de lo que sucede; pero me ha obligado el
honor.
- ¿Lloráis? - exclamó el conde con la voz débil.
En efecto, Rodrigo lloraba ... Un instante después exhaló
el último gemido entre sus brazos el conde Lozano.
- ¡De rodillas! - exclamó Rodrigo con una voz sobre-
natural -. Rendid las enseñas; el conde Lozano ha muerto;
orad por su alma. (p.79)

The scene is not without a certain power, but it is noteworthy
that despite the atmosphere of reconciliation, there is no attempt
to call in question the law of vengeance itself. Rodrigo is no
Calderonian hero, caught in a tragic dilemma, and railing against an
unjust code which forces him to make intolerable choices. Such
appeal as the episode of the duel possesses is of another, less
sophisticated kind. It is the appeal of untrammelled individualism
and assertiveness to readers immersed in a society in which mediocrity
is at a premium, and where life is a matter of moral compromises. It
is the appeal of traditional hidalguía to people who inhabit what
Galdós repeatedly referred to as este siglo prosaico, and who are
obsessionally conscious of national decadence, and of the fading of
those qualities which, in the popular mythology, once made Spain great.
It is the pleasure of contemplating aristocratic brío, arrogance and
aggressiveness in an idealized setting where they can do no real harm.[25]
The representative quality of Fernández y González's portrayal
of these values is thrown into relief if we reflect that the expression
of the honour theme is free from the egregious anachronism of, for
example, the view of the Reconquest which he ascribes to the Cid. Given
that Fernández y González had no pretensions to being a scholarly
historian, given also the essentially commercial character of his
literary activity, we may be reasonably certain that this absence of
anachronism is not due to any scrupulous respect for his sources. It
is rather that the author felt no need to modernize this aspect of the
novel because he knew that he was celebrating ideals which held great
interest and attraction for his readers. As Urbano Serrano wrote in
1879:

Lo que es legendario y tradicional es siempre preferido
por el verdadero artista; porque, aparte su forma y
simbolismo universalmente conocido, expresa aspiraciones
unánimes, ideales históricos, estados de la conciencia
pública, que puestos a contribución por el genio, dan
por resultado obras de general aceptación y que hieren
la sensibilidad de todos.[26]

We thus return, by a circuitous route, to the point which I made
at the outset of this article. Puerile and unsophisticated as second-
rank fiction may often seem to the academic critic, it is a mistake
to be dismissive towards it. As Miss J.M.S. Tompkins has written,
"... no fantasies have a wide popular appeal unless they are fairly
closely linked with popular aspiration and even, though less closely,
with fact".[27] While it is notoriously risky to use imaginative
literature as documentary evidence, this is because imaginative
literature, at its best, is also creative literature: creative in the
sense that the unique and original insights of the author open up to
a particular society, and ultimately to readers of subsequent gene-
rations, the possibility of new patterns of understanding. But the
bulk of imaginative literature is not creative in this sense. It is,
to borrow Fernández y González's phrase, an _evangelio popular_,
ministering to, rather than challenging, the deeply-held assumptions
and self-images of its readers. The historical novel of nineteenth-
century Spain belongs to this kind of literature, and may therefore
be studied for evidence of the myths which both expressed and fostered
the contemporary search for a sense of national identity and purpose.


NOTES

1. I have argued this case at greater length in 'Literary history,
literary criticism and the literary syllabus', Hermathena, CXXI
(Winter 1976), 54-68.

2. It has been well said of the English eighteenth-century novel
that "... at a period when historical knowledge was partial and thinly
spread, while the impressive relics of the past still filled the eye
and served as a focus for easy imagining, when education had hung no
weights on the dreamer's heels, and she could multiply dungeons to
her hearts content and transport without misgivings, herself and her
ideal lover, with all their varnish of modern sensibility fresh about
them into the rust of the past ... then we may conclude that 'historical novel' and 'romance' spell the same sort of entertainment"
(J.M.S. Tompkins, The Popular Novel in England, 1770-1800 [London
1969], 224. First edition 1932.).

3. See Juan Ignacio Ferreras, La novela por entregas 1840-1900.
Concentración obrera y economía editorial (Madrid 1972), especially
chapter 2.

4. See Antonio Serra y Oliveres, Manual de la tipografía española
(Madrid 1849).

5. For a fuller list, see Juan Ignacio Ferreras, <u>Los orígenes de la novela decimonónica 1800-1830</u> (Madrid 1973), 291-294.

6. Quoted by J.F. Montesinos in <u>Galdós</u>, Vol. I (Madrid 1968), 5.

7. B. Pérez Galdós, <u>Obras inéditas</u>, Vol. I (Madrid 1923), 103.

8. op. cit., 109.

9. B. Pérez Galdós, <u>Ensayos de crítica literaria</u>, ed. Laureano Bonet (Barcelona 1972), 116.

10. op. cit., 113

11. See my "Galdós y el 'complejo de inferioridad' español en el siglo XIX", in <u>Nationalisme et Cosmopolitisme dans les littératures ibériques au XIXème siècle</u> (Université de Lille III 1975), 121-131.

12. <u>Spain 1808-1939</u> (Oxford 1966), 105-106. Galdós shared the enthusiasm surrounding Peral's submarine, and wrote in one of his <u>La Prensa</u> articles: "¡Qué honor tan insigne para nuestro país si aclaramos antes que ninguna otra nación el misterioso enigma de la navegación submarina!" (<u>Obras inéditas</u>, VII, 195). Unfortunately, the submarine sank during trials.

13. Carr, op. cit., 260.

14. According to P. Blanco García, in his <u>La literatura española en el siglo XIX</u>, Parte 1a., Vol. II (Madrid 1891), 456.

15. <u>Proverbios ejemplares</u>, Vol. I (Madrid 1864), 232.

16. ibid., 233.

17. <u>Historia crítica de la literatura española</u>, Vol. I (Madrid 1861), li.

18. <u>Ensayos literarios y críticos por D. Alberto Lista y Aragón, con un prólogo por D. José Joaquín de Mora</u>, Vol. I (Seville 1844), vii-viii.

19. Footnote (<u>c</u>) to Agustín Durán's <u>Discurso sobre el influjo que ha tenido la crítica moderna en la decadencia del teatro antiguo español</u> (Madrid 1828), reprinted in Ricardo Navas-Ruiz, ed., <u>El romanticismo español. Documentos</u> (Salamanca 1971), 93-94.

20. From an anonymous <u>Miscelánea</u> in the <u>Revista Contemporánea</u>, XXII (July-August 1879), 122.

21. <u>A Literary History of Spain: The Nineteenth Century</u> (London and New York 1972), 178.

22. "¡<u>Granada</u>! Este nombre es de suyo poético: él evoca recuerdos grandes a la par y halagüeños: él trae a la mente en confuso tropel todo el brillante período de nuestra historia, en que la prepotencia española conquistó gloriosamente el baluarte último de la invasión morisca. ¡Granada! A este nombre soñamos con su dilatada vega, con sus justas antiguas, con su Alhambra dorada, con sus árabes generosos y valientes, con sus historias de amor, con los guerreros que

disputaban dignamente a los castellanos aquel postrer recinto de su dominación pasada." (From a note on Miguel Lafuente Alcántara's <u>Historia de Granada</u> (Granada 1843), in Dionisio Hidalgo, <u>Diccionario bibliográfico</u>, III (1868), 213a).

23. <u>Discurso</u> ..., ed. cit., 95, note (<u>c</u>).

24. See the relevant volumes of the series <u>La Novela Histórica Española</u> for references to this novel and to <u>El Cid Campeador</u>, discussed below. Page references will be incorporated in the text of the article.

25. It is interesting to note in this connexion that López Soler, in the preface to <u>Los bandos de Castilla</u>, felt the need to justify his modifications of the facts of fifteenth-century history by claiming that "la [época] de don Juan el Segundo no es la más a propósito para una novela histórica, a causa de no resplandecer en ella un carácter esencialmente marcado por grandes vicios, admirables virtudes o sobresaliente valor ..."

26. <u>Revista Contemporánea</u>, XXIII (September-October 1879), 156.

27. op. cit., 86.

216

# Exemplary ethics:  towards a reassessment of Santillana's Proverbios

Nicholas G. Round (University of Glasgow)

The date traditionally given for the composition of Iñigo López
de Mendoza's Proverbios de gloriosa doctrina e fructuosa enseñança is
1437. This is the date, apparently, which the great eighteenth-century
antiquary Floranes found in the Cancionero de Martínez de Burgos.
The copy of the Proverbios in that volume, however, belonged to a section which has now disappeared, and which Dr. Dorothy Severin, the
editor of the surviving portions, regards as no earlier than 1458.[1]
Yet in biographical and historical terms Floranes' information seems
credible enough.  The author's prologue makes very clear the circumstances in which the Proverbios were dedicated to Prince Enrique, the
heir of Castile:

> cómo algunas veçes por el muy illustre, poderoso, manífico
> é muy virtuoso señor rey, don Johan segundo, padre vuestro
> me fuesse mandado los acabasse é de parte suya á la Vuestra
> Exçellençia los presentasse.[2]

"Algunas veçes" need not lead us to suppose that Juan II had seen the
copy of verses on several separate occasions.  We know something of
Iñigo López's poetic drafts from the half-formed verse paraphrase which
he jotted in the margin of Juan Gil de Zamora's Alabanças de España.[3]
If the Proverbios, when Juan first saw them, were in a similarly rough
and ready state, it might well have taken several attempts to persuade
their author that they could ever be made fit reading for a prince.
The problem is, when did all this take place?
Obviously it was while Enrique was still young.  The Prologue
with its reference to "la terneça de la vuestra edat" (Amador p.22;
Cortina p.42) would fit the case of a boy of twelve - Enrique's age in
1437.  But a much younger child, unless strikingly precocious, would
get little good from a text like this, while a grown man would probably
resent its pedagogic tone.  We know that the work must have been completed before 4th May 1444 when Iñigo López sent a copy to Violante de
Prades.[4]  Political history, though, supplies a narrower set of limits.
From the end of 1438 Iñigo López was in open opposition to Juan II,
and several times bore arms against him in the sporadic civil wars of
the next few years.  By 1441 Prince Enrique too - his notions of filial
duty not much clarified, evidently, by the Proverbios - was pursuing
an independent and erratic political line of his own.  Only in late
1444 did the three men come together again, to form with Don Alvaro de
Luna the nucleus of that coalition which was to triumph in the following May on the field of Olmedo.  One celebration of that victory was
the grant to Iñigo López of his Marquisate of Santillana.  Another was
Juan II's commission to one of his judges of appeal, Pero Díaz de
Toledo, to compose an extended moralizing gloss on the Proverbios,
and send the work, thus embellished, to Enrique.  By that time Pero
Díaz could describe the original as being "difundido por tan diversas
e estrañas partes".[5]  But its composition clearly antedates the late
1430s.
Equally, the known relationship between poet and king would rule
out any date before the middle of that decade.  Social position,
family ties, and a long friendship with the Aragonese Trastámaras all
predisposed Iñigo López to take a dim view of Juan II's political
dependence on his Constable, Alvaro de Luna.  Nevertheless, in the

crisis of the late 1420s, he had justified his loyalty to the Crown
by a good war-record on the eastern frontier, and some lively patriotic satires.  But in 1432 he again fell foul of Don Alvaro's
security policies:  the arrest of several friends led him to set his
own strongest castle in a posture of defence.  By 1434 the situation
had once more eased, permitting a visit by King and Constable to
Iñigo López's stronghold of Buitrago; a marriage alliance with the
Lunas followed two years later.  At the end of 1436 the wedding feast
itself gave Iñigo López another opportunity to play host to the King,
this time in Guadalajara.  A royal visit there, indeed, was an especial
mark of favour.  It legitimized Iñigo López's de facto sway over a
town of some importance, with its own representation in Cortes.  It
gave hope of a favourable outcome - though the affair remained sub
judice - to the legal dispute between Mendozas and Manriques over
property in the area.  And it gave rise to a gratifying number of
royal grants in Iñigo López's favour.  It must have counted for
something, too, to have the whole business of government conducted
from one's own house.[6]  Did the discussions of poetry which issued in
the Proverbios also belong to this visit of December 1436?  It is
natural enough to think so.  And one piece of internal evidence supports
this view.  This is the reference in the Prologue to a letter sent to
Juan II by the Florentine Chancellor, Leonardo Bruni:

> en la qual le recuenta los muy altos é grandes fechos de
> los emperadores de Roma, naturales de la vuestra España.
> (Amador p.22; Cortina p.42)

The letter in question survives in a Castilian translation, and in
its Latin original as no. VII, 2 of Mehus, eighteenth-century edition.
Hans Baron dates the latter as no earlier than 1435, and no later than
August 1437; the Castilian text is dated 21st March, but with no year
mentioned.  This would rule out the earlier royal visit of 1434 as a
date for the Prologue, and probably for the actual commission to complete the Proverbios.  Much the most cogent reconstruction of events
seems to be this: Bruni's letter was sent on 21st March 1436, and
brought by Juan II to Guadalajara in December to impress his host.
Very possibly the Castilian translation, copied in one of Iñigo López's
own MSS, was made then and there for his benefit.[7]  On the same
occasion Juan II would have pressed him to finish the Proverbios, and
this he would have done, as the Cancionero de Martínez de Burgos
stated, in 1437.
    If that is accepted, however, the place which the Proverbios
occupy in the development of Iñigo López's writing would at first
appear to be an odd one.  His major poems of the two preceding years
illustrate a growing involvement and mastery in a wholly different
poetic idiom - that of ceremonial allegory and declamatory Latinism.
The Defunssión de Don Enrique de Villena of 1435 is unmistakably, not
to say defiantly, a difficult poem, bristling with Latinisms and
intricately structured.[8]  Its ultimate purpose would seem to be to
offer a sense of identity and reassurance to that tiny minority of
readers who were fully able to appreciate Villena's involvement with
ciencia in all its aspects.  Within the social minority of the
Castilian nobles and their immediate clients, and the minority among
these who read poetry at all, the Defunssión singles out a yet more
minoritarian readership.  Less provocatively esoteric, but just as
elevated in its diction, and notably more ambitious in scale, is the
Comedieta de Ponça of 1436.  It is very much more than a mere rhetorical monument to a public disaster - the capture in battle of the

Aragonese Trastámara princes. Through a complex and conspicuous display of learning, it reinterprets adverse fortune, not as mere _caso_
or mischance, but as memorable history, as divine providence, as the
earnest of blessings in store.[9] In so doing, it draws upon the full
resources of Iñigo López's poetic craft and book-learning. Yet instead
of a further development along the same lines, we have, in 1437, the
_Proverbios_, a major poem as limpid, austere and direct in intention
as the preceding allegories were complex, devious, and richly-wrought.
Why, one wonders, this sudden change of style?

Manuel Durán sees it as a matter of conscious poetic evolution
towards a "third manner" of writing:

> La presunción del poeta sabio, culto, superior, cede el paso
> a la sabiduría... del que sabe que es imposible mantenerse
> largo tiempo en el ambiente enrarecido de las cimas que una
> y otra vez intenta escalar.[10]

This is, perhaps, an excessively twentieth-century view. Mediaeval
views of poetry, by contrast with our own, tended to emphasize technique and training rather than individual creativity and inspiration.
The adoption of a particular style could scarcely present itself to
a mediaeval author as a question of self-expression in phase with his
own personal development. Rather, it was a matter of choosing the
particular rhetoric which corresponded to the poetic task in hand, the
inherent dignity or baseness of the subject-matter, and the character
of the audience in view. Thus Iñigo López, who at about the same
period was producing work as diverse as the later _serranillas_ and the
earliest of his Italianate sonnets, had plenty of sound, professional
reasons for composing the _Proverbios_ in a plain and accessible idiom.
They were not intended to idealize living royalties or to commemorate
the illustrious dead, but to offer "moralidades é versos de dotrina."
(Amador p.21; Cortina p.41). They were not addressed to the enlightened
minority of readers who could move securely in the realm of high culture, or even to individuals who, like the Aragonese royal house
apostrophised in the _Comedieta_, could safely be reckoned part of that
minority. They were for Prince Enrique, who was being encouraged and
assisted to join that select band. But he was not there yet; he was
a boy of twelve, whose need at the moment was for "algunos provechosos
metros acompañados de buenos enxemplos".[11] Clearly the ceremonial
strain was not in order here.

It is in this light, too, that we have to view the more learned
aspects of the _Proverbios_. The fact that the poem is "envuelto en una
copiosa masa de comentarios eruditos" is not, as Durán thinks, evidence
that they represent only a tentative first step towards a new simplicity.[12] Indeed, the amount of such material provided by Iñigo López
was neither extensive in itself - Amador's edition identifies only a
score of prose glosses as his work - nor even fully satisfying to
educated fifteenth-century taste; Juan II, after all, was to ask Pero
Díaz for a much longer commentary. To the later commentator, the
poet's own glosses were merely "algunas historias".[13] Their purpose
is to explain the work's array of allusions to classical and Biblical
examples, and to suggest, through reference to sources, some possible
lines of further reading. By contrast with the major allegories, the
_Proverbios_ are not so much a learned poem as a work of induction into
learning. Much of their success with Castilian readers over the next
century or so may well have been due to this.

There remains a problem, though, over the glosses, and for that
matter over Iñigo López's prologue, too. By contrast with the actual

poem, these supposedly informative elements are anything but straightforward easily assimilated Castilian.  A sentence like this, for
example, aims at a certain classical organization and amplitude, but
it falls flat on its face:

> Damnes, fija de Peneo é dada al serviçio de Dianna, deesa
> de castidat, é segund Ovidio lo pone en el su libro mayor,
> mucho amada de Febo ó Apolo, la qual non consintiendo en
> el su loco amor, segund poética ficçión, non pudiendo
> resistir á la fuerça del ardiente enamorado, recomendándose
> á los dioses, é en especial á Dianna, á quien ella servía,
> fué tornada en laurel, árbol de perpétua verdor, odorífero
> é de plaçiente sombra. (Amador p.79)

The erudition here is tediously and clumsily introduced, and if
the Latinisms of voçabulary are tolerable enough, the syntax is
perilously inept.  What sets out to be a nicely balanced descriptive
clause, following "la qual", degenerates into a rather desperate
huddle of adjectival phrases.  The effect - which brings us close to
much of Enrique de Villena's prose - is substantially to confuse,
rather than to impress or enlighten.  And this, from the _Prologue_,
is little better:

> Nin las roncas é soberbiosas ondas del mar ayrado, nin las
> prenosticaçiones vistas, asy de la garça volar en alto,
> como de la corneja passearse presurosamente por el arena,
> nin después de las señales que eran vistas en la luna, las
> quales todas eran amonestaçiones del pobreçillo barquero,
> impidieron la passada del Çésar é Antonio. (Amador p.25;
> Cortina p.43)

It is a bravura piece, of course, directly imitated from Lucan.  But
the effect is less than convincing.  All those connecting words which
ought to knit the sentence together end by making it seem more fragmented, and the homely "pobreçillo" sits uneasily with the grandiose
"prenosticaçiones".  That sort of thing went better in verse.  In
Juan de Mena's rather freer paraphrase of the same lines of Lucan, or
in Iñigo López's own close rendering of a Latin original in the famous
"Benditos aquellos ..." passage of the _Comedieta_, the verse-form
supplies that reinforcement of structure which ought to come in prose
from a Latin syntactical pattern.[14]
   It cannot do so in Castilian at this stage because the ground-
rules for what will prove acceptable in Castilian prose have yet to
be worked out.  These fifteenth-century examples are among the first
efforts at a Castilian prose rhetoric in which Latin syntactic models
are to the fore.  Alfonsine prose, though intensely concerned with
presentation, had sought to develop an independently Castilian mode
of good, communicative language.  Its long-standing influence was the
measure of its success, and was reinforced by that of other tendencies
which pointed away from the direct imitation of Latin syntax.  There
was the oral rhetoric of the sermon; there was also the didactic
tradition deriving from oriental translations.  Iñigo López's prose
shares the faults of Villena's because the latter offered virtually
the only model for a prose which assumed a similar relationship to
Latin.  Juan de Mena had the same problem, and fared no better, in the
prose commentary to his _Coronaçión_, dedicated to Iñigo López within
a few years of the _Proverbios_.[15]  Villena and Mena, who knew Latin
well, and Iñigo López, who almost certainly did not, all strove to

give their prose the dignity and difficulty which they associated
with that language. But the way forward lay through a rather different
approach to Latin, whose primary concern was with rendering what Latin
texts actually said:

> Por ende, guardada cuanto guardar se puede la intençión,
> aunque la propriedat de las palabras se mude, non me
> paresce cosa inconveniente; ca como cada lengua tenga su
> manera de fablar, si el interpetrador sigue del todo la
> letra, nescesario es que la escriptura sea obscura, e
> pierda grant parte del dulçor.[16]

Alonso de Cartagena, who set down these sensible observations in
the early 1430s, introducing his own version of Cicero's De Inventione,
could rise to rhetorical heights as well as most Castilians; indeed,
unlike most of them, he could do it in Latin. But he knew that his
native language made demands which were all its own. His application,
here to Cicero and elsewhere to Seneca, of a principle which dates
back to St. Jerome helped to release Castilian prose from the blind
alley into which its infatuation with Latin rhetoric threatened to
lead it. But it was an example with which Iñigo López's prose was
slow to come to terms.

It may have played some part, even so, in the much more successful adaptation evident in his verse. Certainly there are Senecan
echoes in both the style and the content of the Proverbios. Cartagena's version of the letter on the Liberal Arts, for example, seems
not quite close enough to Iñigo López to rank for certain as a direct
source. Yet both the ideas and the rhythms through which they are
expressed would appear to have been somewhere at the back of the poet's
mind. This is Cartagena's Seneca:

> ... E tanto es de tardar en ellos quanto nuestro coraçón
> no puede hazer otra cosa mayor. Ca comienço son de otras
> obras; no son ellas obras perfectas. E dirás ¿por qué los
> llaman estudios liberales? Yo te lo diré. Porque son dignos
> de onbre libre; mas el estudio verdaderamente liberal uno es.
> E sabes qual: aquel que haze al onbre libre, es a saber
> sabidor, virtuoso, alto, fuerte, de grand coraçón.[17]

And this, Iñigo López:

> A los libres pertenesçe
> Aprehender
> Dónde se muestra el saber
> E floresçe;
> Çiertamente bien meresçe
> Preheminençia
> Quien de dottrina é prudençia
> Se guarnesçe. (st.15)

Topics and sentiments apart, the clipped, elliptical sentences, the
strong but simple parallelisms, the discreet inversions of order –
above all, their secure accommodation within the Castilian idiom –
have all had their impact on the phrasing of the Proverbios.

But Iñigo López was also decisively assisted by the fact that
Castilian verse could offer him a wider range of alternative serious
styles. In particular, if he needed a model for 'proverbs' – accessible,
yet tersely memorable, moral instruction – there were two obvious

instances to hand. In the early 1420s or before, his kinsman Fernán
Pérez de Guzmán had composed a series of rhymed Proverbios. And in
the previous century, a yet more austere rhetoric with strong Biblical
overtones had marked the Romance Proverbios of Rabbi Sem Tob of
Carrión.[13] Among his contemporaries, Iñigo López thought highly of
Pérez de Guzmán, while even Sem Tob's manifest handicaps of status
could not deter him from recognizing the Rabbi as a major poet:
"Púselo en cuento de tan nobles gentes por grand trovador".[19] Between the three sets of Proverbios, moreover, there is a discernible
continuity of metre. Sem Tob's verse-form may be defined, adequately
if unscientifically, as a development of the old four-beat mester de
clerecía. Each hemistich is now experienced (and written) as a
separate line, with its own rhythmic structure, its own occasional
departures from a seven-syllable norm, and its own rhyme. This last
feature is not totally consistent: second and fourth lines, deriving
from the rhymed hemistich of the older metre, always rhyme; first and
third lines show a strong but not universal tendency to do so:

> El cuerdo non consyente
> Tomar de sus bondades
> Plazer quanto en myente
> Le vyenen sus maldades.[20]

Fernán Pérez takes this metre as his point of departure, alternating
the rhymes on a consistent a/b/a/b scheme, and assimilating each line
to a regular octosyllable, thus:

> Del home malo e malvado
> que alcanza grande poder
> si es sabio e esforzado
> quién se podrá defender? (st.5, Foulché-Delbosc
> p.753)

There is still more frequent hiatus between adjacent vowels than
would be tolerated in modern verse, or even perhaps in Villena's Arte
de trovar, but there is an obvious shift towards greater regularity
in the sophisticated forms of cancionero verse. Iñigo López goes
further in the direction of cancionero elegance, while retaining the
basic 'proverbial' pattern of a short, gnomic stanza with frequent
internal rhymes. He adopts a pie quebrado metre, alternating eight-
and four-syllable lines. By using four such pairs to a stanza, he
extends the traditional form by roughly half its length, but he avoids
diffuseness by adopting a rhyme-scheme - a/b/b/a/a/c/c/a - which
neatly integrates the stanza as a whole. This, too, comes from the
cancionero tradition: it is the scheme, for example, of several of
Iñigo López's own dezires.[21] Even so, he found it necessary to defend
his method in the Prologue, in terms less of contemporary practice than
of the Provençal theory set forth in Villena's Arte.[22] In any poem
of more than twenty stanzas, he explains, "cómo ya lo tal pueda ser
mas bien dicho libro ó tractado que deçir nin cançion, balada rondel,
nin virolay", repeated rhymes are permissible, provided all other
rules are kept. These, then, are proverbs in a very up-to-date idiom.
    At the same time, they plainly acknowledge a debt to Fernán Pérez.
The opening phrase, "Fijo mío mucho amado ..." owes something, as the
Prologue explains, to the terms of Iñigo López's commission from
Juan II, and to the example of Solomon. But it also echoes Fernán
Pérez's beginning, "Señor mío mucho amado ...". Again, the latter's
work survives in 102 stanzas; Iñigo López's has come down to us in 101,

of which no.73 is missing in many copies.  The reference in the 1444
prologue to the Comedieta to "los çient 'Proverbios' míos" makes it
almost certain that their number was originally 100;[23] very possibly,
the same was true of Fernán Pérez's work.

A hundred was, in any case, a convenient number, lending a little
formal unity to what appears to be a fairly loosely assembled poem.
The early tradition - apparent, for example, in editions like that of
Seville 1494[24] - of calling the collection "el Centiloquio" suggests
that contemporary readers found this number significant.  Quite
probably, the poem contains other important numbers too; we shall find
that there is a fairly clear division of the subject-matter after
stanza 62 - the nearest approximation to the Golden Section - and
that some other numerical relationships are pleasingly proportionate.
But such analyses ought not to be pushed too far.  The more obvious
numerical patterns were a form of embellishment which a poet like
Iñigo López might well employ, particularly to engage the interest
and direct the attention of a juvenile reader.  But insofar as the
poem is already integrated in its treatment of themes, any numerical
integration must be seen as secondary.  Besides, given that all the
Proverbios are meant to contain memorable advice, there is a danger
that any numerical relationship whatever can be made to seem significant.  It seems wisest to treat such features as largely incidental.[25]

The term "Centiloquio" has other, more important overtones,
recalling the manuals of classical moral lore - the Communiloquium,
Breviloquium, and so forth - assembled by the thirteenth-century
Franciscan, John of Wales.  These latter are a source for Iñigo López's
own glosses, and the title Centiloquio could itself reflect this
indebtedness.[26]  If so, it illustrates very clearly the didactic tradition to which he saw his work as belonging:  a strong mediaeval
tradition, concerned not to derive newly authentic human values from
a revived classical culture, but to assimilate the teaching of the
ancients into a Christian and Biblical framework.  The poem's more
familiar title, and the reality behind it, point in the same direction.
The first known author of a set of Proverbs had, after all, been
Solomon (whom Iñigo López and his contemporaries believed to have
written in verse).[27]  And the transmission of ancient wisdom through
collections of short, memorable sentences was a basic tool of mediaeval education.  Among such collections circulating in Castile, a
significant number, reflecting a wide diversity of types, bore the
term Proverbia in their title:  Proverbia Senecae; Proverbia Senecae
de Vitiis et Virtutibus; Buenos proverbios, to name but three.  In
embodying similar lore in a collection of his own Iñigo López was
following a standard mediaeval practice, and one which he believed to
have been that of the ancients also.  This is the defence which he
offers against the claim that his sentences are all taken from "Plato,
Aristotle, Socrates, Virgil, Ovid, Terence", and so forth:

> ... estos que dicho hé, de otros lo tomaron, é los otros de
> otros, é los otros d'aquellos que por luenga vida é sotil
> inquisiçion alcançaron las experiencias é cabsas de las
> cosas. (Amador p.26; Cortina p.44)

In this he had the support not merely of the mediaeval tradition of
sentence-literature but of the ingrained mediaeval suspicion of
originality.  First-hand insight was less prized than the weight of
tradition and authority.

The study of Iñigo López's sources, then, is likely to be useful
only in a limited sense.  The mere mention of an author's name does

not imply that he ever handled a text of that author; indirect contacts are just as likely. Thus, to take the list just cited, his library contained Castilian versions of Aristotle's Ethics and De Animalibus; Villena had supplied him with a version of Virgil. His awareness of Ovid may or may not have been at first hand. But one doubts if he ever read a play of Terence; he owned no Plato that he could read before the mid 1440s, and he read nothing by Socrates because Socrates never wrote anything. The close and discriminating source-study supplied by Lapesa's article of 1957 tells us less about indebtedness to particular authors than about the general pattern of material used - the preponderance, for example, of classical and Biblical references over mediaeval ones, and still more significantly, the mixture of elements of all these kinds.[28] Already Fernán Pérez, in his own Proverbios, had sought to blend the wisdom of "Séneca e Solomón" in similar fashion. But this in turn was simply a recent example of a long-standing mediaeval tradition - that of bringing such a diversity of sources to the service of a moral truth which was perceived as single, contemporary, and Christian. And so, in Iñigo López's poem, John of Wales and the Flos Sanctorum - possibly also Sem Tob and Walter Burley - keep company with Boccaccio, with Biblical Wisdom literature, and with genuinely classical examples. A high proportion of these last turn out, on Lapesa's evidence, to have been available in Castilian by this date - Valerius Maximus possibly; Cicero's De Officiis and De Senectute, and Seneca on clemency and the Liberal Arts certainly, in Alonso de Cartagena's versions. Other Senecan quotations used by Iñigo López could derive from the same translator's abridged rendering of Bishop Luca Manelli's massive fourteenth-century anthology of Senecan material. For Seneca's Letters there was a version done for Fernán Pérez de Guzmán, whose complex history in translation involved both French and Italian intermediaries.[29] The probable presence of these last two items indicates that Iñigo López was not in touch with Humanistic criteria of textual adequacy; his apparent reliance on translations suggests that he was no Latinist either. The positive aspects of his culture were not these; they have to do with his belief that what could be learned from books was relevant to the better living of a secular life, and ought to be mastered by lay persons of great estate. That was a new conviction in the Castile of his time, even though - as the Prologue implies - the royal family themselves belonged firmly to the minority which shared it.[30] From that conviction, applied to a synthesis of cultural elements which is still in line with mediaeval tradition, comes the belief that an education fit for a prince will draw on the wisdom of the ancients to reinforce the teachings of religious morality. In the words of the full title, "fructuosa enseñança" is to be added to "gloriosa doctrina".

Up to this point, the present analysis has made the content of this teaching appear fairly unstructured, and so to an extent it is. Yet the truth of the matter probably lies somewhere between D.W. Foster's claim that "There is no cohesive line of development discernible", and Lapesa's equally firm assertion "No son un conjunto desordenado de sentencias, sino expresión orgánica de un altísimo ideal humano".[31] The sixteen thematically-titled chapters are, indeed, unevenly divided, and the transitions between them abrupt, but then the proverb-collection is simply not a narrative genre. Yet certain loose-knit patterns do emerge, even at first glance. Prudence (Chapter II), Justice (Chapter III), Temperance (Chapter V), and Fortitude (Chapter VII) are the traditional cardinal virtues; Old Age and Death, which end the poem, end life. Along these lines it seems possible to build up a more coherent view of the poem as a whole.

Chapter I (<u>Amor e temor</u>) sets out a balance of attitudes that
will govern everything which follows. Its initial point of reference
is the position of the "fijo ... mucho amado"; the phrase "o fijo"
recurs in several of these early stanzas. The child is already loved;
in being told "Ama é serás amado" (1), he is being urged to build upon
the possibility for good inherent in this situation. The point is
that moral relations are mutual in character; by the same token, he
will not build on fear (2); that way lies disaster, as the example of
Caesar shows (3). A fuller exploration of <u>amor</u> (4-7) is followed by
a new theme, the proper role of fear - one should be cautious in taking
advice (8). The Book of Esther shows what happens to those who are
not (9-10), but good advice, especially from older men, is always
worth having (11-12):

> Tanto tiempo los romanos
> Prosperaron
> Quanto creyeron é onraron
> Los ancianos. (12)

Three keynotes, then, are struck: mutuality, moderation (virtue as a
balance of qualities), and the need for proper instruction. Each is
made meaningful in terms suited to a pupil who is cherished, and
capable of appreciating such lessons, but not as yet instructed:
Caesar and Ahasuerus are <u>easy</u> examples. Already, the work seems more
coherent than it appeared on the surface.

This is confirmed in Chapters II-VII (stanzas 13-62) which give
a scheme of basic moral instruction, based on the four cardinal virtues.
Significantly, the first to be treated is <u>Prudencia</u>, presented here,
as in the <u>Defunssión</u>, as "prudencia é sabiduría" - wisdom acquired
through learning:

> Inquiere con grand cuydado
> La sçiençia
> Con estudio é diligençia
> Reposado. (13)

The "Arms and Letters" topic has already made its appearance in the
<u>Prologue</u> where both ancient and modern examples (Caesar, Cato, Enrique's
immediate family) were adduced to prove that learning does not weaken
valour. In the poem, Iñigo López does not mention such doubts even
to refute them. Taking his theme from Seneca - who had in mind, of
course, a quite alien social structure - he presents learning as a
natural adjunct of social eminence - "A los libres pertenesçe /
aprehender" (15), and this justifies their "preheminençia". The
minority view of Arms and Letters is affirmed as the norm for a whole
class. Their proper formation, begun in youth (16), must observe a
due balance:

> Non cobdiçies ser letrado
> Por loor,
> Mas sçiente reprehensor
> De peccado. (13)

Again, though fine words are all very well, wisdom itself is something
deeper (18). Learning in this sense is fit for a king, as Enrique
will one day be, and as Solomon (17) once was. But Solomon's disastrous son, Rehoboam (19), was lacking in just this. The emphasis now
shifts to the content of prudence, whose first principle (20)

is the service of God. In secular terms - and here the Stoic note comes to the fore - it means bearing with the vicissitudes of time and Fortune (21-22). Late mediaeval rulers had plenty of that to do; they could hardly start learning too young.

A still adolescent prince was not yet required to exercise justice, and for this a mere four stanzas suffice, ending with the reminder that those who judge must also live rightly. But a second chapter (IV) commends the underlying principle of cool-headed, merciful judgment, in which virtues of many kinds flow together. There is Stoic tranquility:

> ... corrije con reposo
> Al culpado (28);

magnificence, the dignity befitting great estates (Iñigo López enjoyed being addressed as "muy magnífico señor"[32]), as well as Aristotelian magnanimitas:

> Ca de la manifiçençia
> Es perdonar ... (30);

and the specifically knightly and courtly mesura:

> La messurada clemençia
> Es virtut ... (30)

All of these culminate in Christian charity:

> ¿Quál es en humanidat
> Tan pecador,
> Que judgado con amor
> É caridat,
> Se falle la su maldat
> Intolerable? (31).

And here, as before, a balance is to be kept. The death-penalty is to be used sparingly, but the laws must not be overridden, and:

> ... non es de tolerar
> Al que mató,
> Si de lexos contrayó
> Dapnificar. (33)

This reminder of the dangers of overlooking muerte alevosa restates a fairly well-known legal principle,[33] and with it (34), the section on Justice ends.

Temperance is covered under two heads, sobriedat and castidat, though there is a certain overlap, with "loco amor" being upbraided under the former. Naturally enough, with Enrique on the edge of puberty, it is chastity which receives the fuller treatment. Stanzas 39-54 begin with several warning examples (Solomon, David, Tarquin), and one encouraging one (Scipio). But the poem soon moves (44 onwards) into a digression on famous women. Again there is a concern with balance. The harsher antifeminism of the Cynic tradition (very apparent in sentence-collections), and of religious ascesis is here rejected.[34] Well and good for the monastic life, such attitudes could not benefit a future secular ruler who was going to be expected to beget heirs. The pro-feminist case, then, is rooted both in

moderation and practicality. It is presented here through a graded
series of examples - first, of course, the Blessed Virgin (48), then
the saints (49-50), then Old Testament heroines (51), and finally
(52-4) the "gentil nasçion notable". This pleasantly literary excursus
was calculated to arouse Enrique's curiosity to learn more - and he
had Iñigo López's glosses to tell him more at just this point.

Fortitude (55-62) is again decked out with Roman examples, but
that is only one of the ways in which valour in arms is held in a
relationship with book-learning. The first figure of note here is
Cato (56), one of the patterns of "Arms and Letters" mentioned in the
Prologue, though the moral confusion of approving his suicide is
avoided. And Fortitude is not presented as self-sufficient; it is
constantly being linked with other virtues. It involves a Stoic
contempt for self-interest:

> Ca, fijo, si mucho amáres
> Tu persona,
> Non esperes la corona (57),

a Christian preparedness for death (58); and even modesty:

> Porque la mesma loor
> En tu boca
> Non ensalça, mas apoca
> Tu valor ... (61)

The message is that valour is indeed a splendid quality, but that it
implies much more than those who are merely valiant can ever know; only
those who are fully instructed in morality can comprehend it - or, of
course, recognize examples from "Livy and Lucius" (56).

The fifty stanzas dealing with the virtues are, then, tolerably
well-integrated in themselves. Prudence teaches the nature of other
virtues - justice for one. Justice means judging independently of
passions and impulses; the control of these things is the sphere of
temperance. Chastity, an aspect of temperance, leads to the "praise
of good women"; fortitude, in parallel to this last, illustrates a
specifically manly virtue. This is, in two senses, a mediaeval type
of unity: first because it is based on the traditional paradigm of
the Four Virtues, and secondly, because of its linear, discursive
character, more natural to the more oral background of mediaeval
culture (and, of course, to the didactic tradition of the Proverbios),
than a unity of architectural balance.[35] But it is also pleasingly
consequential - just at the very centre of the poem, its human arche-
types (women first, then men), are clustered most thickly. Again, it
fits very well into the process of instructing the boy Enrique - first
as a scholar, then as a future ruler, then as an adolescent coping
with adult passions, and finally as a man in a martial world.

Chapters 8-14 (stanzas 63-97) are harder to reduce to order. But
the Four Virtues section itself offers a clue. The Prince, thus
instructed, will have to cope, not with any foursquare traditional
scheme, but with that authentic jumble of differing demands which
characterizes life in practice rather than theory. These later chapters,
then, offer, a miniature manual of conduct, attuned to just this kind
of complexity; the poem, like life, gets harder as one moves from
learning to doing. But its order is not a random one, even so. Iñigo
López is interweaving just two series of moral situations. The first -
liberality, overcoming covetousness, gratitude - embraces Chapters 8,
10 and 12, and covers those relationships which stem from the Prince's

possession of _bienes de fortuna_. The second (Chapters 9, 11, 13)
deals with those other _bienes_ of the personal life which Aristotle
and the Stoics after him loved to contrast in worth and permanence
with such worldly goods – truth, the avoidance of envy, friendship.[36]
The interrelationship of the two arises inevitably from the attempt
to apply reflective wisdom to the active life of the noble and royal
estates. Yet, if seen aright, the two spheres of conduct must also
converge – gratitude and friendship, after all, are not so very far
apart. Again, the virtues in each nexus are reciprocal and mutual.
Those kings who used liberality got something for it:

> Alixandre con franqueça
> Conquistó
> La tierra é sojudgó
> Su redondeça (64),

which is more than can be said for Darius (67). If someone has been
generous and kind to you, Iñigo López advises "Págalo con buen talente"
(85). Tell the truth, and let this be your guide in friendship (69);
but it is important, too, to avoid the type of friend who merely
flatters you (88). And to follow the advice of stanza 90:

> Nin te reguardas nin velas
> De tu amigo; ...

would involve making sure that your own thoughts were the kind you
could reveal without shame. Besides reciprocity, the other key ideas
of balance and Stoic restraint are again present. Your worldly goods
belong not to you but to Fortune, and that, says the poet firmly, is
that:

> Pues si preguntáres cúyo
> Es, diré:
> _De Fortuna_, é callaré,
> Pues concluyo. (82)

This being so, one has to strive for moderation. Someone who felt
that this imposed too tight a limit on those who were occupationally
liable to gather great wealth may have been responsible for the
doubtfully authentic stanza 73, with its reminder that it is licit to
seek wealth in order to give it away. But Iñigo López is interested
in a different kind of balance; the message of stanza 77 is:

> Quiere aquello que pudieres
> É non mas.

High estates are intrinsically dangerous (79); they go before a fall
(81). That was true both to Stoic doctrine and to the experience of
the fifteenth-century ruling class, from royalty downwards. Better
to play safe, to go for balance and restraint:

> Elige la medianía
> De la gente (75)

is the phrase which governs this section. Enrique, of course, was
destined to have little choice; a _grande del reino_ like Iñigo López
had little enough. The regret in the next stanza at the cares
inherent in "el estado é asçension" rings very authentically indeed:

<pre>
                    Mas acresçientań cuydado
                    Ansia é pena;
                    Al libre ponen cadena,
                    Mal su grado.
</pre>

If bringing arms and letters together raised controversy, bringing
wisdom and worldly greatness together brought a corresponding inner
tension.

   It is with the more positive and stable _bienes propios_ of private
friendship among the morally wise that this "manual of conduct" nears
its close.  But it ends on a particular instance of such friendship -
one which has been, in a sense, present all along - , the relationship
of the father and son, which has led Juan II to commission the work.
At the beginning, the poet himself addressed his reader as "fijo mío",
but it is clear here that he is not talking about himself:

<pre>
                    A los padres es devida
                    Reverençia
                    Filial é obediençia
                    Conosçida. (92)
</pre>

Like Hippolytus in the _Infierno de enamorados_,[37] the _yo_ who utters
the lines (and whose most recent appeal to his own experience occurred
a mere three stanzas earlier) discreetly withdraws, his work of
instruction done.  And Prince Enrique is left at last face to face
with his father.  He is bound to him by Biblical precept (92), reinforced by both pagan and scriptural examples (93-4), and the link is
related to the earlier sections by its crucial element of gratitude
(94).  It also recalls the very first section, where the Romans'
success was linked with their respect for their elders (12).  If
Enrique has heeded the fatherly voice of the poem, he will understand
his relationship with his own father all the better.
   By a further easy transition the topic of parenthood leads into
the last section of all, on the Last Things.  It opens with a view of
old age - not now that of a parent, but Enrique's own:

<pre>
                    Non te desplega la edat
                    Postrimera,
                    Como sea la carrera
                    De bondat. (95)
</pre>

Old age, if prepared for by virtue, is no burden, but a blessing -
not "molesta" but "modesta vejedat".  The process of learning has as
its end not just a dutiful son, nor even a prince equipped for his
worldly responsibilities, but a life complete at its close.  The old
man who has followed virtue lives in the judicious, even-tempered
mode of Stoicism, "... El político vivir / En egualdat" (96).  And,
as the well-formed stanza 97 illustrates, he shares the exemplary
virtues of both arms and letters:

<pre>
                    Esta fiço á los Catones
                    Sapientes
                    Militantes é valientes
                    Los Çipiones,
                    Esta rige las legiones
                    Con destreça
                    É judga con sableça
                    Las regiones.
</pre>

The order here is: Cato (wisdom), (arms) Scipio, arms, wisdom - structurally A a b B B A. But the sense is still more complex. Cato is a type of wisdom with practical success; Scipio of valour with virtue. To command legions demands skill; the judge of territories is a figure of power. The human, secular ideal towards which the poem moves is here presented in a completely integrated form. But it takes its place - as it must - in a religious context. Life is lived under the shadow of death (98); even the Stoics know that. But this is more than a fact to be faced; it is part of a providential scheme, and if it were not so the glory of Jesus Christ as the redeemer of mankind would be diminished (99). There is, then, no cause for fear, rejected here as it was at the start of the poem - there as a basis for human relationships, here as a response to death (100). And this is Iñigo López's final word:

> ... Quel remedio
> De todos viçios es medio
> Ser contigo.
> Si tomares tal amigo,
> Vida inmensa
> Vivirás, é sin offensa
> Nin castigo. (101)

Vices are to be conquered, as the Stoics recommended, by a properly-adjusted relationship with the self ("medio ser contigo").[38] And this counsel, seen in terms of another of the poem's key concepts - friendship - offers both a life of serene fulfillment (the Stoic ideal) and a well-merited immortality. The richness of content in the phrase "vida inmensa" is the product of all that has gone before in the poem.

It is a work of intense didacticism - learned, shrewd, detailed, patient, repetitious. But it is about more than the process of learning as such; it is about the growth to a fuller and more serious humanity. It is not, and does not begin to be, a work of Renaissance Humanism, but it can very fairly be described as a late yet characteristic example of mediaeval humanism. In an essay of that title, R.W. Southern sums up this aspect of Dante (whom Enrique de Villena had translated, and Iñigo López admired) in these words:

> By reason we can see at once the autonomy of nature and the necessity for that which is above nature.[39]

If by "reason" we understand what Iñigo López understood by prudencia and ciencia, and by "nature" the life of secular greatness, informed and reassured as to its proper role, we have the substance of this poem.

Its effectiveness, as we have seen, is real, but it does not derive primarily from those features to which a modern critical sensibility would look first - structure and texture. The structure - basic attitudes, the Four Virtues, the manual of conduct, the Last Things - contains but does not guarantee the poem's real coherence. Numerical symmetries - that the end of the second part coincides more or less with the poem's Golden Section; that the passage on the virtues is exactly half the total length; that the first and second sections together are just twice as long as the third - add an agreeable, but gratuitous neatness. But that is all. The texture, rather than dramatic and imaginatively forceful, is supple and well-mannered. It has the ease and naturalness of utterance of a poet absolutely secure in his medium. Consider the flow of subtly rhythmic highlights in stanza 42:

```
        Fuye de la oçiosidat
        Con exerçiçios
        Honestos, porque los viçios
        Potestat
        Non ayan nin·facultat
        De te prender;
        Que non es poco vençer
        Humanidat.
```

The sense of conflict issuing in achievement is made as concrete here
as one could wish. Within the apparent evenness of tone, indeed,
there is a surprising variety at work - shifts from direct advice to
personal reminiscence, to general maxims, to predictions, to examples,
all of which keep the poem moving, in default of a narrative structure.
The _exempla_ which accumulate in the middle sections offer the sort of
mildly exotic catalogue much loved by serious fifteenth-century poets.
But only a very few phrases or stanzas prove memorable for their
evocative power - "el sueño que acelerado dexarás", for worldly life
in stanza 14; no.76 on the perils of greatness; the blunt conclusion
of 82 on _bienes de fortuna_; the praise of mature age in 95; the last
stanza of all. Significantly, most of these have had to be quoted
already, in our analysis of the poem's content. For its unity and
effectiveness stem in the main from its _intellectual_ coherence, its
inner movement towards a deeper and more integrated understanding.
Its premise is that of the poet's major allegories - that it is both
possible and necessary for learning to be transformed into a better
kind of practical living. Its achievement, different from theirs,
is to transform its own multiple lore into a single, lifelike poetic
meditation.

        The achievement, of course, does not enact Iñigo López's aspiration;
it merely symbolizes it. On the evidence, and with every due allowance
made for the distortions of propagandist history, the _Proverbios_ did
not do very much for the future Enrique IV. And, despite its appearance
in fifteen or more _cancioneros_, neither this nor any other poem was
going, of itself, to alter the sense of responsibility of the rulers
of Castile, taken as a group. That had to come about by other means.
Yet poems like this were designed to play a part, and quite possibly
did play a part, in preparing the ground for change. This one clearly
mattered to the readers of _cancioneros_, and to those who read its
thirty fifteenth and sixteenth-century editions.[40] To write, as Foster
does, of the poem's "scant literary value", and to account for its
success in terms of "facile, 'sweet' moralizing"[41] is to read it with
less attention than it deserves, and perhaps with less than was
accorded it by those who shared Iñigo López's conviction that his
poetry could teach them how to live.[42]


                            N O T E S
                            ‒‒‒‒‒‒‒‒‒

    1. R. Lapesa, _La obra literaria del Marqués de Santillana_ (Madrid
1957), 206n., quoting R. de Floranes, "_Apéndice 16 a las Memorias
históricas de don Alfonso el Noble_ del Marqués de Mondéjar", cxxxix.
Cf. Dorothy S. Severin, The _Cancionero de Martínez de Burgos_ (Exeter
1976), xv, xviii. In his own MS edition of the _Proverbios_ (MS Madrid,
Biblioteca Nacional, 11.264/20, f. 1v) Floranes had suggested the less
plausible date of 1435.

2. Marqués de Santillana, Obras completas, ed. J. Amador de los Ríos (Madrid 1852), 21; Obras, ed. A.Cortina (Buenos Aires 1946), 41. Of modern editions, Amador (pp.21-91) presents the prologue, poem and glosses in full, from MS Madrid, Biblioteca Nacional 3677 (formerly M-59). J.M. Azáceta, Cancionero de Juan Fernández de Ixar (Madrid 1956), II, 428-462, and Appendix VI, 906-912, also supplies all these elements, from the MS which most concerns him, with a good apparatus of variants, and lacunae supplied from elsewhere. J. Rogerio Sánchez, Los "Proverbios" de D. Iñigo López de Mendoza, Marqués de Santillana (Madrid 1928), uses MS Escorial N I 13 for the prologue and verses, and reprints the glosses from Amador. R. Foulché-Delbosc, Cancionero castellano del siglo XV, I (Madrid 1912), 449-460 reproduces only the verses. J.B. Trend, Marqués de Santillana: Prose and Verse (London 1940), 21-27 gives the prologue only. Cortina (pp.41-78) reprints the prologue and verses from Amador (with modernized accents) but omits the glosses. All these will doubtless be superseded by the Castalia Poesías completas edited by M. Durán, but the only volume so far published (Madrid 1975) does not include the Proverbios. In the present study, references are to Amador, and wherever possible to Cortina also.

3. MS Madrid, Biblioteca Nacional, 10172, ff. 97v-98r; 120r-v, cf. M. Schiff, La Bibliothèque du Marquis de Santillana (Paris 1905), 422-423; W.C. Atkinson, 'The Interpretation of romances e cantares in Santillana', HR, IV (1936), 5.

4. Durán, 238.

5. Marqués de Santillana, Proverbios (Seville, M. Ungut and S. Polono, 1494), f. a 6r. For the historical background cf. J. Amador de los Ríos, Vida del Marqués de Santillana (Buenos Aires 1947; reprinted from the 1852 Obras completas), 58-64.

6. Amador, Vida del Marqués, 43-48, 54-55. For the elaborate reorganization of judicial and other offices undertaken by Juan II while on this visit to Guadalajara cf. Crónicas de los reyes de Castilla, II, ed. C. Rosell (Madrid 1877), 529-534; P. Carrillo de Huete, Crónica del Halconero de Juan II, ed. J. de Mata Carriazo (Madrid 1946), 236-245; Lope Barrientos, Refundición de la Crónica del Halconero, ed. J. de Mata Carriazo (Madrid 1946), 206-213.

7. Cf. A. Soria, Los humanistas de la corte de Alfonso el Magnánimo (Granada 1956), 113-114, 122-125; L. Mehus, ed., Leonardi Bruni Arretini Epistolarum Libri VIII (Florence 1741), VII, 77 ff.; H. Baron, Leonardo Bruni Aretino: humanistisch-philosophische Schriften (Leipzig and Berlin 1928), 211; also MS Madrid, Biblioteca Nacional 10212, ff. 17v-18v, and Schiff, 361-363.

8. Cf. J. Gimeno Casalduero, "La Defunsión de Don Enrique de Villena del Marqués de Santillana: composición,propósito y significado" in Estructura y diseño en la literatura castellana medieval (Madrid 1975) 179-195.

9. Cf. Lapesa, La obra literaria..., 137-151; also A.J. Foreman, 'The Structure and Content of Santillana's Comedieta de Ponça',BHS, LI (1974), 109-124, and the references given there.

10. Durán, 23.

11. _Prologue_, ed. Amador, 22; Cortina, 41.

12. Durán, 23.

13. Santillana, _Proverbios_ (Seville 1494), f. a 6 r.

14. Juan de Mena, _Laberinto de Fortuna_, ·st. 172 (in Foulché-Delbosc, _Cancionero castellano_, I, 169), cf. Lucan, _Pharsalia_, V, 550 ff.; Mena also had in mind Virgil, _Georgic_ I, 383 ff.; it is less clear that Iñigo López did so. Cf. also Santillana, _Comedieta de Ponça_, st. 16-18 (Durán 248-249).

15. Cf. Inez Macdonald, 'The _Coronación_ of Juan de Mena: Poem and Commentary', _HR_, VII (1939), 125-144.

16. Alfonso de Cartagena, _La Rethórica de M. Tullio Cicerón_, ed. Rosalba Mascagna (Naples 1969), 31.

17. _De las siete artes liberales_, I, in _Cinco Libros de Séneca_ (Seville, M. Ungut and S. Polono, 1491), f. e iii r-v. Olga Tudoricǎ Impey, 'Alfonso de Cartagena, traductor de Séneca y precursor del humanismo español', _Prohemio_, III (1972), 473-494 - an indispensable article for the history of translation in Castile - quotes this passage (480) from MS Escorial N ii 6, alongside a text of the original Latin (Seneca, _Ep._ LXXXVIII), and offers a valuable commentary.

18. For Fernán Pérez's _Proverbios_ cf. Foulché-Delbosc, _Cancionero castellano_, I, 752-759; for Sem Tob, the edition of I. González Llubera (Cambridge 1957).

19. _Prohemio e carta quel Marqués de Santillana envió al Condestable de Portugal con las obras suyas_, Amador, 14; Cortina, 35. On Fernán Pérez, cf. ibid., 16 (Amador); 37 (Cortina).

20. Lines 13-14, ed. González Llubera, 65. On the metre of this poem, cf. ibid., 52-58; my own description differs chiefly in preferring the convention which counts to the last stressed syllable plus one; thus Llubera writes of "6 + 6 syllables", rather than 7 + 7".

21. For the rhyme-scheme (but not the _pie quebrado_ metre) cf. _El aguilando_, Durán, 91-92; "Gentil dueña, tal paresce ...", ibid., 96-99; "Non es umana la lumbre ...", ibid., 100-102.

22. The authorities cited - "Remon Vidal de Besaduc", "Jufre de Joxa, monge negro", "Berenguel de Noya" of Mallorca, and the Consistory of Toulouse (Amador, 26; Cortina, 44) are all to be found in Villena (cf. I. Bullock, ed., _Villena, Lebrija, Encina: Selections_ (Cambridge 1926), 2).

23. Durán, 238. For the doubtful authenticity of stanza 73 cf. Rogerio Sánchez, 9, 75. It is also missing in the _Cancionero de Ixar_, ed. Azáceta, 452.

24. Cf. the rubric to the _Prologue_ there, cited by Trend, 21.

25. Cf. below, _Appendix_ (b), _Some numerical relationships_. Discussion among Hispanists about numerical methods of composition has been stimulated by two recent works, Dorothy Clotelle Clarke, _Juan de_

Mena's Laberinto de Fortuna: Classic Epic and Mester de Clerecía
(University of Mississippi 1973), and less usefully H. de Vries,
Materia Mirable. Estudio de la composición numérico-simbólica en las
dos obras contemplativas de Juan de Padilla, el Cartujano (Groningen
1972); cf. the reviews by the present writer (BHS, LII (1975), 162-
164) and A.D. Deyermond (Rom.Phil., in press).

26. Lapesa, La obra literaria..., 207n., cf. the glosses to Proverbios,
st. 27 (Amador, 72; Rogerio Sánchez, 95); st. 40 (Amador, 73; Rogerio
Sánchez, 97). Iñigo López, however, does not use the word Breviloquium
for John of Wales' work of that title on the Four Virtues, preferring
to write of "un compendio que figo de las «Quatro virtudes cardinales»".
For John of Wales cf. Beryl Smalley, English Friars and Antiquity in
the Early Fourteenth Century (Oxford 1960), 51-55.

27. Prohemio e carta, Amador, 4; Cortina, 29; Prologue to Proverbios,
Amador, 21; Cortina, 41. Cf. also Pero Díaz de Toledo, Introducción
al dezir que compuso ... Gómez Manrique que intitula la Esclamación
e querella de la gobernación, in Foulché-Delbosc, Cancionero castellano,
II (Madrid 1915), 131.

28. R. Lapesa, "Los Proverbios de Santillana: contribución al estudio
de sus fuentes", in De la edad media a nuestros días (Madrid 1971),
95-111.

29. Cf. Lapesa, "Los Proverbios...", 104 (Valerius Maximus), 107
(Cartagena's versions of Cicero; Seneca's Letters), 109 (Seneca, De
Clementia, translated by Cartagena). For 15th-century translations of
Valerius, cf. Schiff, 134; Margherita Morreale, 'Apuntes para la
historia de la traducción en la Edad Media', Rev. de Lit., XV (1959),
6; for the detailed history of Fernán Pérez's version of Seneca's
Letters, cf. M. Eusebi, 'La più antica traduzione francese delle
Lettere Morali di Seneca e i suoi derivati', Romania, XCI (1970), 1-47.
For Seneca on the Liberal Arts, cf. above, n. 17. The example of
Alexander's liberality from Seneca, De Beneficiis, II, 16 (Lapesa,
"Los Proverbios...", 109) is in Cartagena's Copilación (in Cinco libros
de Séneca (Seville 1491), as De la providencia de Dios, II, extract 38:
"que en el dar principalmente es de considerar el juyzio del dador");
for its derivation via Manelli cf. N.G. Round, 'The Mediaeval Reputation of the Proverbia Senecae', Proc. RIA, 72, C, 5 (1972), 134n.

30. Cf. N.G. Round, 'Renaissance Culture and its Opponents in
Fifteenth-century Castile', MLR, LVII (1962), 206-215; P.E. Russell,
"Arms versus Letters: Towards a Definition of Spanish Fifteenth-
century Humanism" in A.R. Lewis, ed., Aspects of the Renaissance:
A Symposium (Austin and London, 1967), 47-58.

31. D.W. Foster, The Marqués de Santillana (New York 1971), 72;
Lapesa, "Los Proverbios...", 95.

32. Cf. the dedication of St. Basil's homily De Legendis Antiquorum
Libris (MS Paris, Bibliothèque Nationale, Fonds espagnol, 458):
"Suelen, muy magnífico señor Yñigo López de Mendoça, señor de la Vega,
los omes escriuir unos a otros ..." (Schiff, 342).

33. Pero Díaz de Toledo, Proverbios de Séneca (MS Escorial, S II 10),
f. 73r: "Por tanto el que mata a muerte segura es más gravemente
penado que non el que mata en pelea peleada ... E por tanto acordaron

los sabios por la enormedad e graveza del crimen que, caso que el Rey
de su soberano poderío perdone a alguno si injusta e non devidamente
mató a otro, que esto se entienda:  salvo si la tal muerte fue segura
e non peleada ...".

34. Cf. J. Ornstein, ed., L. de Lucena, Repetición de amores (Chapel
Hill 1954), 12-32; Harriet Goldberg, ed., Martín de Córdoba, Jardín
de nobles donzellas (Chapel Hill 1974), 95-96. The pseudo-Senecan
sentence "Aperte cum est mala mulier tum demum est bona" caused some
embarrassment to both its 15th-century Castilian translators: cf.
Alonso de Cartagena, Cinco Libros de Séneca (Seville 1491), f. g i v,
Amonestamientos e doctrinas (De Legalibus Institutis), III, vi; Pero
Díaz de Toledo, Proverbios de Séneca, MS Escorial, S II 10, f. 17r.

35. Cf. A.C. Spearing, Criticism and Medieval Poetry (London 1964),
24-25.

36. Cf. Pero Díaz de Toledo, Proverbios de Séneca, MS Escorial,
S II 10, f. 10v, glossing "Alienum est omne quicquid optando evenit".
The distinction goes back to Aristotle, Ethics, I, viii.

37. Durán, 227, st. LXVII.

38. The language here is extremely dense and elliptical, and other
overtones are almost certainly present - an allusion to the Golden
Mean, and hence to the division of the poem at its Golden Section may
be implied, and it is possible that "amigo" in the next line is a
vocative, marking the growth of the "fijo mío" of earlier stanzas to
full equality with his enlightened elders.

39. R.W. Southern, Medieval Humanism and Other Studies (Oxford 1970),
58.

40. Azáceta, Cancionero de Ixar, II, 432 lists twelve MS cancionero
appearances besides the Ixar copy.  To these may be added MS Madrid,
Biblioteca Nacional, 3677 (Amador's basic text; cf. Lapesa, La obra
literaria..., 281); MS Seville, Biblioteca Colombina - Capitular,
83-6-10, ff. 6v-64v (with Pero Díaz's gloss); MS Yale, Beinecke Rare
Books Library, 482 (Durán, 32), making sixteen in all. Lapesa, loc.
cit., refers to six early copies of the Proverbios alone. The number
of pre-1600 editions is given by both Lapesa and Durán as 29; Azáceta,
loc. cit., lists thirty.

41. Foster, 72, 69.

42. The original version of this article was read to a meeting of
the Medieval Hispanic Research Seminar at Westfield College, London
in June 1977.

# APPENDIX

## STRUCTURAL AND NUMERICAL PATTERNS IN THE PROVERBIOS

(a) A SUMMARY OF STRUCTURE

| | | CAP. | TITLE | | |
|---|---|---|---|---|---|
| A. | Basic attitudes | I | De amor é temor | 1-12 | 12 |

B. The Four Virtues

| | | | | | | |
|---|---|---|---|---|---|---|
| (i) | Prudence | | II | De prudençia é sabiduría | 13-23 | |
| (ii) | Justice | (a) | III | De justiçia | 24-27 | |
| | | (b) | IV | De paçiencia é honesta correpción | 28-34 | 50 |
| (iii) | Temperance | (a) | V | De sobriedat | 35-38 | |
| | | (b) | VI | De castidat | 39-54 | |
| (iv) | Fortitude | | VII | De fortaleça | 55-62 | |

(62)

C. Manual of conduct

| | | | | | |
|---|---|---|---|---|---|
| (i) | Bienes de fortuna | VIII | De liberalidat é franqueça | 63-68 | |
| (ii) | Bienes propios | IX | De verdat | 69-70 | |
| (iii) | B. de f. | X | De continençia cerca de cobdiçia | 71-82 | 31 (no.73 not in original) |
| (iv) | B.p. | XI | De invidia | 83-84 | |
| (v) | B. de f. | XII | De gratitut | 85-86 | |
| (vi) | B.p. | XIII | De amiçiçia | 87-91 | |
| (vii) | B.p. | XIV | De paternal reverençia | 92-94 | |

(38)

D. Last things

| | | | | | |
|---|---|---|---|---|---|
| | XV | De senetut ó vejez | 95-97 | |
| | XVI | De la muerte | 98-100 | 7 |
| | - | Fin | 101 | |

---

(b) SOME NUMERICAL RELATIONSHIPS

(i) Golden Section (61.8): 100:62::62:38. 100 = (62+38)

(ii) $\underline{B} = 50 = \frac{100}{2}$

(iii) $(\underline{A+B}) = (12+50) = 62 = (31 \times 2) = (\underline{C \times 2})$

(iv) $(\underline{D-Fin}) = (7=1) = 6 = \frac{12}{2} = \frac{A}{2}$

(v) $(C-D) = (31-7) = 24 = (12 \times 2) = (A \times 2)$

(vi) $(\underline{A+D}) = 19.31:19::19:12$ (another Golden Section, more or less).

(vii) $\underline{C-(A+D)} = (31-19) = 12 = \underline{A}$.

The first three may well be conscious embellishments on Iñigo López's part. The others, almost certainly, are fortuitous.

La geografía humanística y los historiadores españoles del
siglo quince *

R.B. Tate (University of Nottingham)

Antonio de Nebrija, en un prefacio en verso a su Cosmographia,
impresa hacia 1498 y encuadernada como prólogo al De situ Orbis de
Pomponio Mela, ruega al lector que lea no sólo sus propias palabras,
sino las mismas obras de los grandes cosmógrafos clásicos y modernos:
"Nem designatio terrae maximus est illis praecipuus labor. Interea
contentus abi; nostrumque laborem non aspernatus lector, amice, legas".
Fue un paso más en la tarea que se había propuesto para descartar las
obras anticuadas de "viros obscuros quos ego nunquam legi, neque me
non legisse pudet", y, en sus propias palabras, "sacar a la luz las
antigüedades de España que hasta nuestros días han estado encubiertas
i para que pudiesse, como dize Virgilio, pandere res alta terra et
caligine mersas".[1] Por vez primera en la Península, dio forma concep-
tual a la visión ternaria de la historia, propuesta hacia un siglo por
el Petrarca y ejemplificada en el siglo quince en los tomos históricos
y cosmográficos de Flavio Biondo y Eneo Silvio entre otros. Estas com-
pilaciones, como es bien sabido, fueron facilitadas por la estabilización
crítica de textos clásicos ya conocidos y la traducción del griego al
latín de nuevas fuentes. De este vasto campo historiográfico nos
limitaremos al aspecto geográfico, y por lo tanto a la utilización de
datos recogidos por Plinio, Mela y Solino entre los conocidos, y
Estrabón, Tolomeo y Diodoro Sículo entre los recién descubiertos.
Podría parecer un poco estrecho y rebuscado un tema como la
geografía humanística y los historiadores del siglo quince. Hay que
confesar que no es tiempo todavía para las grandes síntesis en los
estudios humanísticos de la Península. Pero la investigación de cómo
enfocaron su país estos historiadores españoles podría llevarnos a un
más justo aprecio de sus bases críticas, de su valoración de la historia
y cultura de las Españas, de la misma manera, pero mucho más desarrol-
lada, en que los críticos italianos y extranjeros han estudiado las
'prises de position' del Petrarca y de Boccaccio cuando contemplaron
las ruinas de Roma a mediados del siglo catorce.[2] No fue, desde luego,
idéntica la mirada de Pedro el Ceremonioso cuando calificó la Acropolis
como "la pus rica joia que al món sia".[3] Pero es posible que, un siglo
más tarde, la visión de la España clásica presentada por los historiadores españoles pudiese parangonarse con la de los humanistas italianos
mencionados arriba.
Hasta bien avanzado el siglo quince, la organización de la crónica
peninsular tradicional no era de la misma especie que la ternaria
confeccionada por eruditos como Flavio Biondo.[4] El concepto de época
clásica, edad media y moderna era distinta de la línea - colonización
romana, época visigoda y neogótica - sólo interrumpida por la incursión
islámica. Este enfoque es el que contribuye a la formación y a la
localización dentro del esquema narrativo de las primeras descripciones
de la Península. El Toledano transmite a los historiadores posteriores
un panorama elemental de la Península y sus características bajo el
signo de un lamento por la pérdida de España, derivada de Isidoro y de
Justino y colocada, no como prólogo a su historia, sino como pausa
retórica inmediatamente después de la invasión árabe. Esta elaboración
se repite en la serie de versiones vernáculas de la Primera Crónica
General o en forma tratadística en opúsculos como el De praeconiis
Hispaniae de Gil de Zamora.

Sólo con el renacimiento de la historia general en latín a mediados del siglo XV surge un renuevo de interés en el mapa antiguo de
Hispania. A estas alturas, el Laus Hispaniae o el Commendatio Hispaniae
deja de figurar como contrapunto a la narrativa, aunque sigue apareciendo
como tema independiente en tratados romances como los de Pérez de Guzmán
y de Santillana entre otros. En la Anacephalaeosis de Alfonso García
de Santa María vislumbramos las primeras tentativas para restablecer la
perspectiva antigua en comparación con la actual, pero si él intentó
esbozar las provincias romanas, esto no se debe exclusivamente a ningún
ejercicio académico, sino que servía para argumentar una tesis política
en favor de pretensiones territoriales castellanas.[5]

El nuevo enfoque del pasado de España se manifestó, como era de
esperar, en las obras de dos españoles residentes de Roma. En la
Historia Hispanica de Ruy Sánchez de Arévalo publicada en Roma en 1470,
se da el primer paso hacia la fusión del tradicional elogio de España
con los nuevos datos geográficos de los humanistas. En lugar del corto
capítulo inicial del Anacephalaeosis tenemos media docena dedicados a
varios aspectos de la topografía y geografía histórica de la Península.
En lugar del encomio de Isidoro o del lamento de Jiménez de Rada, él
nos presenta el primer panorama detallado, forjado no sólo de sus
lecturas, sino también de observaciones personales del territorio que
"a mare usque ad mari, seriose ac personaliter peragravi atque conspexi".[6]
Por la misma razón saca sus datos con preferencia de escritores que a
él le parecen testigos oculares, como Mela, al cual añade Plinio,
Solino y Estrabón. Estos datos sobre la antigua riqueza del país, los
complementa con otros de la época contemporánea con el propósito de
establecer una estrecha relación, según la vieja tesis aristotélica,
entre el fondo físico del país y la disposición de los habitantes.
Esta aportación suya, valiosa en sí misma, apuntaba una crónica de
España del mismo corte que las historias de Italia contemporáneas, pero
a la moda española, en que el imperialismo romano no era la base, sino
una interrupción del eje hispano-godo.

Sólo cuando Juan Margarit, obispo de Gerona y procurador de
Fernando el Católico en Roma en sus últimos días, se dedica exclusivamente a la época pregótica en su Paralipomenon, empieza a salir de la
oscuridad una visión coherente de la España clásica, acompañada de una
revisión de tradiciones y teorías aceptadas hasta el día como auténticas.
Hay que insistir una y otra vez que Margarit es cronológicamente el
primero que utiliza sistemática y críticamente los datos nuevamente
asequibles en traducciones de historiadores y geógrafos griegos y
romanos. Es él quien echa los fundamentos de un estudio comprensivo
de cada colonización de la Península para poder reconstruir con cierta
seguridad las etapas progresivas hasta la implantación del imperio
romano. La identificación subsecuente de la nomenclatura antigua con
la moderna permite que el lector adquiera una más rica perspectiva
geográfica de la tierra donde habita. No sólo ofrece identificaciones
por su propia cuenta, algunas de las cuales, hay que confesarlo, son
erróneas; no sólo emplea fuentes escritas, sino también mapas carto-
gráficos, y como Sánchez de Arévalo, trae el testimonio de sus propios
ojos, y más que nadie contribuye a la más exacta localización de sitios
como Sagunto, Roda, Emporion y Numancia, todos más o menos dentro del
ámbito político catalano-aragonés. En la utilización de fuentes es muy
ecléctico. Prefiere Mela a Plinio, siendo éste mero catalogador;
prefiere Tolomeo y Estrabón a ambos pero critica a todos con perfecta
independencia, aun a Estrabón de quien discrepa sobre la localización
de las islas Caseritides y la colonización de Cádiz. Además no comparte la fe de éste en Homero como el padre de los geógrafos y omite
las tradiciones poéticas cuidadosamente narradas por el griego. Pero

en su totalidad lo que infunde su presentación de las sucesivas
colonizaciones de la Península es su aprecio de la capacidad adminis-
trativa y cultural de los romanos, ejemplificada en la obra pacificadora
de Augusto desde Tarragona, lo que resuena en su calificación del
casamiento de Fernando e Isabel como la unión de la Hispania Citerior
con la Ulterior.[7]

La búsqueda de la España clásica se vio estimulada en sentido
contrario, es decir, por el creciente interés de los extranjeros residentes en España, como por ejemplo los italianos o sicilianos, secre-
tarios, académicos o tutores. Estos, según su voluminosa correspondencia, querían saber dónde se hallaban las colonias de los patricios
romanos, las columnas de Hércoles, la fuente que disolvía las piedras,
y por donde soplaba el viento que fertilizaba las yeguas.[8] Un tal
Pedro de la Puente, secretario del arzobispo de Toledo, Alonso de
Carrillo, escribió al conocido historiador Alonso de Palencia por los
años ochenta pidiendo que le preparase un pequeño compendio de la
geografía antigua de España, "compendiolum breve quo civitatum, oppidorum atque fluminum nomina a geographis commendatioribus olim indicta,
postmodum autem ob maurorum invasionem ... vel oblitterata vel perversa".
Este tratado, que cae dentro de la fórmula humanística establecida por
Boccaccio en su tratado De fluminibus y tantas veces imitada, está
todavía sin estudiar.[9] Mucho más prosaico e informativo que la obrita
posterior del barcelonés Jerónimo Pau, es el primer reconocimiento
sistemático de la geografía antigua peninsular independiente de un
andamiaje histórico. Empieza en la frontera franco-aragonesa, baja
hasta Cartagena para volver atrás sobre la provincia tarraconense hasta
Galicia, incluyendo a Aragón, la mayor parte de Castilla la Vieja, Léon,
Asturias, las provincias vascongadas y Navarra. Sigue con la Bética y
termina con un breve examen de Lusitania. En el curso de la exploración
rechaza etimologías populares y aunque no abarca tanta información como
Margarit, dado el carácter del opúsculo, es revelador el número de
puntos de contacto con el gerundense en cuanto a tópicos y teorías.
Efectivamente lo nombra en una discusión sobre la etimología de Léon;
y esto será el primer testimonio de que las obras del obispo de Gerona
circulaban tan temprano entre eruditos más allá de las fronteras de
Aragón. Es posible, pues, que estos eruditos no trabajasen tan aisladamente como parece por la lectura de sus obras.

La correspondencia y los tratados de los humanistas extranjeros
que vinieron a España nos inclina a este punto de vista. El círculo
al que pertenecía Lucio Marineo Sículo es sintomático de la misma
curiosidad infatigable. La obra mayor del siciliano, una acumulación
de opúsculos y tratados conocida más tarde por el nombre De rebus
memorabilibus Hispaniae contiene cuatro libros sobre veintidós sobre
la geografía de España, tanto antigua como moderna. Estos cuatro libros
se llamaron originalmente De laudibus Hispaniae, impresos en Salamanca
por los años 1495-1496. Este librito será la primera refundición del
viejo tema bajo el signo humanístico. Nos confiesa que había corrido
por más de 150 ríos españoles, y pasado por más de 700 puentes de los
cuales los más imponentes eran el romano de Alcántara y el acueducto
de Segovia. Citando explícitamente a Boccaccio y su tratado De fluminibus y con la ayuda de los geógrafos Estrabón, Plinio, Mela y Diodoro
Sículo, identifica muchas más colonias romanas que Margarit. Consulta
con un moro sobre el significado de Jaén, cita a Juan de Mena sobre
Madrid y a Juan Sobrarias sobre Alcañiz. No sólo atraen su atención
los restos de la arquitectura clásica sino también las fortificaciones
de Peñafiel y Puñonrrostro, las murallas de Ávila y la plaza de
Valladolid. Tales viñetas intercaladas con reminiscencias clásicas nos
hacen pensar menos en el erudito que en el paciente y ávido turista,

coleccionador de datos heterogéneos, fascinado por todo, incluso la
lengua vasca, pero incapaz de sistematizar o profundizar, si no es
para confesar que todo lo bueno español derivaba de Roma y su cultura.

Leyendo las cartas de Marineo a Nebrija (porque son los únicos
datos que sobreviven de su contacto profesional) fácilmente podríamos
imaginar cómo reaccionaba el quisquilloso andaluz. Tan sospechoso
del sabio extranjero como del pedante indígena, se consideraba a sí
mismo como el único capaz de corregir los errores ajenos. El propósito
de la Muestra de antigüedades de España que cité al principio de esta
comunicación, demuestra cómo él quiere seguir un camino distinto del
de Sánchez de Arévalo o de Margarit. Además de continuar tanto la
labor de revisión de Margarit, Palencia y Marineo, como el examen de
fuentes adicionales como Dionisio Periegetes y Silio Itálico y la
contemplación directa de las ruinas de Evora y Cazlona, explora ahin-
cadamente la etimología toponímica con el propósito de descifrar la
patria de los colonizadores originales. La teoría según la cual el
pueblo invasor recordaba su patria abandonada implantando nuevos
topónimos en las tierras conquistadas se remonta a la obra de Esteban
de Bizancio, obra no conocida que yo sepa en España hasta su aparición
en la lista de los grandes cosmógrafos formulada por Nebrija en el
prólogo versificado a su Cosmographia. Nebrija, por lo tanto, extiende
la perspectiva histórica de España, vinculando su toponimia con civili-
zaciones orientales más antiguas que las clásicas, como los persas,
los masagetos, los curetes y los sármatos, y reduciendo la contribución
de Roma a ser una entre tantas.

Además de esto, es el primer humanista español quien echa mano de
los datos más recientes ofrecidos por los viajes de exploración para
corregir taxativamente a las autoridades clásicas. En su Cosmographia
a la cual aludí en mis primeras palabras, declara incorrecta la obser-
vación del Tolomeo que el Océano Índico está totalmente cercado de
tierra: "Lusitanorum nauigatione compertum est quod ex atlantico mare
per aethiopicum facile in persidis oram commerciorum gratia peruemiunt",[10]
lo que podría referirse tanto al viaje de Bartolomé Díaz, quien volvió
a Lisboa en diciembre 1488, como al de Vasco de Gama que volvió en
setiembre 1499. Más tarde, hablando del continente meridional, predice
que: "breui futurum est ut nobis ueram terre illius descriptionem
asserant, tum insularum tum etiam continentis, cuius magnam partem orae
maritimae nautae nobis tradiderunt, illam maxime que ex aduerso
insularum nuper inuentarum (hispanam dico isabelam reliquasque adiacentes)
posita est",[11] lo que podría ser una referencia a la exploración de la
costa de Cuba por Colón en 1494, o el descubrimiento de la tierra
firme en agosto 1498. Si aceptamos que su Cosmographia (que no tiene
fecha) se imprimió con la de Mela en abril 1498, estas noticias deben
vincularse con el viaje de Díaz y la primera declaración equivocada
de Colón que había pisado el nuevo continente en 1494.

Para resumir; en el espacio de menos de cincuenta años y como
consecuencia de los esfuerzos de media docena de eruditos, el mapa de
la península había adquirido una perspectiva histórica sustancialmente
distinta de la que figuraba en las narrativas tradicionales derivadas
de las obras del Toledano y de Alfonso el Sabio. De las pocas alusiones
a fuentes clásicas, arregladas dentro del marco de un encomio, se ha
amplificado la introducción geográfica a la historia peninsular para
abarcar una visión de conjunto de épocas antiguas y modernas. El siglo
quince trajo un sentimiento más vivo de la continuidad histórica y una
conciencia más clara de las actividades de las épocas clásicas
colonizadoras. Esto se debe tanto a los literatos españoles desplazados
hacia Italia, como a los inmigrados italianos en busca del fondo cultural
común a todo el Mediterraneo.

Esta coyuntura cultural lleva directamente a los primeros estudios arqueológicos de la Península. Jerónimo Pau de Barcelona, que hizo un *Libellus de fluminibus et montibus Hispaniarum* y prometió otro *De situ urbium et oppidorum Cathaloniae*, confeccionó una lista de las estatuas y templos romanos de la ciudad y también algunas de las inscripciones lapidarias con la ayuda de las obras del conocido anticuario Ciriaco de Ancona. Francisco Desplá, el famoso arcediano de la catedral, restauró la fuente romana de Montjuich.[12]

Estos esfuerzos, sin embargo, no arrancan exclusivamente de pruritos académicos. Revelan también de vez en cuando su cariz político. Alfonso García de Santa María y Sánchez de Arévalo apoyan pretensiones castellanas a las islas costeras y a la provincia de Tingitania en la Africa del Norte en el testimonio de sus lecturas clásicas. Margarit justifica la política fronteriza de Juan II de Aragón, señalando que el Rosellón siempre ha pertenecido a la Hispania antigua. Nebrija mira la incorporación de Navarra a Castilla al principio del siglo dieciséis como la "reintegratio Hispaniae". Pero mucho más importante, este último lanza un vigoroso ataque, no sólo contra la ignorancia de sus compatriotas sobre la geografía e historia remota de su patria, sino contra los eruditos extranjeros, algunos de los cuales se creen más adeptos para estas artes y ciencias que los propios españoles: "Non tamen opinor satis tuto peregrinis hominibus historiae fides concrederetur, Italis maxime nullius rei magis que gloriae avaris".[13]

Como consecuencia de esta codicia de la gloria, Nebrija veía a los españoles como víctimas de una conjuración académica que los transformó en objetos de desprecio. En el prólogo a las *Décadas*, su versión latina de la crónica de Pulgar, aserta defensivamente, que los italianos republicanos, viviendo sin reyes, no podían entender la monarquía ni mucho menos describir un país que siempre había reverenciado a sus monarcas. Los italianos, concluye, exportan la corrupción con su cultura de la misma manera que los griegos, según Marco Catón, corrompían a los romanos: "Quodque Marco Cato ad filium de Graecis scribit, possumus et nos de Italia dicere, quandocunque gens ista nobis literas dabit, omnia corrumpet".[14]

Vista aisladamente, la contribución de cada obra comentada corresponde adecuadamente a las circunstancias vitales de cada autor. Vista en conjunto, sin embargo, es posible captar cierta homogeneidad de enfoque debida al juego de las presiones culturales y políticas entre las dos penínsulas. Si hubiéramos podido extender la línea de investigación hasta, por ejemplo, las obras de Damião de Goes, Pedro de Medina y Juan Vaseo a mediados del siglo dieciséis, habría sido posible indicar la elaboración de ciertas líneas directrices según las cuales el legado cultural hispánico casi llegaba a rivalizar con el de Italia. Valgan como remate de este trabajo las palabras con que Juan Vaseo, el erudito flamenco, introduce la sección geográfica de su historia, publicada en 1552. Hablando de sus fuentes, que son exhaustivas, observa que Plinio alaba primero a Italia y después a España, y añade: "Sed nescio equidem an ulla parte laudis Hispania cedere debeat Italiae; de iis loquor quae ad salubritatem ac fertilitatem pertinent utriusque regionis".[15]

## N O T A S

* Esta comunicación fue presentada en el Cuarto Congreso Internacional

de Hispanistas (Salamanca, 1971). Desde esta fecha ha salido mucha
pero no excesiva bibliografía, de la cual sólo hace falta notar aquí
F. Rico, Nebrija frente a los bárbaros (Salamanca 1978).

1.  Rerum a Ferdinando et Elisabe Hispaniarum regibus gestarum
Decades II, ed. A. Schott, Hispaniae Illustratae, I, 842; Muestra de la
istoria de las antigüedades de España, ed. I. González Llubera
(Oxford 1926), 205.

2.  Franco Simone, 'Une entreprise oubliée des humanistes français.
De la prise de conscience historique du renouveau culturel à la
naissance de la première histoire littéraire' en Humanism in France
at the end of the Middle Ages and in the early Renaissance, ed.
A.H.T. Levi (Manchester 1970), 106 - 114.

3.  M. Batllori, 'Alguns aspectes de l'humanisme a la península
ibèrica: Catalunya, Castella, Portugal' en Catalunya a l'època moderna
(Barcelona 1971), 20.

4.  Denis Hay, 'Flavio Biondo and the Middle Ages', Proceedings of the
British Academy, XLV (1959), 97 - 128.

5.  R.B. Tate, 'La "Anacephalecsis" de Alfonso García de Santa María'
en Ensayos sobre la historiografía peninsular del s. XV (Madrid 1970),
67.

6.  R.B. Tate, 'Rodrigo Sánchez de Arévalo y su "Compendiosa Historia
Hispanica"', op. cit., 83 - 84.

7.  R.B. Tate, 'El "Paralipomenon" de Joan Margarit', op. cit., 139 - 143.

8.  Por ejemplo, las preguntas de Antonio Ronzoni en Lucio Marineo
Sículo, Epist. Fam., vii, 4, 5; la carta de Castiglione al siciliano
impresa como prólogo a su De Rebus Hispaniae memorabilibus opus (Alcalá
1530); Jerónimo Pau envió su De viris illustribus Hispaniae a Gregorio
Columbeto, quien sólo sabía de España que había producido a Marcial.

9.  Véase el texto y estudio preliminar por R.B. Tate y A.M. Mundó,
'The Compendiolum of Alfonso de Palencia: a humanist treatise on the
geography of the Iberian Peninsula', JMRS, 5 (1975), 253 - 278.

10. Introductorium in cosmographiae libros, s.a., s.l., f.2$^a$,
líneas 14 - 17.

11. Op. cit., f.2$^b$, líneas 6 - 11.

12. Véase el prólogo de J.M. Casas Homs a su edición del opúsculo
Barcino de Jerónimo Pau (Barcelona 1957), 7 - 15, y el texto pp. 51 - 52.

13. Nebrija, Decades II, ed. cit., 787.

14. Op. cit., loc. cit. Consúltese también O. Di Camillo, El humanismo
castellano del siglo XV (Valencia 1976), 293.

15. Joannis Vasaei Brugensis rerum Hispanicarum Cronicon, ed. A. Schott,
Hisp. Illustr., I, 589 - 590.

Neruda in Transition:   Image and Structure in Tentativa del hombre
infinito

Arthur Terry (University of Essex)

Tentativa del hombre infinito (1925) has so far received very
little critical attention, though Neruda himself clearly regarded it
as a crucial step in his poetic experience.[1] Talking to Alfredo
Cardona Peña in 1950, he said: "es el libro menos leído y menos
estudiado de mi obra; sin embargo, es uno de los libros más importantes
de mi poesía, enteramente diferente a los demás".[2] Perhaps the last
part of this statement is an exaggeration: while it is true that
Tentativa represents a fairly sharp break with Neruda's earlier poetry,
the effort of writing it seems to have carried over into the first few
poems of Residencia en la tierra, and, though I shall not have time to
explore them in the present essay, there are some very striking
similarities, it seems to me, between the two collections.
      We can see why this should be so if we consider two other state-
ments by Neruda, both from his famous Biblioteca Nacional lectures of
1954.   In the first, he is looking back to his earlier volume of poems,
Veinte poemas de amor y una canción desesperada (1924): "este libro
no alcanzó, para mí, aun en esos años de tan poco conocimiento, el
secreto y ambicioso deseo de llegar a una poesía aglomerativa en que
todas las fuerzas del mundo se juntaran y se derribaran.   Era éste el
conflicto que me reservaba".   This is the conflict, we might add, which
is finally brought to a head in the Residencia poems, but which is
already present, in some of its most characteristic details, in
Tentativa del hombre infinito.   But the important phrase is the one
which comes before this:  "una poesía aglomerativa en que todas las
fuerzas del mundo se juntaran y se derribaran".   This desire to write
a kind of poetry which will exclude nothing, this vision of a world in
which reality itself is disintegrating, are familiar enough from the
Residencia poems, but are already gathering weight, I would argue, in
some of the most striking passages of Tentativa.
      The second statement takes us closer to the actual technique of
these poems:  "Este libro, Tentativa del hombre infinito, esta
experiencia frustrada de un poema cíclico, muestra precisamente un
desarrollo en la oscuridad, un aproximarse a las cosas con enorme
dificultad para definirlas... Y ese libro procede, como casi toda mi
poesía, de la oscuridad del ser que va paso a paso encontrando
obstáculos para elaborar con ellos su camino."   Like many of Neruda's
comments on his own poetry, this seems extraordinarily clear-sighted.
Darkness, as we shall see, is one of the central metaphors of Tentativa,
and the "development" Neruda refers to here is conveyed very literally
in the poems, through images of travelling and departure.   The phrase
about the difficulty of defining things also has important implications
for Neruda's poetic language at this stage, particularly when one relates it to a remark he made in 1926, a few months after the publication of Tentativa, about the need to eliminate everything objective
from one's poetry: "despojar a la poesía de todo lo objetivo".[3] What
this means in practice is that the objects Neruda names in his poems
of this period are more often than not removed from their conventional
contexts and used as metáphors for other, less easily definable things.
And, as Neruda himself goes on to suggest, it is the actual difficulty
of this process - the "obstacles" which he encounters in his search
for a truer concept of reality - which creates the general movement, or
"path", of his poems.

In a moment, I shall try to show how these intentions affect both the imagery and structure of certain poems. But before I come to this, there is another kind of difficulty to be considered: one which arises from the actual nature of the text. The original edition of <u>Tentativa</u> was published in January, 1926: it contained fifteen poems, several of which had been published separately in the course of the previous year. What makes the poems disconcerting at first sight is the fact that they are printed without punctuation or capital letters. Later, in 1961, Neruda explained this, rather dismissively, as a blatant and superficial imitation of Apollinaire and possibly Mallarmé.[4] Yet I suspect that this is not quite the whole truth; if it were, it ought to be possible for a careful reader to supply the punctuation himself. However, when one critic - admittedly a fairly hostile one - actually printed several of the poems with conventional punctuation, the results were plainly unsatisfactory. Why should this be so? If my own experience of reading these poems is anything to go by, a good deal of the time it is the actual cadences of the verse which help to confirm the various hints thrown out by the syntax. Yet attention to cadence and syntax is not always enough: even with this, there are times when it is almost impossible to decide where a particular sentence begins or leaves off, or how the various parts of the same sentence should be grouped. In something like half the poems, there are examples of what one might call 'sliding syntax', where certain lines can be read in more than one way without grammatical offence.

There is a striking example of this in the fifth and sixth lines of the first poem in the collection: "ciudad desde los cerros en la noche los segadores duermen / debatida a las últimas hogueras". If one is to make any sense at all of these lines, it is clear that part of the first one has to be read as a parenthesis. Granting this, it is easy to take "los segadores duermen" as if it were a stage direction or an aside. But where does the parenthesis begin? Should one read: "ciudad desde los cerros en la noche (los segadores duermen)..." or "ciudad desde los cerros (en la noche los segadores duermen)"? And how is the second line linked to the first? Does "debatida" refer to "ciudad", as it would have to if "en la noche" were part of the parenthesis, or should it go with "noche", which would be possible if one were to choose the first reading? To see the full implications of either reading, one has of course to take the lines in the context of the whole poem, which I shall shortly be doing. But to generalize for a moment: one has to remember, naturally, that in cases like this, one is reading a poem (that is to say, a pattern of words in which sound may be as important as sense), not merely shuffling round the pieces of a jigsaw; and sometimes the sound itself will help to determine the phrasing where more than one reading is grammatically possible. At the same time, there are a small number of instances - and this, I would claim, is one of them - where Neruda seems to have taken advantage of the absence of punctuation to create a genuine ambiguity which actually enriches the poem. In other words, by compelling the reader's imagination to come to terms with more than one possibility, it is as if he were deliberately steering him away from the idea of a single, definitive reading and producing an effect, not of alternatives, but of mysterious correspondences.

Let us look, then, at the first poem as a whole:

> hogueras pálidas revolviéndose al borde de las noches
> corren humos difuntos polvaredas invisibles
>
> fraguas negras durmiendo detrás de los cerros

```
       anochecidos
la tristeza del hombre tirada entre los brazos del sueño

ciudad desde los cerros en la noche los segadores
       duermen
debatida a las últimas hogueras
pero estás allí pegada a tu horizonte
como una lancha al muelle lista para zarpar lo creo
antes del alba

árbol de estertor candelabro de llamas viejas
distante incendio mi corazón está triste
sólo una estrella inmóvil su fósforo azul
los movimientos de la noche aturden hacia el cielo
```

What strikes one first here, surely, is the suggestion of a landscape.
To put it at its most abstract, one could say that there were three
areas of space: the hills, the distant city, and the frontier between
the two, symbolized by the bonfires.[5] At the same time, it is possible
to glimpse the elements of a plot: to associate the fires with the
presence of the reapers, and to visualize the poet looking out over the
city from the neighbouring hills. Yet the important thing is the
frontier situation, which in a sense is the speaker's own: what gives
the poem its shape is a whole series of polarities - city-country,
day-night, earth-sky, movement-stasis - and the way these are eventually
brought together in the poet's own mood. This process begins with an
impression of dying light which is also an image of movement and transformation: the "hogueras pálidas" which become "humos difuntos" and
"polvaredas invisibles". The "fraguas negras" of the third line are
on the far side of the hills, where the speaker can only imagine them:
their fires, which are a sign of daytime activity, are already extinct,
already swallowed up in the darkness of night. And this leads the
poem to its first general assertion: "la tristeza del hombre tirada
entre los brazos del sueño". One cannot help noticing the suggestion
of a parallel structure in the first four lines: the way the first
line of each pair begins with a similar combination of words (noun-
adjective-participle) and then opens out in the following line into a
parallel action or state. And there is still a trace of the same
pattern in the fifth line, which also begins with a noun: "ciudad
desde los cerros..." Clearly, this is not just a mechanical device for
keeping the poem going; taken along with the sense, this strong syntactical pattern seems to reinforce the parallel between man and the
various natural phenomena: in a way, one might say, the "sadness" is
carried over from the "pale bonfires" and the "black forges".
    The next lines are more difficult, because of the ambiguity I
mentioned earlier. The image of the sleeping harvesters makes the
reference to "la tristeza del hombre" more specific - these are the
people associated with this particular landscape - and at the same time,
perhaps, gives a more realistic basis to the "hogueras" of the opening
line. The real difficulty, as I have suggested, is in knowing how to
take the word "debatida". If one includes "en la noche" in the
parenthesis, it must refer to "ciudad": the poet's attention would be
"divided" between the city and the fires. If one limits the parenthesis
to "los segadores duermen", then it would be natural for "debatida" to
refer to its nearest antecedent, which is "noche"; again, the poet's
attention would be divided, but this time between the fires and night
itself, as if he were contemplating, not the city, but the darkness of
the interior which lies in the opposite direction. And on this second

reading, we could also think of the fires as struggling against the night: a slightly different sense of "debatida", but one which seems quite natural in the context. But does one really need to decide? I am tempted to argue that one can take all these associations together, since none of them conflicts. If the poet's attention is divided, then it seems more than likely that it is divided in both directions at once, and that this reinforces what I have already described as his "frontier situation". That this is both a geographical boundary and a symbolic limit is made clear in the rest of the poem, which takes up the "hoguera" image in a quite unexpected way.

The next three lines refer back to the city: "pero estás allí pegada a tu horizonte..." - the city on its own "frontier", one might say, at the moment static, but implying the potential movement which anticipates day. The actual logical twist which links this to the earlier part of the poem is important: "pero estás allí" ("nevertheless", "the fact remains that"); and if we read "ciudad...debatida" in the previous lines, it is as if the city had moved for a moment to the centre of the speaker's attention.

Near the end, the image of the fire comes back in a more personal sense. The three phrases which come next - "árbol de estertor", "candelabro de llamas viejas", "distante incendio" - are metaphors for the heart: "mi corazón está triste". In a way, the fire, now singular ("distante incendio") has become the heart - a surprising transmutation of what began as a more realistic image. One hardly needs to spell out these metaphors, except to notice that "árbol de estertor" introduces the idea of a vertical thrust (here linked to the dying fire) which reappears in the last two lines. The image of the single star suggests both solitude and stasis, and it reappears in other poems of the cycle associated with order.[6] This is a relatively conventional idea, and the line itself has a distinctly modernista ring to it. The last line, on the other hand, is more complex, partly because of the unusual use of the verb "aturden", as if the speaker were saying: "the movements of the night bewilder us and direct our attention upwards, to the sky". It is this double movement which is important, or rather, the transition from the horizontal to the vertical: as yet, the "movimientos de la noche" are undefined, though they are made more specific in some of the later poems; what seems clear, on the other hand, is that both star and sky are symbols of an order which absorbs the confusion of earth and darkness. The association of night with earth at this stage seems quite deliberate: the earth, of course, suggests the poet's own situation in time and place, and it is easy enough to see the night as a symbol of the unconscious forces which he is struggling to admit. And if the dominant mood of the poem is sadness, there is also an edge of fear in the images of death and in the final verb, "aturden".

There is a passage in one of the poems from Neruda's previous collection, El hondero entusiasta, which reads almost like a starting-point for the present poem. It goes: "Cae, muere el deseo. / Caen, mueren las llamas en la noche infinita...". The parallel, of course, lies in the combination of night and dying flames; at the same time, there is a difference in the place given to desire. In the earlier poem, "desire" is associated quite simply with day: desire fails, like the flames, at the approach of night. In the poem I have just been discussing, "desire" - sexual desire - is not mentioned; but when it does appear, in some of the later poems, it is not left behind in this way. To put it crudely, in Tentativa it is as though Neruda were prepared to carry sexual desire with him into the night. (I use the journey metaphor deliberately, since it is the one he himself uses most often in the poems.) And it is this willingness to associate sexual desire with the other unconscious forces suggested by the passage from day to night which makes for much of the tension and originality of these poems and prepares the ground for the even more comprehensive vision of <u>Residencia en la tierra</u>.

In the earlier poems of <u>Tentativa</u>, however, the emphasis remains on the kind of situation described in the first poem. Here, for example, is the third poem of the sequence:

> oh matorrales crespos adonde el sueño avanza trenes
> oh montón de tierra entusiasta donde de pie sollozo
> vértebras de la noche agua tan lejos viento intranquilo
>     rompes
> también estrellas crucificadas detrás de la montaña
>
> alza su empuje un ala pasa un vuelo oh noche sin
>     llaves
> oh noche más en mi hora en mi hora furiosa y
>     doliente
> eso me levantaba como la ola al alga
> acoge mi corazón desventurado
> cuando rodeas los animales del sueño
> crúzalo con tus vastas correas de silencio
> está a tus pies esperando una partida
> porque lo pones cara a cara a ti misma noche de
>     hélices negras
> y que toda fuerza en él sea fecunda
> atada al cielo con estrella de lluvia
> procrea tú amárrate a esa proa minerales azules
> embarcado en ese viaje nocturno
> un hombre de veinte años sujeta una rienda
>     frenética
> es que él quería ir a la siga de la noche
> entre sus manos ávidas el viento sobresalta

Here, the landscape is directly addressed: in the opening lines, the dominant emotions are exaltation and pain. These are brought together in the second line, where the phrase "montón entusiasta" (like "estrellas crucificadas" two lines later) transfers the speaker's own emotion to nature. And once again, the poet places himself firmly in the "frontier situation" of the earlier poem. At the same time, one cannot entirely separate the emotion from the landscape: "entusiasta" literally means "inspired by a god", but here it is as if the "god" were simply the energy shared by man and earth. And it is from this position that the speaker in his imagination explores the landscape of night. Neruda's way of putting this is very striking: "el sueño avanza trenes". Such train metaphors occur in several poems of <u>Tentativa</u>. The most extraordinary examples come in the fifth poem, which I have no space to examine in detail. There, the starry sky is referred to as "tren de luz": "tren de luz allá arriba te asalta un ser sin recuerdos". The rest of this poem is full of images of travelling: "y la noche como un vino invade el túnel"; "señalarás los caminos como las cruces de los muertos" (perhaps the telegraph poles beside the track suggesting wayside crosses). The last two lines are more difficult to interpret: "donde lo sigue su riel frío / y se para sin muchas treguas el animal de la noche". The difficulty is partly that here, as elsewhere in these poems, Neruda has deliberately avoided giving the object its usual name. But if one puts the sentence in the form of a riddle: "What is it that goes through the night like an animal and keeps stopping, though never for long at once?", the answer, clearly, is "a train". When one reads the whole poem, the effect is not as clear-cut as this; the train metaphor itself, one might say, keeps disappearing into tunnels. Nevertheless, this partly submerged train metaphor is one of the basic structural features of the poem, and again it shows Neruda's skill in detaching an image from its normal, more realistic context, and recreating it in terms of the imagination. And these train images are particularly interesting, I think, because they are rooted in biographical fact, in Neruda's own fascination as a child for the railways which were associated with the remote and yet powerful figure of his father. At the back of such images in Tentativa, I suspect, there is one dominant image of a train of lighted carriages going off at night towards the interior: an image which, in the poems, becomes a metaphor for various kinds of cosmic relationship.

Coming back to the third poem, one notices the strategic placing of the word "vértebras"; as in other poems, there is a tendency for each of the opening lines to unfold from an initial noun. Here, it is the elements of water and air which run through the night, which give structure to it: the wind is both restless and hostile, since it "breaks" the stars: "crucificadas" suggesting both stasis (as in the first poem) and pain. And there is another reminder of the first poem in that night seems to be imagined as in some way behind the mountain; again, the "frontier situation", with the mountain itself as a kind of barrier between day and night.

After this, the tone of the poem changes for a moment: the "ala (que) alza su empuje" suggests aspiration; at the same time, it is one of the "movements of night" referred to in the earlier poem, though the night itself at this stage is unintelligible ("sin llaves"). The rest of the poem is an invocation to night, beautifully sustained, and not especially complex. "Oh noche más en mi hora..." suggests that the night is "greater" through the intensity of the poet's emotion; pain has now been joined by fury - a less passive mood than the "sadness" of the first poem, and one which has already been suggested by the combination of "entusiasta" and "crucificadas".

Immediately after this, one notices a device which Neruda exploits a good deal in the Residencia poems: the use of the neuter eso or aquello to refer back to a whole complex of feelings and intuitions which cannot be defined in a simple way.[7] The action itself - "eso me levantaba como la ola al alga" - once again implies exaltation, this time reinforced by a more concrete metaphor, which seems to identify the speaker with the superior forces of nature. The whole drift of the invocation at this point rests on the wish to be absorbed by night, to become just one more of the "animales del sueño", to be imprisoned within the universal silence. So, by one metaphorical shift after another, the poem moves towards the final extended metaphor of the journey. The heart, confronted by night, is ready to depart; it is night itself which has imposed the confrontation ("porque lo pones cara a cara a ti..."), and it is night which contains the motive power, so to speak, for the journey. "Que toda fuerza en él sea fecunda" refers back to "corazón": a conventional enough wish if taken in isolation, though in the context it suggests a desire to be joined to the actual source of energy and fertility. And the next line adds to this intensity: it is the force itself - "every force" - which is to be "atada al cielo con estrellas de lluvia". It is not difficult to see how "atada" extends the "correa" metaphor of a few lines back and in turn produces "amárrate" a moment later; "estrellas de lluvia" is perhaps rather a strange metaphor in Spanish, though it comes into focus if one remembers the English phrase about stars "raining their influence".

The transition to "minerales azules" is not strictly grammatical, unless one reads it as a kind of aside; in the context, this scarcely matters: the phrase is clearly a synonym for "night", though night seen in a rather special way. "Azul" here, surely, is more than just the conventional colour of night: one recalls that, in the first poem, it was the colour of the star, and elsewhere it is associated with the moon. In the opening poem of El hondero entusiasta, Neruda had already described night as "toda ella de metales azules", and in the Residencia poems, both "metal" and "mineral" are used in a similar sense.[8] So here, the night, and more specifically the stars, are seen as sources of cosmic energy, and perhaps also as a metaphor for the unconscious.[9] The last three lines are simple and powerful: the "viento (que) sobresalta" echoes the "viento intranquilo" of the opening lines; it is the same wind, we might say, only brought closer now to the poet, a force which leaps in his hands, like the "rienda frenética" two lines before. In whichever metaphor one takes it, this is the force which the poet must try to control. It is interesting that Amado Alonso, in another context, should define the Greek word enthousiasmos as "frenesí controlado";[10] this fits perfectly the mood of these closing lines and of much else in Tentativa. And part of the attempt to gain control - part of the poet's own power, in other words - is embodied in the shift from the first to the third person: "un hombre de veinte años...". This effect of desdoblamiento occurs a number of times in Tentativa, as it does in certain of the Residencia poems. I have already quoted one example from Tentativa in a different connection: "tren de luz allá arriba te asalta un ser sin recuerdos", and this is echoed in "Serenata", one of the earliest poems in Residencia, written in 1925: "El joven sin recuerdos te saluda, te pregunta por su olvidada voluntad" (6). In all these examples, the effect is the same: to increase the illusion of control by creating emotional distance.

The two poems I have looked at so far come near the beginning of the cycle. Roughly speaking, the first six poems explore the same situation: the poet as a solitary figure on the confines between day and night, with all the symbolic overtones this opposition implies. In the seventh, woman enters the sequence for the first time:

> torciendo hacia ese lado o más allá continúas
>     siendo mía
> en la soledad del atardecer golpea tus sonrisas
> en ese instante trepan enredaderas a mi ventana
> el viento de lo alto cimbra la sed de tu presencia
>
> un gesto de alegría una palabra de pena que
>     estuviera más cerca de ti
> en su reloj profundo la noche aísla horas
> sin embargo teniéndote entre los brazos vacilé
> algo que no te pertenece desciende de tu cabeza
> y se te llena de oro la mano levantada
>
> hay esto entre dos paredes a lo lejos
> radiantes ruedas de piedra sostienen el día
>     mientras tanto
> después colgado en la horca del crepúsculo
> pisa en los campanarios y en las mujeres de los
>     pueblos
> moviéndose en la orilla de mis redes
> mujer querida en mi pecho tu cabeza cerrada
> a grandes llamaradas el molino se revuelve

                  y caen las horas nocturnas como murciélagos del
                       cielo

                  en otra parte lejos lejos existen tú y yo parecidos
                       a nosotros
                  tú escribes margaritas en la tierra solitaria
                  es que ese país de cierto nos pertenece
                  el amanecer vuela de nuestra casa

Significantly, this is a poem about absence: the poet's own situation
is associated with dusk and solitude as the woman seems to recede into
a still remoter distance. It is hard to be sure how to read lines 2-4:
in the Obras completas of 1962, "golpea tus sonrisas" is altered to
"golpea tu sonrisa", which makes "golpea" a present indicative. My
own preference here is for the original reading, with "golpea" as an
imperative. This in itself conveys a sense of irruption, of breaking
suddenly into a situation. The imperative makes the line into a plea,
though if one takes the two lines together, it is as if there were the
suggestion of a conditional construction: "if you were to smile
suddenly (if you were suddenly to interrupt my solitude with your
smiles), at that very moment ivy would climb to my window". This seems
to me to make better sense: the woman's imagined presence associated
with natural growth, and, in the fourth line, with wind: an energetic,
purifying force, with a suggestion of violence ("cimbra") which echoes
the similar violence of "golpea".
     The mood of what follows is summed up in the conjunction of "ale-
gría" and "pena" in the next line. The reference to time - "en su reloj
profundo la noche aísla horas" - is picked up again nearer the end of
the poem: "y caen las horas nocturnas como murciélagos del cielo",
where the bat image adds a more sinister note. In either case, the
"hours of the night" are both like and unlike those of the clock:
they are distinguishable, but on a different scale, a scale which links
them, perhaps in a frightening way, with the unseen forces of the
universe. The same forces enter into the lines which follow. These
directly concern the woman, and at first sight are very puzzling:
"sin embargo teniéndote entre los brazos vacilé / algo que no te
pertenece desciende de tu cabeza / y se te llena de oro la mano
levantada". This is clearly a memory of an encounter in the past.
But why did the speaker "hesitate", and what is this "something" which
does not belong to the woman? Alfredo Lozada has a good comment on
these lines: "el 'algo' que no le pertenece a la amada y que le hace
levantar la mano como para atraer, nombra con la usual indeterminación
a la sustancia cósmica", and he goes on to connect the woman's gesture
with a similar image from one of the Residencia poems, "Alianza
(Sonata)": "En lo alto de las manos el deslumbrar de mariposas, / el
arrancar de mariposas cuya luz no tiene término".[11] What made the
poet hesitate, therefore, was the sense of powerful cosmic forces
working through the woman - using her, in fact, as their instrument.[12]
     This is an important passage, since it brings into the open a
whole aspect of Neruda's vision at this stage, and one which Lozada
himself has studied in relation to the Residencia poems. To put it
briefly, it is as though in writing the poems of this period, Neruda
had responded imaginatively to something like the basic conception
contained in the philosophy of Schopenhauer, though, as Lozada argues,
he could have found what he needed for his purpose in the novels of
Baroja, to which he appears to have been addicted at the time. This
basic conception is implied in the title of Schopenhauer's major work,
The World as Will and Idea: roughly speaking, it asserts that the

universe is composed basically of undifferentiated matter or energy, whose one aim is to perpetuate itself at all costs, which it does by assuming a whole series of temporary forms, both animate and inanimate. For the most part, it is a hostile process, because of its sheer ruthlessness. This perhaps explains why the poet, at this point, appears to recoil from the woman, because he senses the nature of the forces which are working through her. It is also a cyclical process which works through constant metamorphosis; this is why, in "Galope muerto", the first of the <u>Residencia</u> poems, Neruda refers to "el molino de las formas", and there seems to be an anticipation of this image further on in the earlier poem: "a grandes llamaradas el molino se revuelve". In one sense, of course, this takes us back to the flame-night situation of the first poem, where movement was associated with the transition from light to dark. But there is also a hint of the constant metamorphosis of forms which I referred to a moment ago; and in that first poem, the flames of the bonfires did not simply disappear: they were transformed into smoke and dust – the same energy, but in a different shape.

This helps to explain another image in the present poem: the "radiantes ruedas de piedra (que) sostienen el día". As I read this line, the stones are millstones, another variation on the "molino de las formas". Stones are, of course, important throughout Neruda's work, but here I take another hint from Lozada. In his commentary on another of the <u>Residencia</u> poems, he remarks on the similarity between Neruda's use of stone symbols and the various primitive myths which regard stones as sacred objects: "la veneración de las piedras como solidificaciones de la materia, del ritmo creador". And he goes on: "La materia cósmica, en el poema, es lo denso, lo unitario, lo idéntico a sí mismo".[13] Exactly. And this is why, I think, at the end of this poem, the lovers are described as "parecidos a nosotros": in the ideal state which the speaker can only imagine, the lovers will have realized themselves in terms of cosmic harmony. For once – and this, I am inclined to think, is exceptional in these poems – love will have proved superior to the chaos of the universe: the lovers will be "parecidos a sí mismos", like the sources of energy itself. This in turn explains the play on "pertenece" and "no pertenece": in the earlier passage, the woman was the instrument of forces which did not belong to her; by the end of the poem – though only in an ideal vision – she has become completely identified with these forces, and the lovers exist in a "country" which is genuinely their own.

I have leapt ahead to the end of the poem in order to bring out these connections. If one looks at them in their full context, one sees that there are other details which reinforce the situation I have just sketched in. Half way through the poem, for instance, there is another example of Neruda's characteristic use of the neuter pronoun: "hay esto entre dos paredes...". This refers back to everything he has described in the early part of the poem: at the moment of experiencing both the actuality and the memory, the speaker is in a closed situation, bounded by the walls of his room. Just after this, there is a movement from day to dusk, and eventually to night. The first part of this transition is expressed in a rather curious conceit: "después colgado en la horca del crepúsculo ('colgado' refers to 'día') / pisa en los campanarios y en las mujeres de los pueblos...". A slightly grotesque conception, which belongs to the fantasy rather than to the imagination: and perhaps rightly so, since it occurs "en la orilla de mis redes" – that is to say, on the borders of the speaker's perception. Immediately after this comes a line which stands apart from those on either side of it: "mujer querida en mi pecho tu cabeza cerrada". Because of its relative isolation, I am tempted to read this as another memory, one which echoes the earlier passage which begins "sin embargo teniéndote entre los brazos..."; the woman's head is "cerrada" in precisely the same sense as before: it is impenetrable because if is full of an alien power which the speaker cannot begin to understand.

This brings us back to the ending. There is an idyllic note here, it seems to me, which goes with the imaginary situation I have already described. In this ideal state, as I said before, the lovers will have realized themselves in terms of cosmic harmony: "tú escribes margaritas en la tierra solitaria" suggests that the woman will people the earth with flowers, like the germinating force or energy itself; "vuela", in the last line, implies aspiration, perhaps liberation, and the sense of the whole line - "el amanecer vuela de nuestra casa" - is similar to that of the earlier one: both the man and the woman are one with the processes of time and the cycle of night and day.

This final situation is exceptional in these poems. Even in an imaginary state, as here, love is seldom able to rise above the apparent chaos of the universe. Moreover, the cosmic energy which Neruda so vividly re-creates is normally blind and hostile - something which it is difficult to regard as a source of harmony. In the later poems of the cycle, the woman tends to be overshadowed by the tensions which arise from the speaker's own relations with the universe. On the one hand, there are poems in which the sexual relationship is seen as a source of light, as something which illuminates the poet's experience and gives it a sense of inevitability. But against these, there are others in which the woman recedes further and further into the distance: someone whose return is always hoped for, but which seems increasingly improbable.[14]

The woman makes her last appearance in the thirteenth poem. Here, the greater part of the poem consists of an invocation which begins in the seventh line:

> párate sombra de estrellas en las cejas de un hombre a
>     la vuelta de un camino
> que lleva a la espalda una mujer pálida de oro
>         parecida a sí misma
> todo está perdido las semanas están cerradas...

This should remind us of those lines from the poem I was discussing a moment ago: "algo que no te pertenece desciende de tu cabeza / y se te llena de oro la mano levantada". Gold is one of the metals which give visible shape to the forces of cosmic energy; this is why, once again, the woman is "parecida a sí misma": she has the uniqueness, and also the otherness, of matter itself. And again Neruda uses the device of desdoblamiento: by setting an emotional distance between his speaking voice and his own person - "un hombre a la vuelta de un camino" - he is giving an air of finality to his experience which the rest of the context bears out. The invocation opens with a plea to the stars: "párate sombra de estrellas en las cejas de un hombre..."; if the stars "stopped" or became static, it would mean that the poet was directly under their influence, perhaps that he was a part of their order. It is some such pattern that he is looking for in the opening lines of the poem: "sigo un cordón que marca siquiera una presencia una situación cualquiera..." - anything, that is to say, provided it has a recognizable form. But this is precisely what he is unable to achieve. As in the previous poem, the woman follows him only in his imagination, and even then she stands for a centre of energy which is alien to him. And immediately after this, his vision of her is wiped

out by the sense of total loss: "todo está perdido las semanas están
cerradas".

I want to turn now to the last poem of the cycle, the one which
begins "devuélveme la grande rosa...". This is a beautiful and
difficult poem, and perhaps a little baffling in places if one hasn't
read the other poems in the sequence, since it hints at a number of
images which have already occurred elsewhere. At the same time, this
suggests what I think is true: that the poem earns its place at the
end of the cycle precisely because it combines certain echoes of
previous poems and holds them together in a final chord:

> devuélveme la grande rosa la sed traída al mundo
> adonde voy supongo iguales las cosas
> la noche importante y triste y ahí mi querella
> barcarolero de las largas aguas cuando
> de pronto una gaviota crece en tus sienes mi
>     corazón está cansado
> márcame tu pata gris llena de lejos
> tu viaje de la orilla del mar amargo o espérame
> el vaho se despierta como una violeta es que
> a tu árbol noche querida sube un niño
> a robarse las frutas
> y los lagartos brotan de tu pesada vestidura
> entonces el día salta encima de su abeja
> estoy de pie en la luz como el mediodía en la
>     tierra
> quiero contarlo todo con ternura
> centinela de las malas estaciones ahí estás tú
> pescador intranquilo déjame adornarte por
>     ejemplo
> un cinturón de frutas dulce la melancolía
> espérame donde voy ah el atardecer
> la comida las barcarolas del océano oh espérame
> adelantándote como un grito atrasándote como
>     una huella oh espérate
> sentado en esa última sombra o todavía después
> todavía

This poem begins, like so many others in _Tentativa_, with a division
between aspiration and fact: what the speaker hopes for is the return
of beauty – the rose – which is the symbol of poetic aspiration or
"thirst" in the daylight world; his own journey, on the other hand, is
into night, which makes things equal by merging their identities. At
the same time, there is a certain ironic detachment in the next line –
"la noche importante y triste y ahí mi querella" – as if he could now
regard what earlier was a source of terror and frustration merely
as grounds for complaint. The next lines create an effect of mystery
which nothing else in the sequence quite helps to resolve. Who is
this figure of the "barcarolero" or "singing boatman"? The most one
can say, perhaps, is that he is a presence endowed with the gift of
song, who presides over the waters near the shore. Remembering the
first poem, it is as if one had to do with a different kind of frontier
situation, and one which occurs in a number of the _Residencia_ poems:
the boundary between land and sea which so often in Neruda marks the
passage into reality. Taken separately, the gull is an obvious image
of liberation: something which holds out the promise of new distances.
The "pata gris", I take it, also belongs to the gull; but what makes
the passage puzzling, though at the same time strangely haunting, is

the apparent identification of gull and boatman. This process takes
place in two stages: first, the gull appears as an extension of the
boatman - "una gaviota crece en tus sienes" - and then they appear to
merge completely in "tu pata gris". What is clear, I think, is the
underlying mood: the sense of wishing to be associated with the
journey offshore - to be taken up in it passively, perhaps, in a state
of emotional fatigue.
     . The lines which follow really need to be read with the previous
poem in mind. There, just before the end, there is a moment of naive
celebration: "yo lo comienzo a celebrar entusiasta sencillo / yo tengo
la alegría de los panaderos contentos...". The present passage seems
to come from the same mood of innocence and simplicity. "el vaho se
despierta como una violeta" is an image of sea-mist lifting, like the
awakening of something natural and beautiful; "es que" brings the
explanation: what has caused it to lift is the childlike action of the
boy who is also the poet. And this is followed by a similar image:
"y los lagartos brotan de tu pesada vestidura" suggests the emergence
of quick, spontaneous natural life from the oppressive atmosphere of
night. "Entonces" marks the next stage in the poem: all this has been
leading to the arrival of dawn. The image of the bee, as often in
Neruda, stands for ardour and vitality:[15] the new day, perhaps,
imagined as springing from its original nucleus of energy. In the day,
the poet dominates: "estoy de pie en la luz como el mediodía en la
tierra": "mediodía", that is to say, implying harmony, equilibrium
and control. It is this balance which gives rise to a new wish and a
new emotion: "quiero contarlo todo con ternura". Moreover, he finds
himself, so to speak, in a familiar setting: "centinela de las malas
estaciones ahí estás tú". Here again, Neruda seems to be taking up an
image from an earlier poem - the fourth, which begins: "estrella
retardada entre la noche gruesa los días de altas velas". In both
poems, the star is Venus, the daystar: in the earlier passage, it
symbolizes both order and continuity; it is the "embarcadero de las
dudas", which presides over the difficult passages from night to day,
and, in its capacity as evening star, from day to night. These, I
think, are the "malas estaciones" of the present poem; the star, as
before, is both a comforting presence and a witness.
     This dual rôle of the star - both daystar and evening star - seems
crucial for the ending of the poem and, consequently, of the whole
sequence. To bring the cycle to a close simply with the emergence from
night into day would have been too facile. The poem does, in fact, end
on the threshold of day: "sentado en esta última sombra...". But
before this, there is another reference to dusk. The lines which
introduce this may seem puzzling at first sight: "pescador intranquilo
déjame adornarte por ejemplo / un cinturón de frutas dulce la
melancolía / espérame donde voy ah el atardecer". Again, to bring them
into focus one needs to bear in mind certain images from earlier poems.
"Pescador intranquilo", for example, suggests the metaphor used for
dusk at the end of the eleventh poem: "oh atardecer que llegas
pescador satisfecho / tu canasto vivo en la debilidad del cielo".
There the fish were the spoils of the day which is coming to an end,
and in both cases, as in other poems of Neruda's, fish are associated
with cosmic energy.[16] "Déjame adornarte" suggests an act of homage:
he wishes to pay tribute to evening, in a mood of "dulce melancolía".
The reference to "la comida" is an intrusion - perhaps not a very
effective one - from the poem which comes immediately before, where the
movements of day and night are contrasted with the domestic situation
of the speaker - "yo asustado comía". But, in the context, this
passing allusion is swept up into the expansive movement of the ending.

It is no coincidence, I think, that the previous poem also ends with
a sense of openness: "amanecía débilmente como un color de violín /
con un sonido de campana con el olor de la larga distancia" - a sense
of melancholy and distance which cuts across the mood of naive
celebration I mentioned earlier. Here, the speaker is more directly
involved: the final emotion is one of wanting to be taken on a
journey. Though "sentado en esta última sombra" suggests the
emergence from night, there is no sense of triumph. Instead, the last
four words look forward from this to what may come after, still
hesitating in the face of the unknown, and still hoping to achieve the
"moment outside time".

There is a quiet, deliberately inconclusive ending, an ending of
great integrity, since it refuses to force the poem into a final
attitude which would falsify the whole drift of the sequence. This
last poem, as I have tried to show, completes the cycle which began
on the threshold between day and night. At the same time, it does not
cancel out the experience of night: there is a continuing tension
between night and day which is conveyed in the fluctuating images of
the last part of the poem. The night and all that it implies -
hostility, the unconscious, the sense of a dynamic but ultimately
irrational universe - is still to be explored in the poems of
Residencia en la tierra. If Neruda later came to regard Tentativa del
hombre infinito as "(una) experiencia frustrada", he was equally
correct in seeing it as an essential stage in his poetic development,
and I hope that I have shown at least a few of the reasons why this
should be so.


# NOTES

1. Alain Sicard's article 'La eternidad en el instante: un análisis
de THI', Anales de la Universidad de Chile, CXXIX (1971), 107 - 116
only came to my notice after I had completed the first draft of my own
essay. Sicard's reading of the poems is sensitive and often illuminating, and I refer to it several times in what follows.

2. This statement and the two which follow are quoted by E. Rodríguez
Monegal in El viajero inmóvil: introducción a Pablo Neruda (Buenos
Aires 1967), 187 - 188.

3. Quoted by Alfredo Lozada en El monismo agónico de Pablo Neruda:
estructura, significado y filiación de "Residencia en la tierra"
(Mexico 1971), 339.

4. The remark is quoted by Jorge Sanhueza in the bibliographical note
to his edition of THI (Santiago 1964), 7.

5. It is possible to take "hogueras" metaphorically, as an allusion
to the setting sun. Cf. Sicard: "El sol se hunde sobre la ciudad...
En un sentido literal, esta ciudad y sus habitantes son presas del sol
poniente. Desde lo alto de la colina en que se encuentra, el poeta
escapa a este incendio natural: 'ahí pasan ardiendo sólo yo vivo'
(poem 2)" (art.cit., 108). Nevertheless, the opening lines ("hogueras
pálidas... polvaredas invisibles"), with their succession of plurals
and their hint of movement ("revolviéndose") suggest that these are

real, not merely metaphorical, fires. In more general terms, such details in _Tentativa_ often seem to relate to the actual landscapes described in the prose pieces of _Anillos_ (1926).

6. Cf. Poem 4: "estrella retardada entre la noche gruesa los días de altas velas / como entre tú y tu sombra se acuestan las vacilaciones / embarcadero de las dudas bailarín en el hilo sujetabas crepúsculos" (1-3).

7. Cf. the opening of the second stanza of "Galope muerto": "Aquello todo tan rápido, tan viviente..." (11).

8. Cf. "Unidad": "Me rodea una misma cosa, un solo movimiento: / el paso del mineral, la luz de la piel, / se pegan al sonido de la palabra noche..." (6-8); "Serenata": "Oh noche, mi alma sobrecogida te pregunta / desesperadamente a ti por el metal que necesita" (19-20).

9. Cf. J.E. Cirlot, _A Dictionary of Symbols_, 2nd ed. (London 1967), 208: "metals symbolize cosmic energy in solidified form and, in consequence, the libido".

10. Amado Alonso, _Poesía y estilo de Pablo Neruda_, 3rd ed. (Buenos Aires 1966), 217 - 218.

11. Op. cit., 150

12. Sicard interprets these lines more simply, as a reference to dusk ("oro") and by extension to the woman's vulnerability to time: "Esta mujer... la vemos habitada por el crepúsculo y... amenazada por el tiempo. De ahí la hesitación ("vacilé"), el retroceso un tanto asustado del poeta". This, however, does not affect the basic contrast between this passage and the concluding lines ("en otra parte... de nuestra casa"), which envisage a love "outside time". Sicard's comment on the place of love in these poems seems very just: "Porque él mismo es víctima del tiempo, el amor no podría constituir una forma de eludirlo. Tal vez esto explique que el amor sólo tenga en _Tentativa_ un lugar secundario. Para luchar contra el tiempo, por sobre el acto erótico será preferido el acto poético." (art.cit., 110)

13. Op. cit., 123

14. Compare the end of the twelfth poem:

> te busco cada vez entre los signos del regreso
> estás llena de pájaros durmiendo como el silencio de
> los bosques
> pesado y triste lirio miras hacia otra parte
> cuando te hablo me dueles tan distante mujer mía
> apresura el paso apresura el paso y enciende las
> luciérnagas

Here again, one has something like the interplay between a real and an imagined situation we saw in the seventh poem. Just before these lines, the woman is described as "seguidora de mi alma", but it is clear that she "follows" the speaker only in his imagination; even in the act of urging her to return, it is as if he were acknowledging absence as a final state, and even as he invokes her, she is looking away.

15. See Amado Alonso, op. cit., 236 - 238.

16. See Amado Alonso, op. cit., 239 - 241.

# Juan de Luna, teacher of Spanish, and the 'French picaresque'

M.J. Thacker (University of Liverpool)

The year 1620 saw the publication in Paris of the first picaresque novel to be written on foreign soil, the Segunda parte de la vida de Lazarillo de Tormes.[1] Its author, Juan de Luna,[2] made his living as a teacher of Spanish, being described on the title-page as "castellano, intérprete de la lengua española". Luna's Segunda parte possesses most of the features that the seventeenth-century reader associated with the picaresque genre, but manifests a distinctive tone which critics often consider to be frivolous when compared with novels of the pica-resque canon published in Spain during the previous twenty years. Valbuena's remarks are typical:

> El tono frívolo del libro de Luna va bien al ambiente
> francés así como su especial picaresca sexual, bien
> distinta del estoicismo que en este punto suelen
> ofrecer casi todas las novelas españolas del género.[3]

This alleged deviation in tone is usually attributed to the writer's residence in France, where the reading public, it is held, was used to lighter, more entertaining fiction, with a heavy emphasis on the erotic. Luna is therefore thought to have succumbed, whether consciously or not, to French taste for fiction of this kind. Furthermore, the writer was free, in a foreign environment, from the constraints that would have applied had the book been published in Spain. Luna's novel would thus be the first of a long line of picaresque works that are the products of the sensibility and literary traditions of a foreign culture.[4]

My purpose is to examine those aspects of Luna's novel that suggest a departure from the picaresque in Spain. I shall argue that Luna's occupation as a teacher of Spanish in Paris was of great importance in the genesis of the novel, and helps to explain the special tone that he adopted and some of the subject-matter.

The little that we know about Luna's life has been gleaned from one or two documents and from Luna's works themselves. He emigrated to France around 1612,[5] probably because of a quarrel with the authorities. In the dedication to the English edition of his Spanish grammar, the Arte breve (1623),[6] he asks the Duke of Lennox for his protection because of "la necesidad que de un tal amparo, tiene un forastero, que ha dexado su patria, parientes, y hazienda por una justa y legitima causa". In 1614 he was converted to Protestantism at Montauban, one of the centres of that faith. Sometime after that date he moved to Paris, where he published his first work, the bilingual Arte breve, the privilège of which is dated December, 1615. This grammar was one of a number of similar works timed to coincide with the marriage of Anne of Austria, daughter of Philip III of Spain, to the French King, Louis XIII, in the same year. This event led to an upsurge of interest in the study of Spanish,[7] which Luna and other grammarians were quick to exploit. A document of the following year, in which Luna transferred the right to print his grammar to another, more accurate, publisher, indicates that the author came from Toledo.[8] Luna evidently continued to teach Spanish in Paris, probably with some success, for he published another textbook for learners of Spanish, the Diálogos familiares,[9] in 1619. In the following year there appeared his version of the first Lazarillo de Tormes, "corregida y emendada", so that the

French reader would not be led astray by the 'impure' Spanish of the original. To this he added his own original second part, which was bound with the first <u>Lazarillo</u> and issued by the same publisher.

A document unearthed by Bataillon[10] reveals that Luna married when in France and that his daughter was baptised into the Protestant faith. Her godfather and godmother (le Comte d'Orval and Anne de Rohan) were high-ranking Protestant nobles, a fact that suggests that Luna moved in aristocratic circles. The dedication of the French version of the <u>Arte breve</u>, to Anne of Scissons, a cousin of the King, and that of the <u>Diálogos</u>, to Louis de Bourbon, Anne's son, confirm this impression.

Not long after the publication of the <u>Segunda parte</u> Luna left for England, and settled there. In London all three of his works were translated and published in a short space of time: the <u>Segunda parte</u>[11] and the <u>Diálogos</u>[12] in 1622, and an improved and extended edition of the <u>Arte breve</u> in the following year. It is therefore certain that Luna's interest in the teaching of Spanish continued in his new country of residence. He also continued to practise his faith freely, preaching in Mercer's Chapel, Cheapside, London.[13]

Three important facts relating to Luna's <u>Lazarillo</u> emerge from the sparse information about the author that we possess: first, his long period of residence in France, possibly as many as ten years, which supports the likelihood that his novel was <u>afrancesado</u>; second, his heterodoxy and the possible connexions that it had with his departure from Spain, which might explain the attitude to the clergy and the Inquisition found in his novel; third, the pedagogic nature of his first two works and his willingness to go to the lengths of re-writing a literary classic in the interest of his pupils. This last aspect justifies my intention to re-examine the <u>Segunda parte</u> from the point of view of its value as a reading text for advanced learners. First, however, I shall look briefly at those aspects of Luna's novel that have been labeled <u>afrancesados</u>.

The <u>Segunda parte</u> adheres to most of the typical features of Spanish picaresque novels published before it: the <u>pícaro</u> tells of his adventures in the first person, looking back on the life of a wandering rogue; sometimes he is in service, but more often than not he lives an idle existence; his destiny is in the hands of a capricious Fortune, etc. Luna chose to work certain motifs into this characteristically loose framework. It is the incidence of these motifs and the tone in which some of the episodes are related that give rise to the critics' suspicion of French influence. Luna bends towards his French reader in two of his main themes: his anti-institutional satire (against the clergy and the Inquisition) and his treatment of women (under which I shall discuss the related aspects of eroticism and obscenity).

Luna's rabid anticlericalism and his sarcastic attitude to the officers of the Inquisition ("gente tan santa y perfecta como la justicia que administran")[14] have been examined thoroughly elsewhere.[15] It is sufficient to state that Luna's contribution to the <u>leyenda negra</u> is offered with great relish, at a time when the French had an intense dislike for Spain and her people (despite the official acceptance of Spaniards at court and the enthusiasm among the educated Frenchmen to learn Spanish). Luna's anticlerical remarks are also in tune with the traditional lack of respect accorded to the clergy in France. Luna refers frequently to the promiscuity of the clergy (the <u>pícaro</u> meets two prostitutes whose favourite lovers had been priests; he is himself the victim of the archpriest's designs on his wife), to their meanness (a monk he carries for refuses to pay him, then gives him a beating for demanding payment) and to their idleness and love of pleasure (a monk and a nun join a gypsy band "con deseo de profesar más austera vida").[16]

In his anticlericalism Luna was therefore influenced by his French
environment inasmuch as it provided him with the liberty to satisfy a
personal desire to attack the forces of oppression in Spanish society.
Luna's attitude to women, however, seems to spring from a far more
positive 'contamination' from his French surroundings.

In his treatment of women Luna exploits a theme, the infidelity of
wives, introduced in the first Lazarillo. The whore that Lázaro marries
at the end of the first part and her lover, the archpriest, join forces
against the pícaro in the second part. When Lázaro comes back from
the ill-fated expedition to Algiers, he discovers that his wife is
pregnant by the archpriest, and that she does not want her husband
back. The cuckolded pícaro attempts to sue the pair but runs out of
money to bribe the judge; as a result he is condemned to live the life
of a picaresque wanderer. Lázaro continues to suffer at the hands of
women. A succession of whores, an alcahueta (Chapter X), a licentious
dama (Chapter X), and a scheming gitana (Chapter XI) confirm the
picture of feminine guile and fickleness. To cap it all, Lázaro is
duped by three sadistic women at the end of the novel who pretend to go
through a marriage ceremony between the luckless pícaro and one of them.
They tie him naked to a bed, cut off his hair and prepare to castrate
him. Lázaro manages to fend them off, and escapes, but only after
being tossed in a sheet. Marriage is increasingly debased in the novel:
from the relatively straightforward cuckoldry of Lázaro by his wife,
to the large-scale adultery of an orgy attended by the pícaro in Chapter
XIII, and finally to the sham marriage of Lázaro at the end of the novel.
The husband-wife relationship is shown as a pretence, a cloak of
respectability for wives as they go about indulging their sexual
appetites.

The portrayal of women in the picaresque novel in Spain is in
essence the same as in the Segunda parte. Adultery, conjugal dis-
harmony and prostitution are, after all, part and parcel of low-life
literature everywhere. Where Luna's novel differs from those published
in Spain is in the proportion of the narrative devoted to exposing the
wiles of the fair sex. So insistent is Luna's misogyny that it com-
pels a comparison with French literature of the time, in which, by all
accounts, women were satirized incessantly. The bourgeois prose
writers of this period frequently attacked women and lamented the
rigours of marriage, often in pamphlet form, like Olivier's popular
Alphabet de l'imperfection et malice des femmes (1617). Reynier[17] lists
six works published between 1617 and 1623 which treat the burdens of
the married life. In the comic novels, such as Charles Sorel's Histoire
Comique de Francion (1623, 1626 and 1633), the hero's amorous relations
with women are given far fuller treatment than in Spanish picaresque
novels. Francion's lustful pursuit of Laurette, married to the impotent
Valentin, takes up much of the narrative of the very bawdy first book
of the novel.

More significant than the incidence of episodes involving women is
the tone in which these episodes are related. Luna takes pleasure in
erotic description, an attitude which Cossío rightly characterises as
one of complaciencia.[18] At the clandestine convite witnessed by the
pícaro twelve galanes frolic with half a dozen women, among them
Lázaro's mistress. Luna titillates the reader with the following lines:
'(los galancetes)... retozaban con las señoras, y daban en ellas como
asno en centeno verde. Lo que allí pasó no me es lícito decirlo, ni al
lector contemplarlo'.[19] The police are tipped off, but the revellers
manage to hide before they enter the building. One couple, however, is
discovered by the alguacil in a cask:

y destapándola halló dentro un hombre y una mujer. No quiero
decir cómo los halló, por no ofender las castas orejas
del benigno y escrupuloso lector; sólo digo que la
violencia de su acción había hecho rodar la cuba, y
fué causa de su desgracia, y de mostrar en público lo
que hacían en secreto.[20]

There are similar goings-on in an episode of the <u>Francion</u> where the
libertine Sorel describes how the guests indulge in the pleasures of
the flesh, seeking 'leur advanture d'un costé et d'autre, en folastrant
avec un nombre infiny de <u>plaisirs</u>'.[21] In both Luna and Sorel it is
pointed out that the wives are being unfaithful to their husbands. The
sober, sinful view of illicit relationships that Alemán had given to
the picaresque prevailed in novels published in Spain before 1620, in
sharp contrast with the jocular attitude to debauchery often found in
French low-life fiction.

At this historical moment in France extreme obscenity was commonplace in satirical literature. The <u>libertins</u>, who considered it a
matter of principle that anything they wrote, however obscene, should
be published without censorship, were very influential. Young noble-
men attached themselves to the more scandalous aspects of the philosophy of their leader, Théophile de Viau, whose trial and conviction
took place in 1623. As Adam puts it:

> ... aux environs de 1620, le libertinage devient un
> entraînement qui gagne une bonne partie de la jeune
> noblesse à Paris... Elle ose, dans les églises, se
> moquer d'un prédicateur maladroit, elle se réunit
> dans les "cabarets d'honneur" et y chante des couplets
> blasphématoires, elle ne distingue pas la révolte
> contre la religion et la licence des moeurs.[22]

The audacity of their satire and their obscenity did not prevent their
work being printed in collections like the <u>Parnasse des Poètes satiriques</u>
(1622).[23] Their impact was so great that even the young Queen is said
to have read them avidly. In such an atmosphere it is scarcely surprising to discover a few smutty paragraphs inserted into Luna's novel
to entertain the French reader. These passages, coming towards the end
of the work, were excised or altered by the nineteenth-century B.A.E.
editor of the novel, whose edition has, unfortunately, been reproduced
by all subsequent editors except two.[24] Important omissions and
modifications are:

(Chapter XIII)  Los que veían el anzuelo que por la camisa rompida
                descubría, reían a boca llena.[25]

Valbuena's edition substitutes "las carnes" for "el anzuelo" here.[26]

(Chapter XVI)   ... unas [mujeres] se me colgaban del cuello,
                otras, me trababan de las manos, metiéndome las
                suyas en las faldriqueras, y como estábamos a
                escuras, por buscar la faldriquera encontraron
                la manera. Dió un grito diciendo:
                - ¿Qué es esto?
                Yo le respondí:
                - Un pajarillo que se saldrá si le toca.[27]

Valbuena's edition omits from "y como estábamos" to "si le toca".[28]

(Chapter XVI)   Peláronme [las mujeres] la horcajadura, y una
dellas, la más atrevida, sacó un cuchillo,
diciendo a las otras:

-Teneldo bien, que yo le sacaré las turmas
para que otra vez no le venga la tentación de
casarse.  Creía el dómine ermitaño [Lázaro] que
todo lo que le habíamos dicho era el evangelio:
no era ni aún la epístola.  De mujeres se fiaba:
ahora verá el pago que lleva.

Como vi mis supinos en peligro, hice tanto
que quebré una cuerda y un pilar de la cama.
Eché mano a mis cascabeles y los empuñé de
suerte que, aunque me cortaban los dedos, no
pudieron llegar a ellos.[29]

Valbuena replaces this extract by a completely inoffensive passage.[30]

As these extracts show, Luna had little to fear from the censor (as
surely he would have in Spain).

No single one of the aspects described proves irrefutably that Luna's
novel was afrancesado, but the combination of several factors makes the
suggestion of French influence more than a critical hunch.  Why should
Luna wish to reject the sermonising of an Alemán in favour of a more
'Gallic' approach to picaresque subject-matter?  Part of the answer, I
believe, lies in Luna's occupation as a teacher of Spanish.  The Segunda
parte formed part of an overall approach to the craft of teaching which,
as far as we know, was never fully formulated by Luna, but which can be
deduced in its broad lines from his three works, as well as the corrected
first Lazarillo.  In my view, Luna deliberately tailored the tone and
content of his novel to suit the tastes of his French readers, so that
they might learn Spanish more effectively from a narrative that they
found agreeable.

As we have seen, Luna's enthusiasm for his métier led him to amend
the first Lazarillo in a misguided attempt to improve it and so provide
a text of standard Spanish for advanced learners.  An example of Luna's
colourless re-phrasing of the original for pedagogic purposes comes at
the beginning of the novel, where "Pues sepa vuestra merced ante todas
cosas que a mí llaman Lázaro de Tormes..." is altered to "Yo me llamo
Lázaro de Tormes..." As one might expect, Luna's emendations are
inspired by the grammarian's desire to follow standard syntactic patterns
and to eliminate archaism.  In the Advertencia al lector, Luna justifies
his corrections thus:

... solo me ha movido el bien publico, porque ay tanta
gente que lo lee; y estudia por el la lengua Española,
haviendose imaginado ser un compendio, o recopilacion
de todas las buenas frases della:  siendo muy al
contrario, porque su lenguage es tosco, el estilo
llano, y la fras (sic) mas Francesa que Española.
Tocandome como me toca el dar a mis discipulos pan
de trigo, y no de soma, he querido escardar una
imfinidad (sic) de malos vocablos, peores congruydades,
y malisimas frases que en el havia, y veera el que
conferira esta correccion, con la antecedente impresion:
no he sido muy riguroso en ella, que a serlo, no huviera
dexado nada de mudar, mas he disimulado con loque he
podido, sin perjuycio de barras, digo de la integridad
de la lengua Castellana, rogandote lo agas asi conmi.

Luna's desire to purify the language is surely genuine, but what strikes the reader of this passage is the inflated opinion that he had of himself as the guardian of the Spanish tongue abroad.

The same apparent interest in the progress of the language-learner can be seen in Luna's prologue to the readers of the _Diálogos familiares_. At the same time he once again boosts his own image as a teacher, in this case by pouring scorn on a rival. Of the twelve dialogues that make up the book only the first five are from Luna's pen, the other seven deriving from a very popular work by John Minsheu.[31] Luna is highly condescending about Minsheu's contribution to the book, writing of "unos dialogos hechos en Londres por un Castellano, losquales estan tan corrompidos, que en siete que son, he allado mas de quinientas faltas notables, que se conoce no ser de la emprenta, y tales que si la buena fras (sic) dellos no mostrasse ser Español el que los hizo, los hubiera desconocido, y pensara ser su autor algún Vizcayno; mas esto no puede ser, porque el lenguage, y los muchos, y buenos refranes, muestran de quien son..." Luna, "movido pues de la necesidad que tienen los que quieren aprender la lengua Española de un libro que trate destos ordinarios discursos, y platicas" added to his own dialogues "los siete sobredichos, corregidos, y emendados, que todos, son doce, en los cuales se encierran las palabras, y cumplimientos mas necesarios, y ordinarios". The 'mistakes' that Luna pretends to have found in Minsheu's dialogues are in fact mostly printer's errors,[32] which confirms the impression that Luna was prepared to distort the truth in order to gain the respect of people seeking a thorough, correct textbook.

It has to be remembered that a demand for teachers was created by the arrival of many Spaniards at court in the entourage of Anne of Austria. The language-teaching industry was very competitive; plagiarism among writers of textbooks was rife; claims and counter-claims were made as writers asserted the authenticity of their Spanish and the superiority of their method. Luna, for instance, was very proud of the list of 281 irregular verbs that he compiled for the English edition of the _Arte breve_, comparing it with the short and unreliable list produced by his rival, César Oudin. It appears, however, that Luna plagiarised the list from a lesser-known grammar published in 1619 by Jerónimo de Texeda, whom he attacks in the _Arte breve_.[33] Luna was therefore caught in a competitive situation, in which denigration of rivals and claims for new and improved methods of teaching were expedients to attract pupils.

Despite his preoccupation with maintaining an image of competence before his public Luna was not a pure charlatan. His very sensible introductory remarks to the English edition of the _Arte breve_ reveal much of his thinking about the learning of a foreign language. He considered that language fluency was not easy to acquire; three or four years' residence in a foreign country might not be sufficient to learn a language properly. He insists on the need to begin to learn a language according to grammatical rules as opposed to the _discurso familiar_ method advocated by some teachers, and he points out the importance of seeking a good teacher. Once a bad linguistic habit has been acquired, he states, it is impossible to eradicate. Native speakers are the best teachers, but the learner must be wary, for many native speakers do not speak correctly. A perusal of Luna's two manuals of instruction confirms that he practised what he preached. They are methodical textbooks which reveal Luna as a thorough teacher, conscious of the need for the learner to progress gradually through linguistic exercises of increasing complexity.

The broad lines of Luna's method, although he never explains it precisely, can be deduced from an examination of the three works that

we possess. The principle that he followed seems to have been the
sound one of grading his material so that the knowledge of the pupil
could be extended and reinforced at each stage. Simon and Pelorson[34]
have studied this process, concluding that for Luna there were two
stages in the acquisition of Spanish: an elementary one, during which
the grammatical rules were learnt, corresponding to the Arte breve,
and an advanced one, corresponding to the Diálogos and to good literature, like the two parts of Lazarillo de Tormes. A passage from the
Arte breve confirms Luna's thinking. He begins a 'Familiar Colloquie'
between a Master (Luna) and a 'Scholler' thus:

> Some years past I made in Paris some Dialogues...
> Those that would find phrases and maner of speaking,
> to make ostentation of that which they know, let
> them reade the foresaid Dialogues, or the first part
> of little Lazarus of Tormes, which I corrected and
> caused to be imprinted in the same towne of Paris; or
> the second part of good Lazarus, which cost me much
> paine, labour and toile to bring it to light, out of
> the darknesse of the treasure and records of the rogues
> of Toledo, in which are found the phrases and maner of
> speaking most difficult of the Spanish tongue.

It would be more precise, in the light of what Luna writes here, to
postulate three rather than two stages in the learning process. The
learner would progress from the Arte breve, through the Diálogos, to
the two Lazarillos. The difference between the second and third stage
would therefore be as marked as that between the first and second.
Vocabulary, syntax and idiom would be most difficult in the third stage,
which would also be the least directed. The interest of the advanced
learner would be held by the actual narrative, and so he would assimilate Spanish naturally as useful phrases, proverbs, etc. arose from the
situations in which the pícaro found himself.
     The three works reveal clearly an 'overlapping' principle employed
by Luna, whereby the reader is prepared for the next stage in the
process by the inclusion of material that anticipates it; the later
stages also look back to the method and content of the earlier levels.
In the first edition of the Arte breve some dialogues were included,
which could have been the basis for the later volume. That this is
possible is indicated by the second edition of the work,[35] from which
the dialogues have been removed, presumably so that they could form
part of a separate volume. None the less Luna retains the semblance
of a dialogue in his basic grammar in the colloquy between master and
scholar which, although it does not amount to much more than a list of
useful vocabulary, is couched in a form that anticipates the second book.
     The second stage consists of the twelve dialogues, each of which
places characters in typical situations which enable Luna to introduce
a range of vocabulary and idiom in a more dynamic form than in the
Arte breve. For example, Luna's first dialogue covers forms of greet-
ing, his second the commonplaces of amorous conversation between a dama
and a galán; etc. At the same time Luna introduces spicy tales that
anticipate the third stage, the novel. In the third dialogue, for
example, Luna reduces the artificiality of the conversation by allowing
the language to emerge naturally from the anecdotes of two gossips.
One such tale, about a monk who is discovered under the bed of a whore,
looks ahead to the two main targets of Luna's satire in his picaresque
novel.

In his third stage Luna is able to dispense with the stiffness of the dialogue form, but harks back to it in several ways. The most obvious of these are: (i) the inclusion of proverbs, (ii) the employment of standard 'dialogue' subject-matter and (iii) detailed description which conveys basic vocabulary.

(i) In the Diálogos sayings and proverbs, often several strung together, are italicised and so stand out from the text as pieces of received wisdom that need to be committed to memory. This procedure (without the italics) is also present in the novel, where Luna frequently sums up a situation by means of one or more popular sayings, more often than not at the beginning of chapters. On the first page of the book we meet a good example of the blending of Luna's satirical and linguistic aims: Lázaro is "... gozando el mejor tiempo que patriarca gozó, comiendo como fraile convidado, y bebiendo más que saludador, mejor vestido que teatino..."[36]

(ii) A comment on national psychology, so typical of the dialogue, is inserted into chapter VII for the benefit of the French reader: "Cuando los españoles alcanzamos un real, somos príncipes, y aunque nos falte, no lo hace la presunción... Si preguntáis a un mal trapillo quién es, responderos ha, por lo menos, que deciende de los godos... y morirá antes de hambre que ponerse a un oficio; y si se ponen o aprenden alguno, es con tal desgaire que, o no trabajan, o si lo hacen, es tan mal, que apenas se hallará un buen oficial en toda España".[37]

(iii) In his description of the escudero, the master who deserted Lazarillo in the first part of the novel and whom he meets again in Chapter I of the second part, Luna dwells on the detail of his person and his clothing, as if inviting the reader to revise some basic vocabulary. He includes sombrero, cara, mano, mejilla, pierna, espada, vaina, cabeza, camisa, carne, calzas, medias, tobillos, zapatos, pluma, as well as a wealth of descriptive words associated with clothing.[38]

How far Luna used his novel and the amended first part of the Lazarillo as classroom texts is impossible to ascertain. The evidence however that they had their part to play in the learning process is strong. Luna's effort to instruct the learner as he read was complemented by his adoption of a light tone, together with some fashionable misogyny and obscenity, making the novel doubly attractive. Furthermore, Luna's choice of the picaresque genre, then at the height of its popularity in Paris,[39] shows that he was prepared to court the French reader by exploiting a literary form in vogue.

The Segunda parte, whether it was used widely as a Spanish reader or not, cannot be denied its success as an entertaining novel. The simultaneous publication of the novel and its translation is an indication of the confidence of publisher and author. The novel displaced the anonymous second part of 1555, and in the next hundred years at least seventeen editions of the French translation of both parts were printed. It is perhaps surprising that the two Lazarillos were not issued bilingually in 1620 (as happened in 1660), especially when bilingual versions of Spanish books (for example, the 1615 edition of the first part of Lazarillo de Tormes) were so common. There is a possible explanation for this. The novel was bound with the first part in both Spanish and French versions. The French translation of the first Lazarillo, however, does not take into account Luna's alterations to the Spanish — the translation used was that of M.P.B.P., first published in 1601 — and so would seem inaccurate when placed alongside Luna's version. This inaccuracy would of course mislead the learner who used the Spanish text as a reader, but relied on the French text for deciphering linguistic difficulties.

The translation of the Segunda parte was, however, remarkably
literal at a time when translators in France thought that they were
failing in their art if they did not embroider the original.[40] The
initials of the translator on the title page, 'L.S.D.', were probably
those of Le Sieur D'Audiguier, a prolific translator and novelist in the
first quarter of the seventeenth century. D'Audiguier was a rather
slapdash and inaccurate translator, and he was guided principally by
mercenary considerations.[41] It is therefore all the more surprising
that in this case he placed literal accuracy above all other considerations. The most likely reason for this is that Luna insisted on an
exact rendering into French so that his pupils would be in no doubt
about the meaning of the Spanish when confronted with linguistic
difficulties. Language teachers made substantial use of bilingual
readers and grammars, as a glance through the grammatical works
published during that period testifies. Judging from some of Luna's
introductory remarks to his works he seems to have been a fastidious
supervisor of their translation. He states in his introduction to the
English version of the Arte breve that he "caused it to be very exactly
and cleanly translated". This statement suggests that the translation
was a combined operation between Luna and the translator to produce
the most accurate version possible.

It is therefore not mere guess-work to suggest that Luna used his
novel as a reader. Several pieces of evidence - Luna's emendations of
the first Lazarillo, his recommendation to the learner of Spanish that
the first and second parts of the novel be used as reading texts,
internal features that suggest that Luna was consciously instructing
his reader in the language as well as entertaining him, the simultaneous
publication of the Spanish original and its very literal translation
into French - support this hypothesis. Luna deliberately geared the
subject matter to the taste of his Parisian pupils and related the
pícero's adventures in a tone calculated to hold their interest,
following the sound principle that the more attractive the material the
better the pupil will learn. Thus Luna's afrancesamiento is in my view
another facet of his art as a teacher.


## N O T E S

1. Segunda Parte de la vida de Lazarillo de Tormes, sacada de las
Coronicas antiguas de Toledo por I. de Luna Castellano, Intérprete de
la lengua española. En París, en casa de Rolet Boutonné... M.DC.XX.
Carlos García's La desordenada codicia de los bienes ajenos was
published in Paris in the previous year, but it is inaccurate to
describe this tract about thieves and their art as a picaresque novel.
See my article 'La desordenada codicia... -a caso límite of the
picaresque?', BHS, LV (1978), 33 - 41.

2. The novel was certainly written by Juan de Luna, despite the fact
that the title-pages of the two editions of 1620, Paris and 'Zaragoza',
bear the initial 'I.' and 'H.' de Luna respectively. Critics persist
in reproducing either one of the wrong initials. The Zaragoza edition
was almost certainly spurious; probably the publisher wished to convince
the reader of the authenticity of the novel.

3. La novela picaresca española, ed. A. Valbuena Prat, 5th ed. (Madrid 1966), 113; Valbuena's text of the Segunda parte is contained in this volume, 114 - 146. Unfortunately this text is defective, and so all references will be to the faithful edition of M. de Riquer, in La Celestina y Lazarillos (Barcelona 1959), 685 - 805.

4. See A.A. Parker, Literature and the Delinquent (Edinburgh 1967), Chapters IV and V, for a study of these works.

5. See M. Bataillon's review of La Celestina y Lazarillos, BHi, LXII (1960), 339 - 340.

6. Originally published in France, probably in 1615. The title of the second edition (Paris 1616) is: Arte breve, y ccmpendiossa, para aprender, a leer, pronunciar, escrevir, y hablar la lengua Española compuesta por Iuan de Luna Español, Castellano / Briefve et abregee methode pour apprendre à lire, prononcer, escrire et parler la langue Espagnolle composee par Iean de Lune, Espagnol Castillan. There does not appear to be a copy of the first edition extant, but Luna refers to its existence in his second edition.

7. See G. Hainsworth, Les "Novelas ejemplares" de Cervantes en France au XVIIe siècle (Paris 1933), Chapter II.

8. See J-M. Pelorson, 'Un document inédit sur Juan de Luna', BHi, LXXI (1969), 218 - 230. It was thought that the best Spanish was spoken by Toledans (see A. Morel-Fatio, Ambrosio de Salazar et l'étude de l'espagnol en France sous Louis XIII [Paris 1901], 176 - 184). Critics have noted Aragonese features of language in the novel (Riquer, ed. cit., 129, and E.R. Sims, in the introduction to his edition of the Segunda parte [Austin, Texas, 1928]). It is quite consistent with what we know about Luna that he might have feigned Toledan origin in order to impress his pupils.

9. Diálogos familiares, En los quales se contienen los discursos, modos de hablar, proverbios, y palabras Españolas mas comunes / Dialogues familiers, Où sont contenus les discours, façons de parler, proverbes, et mots Espagnols plus communs.

10. Art. cit., 340

11. Published under the title The Pursuit of the Historie of Lazarillo de Tormes. Translated by Thomas Walkley. The original Spanish version does not appear to have been published in England.

12. There is not a separate edition. The dialogues were annexed to César Oudin's Spanish grammar "Englished by I.W. Who hath also translated out of Spanish the five Dialogues of Juan de Luna, Castellano..."

13. See R. Rudder's introduction to his translation of the novel (New York 1973), xv.

14. Ed. cit., 769

15. Bataillon, Introduction to his edition of La vie de Lazarillo de Tormes (Paris 1958), 60 - 68; J.L. Laurenti, Vida de Lazarillo de Tormes: estudio crítico de la Segunda parte de Juan de Luna (Mexico 1965); A. Francis, 'La estrategia satírica en el Lazarillo de Luna', NRFH, XXV (1976), 363 - 373.

16. Ed. cit., 763

17. G. Reynier, <u>Les origines du roman réaliste</u> (Paris 1912), 93.

18. J.M. de Cossío, 'Las continuaciones del <u>Lazarillo de Tormes</u>', <u>RFE</u>, XXV (1941), 522.

19. Ed. cit., 779.

20. Ibid., 782.

21. In <u>Romanciers du XVIIe siècle</u>, edited, with an introductory study, by A. Adam (Paris 1968), 317.

22. A. Adam, <u>Les libertins au XVIIe siècle</u> (Paris 1964), 7 - 8.

23. Adam remarks that "Ces recueils où foisonnaient les pièces obscènes n'étaient pas publiés sous le manteau, mais au grand jour, et portaient le nom de libraires fort honorablement connus...", ed. cit., 26.

24. Riquer and Sims.

25. Ed. cit., 776.

26. Ed. cit., 137.

27. Ed. cit., 796.

28. Ed. cit., 143.

29. Ed. cit., 804.

30. Ed. cit., 145 - 146.

31. First published in London in 1599 as part of R. Percivale's Spanish grammar.

32. See 'M. Gautier' (pseudonym for R. Foulché-Delbosc), 'Diálogos de Antaño', <u>RHi</u>, XLV (1919), 75. Foulché-Delbosc reproduces both Minsheu's and Luna's dialogues.

33. See J.M. Lope Blanch, 'Las gramáticas de Juan de Luna y de Jerónimo de Texeda', <u>NRFH</u>, XXVI (1977), 96 - 98.

34. H. Simon and J-M. Pelorson, 'Une mise au point sur l'"Arte breve" de Juan de Luna', <u>BHi</u>, LXXI (1969), 218 - 230. This article establishes for the first time the connexion between Luna's novel and his profession.

35. In the second edition Luna refers to their removal from the first one.

36. Ed. cit., 695.

37. Ibid. 730 - 731. There is a similar passage in Luna's first dialogue, in which a <u>maestro</u> says to his <u>discípulo</u>, after discussing the differences between Frenchmen and Spaniards, "... los Españoles, siendo, como son, altivos, no quieren ir adonde los menosprecian y adonde no les permiten mandar..." 'Gautier', art. cit., 161.

38. Ed. cit., 697. Further examples of the links between the Diálogos and the Segunda parte, as well as reminiscences of Cervantes and other prose writers can be found in Simon and Pelorson, art. cit., 224 - 226.

39. See Adam, ed. cit., 26

40. As Parker, op. cit., Chapter V, points out, picaresque novels, especially Guzmán de Alfarache and the Buscón, suffered badly from the alterations made by French translators, whose chief aim was to make the novels more acceptable to French taste. It is therefore conceivable that the translator thought Luna's Lazarillo sufficiently 'Gallic' to render any modifications of the original unnecessary.

41. See F.W. Vogler, Vital d'Audiguier and the early XVIIth-century French Novel (Chapel Hill, N. Carolina, 1964), 28 - 34.

En torno al modernismo de las Soledades de Antonio Machado

Enrique Vinuesa (The Queen's University of Belfast)

En 1900 el movimiento en boga en las letras hispánicas es el modernismo. El propio Machado evocaría en su "Poética" de 1931 "los años del modernismo literario (los de mi juventud)", y en "Los trabajos y los días. Por equivocación" (1920) ya ironizaba sobre su carácter de "pobre modernista del año tres".[1]

No es éste el lugar para ensayar una, creemos que imposible, definición que nos lleve más allá de la noción del modernismo poético más generalmente aceptada: la coincidencia en la literatura posromántica de lengua española de, esencialmente, las corrientes francesas parnasiana y simbolista. Sí se tratará de exponer qué aspectos de Soledades, tal y como fue ofrecida esta colección al lector en 1903 (no en la reelaboración aparecida en 1907), harían que su autor la considerase retrospectivamente fruto de su modernismo juvenil.[2]

Juan Ramón Jiménez habla de A. Machado y de sí mismo como poetas más simbolistas que parnasianos: "Nosotros, en realidad, aceptamos el simbolismo bajo el nombre de modernismo, pero eso no impidió que el parnasianismo nos influyera también"; y esto, a tono con la esencia del movimiento todo: "Lo mejor del modernismo es lo que representa una plenitud simbolista".[3] El mismo Machado, que apenas recordará el parnasianismo, aludiría en repetidas ocasiones a la que consideró "una escuela perfectamente lograda: el simbolismo francés".[4] Recientemente, J.M. Aguirre ha dejado bien sentado en un excelente estudio este carácter "simbolista-modernista" de la lírica machadiana.[5]

La reseña de S por J.R. Jiménez en El País en 1903[6] es en extremo reveladora por sus aciertos al analizar el volumen con criterio semejante, entonces, al del autor. El artículo se inicia con un tono polémico y elitista al que corresponde Machado de forma análoga en las cartas que envía a Juan Ramón por estas fechas, y por fechas muy posteriores.[7]

"Libro de Abril, triste y bello", escribe Juan Ramón en su crítica de S. Tristeza y belleza son, en efecto, notas predominantes en el libro. Tristeza muy modernista: "quimera doliente de nuestra alma" (JRJ), tristeza inefable de poeta sin amor, apartado de "la estúpida ciudad", según la versión del poema "La fuente" publicada en la revista Electra en 1901 (pp. 1057-1059). Melancolía, para usar el término obligado, que va de un extremo a otro de esta colección en que Machado hace de su íntimo sentir el objeto único, y generalmente bastante directo, de la mayoría de las composiciones. Melancolía, y soledad: "Tranquilos, dichosos en nuestro retiro, en nuestra soledad de alma, abramos este libro de soledades" (JRJ); soledad que se impone al autor y que él necesita preservar del "sucio ambiente español, infectado por las rimas de caminos, canales y puertos de los señores premiados en el concurso de El Liberal" (JRJ).

Belleza, señala Juan Ramón al uso modernista:

[...] libro de Abril, amargo y azul [...], música de fuentes y aroma de lirios [...], bello ritmo, rico y diamantino [...], jardín de gracia y de sueño [...], las fuentes y las ventanas floridas a la luna, con el misterio de la sombra de las largas galerías [...]. Libro de Abril, triste y bello: gris y triste [...], verde y triste [...], triste y rosa [...], rojo y triste y negro [...].

Otra de sus observaciones: "es maravillosa la riqueza de orquestación [,] y el verso y la frase y la palabra llevan, verdaderamente, color y son y luz", plenamente justificada por la marcada preocupación estetizante presente en S, parece formular unos principios estéticos diametralmente opuestos a los que don Antonio expuso más tarde en diversas ocasiones.[8]

Pero no estamos todavía ante el Machado a quien J.R. Jiménez acusaría (en líneas muy superiores a las de la reseña de El País) de haber abandonado "sus espejos, galerías, sus laberintos maravillosos, mezcla confusa del simbolismo y de Bécquer, para enseñar francés con énfasis doctoral; para cantar los campos de Castilla con descripción excesiva, anécdota constante y verbo casticiero".[9] Con anterioridad a 1903 Machado prodiga, junto a poemas magistrales, otros muy influidos por el romanticismo más decadente. Sirva de muestra el dedicado "Al libro Ninfeas del poeta Juan Ramón Jiménez" (p.29), cuyo sentimentalismo refinado y vocabulario mismo son tan reminiscentes del propio Juan Ramón como del primer volumen machadiano.

Diez composiciones integran la primera sección del libro, Desolaciones y monotonías. Cuatro tienen rima asonante y seis, consonante. Sólo dos de cada grupo pasarían en 1907 a Soledades. Galerías. Otros poemas. Vemos al poeta junto a la fuente en cuatro de los poemas; en siete de ellos aparece, más o menos prominente, la imagen de la tarde, de gran continuidad en su obra.

"Tarde", de inspiración verleniana, es composición muy de época: en la soledad del parque la fuente incita con su encanto al personaje poemático a sumirse en la intimidad del recuerdo:

>           La fuente cantaba: ¿Te recuerda, hermano,
>       un sueño lejano mi copla presente?...

La ilusión, momentáneamente despierta:

>           —No sé qué me dice tu copla riente
>       de ensueños lejanos, hermana la fuente.
>           ...,
>       mas cuéntame, fuente de lengua encantada,
>       cuéntame mi alegre leyenda olvidada[,]

queda concluyentemente defraudada por la fraternal confidente, cuya "clara harmonía" y "claros cantares" no brindan, en definitiva, alivio alguno al enamorado que un día contemplara el ansiado "fruto [...] dorado y maduro" con inmediatez velada por la sombra de "mirtos talares" que le separan del que resultara ser su "árbol obscuro". Después de aceptar la invitación que ha de llevarle de su soledad presente a algún destello de felicidad perdido en su pasado amoroso, el poeta termina, muy al contrario, enfrentado por la fuente a las raíces mismas de su ansia insatisfecha:

>           —Yo no sé leyendas de antigua alegría,
>       sino historias viejas de melancolía.
>           ...
>       Fue una clara tarde del lento verano...
>           ...
>       Dijeron tu pena tus labios que ardían:
>       la sed que ahora tienen, entonces tenían.

Agravada la pesadumbre en esta segunda visita por la sensación final de la imposibilidad del consuelo ("— Adiós para siempre, la fuente sonora"), queda planteado el motivo central de S: la evocación tardía de un amor

fracasado, de una decepción irreparable, vivencia vaporosa de su personaje que podríamos glosar, anticipadamente, con versos al misterio de
la "irrealidad" de otro amor muy posterior:

> No prueba nada
> contra el amor, que la amada
> no haya existido jamás
> > (CLXXIV. "Otras canciones a Guiomar",
> > ii).10

Los indicios amatorios son raros: "delirios de amores", "tus labios
besaron [...]", "tus labios que ardían"; no lo son tanto los de soledad
y tristeza, no menos notorios en "La fuente", poema con elementos como
"la historia / de mi largo camino sin amores", muy afines a los de una
de las Rimas de J.R. Jiménez:

> Como estoy solo se pierden
> entre perfumes mis quejas
> ...
> ¿Por qué es tan larga y tan triste
> la vida de los poetas?
> > ("Llanto")11

En "La fuente", composición muy discursiva, la admirada contemplación de agua y estatua cristaliza en una alegoría del dolor y aparente
felicidad con que misteriosamente se teje nuestra existencia terrenal:

> Pero una doble eternidad presiento
> que en mármol calla y en cristal murmura
> alegre copla equívoca y lamento
> de una infinita y bárbara tortura.

Fuente - atractivo de vida y amor - y titán - frustración y sufrimiento
humanos - componen un "símbolo [...]" de agua y de piedra" en que el personaje
siente reflejada su propia trayectoria vital: el agua de esta fuente
bien amada, de "frívolo, erótico rumor", es "carcajada", "risa", "alegre
copla" (subrayados nuestros) y "espejo sonriente" que la insatisfacción
de una sed nunca saciada torna (a tenor de los acentuados contrastes
característicos del estilo inicial de Machado) en carcajada "fría", risa
con "ondas de ironía", copla "equívoca" y espejo "lánguido" tras los que
sólo cabe aspirar a la paz y la armonía con que la muerte nos librará
del tormento del existir:

> Y en ti soñar y meditar querría
> libre ya del rencor y la tristeza,
> hasta sentir, sobre la piedra fría,
> que se cubre de musgo mi cabeza.

"Tarde", como tantos otros poemas de este libro, se nos muestra
recargado de tópicos abundantes (monotonía, melancolía, "harmonía") y
de esa adjetivación desbordante y reiterativa ("clara tarde, triste y
soñolienta", "claro cristal de alegría", "claros, alegres espejos
cantores", "bellos espejos cantores", "sonora / copla borbollante del
agua cantora", etc.) que volvemos a encontrar en "La fuente": "claro
rebosar riente", "cejijunto gesto contorcido", "éxtasis convulso y
doloroso", "claro y loco borbollar riente", etc. Esta "música de fuentes"
de que habla Juan Ramón en El País ("sinfonías - sinfonías sabias -"
llama a las composiciones "Tarde" y "La fuente" y el elogio no puede ser

más modernista) no destacará como faceta fundamental de ningún otro libro
machadiano. La poesía de Machado se irá despojando de este tipo de
musicalidad altisonante, que tanto prodigó su musa por 1900, a medida
que los símbolos se enriquezcan por calar en aguas más profundas y la
voz adquiera sus tonos más originales.[12] (Sobre este aspecto volveremos
más detalladamente en nuestros comentarios a la tercera sección,
Salmodias de Abril.)

Las alusiones a su soledad y la vaga evocación de su fracaso amoroso,
que hemos hallado en "Tarde" con tal insistencia en lo prolongado de su
aflicción ("tu pena", "historias viejas de melancolía", "lejanos dolores"
- subrayados nuestros -), reaparecen en el poema "Los cantos de los
niños", cantos en los que el poeta percibe

> tristezas de amores
> de antiguas leyendas
> ...,
> canciones ingenuas,
> de un algo que pasa
> y que nunca llega.

Cuanto los dos últimos versos retienen de ambigua indecisión, se des-
vanece pocos años más tarde en el recuerdo de días de la niñez pasados

> soñando... no sé con qué,
> con algo que no llegaba,
> todo lo que ya se fue
>
>                     (XCIII).

La mayor concreción que el entorno de su infancia confiere al último
ejemplo, le impregna de una conciencia de lo irrecuperablemente perdido
de que no están tan decididamente contaminadas las aguas cantoras de las
fuentes de Desolaciones... Para el autor de S, que ensaya de nuevo el
tema y los elementos más manidos por los poetas del día,

> [...] los niños cantan
> ...
> cual vierten sus aguas
> las fuentes de piedra:
> con monotonías
> de risas eternas
> que no son alegres,
> con lágrimas viejas
> que no son amargas
> y dicen tristezas [...]
>                 ("Los cantos...").[13]

En la composición "Cenit" se insiste de forma alegórica en el tema
de la busca infructuosa iniciada en "Tarde". Las dudas atormentan al
caminante que, tras emprender esperanzado su viaje, sólo ha alcanzado
a distinguir "el desdeñoso gesto" de la encarnación del amor entrevista
en el poema "Noche". La fuente, de "alegre canturía" al comienzo de la
jornada, anuncia para el fin de la misma "tristes jardines" a los que le
conducirán fatalmente sus tentativas vanas; las revelaciones son, una
vez más, desoladoras:

> Tu destino
> será siempre vagar, ¡oh peregrino
> del laberinto que tu sueño encierra!

La peregrinación[14] se trunca y convierte en un "vagar" por el "laberinto"
de un solipsismo que se declara definitivo. El peregrino ha perdido
la senda, su norte, quedando, como el "rojo bergantín" de la composición "El mar triste", a merced de las "olas grises". No habiendo sido
escuchada su súplica: "Detén el paso, belleza / esquiva, detén el
paso..." ("Noche"), su existencia se torna gris y monótona. Con las
debidas salvedades, Desolaciones... es, por su intención, que no por
su calidad, la sección de S en que los pasos del caminante machadiano
se hunden "Dans l'interminable / Ennui de la plaine" de los famosos
versos de Verlaine.[15]

El agua de estas fuentes, "eterna risa del camino" ("Cenit"), como
las "risas eternas" de los niños ("Los cantos..."), no menos radicalmente
ajenas al sentir adulto, pregona una alegría constante erigida por el
poeta en dramático contrapunto al dolor de su personaje solitario, a
la monotonía de una vida sin amor.[16]

La tarde de verano, en toda su belleza crepuscular, le acoge también, mientras recuerda su desengaño amoroso, en el poema titulado
"Crepúsculo". Si en la composición "La fuente" ésta le "desarma de
brumas y rencores", el atardecer dispersa ahora sus "cárdenos nublados
congojosos". La "mirra amarga de un amor lejano" ("antiguos delirios
de amores" en "Tarde") vuelve a entristecer su corazón:

> locura adormida, la primera
> que al alma llega y que del alma huye
> y la sola que torna en su carrera
> si la agria ola del ayer refluye[;]

en este poema, luego suprimido, la soledad, circunstancia habitual y
decisiva del personaje, es cantada por Machado de la forma más repre-
sentativa de su modernismo juvenil:

> La soledad, la musa que el misterio
> revela al alma en sílabas preciosas
> cual notas de recóndito salterio [...].

La misma fusión de sentimiento y paisaje se da en "Horizonte",
otra composición que sobrevivió con correcciones que, como las de "Tarde",
revelan preocupación por eliminar lastre sentimental.[17] En este
poema, como ocurre en gran parte de la sección, la tarde (día que
declina, ciertamente) es la de estío, precisión machadiana muy coherente
porque, tras la primavera del amor (evocación central de las Salmodias
de Abril), el verano del peregrino es plenitud más madura que joven y
estación de un rigor que le obliga, abatido "cuando su lanza tórrida
blande el viejo verano", a buscar refugio en la sombra, en el parque,
en la plaza, junto a la fuente. Cuando sus intentos resultan estériles,
el consuelo y la satisfacción auténticos sólo cabe esperarlos de "la
alegre canción de un alba pura", formulación diáfana con que se cierra
la composición. Unicamente esta "mañana pura" (un eco, quizás, de uno
de los versos verlenianos más hermosos: "Amour pâle, une aurore
future!"),[18] según se nos repite en la segunda sección, se alzará por
encima de todo sufrimiento y de todo temor:

> ... ¡Mi hora! - grité - ... El silencio
> me respondió: - No temas:
> ...
> [...] encontrarás una mañana pura
> amarrada tu barca a otra ribera
>                    (Del camino, i).

Y en un característico diálogo con dicha primavera del amor, que también floreció en su corazón, el romero nos confía la esperanza que ha
resistido al paso de los años:

> [...] si aguardas la mañana pura
> que ha de romper el vaso cristalino,
> quizás el hada te dará tus rosas,
> mi corazón tus lirios
>
>                        (Del camino, xv).

Esta alborada de un posible y esperado renacer se irá extinguiendo
gradualmente ante las notas más angustiadas de "un canto de frontera /
a la muerte, al silencio y al olvido" (CLXVII. "Abel Martín", 'Al gran
cero'), nocturno sin recurso ni a las fuentes ni a los parques de la
etapa modernista, a la que Juan de Mairena alude al recordar a su "maestro,
en sus años románticos", o - como se decía entonces con frase epigramática
popular - 'de alma perdida en un melonar'" (p.410).

La segunda sección, Del camino, conservada casi íntegra en 1907, ha
sido considerada la mejor del libro desde la reseña de J.R. Jiménez en
El País.

La asonancia predomina netamente en ella: quince de sus diecisiete
poemas tienen rima asonante con los impares libres; dos metros, hepta-
sílabo y endecasílabo, son usados exclusivamente a excepción de los
alejandrinos del "Preludio". Salvo la composición xiii, "¿Mi amor?...
¿Recuerdas, dime, [...?]", los versos de siete y once sílabas aparecen
combinados: estamos ya ante una silva-romance, la estructura de lo que
R. de Zubiría considerara "el poema típico machadiano".[19]

Junto a esta perfección formal, el tono sereno de muchas de sus
composiciones hace de Del camino la sección de S más acorde con SGOP;
el "Preludio" es un fiel anuncio de esa serena evocación del pasado amor
que integran buena parte de estos poemas:

> Mientras la sombra pasa de un santo amor hoy quiero
> leer un dulce salmo sobre mi viejo atril.

No contemplamos ya "la agria ola del ayer" ("Crepúsculo") que rompe
en Desolaciones..., sino el momento apacible en que, extinguida la angustia, el recuerdo se idealiza. En contraste claro con las Salmodias de
Abril, de cuya primavera (y "pífano de Abril") nos ocuparemos más
adelante, la rememoración amorosa se dulcifica y eleva al plano de una
devoción grave e inalterable:

> Acordaré las notas del órgano severo
> al suspirar fragante del pífano de Abril.

Las imágenes y pausado ritmo del "Preludio" nos transmiten la
armonía ("Acordaré las notas...") que reina ahora en el corazón resig-
nado del poeta. "En la miseria lenta del camino" (iii), poema que tanto
tiene en común con el "Preludio" y que conviene leer en conjunción con
él, nos habla de la agitación y despecho ante el fracaso, que ya han
dejado paso a la serenidad de ánimo:

> Mis viejos mares duermen; se apagaron
> sus espumas sonoras
> sobre la playa estéril. La borrasca
> camina lejos en la nube torva.
> Vuelve la paz al cielo.

Tras la tormenta en mares de olas grises y amenazadores, "la brisa
tutelar esparce aromas / otra vez sobre el campo" (iii).

Permanece el personaje en los confines de "la bendita soledad" (iii),
pero no es tal soledad lo que ahora canta, sino que oiremos de nuevo la
voz apacible que antaño tuvo el poeta enamorado:

> Al grave acorde lento de música y aroma
> la sola y vieja y noble razón de mi rezar,
> levantará su vuelo suave de paloma
> y la palabra blanca se elevará al altar
> ("Preludio").

En gran medida, Del camino constituye un remanso de paz en el dolor
de S. Si la "copla riente / de ensueños lejanos" y el "claro cristal
de alegría" de la fuente ("Tarde") resultaron inalcanzables, la humilde
llama del recuerdo aparece ahora envuelta en la dorada añoranza del
mejor Machado, lejos del desasosiego que el "rencor y la tristeza"
originaron en Desolaciones...

No veíamos en las fuentes de la primera sección conciencia inequí-
voca del fugit irreparable tempus,[20] mientras el autor perseguía en la
limpidez o murmullo de sus aguas el reflejo o eco - la pervivencia - de
gratas experiencias olvidadas. En Del camino la fuente es "alberca
helada" (iv), "fuente helada" (xiii) o fuente en que "reposa el agua
muerta" (xii), y simboliza, esencialmente, la muerte del amor.[21] En el
único caso en que el agua fluye, lo hace en "manso río" (ix) de calma
aceptación.

Nos hallamos en el momento de la más plena idealización, que se
traduce en verso de cariz religioso, rasgo adecuadamente modernista
("santo amor", "salmo", "incienso", "rezar", "altar", etc.). Y con fondo
religioso asistiremos en las composiciones viii y xi respectivamente,
al paso de la "ilusión velada" y de "las blancas sombras" anunciado desde
el primer verso del "Preludio": "Mientras la sombra pasa de un santo
amor [...]".

Coinciden estos cuatro poemas ("Preludio", iii, viii y xi) en la
vaguedad de sus alusiones al amor, aspecto presente ya en Desolaciones...
y que se extremará aún más en SGOP. Prueba evidente de ello es la
revisión de un verso de iii ("En la miseria lenta del camino"):

> la hora florida brota / de tu amor, como espino solitario (1903),
> la hora florida brota, / espino solitario (1907).

Nos quedamos así en esta composición, por la magistral economía del
poeta más maduro, con sólo la alusión final: "y aparece / en la bendita
soledad tu sombra", aldabonazo certero en la indecisa, pero ya despierta
sensibilidad del lector. De forma semejante, la compasión que corre por
los versos de los poemas viii y xi mientras contemplamos el cuadro de
los mendigos en su pobreza, en el desamparo de su vejez, precede a la
sugerencia final ("su mano / era una rosa blanca" - viii -, "las blancas
sombras" - xi -), que encauza nuestra emoción con redoblada intensidad,
sin necesidad de referencias más explícitas, hacia esa llamada -
recuerdo - del amor, que alivia el desconsuelo del poeta mismo.[22]

A tono con esta vaguedad de los indicios amorosos, el poema iv
("Dime, ilusión alegre,") se abre con una invocación inmediata al
sentimiento del amor y sólo mediata a la amada, de quien se nos ofrece
un retrato sumamente espiritualizado: porque no es la amada, sino el
recuerdo y la ilusión amorosos, lo que se canta en Del camino. Y así,
en varias de sus composiciones asoma el vocablo "ilusión", que habíamos
encontrado una sola vez en Desolaciones..., en forma, significativamente,

de "ilusión amarga" ("El mar triste"). "Ilusión alegre" ahora (iv),
porque es el amor, aunque sólo aliente en la vivencia del recuerdo, el
que ilumina tantos versos machadianos. Desde este primer libro vemos
perfilarse dos constantes de su obra: amor (recuerdo - ilusión) o,
su reverso, soledad (desolación - monotonía). Entre ambas riberas dis-
curre una gran parte de su caudal lírico.

Otras correcciones a los poemas iii, ix y xvi nos muestran cómo
Machado va continuando en esta sección la sana poda, señalada en
Desolaciones..., de las ramificaciones más sentimentales, en su búsqueda
de un mayor recato y de una mayor concisión:

> iii:  En la miseria lenta del camino (1903),
> En la desnuda tierra del camino (1907);
>
> lento a mi corazón y da a mis labios (1903),
> al corazón, y al labio (1907);
>
> ix:  Quizás la tarde lenta todavía (1903),
> La tarde todavía (1907);
>
> xvi:  aunque he escuchado atenta el salmo oculto
> que hay en tu corazón, de ritmo lento
> (ambos versos suprimidos en SGOP).

Cuatro veces ha eliminado el adjetivo lento, cuya reiteración no puede,
ciertamente, sugerir "fugacidad del tiempo". Contribuyen asimismo estas
omisiones a la mayor sutileza con que SGOP suscitará la sensación de
hastío, mientras que en el contexto de Desolaciones... la repetición de
lento era uno de los recursos más obvios para acentuar la monotonía de
la existencia. Viejo, en cambio, es retenido en uso excepcionalmente
abundante, como puede verse en la siguiente enumeración (no exhaustiva):
"mi viejo atril" y "la [...] vieja [...] razón de mi rezar" ("Preludio"),
"juguetes melancólicos de viejo" (ii), "Mis viejos mares" (iii), "campanas
viejas" (vii), "mantos viejos" (viii), "piedra vieja" y "vieja [...]
alma" (xi), "viejo aroma" y "viejos lirios" (xv). Influyen decisivamente
estas frases en el establecimiento de una perspectiva distinta en Del
camino a la de Desolaciones...: el mayor predominio de viejo subraya
la distancia del pasado, la lejanía de la primavera juvenil, distancia
y lejanía que han permitido al tiempo curar las heridas de un antiguo
amor desafortunado, el "espino solitario" de "En la miseria lenta del
camino" (iii). Al cénit y a la tarde del lento verano ha sucedido un
ocaso con "aroma" de "pomas otoñales" ("Preludio"), con aires de "tarde
fría" (iv) o de "mañana(s) fría(s)" (viii y xi), un ocaso apacible que
viene a traer al "caminante viejo" (xv, subrayado nuestro) su última luz:

> —Abre el balcón. La hora
> de una ilusión se acerca...
> (Dc, vii).

Alcanzadas estas nuevas lindes, puede escribir el poeta:

> no tu sandalia el soñoliento llano
> pisará, ni la arena del hastío
> (Dc, ix),

y sentir que en las postrimerías del viaje el peregrino ha recobrado su
rumbo:

Muy cerca está, romero,
la tierra verde y santa y florecida
de tus sueños [...]
                              (Dc, ix).

Abundantes eran en Desolaciones... las referencias al sueño como
recinto en que soledad y desamparo se atenúan, y también como ámbito para
una introspección doliente a que el poeta se siente fatalmente atraído.
Ambas orientaciones se armonizan en la composición "Sobre la tierra
amarga" (ii) para mostrarnos este orbe del sueño machadiano penetrado de
la honda serenidad que distingue a Del camino. La faz más acogedora de
sus sueños y recuerdos se ilumina de forma semejante en el poema "Algunos
lienzos del recuerdo tienen" (x), que comienza introduciéndonos en el
mundo mágico capaz de albergar

            luz de jardín y soledad de campo;
            la placidez del sueño
            en el paisaje familiar soñado.

En la segunda parte de esta composición, influidos ya por la primera,
pasamos por la referencia al "amor amargo" con la misma tristeza, más
melancólica que triste, que el poeta nos comunica en casi toda la
sección; el escarnio de su fracaso amoroso en el verso final se amorti-
gua con el uso de la tercera persona y con imágenes previas ("balcón
florido", "resol bermejo","muros blancos") que nos conducen a una calle
cuya sombra, según es frecuente en el libro, está más próxima al misterio
y ensueño que a la oscuridad y pesar.
      Pero el "dulce salmo", en el que ya han sonado notas especialmente
graves (los poemas v, xii y xiii, p. ej.), llega a interrumpirse al final
de la sección. La composición (también publicada en Electra en 1901)
"Siempre que sale el alma de la obscura" (xiv), de imágenes harto
explícitas, es ya un ejemplo de sueño infructuoso y, todavía más, de
amargo despertar. Y en el último poema, "¡Oh!, dime, noche amiga,
amada vieja," (xvi) el sueño llega a darse, más decididamente aún, en
"retablo [...] / siempre desierto y desolado y solo". La conexión con
el "Preludio" se ha perdido totalmente en esta introspección extrema y
fallida; la "palabra blanca" es ahora "llanto". Muy apreciada por la
crítica, no carece esta composición de facetas que, abundantes en el
libro de 1903, pronto tienden a desaparecer de la poesía machadiana:
el empleo más retórico del vocativo; aflicción explícita en léxico de
desnuda sensiblería ("pobre sombra triste", "lágrimas", "dolor",
"desolado fantasma", "lloran", "queja", etc.); estilo en algún momento
sumamente artificioso ("o soñando amarguras / en las coplas de todos
los misterios"), y el diálogo formalmente más egocéntrico y envarado,
a diferencia del que apunta sin trabas en otros versos de la sección,
la única, por lo demás, en que predominan los poemas carentes de verbos
en primera persona del singular.
      La tercera sección, Salmodias de Abril, contiene el "Nocturno"
("A Juan Ramón Jiménez"), que éste no apreció en mucho, denunciándolo
años más tarde como uno de los "momentos de parnasianismo agudo" de su
autor.[25] Ya en El País sus elogios a estas composiciones parecen
acompañados de cierta reserva: "Las Desolaciones y monotonías y aun
las mismas" - subrayado nuestro - "Salmodias de Abril, tienen una
fuerza florida y luminosa". Son, en efecto, de un tono tan acentuada-
mente modernista como el de Desolaciones... y, como ellas, ricas en
consonancia. Nos parece significativo el que los cuatro poemas de
Salmodias... suprimidos luego, figuren entre los de rima consonante.

Con su radiante "salmo de Abril" ("salmo de amor", más explícitamente, en "Fantasía de una noche de Abril"), la naturaleza trae de nuevo
una dulce melodía al personaje solitario. En su corazón abierto al amor
dejaron huella profunda otros días, cuyo recuerdo despierta en una nueva
visita al parque:

> En tus veredas
> silenciosas, mil sueños resucitan
> de un ayer [...]
> ...
> donde sangran amores los rosales
> ("La tarde en el jardín").

Mas hoy, sintiéndose envejecido, ha de pugnar por entonar su adiós a la
esperanza primaveral, trocada la flor del sueño en "flor sombría"
("Preludio"), cambiadas las ansiadas rosas del amor por las blancas de
connotaciones mortuorias.[24] A la naturaleza engalanada dará amarga
réplica una voz menos mudable:

> El pífano de Abril sonó en mi oído
> lento, muy lento y sibilante y suave...
> De la campana resonó el tañido
> como un suspiro seco y sordo y grave
> ("Preludio").

Ausente, pues, entre pífano y campana la armonía con que órgano y pífano
acordaron sus notas en Del camino. El esplendor primaveral de Salmodias...
es símbolo empleado con intención plenamente modernista: primavera
florida, renacer que el poeta sólo canta en cuanto ajeno a su sentir;
fondo rosado que da realce a su luto y postración, verdaderos temas de
su salmodia. Como en torno a la fuente, el léxico se recubre de alegre
apariencia. Unicamente la voz inexorable de la campana se alza por
encima de todo encanto engañoso, brindando sus ecos al dolor y la muerte
en el marco indefectiblemente luminoso de abril:

> Lejanas tañían / tristes las campanas
> ... ;
> al son dolorido / de lentas campanas
> ("Canción").

Recrudecen en esta sección los marcados contrastes de que suele
acompañarse la fusión de sentimiento y paisaje en los poemas más modernistas del volumen:

> Las fuentes melancólicas cantaban. / [...] un tenue sollozar riente
> [...]
> ("La tarde en el jardín");

> [...] un doble acorde [...] / de tierra en flor y sideral lamento
> ("Nocturno");

> Fue una clara tarde de melancolía. / Abril sonreía
> ("Mai più").

El sentimentalismo (formal y temático) de estas tres composiciones
se desborda en adjetivación profusa y en colorismo y musicalidad intensos:
"alegres gárgolas", "son doliente", "inmóviles secretos verticales",
"árbol cantor, negro y de plata", "silbante suspirar sonoro", "tenue

ligera quimera", "rosa mañana", "plañir de campanas lejanas, llorosas",
"suave de rosas aromado aliento", etc.
"La tarde en el jardín (Fragmento)" ofrece, además, un cántico al
"¡Noble jardín [...!]" que le hace desempeñar en Salmodias... un papel
expositivo semejante al del poema "La fuente" en Desolaciones...  Se
nos introduce en este parque con una primera estrofa en la que resaltan
los tonos sombríos:  "jardín umbrío", "sueño inerte", "ramaje frío",
"fuentes melancólicas".  En él encuentra el poeta su refugio:

> Era un rincón de olvido y sombra y rosas
> frescas y blancas entre lirios.  Era
> donde pulsa en las liras olorosas
> recónditas rapsodias Primavera
>                           (subrayados nuestros).

Fuera del parque, del otro lado de "la tapia ennegrecida",

> [...] el sol esplende
> oculto [...]
> [y] el aire sueña, donde el campo tiende
> su muda, alegre soledad florida.

Enclaustrado en la sombra y el silencio del "parque viejo", "inerte
fantasma de paisaje" ("La fuente" - Electra -), el "corazón cobarde"
renuncia a la ansiada - y esquiva - alegría del campo; se abandona al
consuelo agridulce del recuerdo "en las horas más áridas y tristes"
("La fuente" - Electra -), compartiendo en la intimidad familiar del
jardín los

> secretos viejos del fantasma hermano
> que a la risa del campo, el alto muro
> dictó y la amarga simetría al llano[;]

"fantasma hermano" confinado en la melancolía de "un sueño inerte",
marginado, como el personaje, de la plenitud del goce del vivir ("la
risa del campo"), y capaz por ello de brindar esa comunión tan grata
al alma modernista.
Pero el consuelo ambiguo del jardín ("estrecho ritmo al corazón
cobarde / y húmedo aroma al alma"), triste melodía aliviadora ya
presente en otro parque de Del camino:

> y algo, que es tierra en nuestra carne, siente
> la humedad del jardín como un halago
>                           ("Crear fiestas de amores", v),

no basta a reprimir los impulsos incontenibles y rebeldes a toda sime-
tría o monotonía.  Tras "el alto muro" late la vida con irresistible
encanto, el que inspira la composición "Campo", himno en absoluto ele-
gíaco a la primavera y al amor, a la deseada diosa del poeta, ya cantada
en Desolaciones... ("Noche") y en Del camino ("Arde en tus ojos un
misterio, virgen", vi); la ilusión incumplida que no puede olvidar ni
por la más dulce melancolía del jardín:

> [...] tu paz en sombra, parque, el sueño
> de tus fuentes de mármol, el murmullo
> de tus cantoras gárgolas risueño,
> de tus blancas palomas el arrullo
>                           ("La tarde...");

murmullo risueño, gárgolas cantoras, arrullo de palomas blancas, sueño
(que ya no es inerte) de fuentes: han desaparecido de estos versos
los toques más sombríos de la estrofa inicial, mas no es esta "paz en
sombra" la que reina en el ánimo del poeta, estremecido por el paso
huidizo de la "fugitiva ilusión de ojos guerreros", a la que, como ya
hiciera en <u>Desolaciones</u>... , dirige la súplica más sentida:

> ¡Tiemble en mi pecho el oro
> que llevas en tu aljaba!
> ("Campo").

La herida del amor "a la hora del cenit", no el dolor reconfortante
del "¡Noble jardín [...], / que eternizas el alma de la tarde [...!]",
es la experiencia que añora desesperadamente. Falto de ella, la resig-
nación (postulada en el poema "Ocaso") y la paz del inerte fantasma
hermano serían un consuelo imposible por insincero para el "orgulloso
corazón" inconsolable:

> Abandoné el jardín, sueño y aroma
> bajo la paz del tibio azul celeste
> ("La tarde...", subrayado
> nuestro).

Al personaje poemático le espera en la noche primaveral una
vivencia más amarga en su encuentro con el "árbol sonoro", predecesor
del viejo olmo castellano, que eleva su hermosura en el campo modernista
del "Nocturno".
De acuerdo con la técnica ostensiblemente contrastada a que nos
referimos más arriba, el viento sopla en la noche con "doble acorde" y
el árbol se alza en el llano como

> <u>dulce cantor</u> del campo silencioso,
> que guardaba un <u>sollozo de amargura</u>
> ahogado en el ramaje tembloroso
> (subrayados nuestros);

su "dulce salmo" ("beso del viento susurrante", "brisa que las ramas
besa", "agudo suspirar silbante / del mirlo") es una clara variación
sobre el tema del amor primaveral cantado en "Campo", de que el poeta
no puede participar en su corazón solitario, pese a sentir en él su
propia voz enamorada:

> - que hay en el alma un sollozar de oro
> que dice grave en el silencio el alma,
> como un silbante suspirar sonoro
> dice el árbol cantor la noche en calma -.

Como preludiaran el "sideral lamento" y el "sollozo de amargura"
del viento y el ramaje, la "paz en llanto" de abril no puede (ni lo
pudo antes la "paz en sombra" del jardín) calmar la profunda angustia
que estalla incontenible en su pecho "con eco de cristal y espanto".
Porque, dentro del esquema, ya familiar: mañana - tarde, Oriente -
Occidente, esperanza - decepción, en el poema "Mai più" el personaje
ha descubierto al final de la jornada que la luz - "alegría" - que
inundara su "alcoba triste" en la mañana es irrecuperable. Al final
de la jornada, ya que, a pesar de toda la "temporalidad" de que esta
composición, como su título indica, está cargada, la pregunta "a la
<u>tarde</u> de Abril que <u>moría</u>" (subrayados nuestros) se hace todavía con

ánimo expectante. Es una esperanza viva la que recibe todo el impacto
de la sentencia irrevocable; estamos ante una transición súbita, no
ante una desilusión largamente padecida.

El carácter definitivo de esta vivencia culminante de "Mai più"
se acentúa en el poema "Nevermore". Emplazada en la perspectiva, más
frecuente, de tarde – Occidente – decepción, y dentro del ámbito primaveral específico de Salmodias..., esta composición desvela de forma
directa la faz seductora de la tarde de abril desde sus primeros versos.
En oposición a la "alcoba", "rincón obscuro", del personaje, el entorno
se llena de luz para, "¡Amarga primavera!", conjurar todos los recuerdos
amorosos, la fallida ilusión del amor juvenil:

> ¡Espíritu de ayer! ¡sombra velada,
> que prometes tu lecho hospitalario
> en la tarde que espera luminosa!
> ¡fugitiva sandalia arrebatada,
> tenue, bajo la túnica de rosa!

Túnica, lecho y sandalia claramente sugieren el contenido de ese ayer
primaveral, circunscribiéndolo a la amada ideal de juventud, una vez
más en atuendo modernista. El recuerdo más desasosegado, que excepcionalmente enturbia incluso a la voz de la campana ("Lejos miente otra
fiesta el campanario"), convierte a la antigua ilusión amorosa en
"grotesca ilusión"; "lejana y fría", aquella esperanza de amor aparece,
al igual que en "Mai più", expresamente asociada con un pasado irrepe-
tible y, ahora, distante, al ser contemplada en el "ajuar ya viejo"
(subrayados nuestros). ¿Cuál es el alcance de esta enfática asociación
en la "¡Tarde vieja en el alma y siempre virgen!", como leemos en versión
anterior de este poema publicada también en Electra en 1901? (p. 1060).

Muy pocos meses después de aparecer S, se publica en Helios la
composición "El limonero lánguido suspende" (Poesías completas: VII),
bajo el título de "El poeta visita el patio de la casa en que nació".
Poema también de "tarde clara", no carece de elementos modernistas,
dado lo temprano de su fecha. Citemos el más próximo a "Nevermore":

> [...] en el aire, / algún vagar de túnica ligera (VII),
> [...] leve / aura de ayer que túnicas agita ("Nevermore").

Recordemos asimismo algunas correcciones al poema de Helios, de claro
signo:

| | |
|---|---|
| fuente límpida | (Helios), |
| fuente limpia | (SGOP); |
| | |
| tarde sin flores, ¡ay! tú me traías | (Helios), |
| tarde sin flores, cuando me traías | (SGOP); |
| | |
| para alcanzar encantados los frutos | (Helios), |
| para alcanzar los frutos encantados | (SGOP); |

añadamos la supresión de los dos primeros versos ("El suelo de piedra
y musgo; en las paredes / blancas agarra desgreñada higuera...") y nos
quedamos en 1907 con un comienzo en que "encanto – limpia" vivifican y
matizan de antemano, contrastados con "lánguido – pálida – polvorienta",
el sueño de los frutos; imperceptiblemente casi, dada la mayor adecuación de los adjetivos a los objetos que califican. Por el contrario,
en "Nevermore" la subjetividad estalla rotunda desde los primeros versos:
"¡Amarga primavera! / ¡Amarga luz a mi rincón obscuro!"

Por otra parte, los polos de la tensión, "Fiesta de Abril - rincón obscuro", se han desplazado en "El poeta visita...", se han interiorizado: "corazón - alma luminosa" (confusamente diferenciados en "La tarde en el jardín" y en "Nocturno"), con lo que la naturaleza viene a desempeñar un papel nuevo. De la Primavera - fuente - campana, cuya utilización modernista hemos señalado, pasamos a la primavera - fuente - limonero, símbolos continuos y originales de su poesía posterior; del parque - jardín (raramente huerto), al patio y huerto de Sevilla, concretos - anecdóticos - , menos acordes con su estética primera, pero impregnados de honda conciencia de su pasado.[25]

En "El poeta visita..." desaparece la primavera florida, ornamental, cobertura de quebrantos ("plañido solitario", "un nunca más que dolorido plañe" -"Nevermore"-), dejando paso al estilo más sobrio y frecuente en la poesía machadiana: "tarde alegre y clara / casi de primavera, / tarde sin flores".

Imágenes como "una ilusión cándida y vieja" o "los fantasmas / de las fragancias vírgenes y muertas", tan próximas a la "Tarde vieja en el alma y virgen" de "Nevermore", adquieren una justeza admirable en la evocación de la infancia, y la rememoración se llena de vida a medida que se introducen realismo y objetividad a expensas del esteticismo más alambicado:

> y allá en el fondo sueñan
> los frutos de oro
> (VII),

(los de limonero), frente a:

> y hay más allá un plañido solitario,
> cual nota de recóndito salterio
> ("Nevermore");

o bien:

> En el ambiente de la tarde flota
> ese aroma de ausencia
> (VII)

(seguido de una referencia a "el buen perfume de la hierbabuena, / y de la buena albahaca"), por:

> ¡Salmodias de Abril, música breve,
> sibilación escrita
> en el silencio de cien mares [...!]
> ("Nevermore"),

para llegar a un final de contornos claros en "El limonero lánguido suspende", donde todo era harto difuso en "Nevermore".

Estimamos, pues, que la invocación al "Espíritu de ayer" del poema de Salmodias... dista mucho de la rememoración característica de la poesía machadiana, por quedar bastante más próxima a las "vagas impresiones, puestas en perspectiva de recuerdo" (p. 838) que el mismo Machado atribuye a J.R. Jiménez en su reseña de Arias tristes (El País 1904).[26] El paso del limonero inusitado de la composición "La fuente" ("el amarillo esplende / del limonero") y del "Espíritu de ayer" de "Nevermore" (ambos poemas de 1901) a los de "El poeta visita el patio de la casa en que nació"; de los primores y el consonante de aquéllos a la silva-romance y naturalidad y frescura de éste; de Desolaciones

y monotonías y Salmodias de Abril, en suma, a SGOP, es difícilmente
concebible sin un intervalo al que corresponderían, con toda probabili-
dad, casi todas las composiciones de Del camino.
    Concluyamos insistiendo en primer lugar en que el enjuiciamiento
de Soledades (1903) no puede intentarse tomando por base lo que de ellas
nos queda en Soledades, galerías y otros poemas, en la forma en que
allí nos queda.  El efecto de "Tarde", por ejemplo, encabezando
Desolaciones y monotonías, no es el mismo que el que "Fue una clara
tarde, triste y soñolienta" (VI) produce entre los diez primeros poemas
de SGOP (de los que sólo dos proceden del primer libro).  Juicios muy
autorizados sobre SGOP o PC, incluidas sus primeras secciones, no son
válidos para el volumen de 1903.  La explicación de tal disparidad
reside, principalmente, en la índole tan modernista de éste.
    S tiene como tema central la soledad y aflicción de su personaje
a causa de la pérdida y ausencia consiguiente del amor; lo más modernista de su tratamiento es la afectación.  Tales son las claves de la
unidad del libro.
    Una decepción amorosa de juventud ha sido evocada en tres etapas
sucesivas que ordenaríamos así:  el verano de la madurez, una primavera críticamente tardía y un otoño apacible, culminación natural de
las dos anteriores que sería inútil buscar en los Humorismos (sección
muy breve en 1903 y carente de referencias amorosas); recuerdos
generalmente sentidos al filo de la tarde, mirador de unos días ya
vencidos hacia la espera, y la esperanza, de la "mañana pura" que ponga
término a la monótona reanudación de la peregrinación laberíntica y
estéril de la existencia.
    Pese a la afectación de S (preciosismo formal, alienación,
dilatación del tiempo, "auto-miseración" complaciente), el caminante
"sobre la tierra amarga" es peregrino en marcha hacia "la tierra verde
y santa y florecida / de [sus] sueños"; es decir, romero que canta su
soledad sin la angustia de sentirla insuperable.  De la reseña de
Arias tristes, antes citada, salta a nuestra memoria la afirmación
machadiana de que "la poesía de Juan Ramón Jiménez [...] se alimenta
de vaguísimas nostalgias y tiene acaso un fondo placentero, y que es
así como una nebulosa esperanza de algo que ha de vivirse un día"
(p. 839); las implicaciones serán muy diferentes cuando, treinta años
después, la "sombra talar" de "doble vuelo" y "sandalia equívoca" "en
el Abril de Ocaso" ("Nevermore") aparezca tras el último atardecer ante
"Martín el solitario" en versos estremecedores de "esperar desesperado"
en los que continuidad y evolución machadianas quedan a un tiempo fiel-
mente plasmadas:

> Aquella noche fría
> supo Martín de soledad;
> ...
> Y vio la musa esquiva,
> de pie junto a su lecho, la enlutada,
> la dama de sus calles, fugitiva,
> la imposible al amor y siempre amada.
> Díjole Abel:  Señora,
> por ansia de tu cara descubierta,
> he pensado vivir hacia la aurora
> hasta sentir mi sangre casi yerta.
> Hoy sé que no eres tú quien yo creía;
> mas te quiero mirar y agradecerte
> lo mucho que me hiciste compañía
> con tu frío desdén.
> (CLXXV. "Muerte de Abel Martín", ii-iii.)

No es el modernismo de S parnasiano, si entendemos que al Parnaso le define el sacrificio de toda "honda palpitación del espíritu" al culto de la perfección formal. Sí se pueden tachar de parnasianos algunos de sus poemas, si queremos así aludir a su acentuado esteticismo. En cuanto al simbolismo del libro, su faceta más madura y, por tanto, mejor estudiada por la crítica, solamente se extiende a un puñado de composiciones, casi todas ellas pertenecientes a la segunda sección, Del camino.

Si bien es cierto que el mejor modernismo español es simbolista, S contiene en 1903 bastante de cuanto en él hay de menos bueno. No es demasiado sorprendente que su autor prefiriese olvidar muchos tanteos iniciales, hasta el extremo de emitir juicios aparentemente tan extraños como el muy citado del prólogo a S de 1917: "Esta obra fue refundida en 1907, con adición de nuevas composiciones que no añadían nada sustancial a las primeras, en Soledades, galerías y otros poemas. Ambos volúmenes constituyen en realidad un solo libro" (p. 51). Fuera de él, y por debajo de la gran lírica machadiana, quedaron, sin embargo, los frutos nacidos al calor de las "mandangas y garliborleos de los modernistas cortesanos", de que habla a Unamuno en carta escrita desde Baeza (p. 1014).[27]

No es sólo que los poemas más flojos sean demasiado explícitos, digan demasiado (como los críticos han repetido); el problema es doble: al componer el poeta su "chanson grise / Où l'Indécis au Précis se joint", para darnos en su obra de 1903

> confusa la historia
> y clara la pena[,]

se ha excedido en ambos propósitos, por lo que el equilibrio de la sugerencia no ha prevalecido entre los extremos de la grandilocuencia y de la vaguedad, salvo en gran parte de Del camino y en alguna otra composición aislada; allí donde el peregrino eleva con melancolía entrañable "la sola y vieja y noble razón de [su] rezar" entre la felicidad ("alegría") que persigue y la tristeza de su caminar.


N O T A S

1. Antonio Machado, Obras. Poesía y prosa, ed. Aurora de Albornoz y Guillermo de Torre, 2ª ed. (Buenos Aires, Losada, 1973), 54 y 882 (citamos siempre a M. por esta ed.). Ricardo Gullón ha señalado en el estudio de "Las Soledades de A.M." incluido en Direcciones del modernismo (Madrid, Gredos, 1963) la patente vinculación de M. con el modernismo (pp. 114-117 especialm.). Su adscripción por Guillermo Díaz-Plaja (Modernismo frente a Noventa y Ocho, 2ª ed., Madrid, Espasa-Calpe, 1966) al segundo grupo, ya insostenible ante SGOP, es evidentemente contradictoria a la vista de S. Sobre este punto véase el comentario de Geoffrey Ribbans, Niebla y soledad (Madrid, Gredos, 1971), 255-256.

2. La dificultad de las aplicaciones de una concepción global puede ilustrarse contrastando, entre otras, las apreciaciones siguientes: "algún crítico modernista ha pretendido identificar dicho movimiento con el simbolismo, identificación errónea desde cualquier punto de vista. El modernismo [...] parte del romanticismo francés, pasa por lo

parnasiano, pero se detiene precisamente donde comienza el simbolismo" (Luis Cernuda, Estudios sobre poesía española contemporánea, 2ª ed., Madrid, Guadarrama, 1970, 65-66); "nuestro modernismo [...] es un arrastre de todos los modos franceses del siglo XIX (Hugo, Parnaso, Simbolismo). En Antonio Machado y·Juan Ramón Jiménez [...] han desaparecido las trazas del parnasianismo y de Hugo; pero es fuerte la vinculación con el simbolismo, sobre todo con Verlaine" (Dámaso Alonso, Poetas españoles contemporáneos 3ª ed., Madrid, Gredos, 1965, 131, nota).

3. Véase Ricardo Gullón, Conversaciones con Juan Ramón Jiménez (Madrid, Taurus, 1958), 103 y 112.

4. "Proyecto de discurso de ingreso en la Academia de la Lengua" (p. 940); no todas sus referencias al simbolismo son, sin embargo, igualmente elogiosas, como puede verse en el mismo "Proyecto...".

5. Véase J.M. Aguirre, A.M., poeta simbolista (Madrid, Taurus, 1973); este ensayo, centrado en SGOP, no incluye los poemas preteridos de S: "La razón es muy simple: se piensa que al final del presente análisis, el lector avisado podrá por sí mismo entender las razones que movieron al poeta a desechar los poemas en cuestión" (p. 220).

6. Recogida en A.M., ed. Ricardo Gullón y Allen W. Phillips (Madrid, Taurus, 1973), 345-348.

7. Véase, especialm., la carta no.13, de 1912 (pp. 1000-1002): "Trato [...] de colocarme en el punto inicial de unas cuantas almas selectas y continuar en mí mismo esos varios impulsos en un cauce común, hacia una mira ideal y lejana. Creo que la conquista del porvenir sólo puede conseguirse por una suma de calidades. De otro modo el número nos ahogará" (p. 1000); "No creas que soy un agriado por la soledad. No ¡santa soledad!" (p. 1001), confidencia hecha por los meses en que compone (sin signos de admiración) su conocidísimo poema "Señor, ya me arrancaste lo que yo más quería" (CXIX), en que alude a su soledad en tono tan distinto. La carta no.12, de febrero del mismo año (pp. 999-1000), no es menos reveladora.

8. Recuérdense, entre los textos más conocidos, las composiciones con que, bajo el epígrafe "De mi cartera", se cierra "Glosando a Ronsard y otras rimas" (CLXIV); p. ej., la primera ("Ni mármol duro y eterno") o la quinta ("Prefiere la rima pobre"). Respecto de aquélla, consideramos con Antonio Sánchez Barbudo (Los poemas de A.M., Barcelona, Lumen, 1967, 380) que la fecha de 1902 es muy probablemente inexacta. En prosa, el prólogo de 1917 a S contiene un testimonio muy pertinente: "Pensaba yo que el elemento poético no era la palabra por su valor fónico, ni el color, ni la línea, ni un complejo de sensaciones, sino una honda palpitación del espíritu" (p. 51), y en el "Proyecto de discurso...", ya citado, leemos: "soy poco sensible a los primores de la forma, a la pulcritud y pulidez del lenguaje, y a todo cuanto en literatura no se recomienda por su contenido" (p. 933).

9. Véase Ricardo Gullón, "Relaciones amistosas y literarias entre A.M. y J.R.J.", en A.M., ed. cit. de R. Gullón y A.W. Phillips, 163.

10. Recuérdese también, de un poema cronológicamente mucho más próximo: "¡Y de nuestro amor primero [....]!" (XXXIX. "Coplas elegíacas").

11. Primeros libros de poesía de J.R.J., Madrid, Aguilar, 1959, p. 76.

12.   Dámaso Alonso, op. cit., 141-143, en su análisis de las correcciones de "Tarde" para su publicación en SGOP, ha mostrado cómo el poeta
ha sabido con ellas eliminar "buhonería modernista"; el fenómeno es
general:  a lo largo del primer decenio de nuestro siglo, máximos
exponentes del modernismo, Darío a la cabeza, van reduciendo énfasis en
la belleza formal o, más bien, decorativa.  Tiene conciencia de ello M.:
"Yo también admiraba al autor de Prosas profanas, el maestro incomparable
de la forma y de la sensación, que más tarde nos reveló la hondura de
su alma en Cantos de vida y esperanza" (Prólogo a S, 1917, p. 51, subrayado nuestro); también Juan Ramón opina que el esteticismo modernista
duró poco, para dejar paso a la interiorización ejemplificada por
Bécquer y Unamuno (véase R. Gullón, Conversaciones..., p. 51).

13.   Compárese con estos dos ejemplos de SGOP:

> ¡Oh tiempo en que mis dolores
> tenían lágrimas buenas,
> y eran como agua de noria
> que va regando una huerta!
> > (LXXXVI);
> Adiós, lágrimas cantoras,
> lágrimas que alegremente
> brotabais, como en la fuente
> las limpias aguas sonoras
> > (XCV. "Coplas mundanas").

El primero de estos poemas vio la luz en CC (1912) y fue añadido a
Galerías en 1917, pero no parece muy posterior al segundo, publicado
por primera vez en la revista Renacimiento en 1907.

14.   Véase Domingo Ynduráin, Ideas recurrentes en A.M. (1898-1907)
(Madrid, Turner, 1975): "el romero o el peregrino van a un sitio,
quieren llegar a un lugar que es la razón de su camino" (pp. 106-107).

15.   Paul Verlaine, Romances sans paroles, "Ariettes oubliées", viii,
en Oeuvres poétiques complètes (Paris, Gallimard, 1962), 195-196.  (Las
"Ariettes..." fueron incluidas en Choix de poésies.)

16.   S, dentro de su modernismo, de que aquí nos ocupamos, confirma
plenamente una de las tesis de J.M. Aguirre:  "Ya se ha señalado que el
sentimiento de la persona machadiana es de raíz erótica.  Se ha podido
afirmar que la emoción del viajero se debe al fracaso en su búsqueda
del amor" (op. cit., 261).

17.   El "viejo verano" se transforma en "tórrido verano", y "triste",
dos veces, en "grave", si bien solamente la corrección "grave soñar"
es, de las tres mencionadas, de 1907, datando las otras dos de 1917.
Conviene retener la sustitución de "viejo", vocablo de cuyo uso nos
ocupamos más abajo al comentar los poemas de la segunda sección.

18.   Paul Verlaine, op. cit., "Ariettes...", ii, 191.

19.   Ramón de Zubiría, La poesía de A.M., 3ª ed. (Madrid, Gredos, 1966),
179.

20.   Véase J.M. Aguirre, op. cit.:  "La fuente no debe relacionarse con
el tiempo [...]; sí, con el amor" (p. 354).

21. Véase Concha Zardoya, _Poesía española contemporánea_ (Madrid, Guadarrama, 1961): "La fuente helada [...] deviene espejo de la muerte o de lo muerto" (p. 198). Algún crítico ha mencionado la posible muerte de la amada, y el simbolismo de _Del camino_ se presta a tal interpretación en algunos poemas. Sin embargo, diversas alusiones a lo largo del volumen ("mi largo camino sin amores", "desdeñoso gesto", "lecho inhospitalario", "belleza / esquiva", "la mirra amarga de un amor lejano", "espino solitario", "un pájaro [...] / silba burlón", "virgen esquiva", "cita de un amor amargo", "un fantasma irrisorio", "mi orgulloso corazón", "¡fugitiva ilusión [...:]", "el sol [...] reía / su risa más vieja", "fugitiva sandalia", etc.) apuntan más bien en su conjunto a un amor no correspondido, como venimos sugiriendo.

22. A este respecto véase el juicio (de carácter general, aunque inserto en el estudio de "El símbolo en la poesía de A.M.") de Carlos Bousoño: "El escritor romántico usaba demasiadas veces el subjetivismo de una manera que llamaríamos impúdica. El poeta inmediatamente posterior no es menos subjetivo, sino, al contrario, lo es más. Pero se ha dado cuenta de que la eficacia artística acrece cuando el autor se impone una distancia con respecto a su obra. Uno de los medios de que se sirve para lograr esto es [...] el trasvasamiento de las subjetivas emociones hacia soportes objetivos" (_Teoría de la expresión poética_, 4ª ed., Madrid, Gredos, 1966, 165). En M. esta evolución se da, en buena medida, dentro de _S_, como pretendemos demostrar con nuestro análisis del distinto tratamiento del tema central del libro en sus tres secciones mayores. Sólo podemos, por tanto, aceptar a medias la opinión de R. Gullón, para quien M. toca ciertos temas modernistas "sin la blandura y el sentimentalismo predominantes. Siempre hallaremos en él la sobria contención, el dominio de sí y la reducción del sentimiento a sus límites legítimos" (_Direcciones_..., 117).

23. Véase R. Gullón, _Conversaciones_..., 103.

24. Acerca del simbolismo de la rosa, y especialm. de la blanca, véase J.M. Aguirre, op. cit., 307-308.

25. Véase la sección dedicada al "Tema del huerto" por D. Alonso, op. cit., 132-136.

26. Para un análisis de la profunda significación de las reflexiones que M. vierte en este escrito, así como de su intención autocrítica, véase G. Ribbans, op. cit., 208-213 y 283-285.

27. De "mandangas" (y de "soñolientas melopeas") le venía hablando don Miguel desde agosto de 1903 en que aparece en _Helios_ la carta abierta de éste, reproducida por G. Ribbans, ibid., 289-292; véanse también pp. 300-302 para la reacción directa y temprana (1903-1904) de M., y pp. 207-216, parcialmente citadas antes, para la evolución trascendental que se inicia en _SGOP_.

**Laus Deo**